Multiculturalism
and the **Jews**

Multiculturalism
and the Jews

Sander L. Gilman

Routledge
Taylor & Francis Group
New York   London

Routledge is an imprint of the
Taylor & Francis Group, an informa business

Routledge
Taylor & Francis Group
270 Madison Avenue
New York, NY 10016

Routledge
Taylor & Francis Group
2 Park Square
Milton Park, Abingdon
Oxon OX14 4RN

© 2006 by Taylor & Francis Group, LLC
Routledge is an imprint of Taylor & Francis Group, an Informa business

Printed in the United States of America on acid-free paper
10 9 8 7 6 5 4 3 2 1

International Standard Book Number-10: 0-415-97918-8 (Perfect) 0-415-97917-X (Hardcover)
International Standard Book Number-13: 978-0-415-97918-4 (Perfect) 978-0-415-97917-7 (Hardcover)

Library of Congress Cataloging-in-Publication Data

Gilman, Sander L.
Multiculturalism and the Jews / Sander L. Gilman.
p. cm.
Includes index.
ISBN 0-415-97917-X (hb) -- ISBN 0-415-97918-8 (pb)
1. Jews--Identity. 2. Multiculturalism--Religious aspects--Judaism. 3. Plural-ism (Social sciences) 4. Judaism--Relations--Islam. 5. Islam--Relations--Judaism. 6. Multiculturalism in literature. 7. Ethnic relations--Religious aspects--Judaism. I. Title.

DS143.G425 2006
305.892'4--dc22
2005035746

Visit the Taylor & Francis Web site at
http://www.taylorandfrancis.com

and the Routledge Web site at
http://www.routledge-ny.com

CONTENTS

PREFACE   IX

1 CAN THE EXPERIENCE OF DIASPORA JUDAISM SERVE AS A
MODEL FOR ISLAM IN TODAY'S MULTICULTURAL EUROPE?   1

2 JEWS AND THE CULTURE OF DECORUM IN ENLIGHTENMENT
AND POST-ENLIGHTENMENT GERMANY   23

3 JEWS AND THE CONSTITUTION OF THE MULTICULTURAL ETHNIC   45

4 JEWS, MULTICULTURALISM, AND ISRAEL ZANGWILL'S
"MELTING POT"   65

5 FRANZ KAFKA'S DIET: AN ANSWER TO HYBRIDITY   85

6 ALBERT EINSTEIN'S VIOLIN: JEWS, MUSIC, AND THE
PERFORMANCE OF IDENTITY   99

7 WHOSE BODY IS IT ANYWAY? HERMAPHRODITES, GAYS, AND
JEWS IN N. O. BODY'S GERMANY   111

8 THE FANATIC: PHILIP ROTH AND HANIF KUREISHI CONFRONT
SUCCESS   125

9 "WE'RE NOT JEWS": IMAGINING JEWISH HISTORY AND JEWISH
BODIES IN CONTEMPORARY NON-JEWISH MULTICULTURAL
LITERATURE   145

10 ARE JEWS MULTICULTURAL ENOUGH? LATE TWENTIETH-
AND EARLY TWENTY-FIRST-CENTURY LITERARY
MULTICULTURALISM AS SEEN FROM JEWISH PERSPECTIVES   179

11 POINTS OF CONFLICT: CULTURAL VALUES IN "GREEN"
AND "RACIAL" ANTI-SEMITISM   225

NOTES   243

INDEX   275

DEDICATION

Dedicated with thanks for his intellectual stimulation
and ethical teaching to Arnold Jacob Wolf

PREFACE

This book provides a series of approaches to the question of the "multi-cultural" as a place where the question of "particular" cultural manifestations is seen as possible. It is also a book about the negotiations that need to take place to make this possibility exist and about the constant, ongoing compromises that are implied in such negotiations. I have framed this as a question of the relationship between Jews and Muslims, as many of the contemporary texts examined come out of a multiculturalism shaped by the rhetoric of Islam and Jewry in the twentieth and twenty-first centuries. The reason for this emphasis is my own context in a post-9/11 world. Suddenly, it is Islam that has taken center stage in our concerns about the meaning and direction of "civilization." This word, so redolent of Samuel Huntington's 1993 article in *Foreign Affairs* (and subsequent book) on "The Clash of Civilizations and the Remaking of the World Order," is echoed in the subtitle of Jonathan Sacks, *The Dignity of Difference: How to Avoid the Clash of Civilizations* (London: Continuum, 2002).

It was Sacks, the sixth chief rabbi of the United Hebrew Congregations of the British Commonwealth, in a most controversial book, who set the stage for the debate about the value of multiculturalism and the importance of a debate about difference in a post-9/11 world as a Jewish question. Sacks's argument about globalization points out that the great danger is not economic but cultural: it is a loss of the value of the particular and the different. And he sees the Jews as the litmus test for the importance of difference. He believes that Jewish particularism is the answer to God's covenant "with all humanity." God "then turns to one people and commands it to be different *in order to teach humanity the dignity of difference*" (emphasis in the original: 53). Jewish difference is, for Sacks, exemplary and divinely ordained. It can also be read, and I have done so in this volume, as a reflex of the Jewish experience in the modern Diaspora, in which as David Roskies has shown in his *Against the Apocalypse: Responses to Catastrophe in Modern Jewish Culture* (Cambridge, Mass.: Harvard University Press,

1986), Biblical models may well structure Jewish responses to a world with very different presuppositions and claims. My argument is that the Jewish experience in the modern Diaspora served to be the exemplary case for the possibility (or the impossibility) of such models of multiculturalism. The Jewish experience remains in complex ways the litmus test for its success or for its failure.

Sacks argues against universals of human action and values and for the necessary differences that make human beings human, if not humane. "Universalism," he argues, "is an inadequate response to tribalism, and no less dangerous. It leads to the belief—superficially compelling but quite false—that there is only one truth about the essentials of the human condition, and it holds true for all peoples at all times. If I am right, you are wrong. If what I belie[ve] is the truth, then your belief, which differs from mine, must be an error from which you must be converted, cured and saved" (50). When the book first appeared, Sacks was accused quite wrongly of relativism by some of his rabbinic critics. Did he argue that the Jews, the chosen people, were just one more version of monotheism? His reading of the ideal sacred text is that it would "declare that *God is God of all humanity, but no single faith is or should be the faith of all humanity*" (emphasis in the original: 55). Sacks's view is that "religious truth is not universal. What it does not [mean] is that it is relative" (55). Religious truth allows one to think that one is simultaneously universal in the love of God and particular in the means by which he is understood and worshipped. For him, it was the moment of the confusion of tongues at the Tower of Babel that sealed the necessity for multiple cultures. This is God's answer to the claim of a universal, totalitarian culture that assumed cultural uniformity. (The intense debate within the Anglo-Jewish community led to a revised second edition of Sacks's book.)

Sacks implicitly argues against the empirical experience of the Jews confronted by proselytizing religions such as Christianity that see the conversion of the Jews as a central goal. He also argues against the claims of a hybrid notion of the multicultural. This view, so often dominant in the Western Diaspora, is the ultimate form of an integration that results in total cultural effacement. This is what the early Christianity claimed: *extra ecclesiam nulla salus*, or that no truth can exist beyond the Church. What Sacks argues for is the possibility of pluralism without a clear acknowledgement that pluralism can generate conflict as well as harmony.

Within Sacks's concept of pluralism, however, the "Jewish case" is the initial statement for the value of difference. His is an argument that examines the claims of the multicultural in a post-9/11 world, especially in terms of the presuppositions that certain models ensure "progress" through harmony. Against Plato's claims of universal harmony, at least as read by Sacks, he sets the dissolution of the Edenic moment, and the gradual movement to difference in the Biblical narrative. This difference can have its cruel and destructive moments—the murder of Abel, the Tower of Babel—but it is the establishment of "civilizations" that helps define the general struggle of human beings for their own sense of self and sense of community. That communities can be destructive as well as productive is one of the lessons of twentieth-century history. The same can be held for multiculturalism.

Sacks's resolution to the conflicts inherent in his depiction of "difference" echoes that of Jürgen Habermas: it is "conversation" (83). In real terms, my book is about a hundred-year-old conversation about the Jews and multiculturalism and is itself part of a contemporary conversation about the same topic. It looks at the construction of the two primary ideas of "multiculturalism" through the prism of the Jewish contribution to and function in high culture from the Enlightenment to the present. The two ideas are that of the possibility or fear of integration and the necessity or danger of separation. It is framed in terms of 9/11 in that I have placed special emphasis on the role of Islam in this process, especially in the contemporary world. It is clear, however, that many other "civilizations" are present in the European and North American multicultural mix and that the general context of this debate is the struggle with or for a secularized Christian perspective of the world. Here, too, the position of the Jews is problematic. Now seen as part of a Judeo-Christian world; now part of a secular, national world; now in opposition to both and seen from a religious perspective focusing on Jewish particularism (whether liberal or Orthodox)—the self-definition and definition of the Jews in this multicultural mix are the subjects of my tale. Secularization, at least in its initial conception by George Jacob Holyoake in 1851, included religious belief—but within the acceptable bounds of Enlightenment theism. Thus, the promise of the multicultural seems to afford the Jews, however defined, with a cultural space that will protect and encourage a role for them in a modern, global culture, but within the ever newly negotiated bounds of the secular world.

Beginning with the contemporary question of how Jews and Muslims parallel their understanding of the world they inhabit, I turn, in chapter 2, to the question of the failure of the Enlightenment project, or, perhaps better, the contestation of that project, around the question of public decorum. This is a theme that will run like a red thread through the volume. Rather than rehashing the oft-told tale of how Jews enter into the cultural world of European and American "civilization," I have chosen, as is my wont, a more oblique question about the integration of Jews into European culture, that of the claims of Jewish difference in terms of socially unacceptable behavior rather than cultural creativity. In this chapter, I ask, How do Jews imagine that they can enter into the public sphere, into the encoded Christian world of eighteenth- and nineteenth-century European and American society? How are they represented when they do so?

With the first and second chapters, the contemporary, twenty-first-century world and the world of Enlightenment civic emancipation frames the overall problem that Sacks had raised: what is the function of the Jews in understanding "difference" as it is now contested in our globalized economy and world "civilizations"? Chapter 3 looks specifically at the debates about ethnicity and cultural decorum at the beginning of the twentieth century that provided a vocabulary for the position of the Jew in the debates about culture. Here I show that Jewish scholars and writers provide a model by which Jews can be freed of the curse of being without or beyond culture. Central to this is the development of a parallel Jewish culture within a Diaspora setting; it is the notion of cultural pluralism that evolves to answer the assumption that Jews are driven solely by their own economic motivation. It is Shylock's curse that Derek Penslar, in his *Shylock's Children: Economics and Jewish Identity in Modern Europe* (Berkeley: University of California Press, 2001), presents as a core reference for Jewish identity in the Western Diaspora. By the end of the nineteenth century, its primacy in defining Jewish difference is debated both within and without the Jewish community, only to reappear again after the Shoah in critiques of the vapidity of capitalism.

Two models evolve out of this rethinking of the cultural position of the Jews: both are central to our contemporary idea of multiculturalism. One is the idea of cultural pluralism, which has true resonance only in many of the early twentieth-century thinkers of cultural Zionism such as Ahad Ha-am and then, to a much greater degree, in Western letters after the Shoah.

In chapter 4, I examine the first and most successful model for the cultural refiguring of the Jew in Western "civilization." There I present the implications of "the melting pot" and reflect on how the debate about Jews in culture shaped this powerful metaphor. Answers to the "melting pot" are already present in the world that generated this resolution to Jewish particularism. Chapter 5 turns to Franz Kafka, whose world cannot fathom how the melting pot can work given its powerful biological and cultural underpinning. Kafka's views on culture, especially the culture of the abdomen, have fascinating analogies in debates today with the Muslim communities in the Western Diaspora. Yet there are those who, consciously or unconsciously, are able to both function in high culture and *Bildung* (education) as well as maintain a secular, self-conscious Jewish identity. In chapter 6, I examine how high culture and Jewish identity play their way out in the life and thought of the exemplary "smart" Jew of the twentieth century, Albert Einstein. Yet there are other, more hidden tales to be told about the negotiation and performance of Jewish identity in a multicultural world. Chapter 7 looks at another take on the multicultural—what happens in early twentieth-century Germany, the world of Kafka and Einstein, when there is a "real" (read: physical) transformation of the body, in the case of N. O. Body from female to male, to an understanding of her or his Jewish identity.

Much of what has been examined to this point tracks the tale of the multicultural from the Enlightenment to the Shoah. What is extraordinary are the continuities in these debates by the 1950s and how these debates begin to serve both as models for other "minorities" now entering into the world of high culture and as part of a political power notion of the multicultural. Simultaneously, it is the tale of how the Jews, now seen as the ultimate victims of inhumanity, an inhumanity to be answered by the multicultural, are now excluded from the multicultural as too successful, too white, and too Jewish. The curse of all promises is that they are realized: the Jews enter into the world of the multicultural and become successful within it. Thus, they become the new "establishment" when, by the 1960s, other groups in Germany, France, Britain, the United States, and South Africa begin to seek their multicultural space. The trajectory of the image of Israel from the embattled, overwhelmed, rescued fragment of European Jewry to "Super-Jew" and then to "racist" archvillain parallels this cultural tale, as Paul Breines noted in his *Tough Jews: Political Fantasies and the Moral Dilemma of American Jewry* (New York: Basic Books, 1992). Chapter 8 provides a close reading of the pitfalls of economic success and religious belief in the work of two major figures of mid-twentieth-century writing, Philip Roth and Hanif Kureishi. In these tales of parents and children, the older models seem to be turned on their heads, but the end result remains the primacy of the aesthetic and the cultural. Chapter 9 continues my reading of Hanif Kureishi in the light of a wide range of Muslim and non-Muslim readings of the position of the Jew within the fantasy world of global, literary multiculturalism from the 1990s to the present. Here writers in the United Kingdom, South Africa, and the United States provide complex images of the "Jew" excluded by their multicultural world.

The other side of the multicultural coin is examined in chapter 10. Given the primacy at the close of the twentieth century of the myriad readings of the multicultural, I have also read a range of texts by Jewish writers from India to Israel to England, from the United States to France, Germany, and Belgium, who play with the notion of a multicultural space in which the Jews can and do function. Here the notions of cultural difference and the melting pot take on new and nuanced meanings depending of the context in which these writers live and are read. Transformation, the key to the Enlightenment promise, turns out to be not only a concept that is still flourishing, but also one that Jewish writers still employ in terms of both their own identity as writers and their construction of their characters. That such an ongoing struggle is still taking place in the realm of high culture may well illustrate Jonathan Sacks's claim that conversation is the answer to competing claims of difference, for no matter how parochial a work of literature, once it is present in the public sphere, a virtual conversation is inevitable. Indeed, it is the essence of this present book. Yet I do not want to be accused of being a Pollyanna in terms of today's public debates about Jewish difference, especially in light of the politics of the present world and the "clash of civilizations" bemoaned by Huntington and countered by Sacks: my final chapter looks at the negative side of the rhetoric of Jewish difference through the lens (again) of a Muslim thinker and the anxiety about Jewish success and accomplishment as a mode of distancing the Jews in the contemporary world. The debate about Jewish difference in the present world continues. It takes on different contexts and different articulations over time—but it remains one of the touchstones for any contemporary understanding of modernity.

The chapters in this volume were initially delivered as lectures in my role as the 2004–2005 Weidenfeld Professor of European Comparative Literature at Oxford University. St. Anne's College hosted me, and I wish to thank the principal, Tim Gardam, and the Weidenfeld Committee that extended me the invitation. I also wish to thank George Lord Weidenfeld, whose generosity made this appointment possible.

As is evident, this is a wide-ranging book; the lectures were equally so. They demanded both patience and engagement on behalf of my audiences at Oxford. I found both there. I am therefore doubly grateful for their forbearance. My best reader, my friend and collaborator Zhou Xun, has listened to these ideas with her extraordinary critical ear over the past decade; my editors at Routledge read them with a critical eye. I thank them especially when we disagree.

Oxford, June 2005

CAN THE EXPERIENCE OF DIASPORA JUDAISM SERVE AS A MODEL FOR ISLAM IN TODAY'S MULTICULTURAL EUROPE?

Two moments in modern history: a religious community in France is banned from wearing distinctive clothing in public schools as it is seen as an egregious violation of secular society; a religious community in Switzerland is forbidden from ritually slaughtering animals as such slaughter is seen as a cruel and unnatural act. These acts take place more than a hundred years apart: the former recently in France, the latter more than a century ago in Switzerland (where the prohibition against ritual slaughter still stands). But who are these religious communities? In France (among others), the order banning ostentatious religious clothing and ornaments in schools and other public institutions impacts as much on religious Jewish men who cover their heads (and perhaps even religious Jewish married women who cover their hair) as it does the evident target group, Muslim women. (The law is written in such a p.c. way as also to ban the ostentatious wearing of a cross: "Pierre, you can't come into school carrying that six-foot-high cross on your back. You will have to simply leave it in the hall.")

In Switzerland, even today the prohibition against kosher Jewish slaughter also covers the slaughter of meat by Muslims who follow the ritual practice (*dabh*) that results in halal meat. In Great Britain these debates raged in the nineteenth century, as we shall discuss in chapter 5. The Jewish practice was banned by the Nazis in Germany with the *Gesetz über das Schlachten von Tieren* (Law on the Slaughtering of Animals) of 21 April

1933; it was sporadically permitted after 1945 through exceptions; only in 1997 were these exceptions made part of the legal code. The Islamic practice was outlawed in Germany until 1979 and even today is tolerated but not sanctioned.[1] These prohibitions impact on Jews and Muslims in oddly similar ways when Western responses to "slaughter" are measured. Very different is how the meat is used, whether in "traditional" dishes or in a Big Mac. The question is, How did and will these two groups respond to such confrontation with the secular, "modern" world?[2]

Why should the focus of concern in secular Europe from the Enlightenment to today be on the practices and beliefs of Jews and on the Muslims? Indeed, when the Sikhs in France raised the question of whether their turbans were "cultural" or "religious" symbols under the terms of the new regulations, the official French spokesperson asked, in effect: are there Sikhs in France? Indeed there are.

Yet in September 2004, two French journalists were seized in Iraq and threatened with death unless the law limiting headscarves was not instituted the following week when school was to begin in France. The reaction was not a sense of support for the struggle for an Islamic identity in France. Indeed, virtually all of the French Muslim institutions, from the official French Council of the Muslim Faith to the radical Union of Islamic Organizations in France (UOIF), spoke out against the outside pressure even though it came from the "Islamic" world. As Olivier Roy, a leading French scholar of Islam, noted, "They may disagree on the law of the veil, but they are saying, 'This is our fight and don't interfere.' This is a pivotal moment."[3] Indeed, Lhaj Thami Breze, the head of UOIF, who had been opposed to the law, proposed a compromise in which a moderate interpretation of the law would permit "modest head covering."[4] It was indeed a public change of attitude, as the unity of the Islamic community in France in opposition to "foreign" interference concerning the "law of the veil" suddenly was seen as a sign of the development of a secular consciousness in this religious community. What was striking is that the majority of Muslim schoolgirls did not wear or quickly removed their head coverings the day school began. Only about 200 to 250 girls, mainly in Alsace, wore their scarves to school, and all but about 100 removed them before entering the buildings. These girls were removed from the classroom and provided with "counseling" in the schools. For them the *hijab*, which had been seen as "a way to reconcile modernity, self-affirmation and authenticity," was a sign of the Western rights they demanded as Muslims.[5] These were less central than the rule of law. Three male Sikh students in Bobigny, a Paris suburb, were sent home the first day of class for wearing their traditional head covering. This was true whether they saw the headscarf as a political, ethnic, or religious symbol. The demand that one see oneself as a citizen with the rights of the citizen to contest the claims of the secular state overrode any sense of the primary identification as a member of the Ummah, the Islamic religious community. Jacqueline Costa-Lascoux, research director at the Political Science Center of the National Center for Research in Paris (CEVIPOF), noted that "the hostage taking has helped the Muslim community in France, mainly the young people, to understand that they can live in a democratic society and still be Muslims."[6] The operative terms here are "democratic society" and "Muslim." It is the constitution of the modern secular state and the need for religions such as Islam and Judaism to adapt to it that are at the heart of the matter.

Yet what does it mean to be a Muslim in this secular world of modern France? Scratch secular Europe today, and you find all of the presuppositions and attitudes of Christianity concerning Jews and Muslims present in subliminal or overt forms. Secular society in Europe has absorbed Christianity into its very definition of the secular.[7] Indeed, one can make an argument that "secular" society as we now see it in Europe is the result of the adaptation of Christianity to the model of secularism that arose as a compromise formation out of the wars of religion following the Reformation. The integration of the Jews into Enlightenment Europe, as Adam Sutcliffe has shown in his *Judaism and Enlightenment*, was integration into Christian Europe (with Christianity having different textures in England than in Holland than in Bavaria, etc.).[8] Whether one thinks this provided an ideal model for all modern states, as does the philosopher Charles Taylor when he claims that secularization provides "people of different faiths, or different fundamental commitments," the ability to coexist (33, 34); or whether one is leery of such claims, as is Talal Asad, who sees this merely as a "political strategy" (3), the "Jewish template" may well provide a clue to the potentials for the processes that religious communities with specific ritual beliefs and practices confront.[9]

The veneer was that of a secular state, a veneer that did alter the nature of Christianity itself. Even if today it is true, as Richard Bulliet claims, that "Christianity and Judaism pass by definition the civilizational litmus tests proposed for Islam even though some of their practitioners dictate women's dress codes, prohibit alcoholic beverages, demand prayer in public schools, persecute gays and lesbians, and damn members of other faiths to hell,"[10] this was certainly not the case for Jews in the secularizing Christian world of the European nations and their colonies following the Reformation. Indeed, Jews were regularly seen as being inherently unable to pass "civilizational litmus tests" in the Western Diaspora in virtually all areas.

Yet even today there are odd and arcane echoes of older views about the meaning of Jewish ritual. In the mid-1990s, there was a general acknowledgement in the Catholic Church that the *Bible for Christian Communities* (*La Bible Latino-américaine*), written by Bernard Hurault, a Catholic missionary based in Chile to combat the rising tide of Evangelical Christianity, was blatantly anti-Jewish. Eighteen million copies in English and Spanish were distributed in South America, and hundreds of thousands sold in France and Belgium since it was published in May 1994. According to the text, the Jewish people killed Jesus Christ because they "were not able to control their fanaticism" and thus showed a true lack of decorum. It was also clear that Judaism was represented as a religion of meaningless rituals, mere "folkloric duties involving circumcision and hats."[11] (After a legal challenge from the French Jewish community, the text was officially withdrawn; it still circulates in South America.)

How this is contested, sometimes successfully, sometimes unsuccessfully, is central to the tale told in this book; it also provides an interpretive framework through which to understand the debates about the meaning and function of Islam in the West that have taken place since 9/11. The focus of this present book is, for the most part, on the products of high culture and their constitution as well as their reception. It recounts in some detail the complex rethinking of what it meant and means to be Jewish in what in all intents and purposes remains a society rooted in specific images about Jewish adaptability and change.

Little has altered concerning the deep cultural legacy of Europe over the past two hundred years. Recently, German, Italian, Polish, and Slovakian delegates demanded that the "Christian heritage" of the new Europe be writ large in the (failed) European constitution of 2005. It was only the post–September 11 anxiety of most states that enabled Valéry Giscard d'Estaing, as president of the convention writing the constitution, to persuade the group that such a reference would be "inappropriate." The demand was transformed into a reference in the preamble to the "cultural, religious, and humanist inheritance of Europe." No one missed what was meant. Certainly one of the things that the French and Dutch referenda about the constitution in 2005 tested was the likelihood of admitting Turkey, a majority Muslim state, into the European Union. Judaism and Islam have an all-too-close relationship to Christianity and raise questions that remain troubling in Europe.

It is important not to reduce the relationship between Judaism and Islam to the role that Jewish ideas, concepts, and practices did or did not have in shaping the earliest forms of Islamic belief. It is clear that nineteenth-century Jewish scholars in Europe had a central role in examining the "Jewish roots" of historical Islam. Scholars from Abraham Geiger in the 1830s to Ignaz Goldziher at the end of the century stressed the Judaizing nature of early Islam. These roots, true or not, are not sufficient to explain the intense focus on the nature of Islam in Europe today. Islam is not simply a surrogate for speaking about the Jews in today's Europe because of superficial similarities to Judaism. Among Jewish scholars in the nineteenth century, the search for the Jewish roots of Islam was certainly more than simply a surrogate for speaking about the relationship between Judaism and Christianity in the nineteenth century, as Susannah Heschel so elegantly shows in her study *Abraham Geiger and the Jewish Jesus*.[12] At one moment, the examination or construction of Islam provided one major Jewish scholar with a model for the potential reform of contemporary Judaism. One can quote Goldziher's diaries: "I truly entered into the spirit of Islam to such an extent that ultimately I became inwardly convinced that I myself was a Muslim, and judiciously discovered that this was the only religion which, even in its doctrinal and official formulation, can satisfy philosophic minds. My ideal was to elevate Judaism to a similar rational level. Islam, so taught me my experience, is the only religion, in which superstitious and heathen ingredients are not frowned upon by the rationalism, but by the orthodox teachings."[13] For him, the Islam he discovered becomes the model for a new spirit of Judaism at the close of the nineteenth century.

It is the seeming closeness of these "Abrahamic" religions and their joint history that draws attention to the real or imagined differences to the majority religion and its new form: secular society. "The 'Abrahamic' religions" is the newest p.c. phrase: the "Judeo-Christian tradition" was the catchword for common aspects shared between Judaism and Christianity after the Holocaust made this an acceptable notion, whereas "the Abrahamic religions" is the new buzzword including Islam into the Judeo-Christian fold that has become current only after 9/11. Both phases attempt to defuse the clearly Christian aspects of modern Western secular society by expanding it, but, of course, only reemphasize it. Here Jonathan Sacks's notion of difference is helpful: in creating categories that elide difference and that stress superficial similarities, one believes that one is bridging "differences."[14] Actually one is submerging them.

The closeness of Christianity to Judaism and Islam results in what Sigmund Freud called the "narcissism of minor differences." Those differences are heightened in this secular society, which is rooted in the mindset and often the attitudes, beliefs, social mores, and civic practices of the religious community in Western Europe—Christianity. Thus, in Western Europe there is a radical secularization of religious institutions in the course of the nineteenth century. Marriage is shifted from being solely in the control of the Church to being in the domain of the State: but this form of secularization still maintains the quasi-religious aura about marriage, something we see in the debates in France about gay marriage. No secularizing European state simply abandons marriage as a religious institution that has outlived its time as nineteenth-century anarchists and some early twentieth-century radical Zionists claimed.[15] The new minority is promised a wide range of civil rights—including those of freedom of religion—if only they adhere to the standards of civilized behavior as defined by the secular society. This is rooted in the desire to make sure that that society with its masked religious assumptions redefines the minorities' religious practice or "secularizes" a religious minority into an "ethnic" one.

Equally, it is vital not to confuse the experiences of contemporary Islam with the rhetoric of victimization often heard within Muslim communities in countries such as Germany. There the evocation of the Holocaust becomes a means of identifying with the iconic victims of German history, the Jews. Y. Michal Bodemann and Gökce Yurdakul have noted quite correctly how the competition for the space of the victim or of the essential Other has allowed Turkish writers, such as Yadé Kara, to call upon the Jews as the model, for good or for ill, for Turkish acculturation.[16] The Turkish community regularly evokes the Holocaust when it imagines itself. Thus, at the public events in Berlin on 23 November 2002 commemorating the horrendous murder of Turkish immigrants in Mölln in 1992, one heard the

Turkish spokesman, Safter Çınar, evoke the experience of the Jews in the Holocaust as the model by which the contemporary experience of Turks could be measured. The power of this analogy is clear. But this self-conscious evocation of the experience of the Jews is only one aspect of contemporary parallels of Jews and Muslims.

Can we now look at the experiences within the various strands of Jewish religious (and therefore social) ritual practice from the late eighteenth century (which marked the beginning of civil emancipation) that parallel those now confronting Diaspora Islam in "secular" Western Europe?[17] The similarities are striking: a religious minority enters into a self-described secular (or secularizing) society that is Christian in its rhetoric and presuppositions and that perceives a "special relationship" with this minority. The co-territorial society sees this as an act of aggression. This minority speaks a different secular language but also has yet a different religious language. This is odd in countries that have a national language and (in some) a religious language but not a secular language spoken by a religious minority as well as a ritual. Religious schools that teach in the languages associated with a religious group are seen as sources of corruption and illness. Religious rites are practiced that seem an abomination to the majority "host" culture: unlike the secular majority, these religious communities practice the mutilation of children's bodies (infant male circumcision, and, for some Muslims, infant female genital cutting); the suppression of the rights of women (lack of women's traditional education, a secondary role in religious practice, arranged marriages, and honor killings); barbaric torture of animals (the cutting of the throats of unstunned animals, allowing them to bleed to death); prohibit the creation of "graven images" of all types, including representations of Mohammed or God; disrespect for the dead through too rapid burial; ritual excess (in the case of the Jews, drunkenness at Purim; feasting during Ramadan in the case of the Muslims); ostentatious clothing that signals religious affiliation and has ritual significance (from women's hair covering such as the Muslim *hijab* to Jewish *sheitels* to men's hats such as the Jewish *stremil* or the Muslim *taqiyah*); and, centrally relating all of these practices, a belief in the divine "chosenness" of the group in contrast to all others. The demonization of aspects of religious practice has its roots in what civil society will tolerate and what it will not, what it considers to be decorous and what is unacceptable as a social practice. Why it will not tolerate something is, of course, central to the story. Thus, Alan Dundes argued a decade ago that the anxiety about meanings associated with the consumption of the body and blood of Christ in the Christian Mass shaped the fantasy of the Jews as slaughtering Christian children for their blood.[18] But it is equally present in the anger in secular Europe directed toward Jewish ritual practices such as ritual slaughter with its obligatory bloodletting.

One of the most striking similarities of the process of integration into Western secular society is the gradual elision of the striking national differences among the various groups. Muslims in Western Europe represent multiple national traditions (South Asian in the United Kingdom, North African in France and Spain, and Turkish in Germany). But so did the Jews in Western Europe who came out of ghettos in France and the Rhineland, from the rural reaches of Bavaria and Hungary, who moved from those parts of "Eastern Europe"—Poland, the eastern marches of the Austro-Hungarian Empire—which became part of the West and from the fringes of empire to the center. To this one can add the Sephardic Jews from the Iberian Peninsula who settled in areas from Britain (introducing fish and chips) to the fringes of the Austrian Empire. The standard image of the Jews in eighteenth-century British caricature was the Maltese Jew in his oriental turban. By the nineteenth century, it was that of Lord Rothschild in formal wear receiving the prince of Wales at his daughter's wedding in a London synagogue. Religious identity (as the Jew or the Muslim) replaced national identity—by then, few (except the anti-Semites) remembered that the Rothschilds were a Frankfurt family who escaped the Yiddish-speaking ghetto. The "Jews" are everywhere and all alike; Muslims seem to be everywhere and are becoming "all alike." Even ritual differences and theological antagonism seem to be diminished in the Diaspora, where the notion of a Muslim Ummah (or community) seems to be realized. It is the ideal state, to quote Talal Asad, of "being able to live as autonomous individuals in a collective life that exists beyond national borders."[19] But this too has its pitfalls, as the "Jewish template" shows.

Now for Jews in those lands that will become Germany, in the Austro-Hungarian Empire, in France, and in those lands that will become Great Britain, the stories are all different: different forms of Christianity, different expectations as to the meaning of citizenship. Different notions of secularization all present slightly different variations on the theme of "What do you have to give up to become a true citizen?" Do you merely have to give up your secular language (Western and Eastern Yiddish, Ladino, Turkish,

Urdu, colloquial Arabic)? Today there has been a strong suggestion in Germany and the United Kingdom that preaching within the mosques be done only in German or English—for security reasons. Do you have to abandon the most evident and egregious practices: or, as the German philosopher Johann Gottlieb Fichte (1762–1814) states (echoing debates about Jewish emancipation during the French Revolution), do you have to "cut off their Jewish heads and replace them with German ones"?[20] And that was not meant as a metaphor, but as a statement of the impossibility of Jewish transformation into Germans.

This book presents aspects of what Jews thought it possible to change in Jewish religious practice and belief in the eighteenth and nineteenth centuries, what it accomplished within various national states, and what it did not accomplish. That is, what was gained and what was lost, both in terms of the ability of living religions to transform themselves and the clear understanding that all such transformations have resistance and such transformations that call forth other forms of religious practice in response. All of these changes deal in general with the question of Jewish "identity," but in a complex and often contradictory manner. For the history of the Jews in the European Diaspora, the late eighteenth century called forth three great "reformers" who took on different reforms in light of the Diaspora status of the Jews: Moses Mendelssohn (1729–1786) and the followers of the Jewish Enlightenment in Germany (and their predecessors in Holland), who confronted a secularizing world; Rabbi Eliyahu of Vilnius—the Vilna Gaon (1720–1797)—in the Baltic, who desired to reform traditional Orthodox Judaism to make it more able to function in a self-contained Jewish world; and the first modern Jewish mystics, the Hasidim, typified by Rabbi Yisrael, the Baal Shem Tov (the Master of the Good Name; 1698–1760), who fought, like their contemporaries in Berlin and Vilnius, against what they saw as the stultifying practices and worldview of contemporary Judaism. All lived roughly simultaneously. In their wake came radical changes in what it meant to be a Jew in belief and practice. For contemporary Islam, all can serve as answers to the pressures found throughout the Diaspora. All offer parallels to the dilemmas faced by Islam in the West today. Thus, the list of "abominations" that secular Europe saw in Jewish ritual practices became the earmark for the question of what Jews were willing to change in order to better fit the various national assumptions about citizenship. These were as different in the nineteenth century as the debates about Islamic head covering in the twenty-first century in France, which is opposed because it violates the idea of a secular state; Germany, which is supportive under the very different meanings of multiculturalism); and the United Kingdom, where in March 2005 the courts allowed full traditional South Asian clothing (the *jilbab*) as an exception to the "school uniform" rule in a predominantly Muslim school where the dress code had been worked out with the parents.[21] These are themes, and their literary echo or prefiguration, that we shall explore in this book. How cultural difference becomes located within high or popular culture is one of the major themes of these chapters.

Now I know that there are also vast differences between Jews in the eighteenth and nineteenth centuries and Muslims today. There are simply many more Muslims today in Western Europe than there were Jews in the earlier period. The Jews historically never formed more than 1 percent of the population of any Western European nation. Muslim populations form a considerable minority today. While there is no Western European city with a Muslim majority, many recent news stories predict that Marseilles or Rotterdam will be the first European city which will have one. In France today, there are 600,000 Jews while there are between 5 and 6 million Muslims, who make up about 10 percent of the population. In Germany, with a tiny Jewish population of slightly over 100,000, almost 4 percent of the population is Muslim (totaling more than 3 million people). In Britain, about 2.5 percent of the total population (1.48 million people) is Muslim.[22] Demographics (and birthrate) aside, there are salient differences in the experiences of the Jews and Muslims in the past and today. The Jews had no national "homeland"—indeed, they were so defined as nomads or a pariah people (pace Max Weber and Hannah Arendt). They lived only in the *Goles*, the Diaspora, and seemed thus inherently different from any other people in Western Europe (except perhaps the Roma). Most Muslims in the West come out of a national tradition often formed by colonialism in which their homelands had long histories disturbed but not destroyed by colonial rule. And last but not least, the Israeli-Palestinian conflict over the past century (having begun well before the creation of the state of Israel), the establishment of a Jewish homeland, as well as the Holocaust seem to place the two groups—at least in the consciousness of the West—into two antagonistic camps.[23]

Religion for the Jews of pre-Enlightenment Europe and for much of contemporary Islam, which has its immediate roots in majority Islamic states, became for many a "heritage" in the Western, secular Diaspora. What had been lived experience in a *milieux de memoire* (environment of memory), to use Pierre Nora's often cited phrase from 1994, becomes *lieux de memoire* (places of memory) that refigure meaning constantly within the Diaspora.[24] What is it that such memory of ritual and practice can or must abandon? What must it preserve to maintain its coherence for the group? The answer depends on time and place, and yet the experience of Jews in the Western European Diaspora seems to offer a model case clearly because of the "narcissism of minor differences" among the three Abrahamic religions. The Jews maintain, in different modalities, their religious identity, even if the nature of the options explored created ruptures that produced their new problems and, over time, partial resolutions and yet further conflicts and resolutions. Thus, the ultraconservative Sephardic Rabbi Ovadiah Yosef, former chief sephardic rabbi of Israel, today applauds the use of aesthetic surgery to improve the marriageable status of women and men.[25]

The central cultural of the New Europe is not European integration in national terms, but the relationship between secular society and the dynamic world of European Islam. As the Syrian-born, German sociologist Bassam Tibi noted decades ago, it is the struggle within Islam to become a modern religion, whether within the Islamic world or in the Islamic Diaspora in the West, that is central.[26] Recently further voices, such as that of Tariq Ramadan and Feisal Abdul Rauf, have noted the need for a "modern" Islam.[27] There are certainly moments of confrontation in which Islamic ritual and practices have changed in specific settings. One can think of the entire history of Bosnian Islam from the nineteenth century until its destruction in the past decade and the resultant fundamentalist cast given Bosnia over the past decade. There is, however, a substantial difference between the contexts. Anyone interested in contemporary Europe before 11 September 2001, knew that the eight-hundred-pound gorilla confronting France, Germany, and the United Kingdom—and, to a lesser extent, Spain and Italy—was the huge presence of an "unassimilable" minority. Given Samuel Huntington's recent pronouncements about Hispanics in the United States—"The persistent inflow of Hispanic immigrants threatens to divide the United States into two peoples, two cultures, and two languages. Unlike past immigrant groups, Mexicans and other Latinos have not assimilated into mainstream U.S. culture, forming instead their own political and linguistic enclaves—from Los Angeles to Miami—and rejecting the Anglo-Protestant values that built the American dream. The United States ignores this challenge at its peril"[28]—the question of Muslims in Western Europe seemed to forecast the same set of problems. But, of course, exactly the same things were said (with correction for national self-image) about the Jews for two hundred years.

This book explores how Jews (however defined or self-defined) were able to deal with their integration into a secular state as Jews, what negotiations and compromises occurred, and what radical response from Zionism to neo-Orthodox fundamentalism answered them. It shows how the shift from a religious to an ethnic identity was part of a strategy of dealing with questions of difference, defined in terms such as decorum, in a Western Diaspora. And it argues that such a transformation becomes located within the world of high and popular culture as the production of literary texts comes to be a venue in which to present the fantasies of successful and unsuccessful integration or acculturation. Similar strategies are easily traced among Hispanic writers and thinkers in North America over the past decades. Indeed, it is the topic of Richard Rodriguez's recent book *Brown: The Last Discovery of America*.[29] While not producing a map for future action—historians, unlike political scientists such as Huntington, abjure prediction—I hope to sketch a set of debates that are now or soon will be present within Europe's sense of the future of Islam in Western Europe and the new EU—with or without the predominantly secular Muslim states of Turkey and Albania.

Central to our contemporary understanding of the role that Islam may and does play in the new Europe is the concept of multiculturalism that seems to provide a new model for understanding ethnicity and religion today. The multicultural can be understood, according to contemporary self-defined multicultural thinkers such as the late Gloria Anzaldúa, as the space where "this mixture of races, rather than resulting in an inferior being, provides hybrid progeny, a mutable, more malleable species with a rich gene pool."[30] Contemporary multicultural theory provides a further rehabilitation of notions of hybridity, of continually crossing categories of ethnicity, race, and culture. The Canadian filmmaker Christine Welsh effects a similar, necessary rehabilitation of the anxiety about being *Métis*, of mixed race: the *Métis* becomes a type of one on the Canadian frontier.[31] By positing the "cosmic race" as "healing the split at the foundation of our lives," she removes the stigma of "illness" from those at the borderlands. Here one must note that the very meaning of the "multicultural" is very different when one looks north and south of the United States border. Mexico, at least since the 1910 Revolution, has represented the hybrid as encompassing the wide range of native peoples as well as Spain but not necessarily other immigrant groups.[32] Canada for a very long time focused on the Anglophone-Francophone divide but now sees itself as a broadly multicultural nation encompassing the widest range of immigrants, many of whom are also present in Mexico.[33] American academics such as Edward Said could state simply years ago that "every cultural form is radically, quintessentially hybrid."[34]

And yet the multicultural is also the antithesis of hybridity, just as "cultural diversity" countered the "melting pot," one of the themes in this book. It can just as frequently be the reification and commodification of ethnic identity. The advocacy of and attacks on Afrocentric culture over the last thirty years stress the autonomy of cultural entities often described as "races." Thus Martin Bernal's important study of the denial of the African roots of Greece, in the first volume of his *Black Athena* (1987), gave way to an attempt to "prove" the African (loosely defined) roots of Greek culture.[35] The argument was not one of hybridity but of the authenticity of the African roots. Its project can be to stress the boundaries and borders between ethnic, cultural, religious, or class groups. If the *Métis* is hybrid, then hip-hop is multicultural. (And "world music" can be both!) While multiculturalism can allow for, and indeed celebrate, the merging of cultures so as to eliminate boundaries, one of its strongest claims (in the new global culture that is both hybrid and multicultural) is its insistence that each of us has a "culture" in a reified, ethnic, or class sense, and that the products of these cultures can be displayed, sold, consumed, and exchanged across borders. More important, central to both models of multiculturalism is that "culture" is the basis for our identities. "Biological" difference, the difference of the older and some of the present views of "race," is displaced onto a symbolic, cultural level. But at the same moment, this cultural heritage is commodified and thus made available for all consumers.

Indeed, it is the very concepts of multiculturalism as hybrid or autonomous, parallel culture that were shaped about the conflicts that arose in the late nineteenth century over the status of the Jews in high culture. This debate continues the debate about how the experience of the Jews in Western European cultures shapes the discourses that now impact on Islam. One of the complex litmus tests for Jewish difference in the age of civic emancipation is the ability of Jews to abandon all of their religious particularity and enter into the world of high culture. This world made ethical and aesthetic claims that seemed to validate an abandonment or at least a moderation of the older claims of particularism inherent in Jewish practices as seen through the lens of Christian Europe. "Multiculturalism" (in all of its varieties) comes to be the site where religion becomes ethnicity; where the aesthetics of culture comes to replace or at least parallel the formal aspects of religious practice; and where the "holy" language of art comes to replace the *lashon kodesh*, the Holy Language.[36] Here, too, there are fascinating parallels among Muslim writers and thinkers in our contemporary Western Diaspora, as Talal Asad has noted about the "New Arab" poets who, "strongly influenced by modernist European poetry, have resorted to ancient Middle Eastern mythology to signify the authentically modern."[37] How close to Martin Buber and his contemporary Franz Kafka, who comes to define "the authentically modern."

In the twenty-first century, we seem to be very skeptical about the claims of multiculturalism. Pierre Bourdieu and Loic Wacquant dismissed "multiculturalism" in 2000, in an essay in *Le Monde Diplomatique*, as

> recently imported into Europe to describe cultural pluralism in the civic
> sphere, whereas in the United States it refers, in the very movement
> which obfuscates it, to the continued ostracization of Blacks and to the
> crisis of the national mythology of the 'American dream' of 'equal op-
> portunity for all,' correlative of the bankruptcy of public education at the
> very time when competition for cultural capital is intensifying and class
> inequalities are growing at a dizzying pace. The locution 'multicultural'
> conceals this crisis by artificially restricting it to the university micro-
> cosm and by expressing it on an ostensibly 'ethnic' register, when what
> is really at stake is not the incorporation of marginalized cultures in the
> academic canon but access to the instruments of (re)production of the
> middle and upper classes, chief among them the university, in the con-
> text of active and massive disengagement by the state. North American
> 'multiculturalism' is neither a concept nor a theory, nor a social or politi-
> cal movement—even though it claims to be all those things at the same
> time. It is a screen discourse, whose intellectual status is the product of
> a gigantic effect of national and international allodoxia, which deceives
> both those who are party to it and those who are not. It is also a North
> American discourse, even though it thinks of itself and presents itself as a
> universal discourse, to the extent that it expresses the contradictions spe-
> cific to the predicament of US academics. Cut off from the public sphere

and subjected to a high degree of competitive differentiation in their professional milieu, US professors have nowhere to invest their political libido but in campus squabbles dressed up as conceptual battles royal.[38]

Whatever the truth about this comment on the academic world of North America, this view of multiculturalism (defined here as an American discourse of victimization) retains one strong element inherent to the general sense of the multicultural: that of the multicultural as the invention of theorists arguing their own case. This would apply equally well to the theory debates of the early twentieth century, within the academy and beyond it, that created the very concept in its formulation of the ability or inability of the Jews to enter into or be isolated from modern high culture. Indeed, inherent in the very history of multiculturalism, as Bourdieu and Wacquant see it, is a clear rejection of it as incomplete, limited, compromised, and predictable. This was a hallmark of the debates in the early 1990s about the limits of the multicultural, but it was also a sign of the meanings associated with the multicultural almost a century prior. When the Chicago Cultural Studies Group tabulates "a variety of means for the idea of multicultural: the corporate multiculturalism of global capital; the interdisciplinary cultural criticism that conjoins different publics around discourse, identities, and difference; the international comparativism that crosses boundaries to produce new knowledge and new challenges to the means of knowledge; as well as countless local impulses that appear to derive from pluralism, nationalism, or insurgent subcultural formations and alliances," they are reflecting the complex origin of the multicultural in the image of the Jew as well as its "postmodern" history.[39] Today, in the polemics surrounding the integration of Islam into Western culture, or, according to Canadian Islamic activist Irshad Manji, the modernization of Islam, she dismisses the multicultural (read now as radical cultural pluralism) as a sop to the inhumanity of Islam: "As Westerners bow down before multiculturalism, we often act as if anything goes. We see our readiness to accommodate as a strength—even a form of cultural superiority (though few of us will admit that). But foundamenalists [sic] see our inclusive instincts as a weakness that makes us soft, lardy, rudderless."[40] Yet multiculturalism is in the twenty-first century still seen as a goal for the transformation of the separatism of Diaspora groups into members of a cultural community through the production of high culture. Indeed, Irshad Manji over and over again evokes even the hybridity of contemporary Israeli society as an example of such productive multiculturalism. The origin of both models of the multicultural, as I shall show, lies not in North America but in Europe; its adaptation and inflection vary from national culture to national culture. It seems inescapable. Even such pessimistic accounts of the afterlife of the multicultural articulated as Paul Gilroy's *After Empire: Melancholia or Convivial Culture?* postulated a new variant on the hybrid multicultural, the "feral beauty of postcolonial culture."[41]

The variant meanings of "culture" (the discourses that define, according to participant and/or observer, a network) and "Culture" (the production of aesthetic objects) are linked in the modern period by the central notion that both seemed to be defined by fixed ideas of "nationhood." Yet, as Norbert Elias observed decades ago, "the German concept of *Kultur* places special stress on national differences and the particular identity of groups; primarily by virtue of this it has acquired in such fields as ethnological and anthropological research a significance far beyond the German linguistic area and the situation in which the concept originated. But that situation is the situation of a people, which by any Western standards, arrived at political unification and consolidation very late and from whose boundaries, for centuries and even down to the present, territories have again and again crumbled away or threaten to crumble away."[42] It is the very indeterminacy and porosity of the concepts of "culture" and "Culture" that make the reading of cultural objects a means of understanding the strategies and rhetoric of the multicultural and the importance of multicultural objects, such as novels, poetry, art, theater, and film, in both presenting and constituting multiculturalism.

We can take one salient example from contemporary German-Turkish (Turko-German) writing. It is clear that some contemporary writers, at least, recognize the parallels between Jewish and Muslim experience. Here, too, the Jewish experience is that of the past, the Shoah, rather than that of the present. What is striking about the debates in Europe today is that they not only echo the debates, reforms, and reactions of the nineteenth century, but also impact on Jews and Muslims in Europe today. As with the Jewish writing of the eighteenth century in German, French, and Latin, it reflects by definition "liberal" attempts to engage the "enlightened" Europe. Today, as Olivier Roy notes, "neofundamentalist[s] . . . are not interested in creating or asserting a 'Muslim' culture. They reject the concept, even if they sometimes use the term to find a common language with Western societies, where the language of multiculturalism is the main idiom through which we deal with otherness. Conspicuous by their absence are neofundamentalist novelists, poets, musicians, filmmakers, or comedians."[43] Thus, the Muslims (now understood as "ethnicity" rather than "religion") engaged in the creation of high culture are by definition those engaged in a process of acculturation, even if they deeply mistrust this process. One needs only note that it is in the process of acculturation that the attack against Salman Rushdie's "heretical" novel *The Satanic Verses*, initiated by the Bradford Council of Mosques in 1989, was launched.[44] In the Muslim Diaspora in the United Kingdom, high culture, defined as the space of the multicultural, is and remains the place of contestation.

Zafer Senoçak's *Dangerous Relations* (*Gefährliche Verwandtschaft*; 1998) presents the Shoah as forming the back story to the novel.[45] While it does use Jewish identity to provide a model for the Turkish experience, it also imagines such an experience within the new multicultural model of hybridity or cultural synthesis. Senoçak provides the reader with a novel about Germany after the Shoah that is also an account of the tribulations of modern Turks in that Germany. Senoçak, while born in Ankara in 1961, has lived in Germany since he was nine years old. He writes in German (needless to say) from a self-consciously and ironic multicultural perspective. To do so, he evokes the "Jewish" experience as "historical," while the "Turkish" (but not necessarily Muslim) experience is contemporary. As Olivier Roy has argued, one of the processes that happens is the creation of a virtual Ummah by believers that is deterritorialized. This is a form of empowerment that transcends national limits and ethnic identity and can take on "secular" form. For secular writers, this process is the hyperawareness of an "ethnic" identity merged with an assumption that such a multicultural identity is simultaneously that of the victim. The problem that this evokes in the denial of the contemporary experience of Jews in Germany does raise further questions, but for the moment let us focus on his claims.

Senoçak's novel recounts the adventures of Sascha Muchteschem, the son of a German-Jewish mother and a Turkish, middle-class father. After the death of his parents, he inherits a box with the notebooks of his Turkish grandfather, which he cannot read as they are written in Arabic and Cyrillic script. These unreadable texts place him on the search for his roots just as he begins to write his first novel. Central to this novel are both of his grandfathers, the German-Jewish Orientalist and the Turkish adventurer. Both are radically secular, but what "secular" comes to mean in the context of a

German "secular" Diaspora is shaped by German expectations, not necessarily Turkish ones.

Senoçak presents a self-designated "hybrid" author who in his own estimation is the exemplary cosmopolitan German: "I don't have an identity. People in my world have more and more problems with this. It is as if the fall of The Wall, the collapse of the old order, did not only have a liberating function. Without The Wall one no longer feels oneself protected. Identity is a substitute concept for being protected" (47). He is, however, seen in the Berlin Republic as a Turkish writer. "Are you a foreigner? I am asked when I spell my name. Earlier I spelled it without being asked. Indeed, according to the passport I am German" (128). He is "seen" as Turkish, nevertheless: "Do you write in Turkish? I offer many contradictory answers to this question if only to confuse those who are already confused. Who could know that I hardly speak a word of Turkish . . . ? Colleagues of mine, who are more evidently foreigners than I, who are dark skinned or speak German with an accent, seem to have little problem with their reception as 'Foreign Writers'" (130). Forgotten, or at least repressed, is the powerful stereotype that no Jew could ever command a European cultural language, that hidden within the nuances of pronunciation or style is a "foreignness" that revealed the Jew within. It is visibility (skin color) and language that define difference. He is seen as different, and the assumption is that his language must also be different. He, however, does not see himself as appearing different because of his "Jewish" background. For him this appears "white," but not for the Germans.

Sascha Muchteschem is very dismissive of "Germanness." "Am I a German? This question never interested me. It seems to interest no one. The question about a German identity was an old fashion question, a theme heavy with clichés and stereotypes, a type of heretical question, that any intelligent person would dismiss with a gesture that indicated that it was unimportant" (127). Yet it is, of course, the history of the German Jews who saw themselves as Germans that haunts his own family: "In the family of my mother there were no survivors. One didn't speak about this. My mother crossly answered the questions that I asked about the photos I found in the drawers in the library. She took the photos away and, as I later learned, called aunts and cousins merely strangers or friends of grandfather" (59). That this vanished family wanted to be German did not mean that they wanted to become Christian. "My grandfather was one of those German Jews, for whom Judaism was nothing more than the belief of their fathers. My maternal family felt itself for generations indebted to the Enlightenment. . . . It would have never occurred to him to convert to Christianity, because this religion was just as passe as Judaism" (57). Could one be a German who just happened to be a Jew, just as the narrator desires to be a German with Turkish and Jewish ancestry? The historical answer is clearly "No." And what has happened to the ethnic or religious in each case? Is the Turk not a Muslim and the Jew not a German? The answer is a historical one: after the Young Turks, Turkish identity is consciously distanced from Muslim identity; and after the Shoah, the idea of a German Jew in the older model of a cultural symbiosis is unthinkable.

Certainly, the narrator sees his "Jewish" grandfather as a German. He reads his way through the library that his grandfather had built up in the 1920s and that survived the Nazis. It is filled with authors such as Thomas Mann (59). He shares the cultural prejudices of the Germans toward other peoples, especially the Turks. In other words, he has been completely acculturated into German society, and the sign of this is his idealization of high culture. His mother accepted his father, who was upper middle class and well educated, only after a five-year courtship. "The arrogance and disdain for the poor and primitive Turks that the German Jews expressed [were] a sign of their assimilation. . . . Many Orientalists were German Jews. They attributed to the Orient eternal tyranny, fatalism, immutability, and difference. Who would have thought that their grandchildren would become Orientals like their ancestors" (92). The irony is double-edged, for the "Orientals" (i.e., the Turks) are simultaneously becoming Germans as the Jews are becoming Israelis. They are becoming Israelis because the project of their becoming Germans failed horribly.

Belonging to the German cultural sphere is not sufficient to define "Germanness." There is the double problem, as Gershom Scholem noted about the "German Jewish symbiosis," that I shall discuss later in this book, that the Jews never really belonged to it in the eyes of the Germans and that the Jews fantasized that they were included. And it is in the realm of high culture that Scholem sees the fantasy having failed the Jews most egregiously:

> I deny that there has ever been such a German-Jewish dialogue in any
> genuine sense whatsoever, i.e., as a historical phenomenon. It takes two
> to have a dialogue. . . . Nothing can be more misleading than to apply

such a concept to the discussions between Germans and Jews during
the last 200 years. . . . To be sure, the Jews attempted a dialogue with
the Germans, starting from all possible points of view and situations,
demandingly, imploringly, and entreatingly, servile and defiant . . . and
today, when the symphony is over, the time may be ripe for studying
their motifs and for attempting a critique of their tones.[46]

Will the Turks simply replicate this error? "One day a woman said to me,
who lived in a very elegant and very well kept house in Dahlem, that today's Turks are much worse than the Jews of the past. The Jews would have
masked themselves in Germanness. They acted as if they were Germans.
One didn't believe them. But that was their problem" (66). The "mask"
is what is central to the German Jews in Senoçak's image of history. It is a
mask as seen by the Germans, but it was the only face that the German Jews,
such as the narrator's grandfather, actually had.

To understand the distinction between appearance and reality of Jew
and Turk is the key to the novel. The narrator enters into an exchange with
his friend Heinrich, who is an expert on nineteenth-century German-Jewish
history, as to what defines a human being:

> "The body is the only home that a human being has," Heinrich
> claimed categorically.
>
> I contradicted him. "Language is essentially more important. Only in
> language can you be at home."
>
> "Language alienates man from himself." He argued. "Man is a being
> without name." (82)

It is in the body that the essence of "Jewishness" lies for the Germans.
Language, the utopian space of the writer, is secondary. One thinks of Stefan
Zweig's claim, shortly before his suicide in Brazilian exile, that language is
the only home of the writer. It is a body that betrays even as it changes:

> Many generations of German Jews have concerned themselves with the
> question, when and how a Jew can overcome his Jewishness in order to
> become a total German. Lightening the skin and the hair, Germanizing
> language and belief did not free the Jews from the Jewish illness that they
> brought from Germany. The Jews took over these tortuous questions

from the German society in order to belong to that society. They made them more sophisticated and asked them again. And they became the same questions in return. And so on. This reciprocal process continued until the question was reformulated in: "When will Germany be free of its Jews." (89)

Historically, this is quite accurate if teleological in its argument that nineteenth-century anti–Semitism led directly to the Shoah. By the latter half of the nineteenth century, Western European Jews had become indistinguishable from other Western Europeans in matters of language, dress, occupation, the location of their dwellings, and the cut of their hair. Indeed, if Rudolf Virchow's extensive study of over 10,000 German schoolchildren published in 1886 was accurate, they were also indistinguishable in terms of skin, hair, and eye color from the greater masses of those who lived in Germany. Virchow's statistics sought to show that wherever a greater percentage of the overall population had lighter skin or bluer eyes or blonder hair, there a greater percentage of Jews also had lighter skin or bluer eyes or blonder hair.[47] But although Virchow attempted to provide a rationale for the sense of Jewish acculturation, he still assumed that Jews were a separate and distinct racial category. George Mosse has commented that "the separateness of Jewish schoolchildren, approved by Virchow, says something about the course of Jewish emancipation in Germany. However, rationalized, the survey must have made Jewish schoolchildren conscious of their minority status and their supposedly different origins."[48] Nonetheless, even though they were labeled as different, Jews came to parallel the scale of types found elsewhere in European society. They "became" German in their very bodies, but these bodies were distrusted by the culture in which they found themselves.

At the close of the twentieth century, it was the turn of the Turks. Can Turks, even hybrids like the narrator, really become Germans? Heinrich claims, "The Germans have learned nothing from history . . . now they have brought the Turks here. And they never came to terms even with the Jews" (82). Physical assimilation through surgery or intermarriage seems to be no prophylaxis for persecution in Senoçak's world. Hybridity, such as that of the protagonist, means only that one is exposed to a double risk. One is at the end an Oriental, no matter what one's identity or language. Being hybrid only reinforces this. The protagonist's desire is not to be cosmopolitan but to be "simply" German. This is denied to him by his Turkish identity, and his Jewish ancestry reinforces this in his own estimation. Indeed, the search for someone to "translate" his Turkish grandfather's notebooks from the Arabic (presumably Turkish) and Cyrillic (presumably Russian) fails when it becomes clear that what is written is disguised in a personal code, not in a national language. This rather pessimistic view can only work if a specific idea of a Jewish history that ends in the catastrophe of the Shoah in Europe dominates. If modern Judaism as a series of cultural negotiations is taken as a whole, a wider range of possibilities exist.

The study of the history and the culture of the Jews of Germany has been formed for good or for ill on the notion of the "reconstruction of a lost tradition." Whether following the ideology of the *Wissenschaft der Juden* (the science of the Jews) in the nineteenth century, or the post-Holocaust fascination with the "lost world" of the *Ostjuden* (Eastern Jews), or the *Beitrag* (contribution) of Jews to German culture before 1933, little thought has been given to the question of whether and how the model of the Jewish experiences in Germany (and Western Europe) may provide some hint of options and pitfalls for Muslims in today's Europe. What make Senoçak's novel striking is not that he answers these questions or questions these appropriations, but that he writes about them in the form of a novel. It is in the world of multiculturalism that literature (especially "serious" works of fiction) generates the cultural capital to allow an "outsider" to become a multicultural insider. This is one of the major means by which Jews entered into Diaspora culture as the model case for the multicultural. Jews become part of and then see themselves in opposition to Diaspora high culture. That Senoçak can turn this conflicted relationship to high culture and *Bildung* into the theme of his novel is one of the ironies of contemporary multiculturalism. This process of acculturation among Jews in Diaspora Europe may provide some indicators for the world of European Muslims in regard to their rethinking of their identity as ethnic culture bearers. Today such a rethinking may also provide a new focus for German-Jewish studies and a bridge to collaborative work with Muslim scholars in the Diaspora today. As such, it could have a political as well as cultural function in addition to its indubitable role in illuminating the ever-changing nature of Diaspora identities.

TWO

JEWS AND THE CULTURE OF DECORUM IN ENLIGHTENMENT AND POST-ENLIGHTENMENT GERMANY

By the close of the nineteenth century, the claims and failure of the Enlightenment promise impact on the manner in which Jews see themselves in society. It is not merely that the promises of absolute equality are violated by the claims of nineteenth-century racial science, but that Jews themselves begin to suspect that there is a modicum of truth in many of the claims of Jewish difference. No stronger case can be made, for this is the claim that Jews are unable or unwilling to ascribe to Western codes of social and therefore cultural decorum. Jews, no matter how well integrated into society, would always be different in the way they saw and thus represented the world. The multicultural as hybrid or as autonomous structure comes to reify, answer, or contradict the failures of the Enlightenment project. It is reflected in the very construction of the "Jew" as an image in Europe, but also impacts on late nineteenth- and twentieth-century self-representations of the Jew as part of or beyond the "multicultural." This shapes Jewish self-awareness in complex ways and clearly impacts on Jewish constructions of their role within European (and Western) culture. Let us take a single claim, that of Jewish immunity to alcoholism, and trace its history from the Enlightenment to the late nineteenth century (and beyond). In it, we can see how this discussion constantly creates expectations and then destroys them; constantly identifies and constructs categories while undermining them, and generates ever new ones; and serves as a focus for Jewish self-under-standing as well as European constructions of the image of the Jew.

Today, there is a commonplace that Jews do not drink to excess. Most recently, John Efron in his magisterial *Jews and Medicine* has argued for the genetic hypothesis: Jews are genetically not predisposed to alcoholism.[1] Ephron evokes the medical model seeing alcoholism as inherited, which has been dominant over the past fifty years. It was introduced after World War II as a calculated attempt to replace the moral model of the lack of will by a model of collective predisposition.[2] Such a model freed, it was assumed, individuals who were "alcoholic" from the stigma of individual responsibility for their "addiction." It was a genetic fault or mutation in the collective (race) that was at the heart of the matter.

The high (or low) point of this came in 2001 when the gene for the resistance to alcoholism in "Jews" supposedly was discovered.[3] In a paper published that year, a group of researchers based in San Diego argued that they had "evaluated 84 Ashkenazic Jewish American college students to determine the prevalence of the ADH2*2 allele (0.31). Carriers of ADH2*2 reported significantly fewer drinking days per month. ADH2*2, however, was not related to alcohol use disorders, alcohol-induced flushing and associated symptoms, number of binge drinking episodes in the past 90 days, maximum number of drinks ever consumed, or self-reported levels of response to alcohol. Results suggest that Ashkenazic Jewish Americans with ADH2*2 alleles drink less frequently, which might contribute, in part, to the overall lower rates of alcoholism in this population" (231). In other words, among Jewish college students of "Ashkenazic" descent, alcoholism is less apparent. But what does this actually mean? The authors understand the dangers of the claims and dismiss them. "Other limitations of this study included the use of self-report data, which may have produced increased variability. Study measures, however, were shown to have good reliability and validity and ADH2 gene status was not known at the time of data collection. Moreover, the sample consisted only of Ashkenazic college students, so the findings may not generalize to all Jewish Americans, such as Sephardic Jews or older populations" (237). But it is not just alcohol use that is self-reported; even the category of "Ashkenazic college students" is a self-reported category. What does this mean in the United States in 2001, looking at the fourth or fifth generation of Americans from Central and Eastern Europe? The assumption is that these cadres continued to follow those romanticized marriage practices of Eastern Europe, a fact that the anxiety about intermarriage over the past forty years in the United States seems to obviate. The "Jews" in this study respond similarly to the "Asians": "A variety of genetically influenced alcohol-related phenotypes relate to risk for alcohol dependence. In Asians, variation in the alcohol dehydrogenase (ADH2*2) gene relates to alcohol dependence, alcohol consumption, and reported alcohol-related symptoms, even after controlling for variation in the aldehyde dehydrogenase (ADH2*2) gene. The association of ADH2*2 polymorphisms with alcohol-related behavior, however, has not been well characterized in non Asians" (236). But, of course, "Asians" is a very American category lumping diverse cultures, histories, and geographies into a handy category for census purposes. Likewise, "the Ashkenazic Jews" is a construction of often contradictory meanings. Both are attempts to create a genetic homogeneity out of diverse and ever changing populations. The authors are, of course, inchoate in their attempt to define the categories of "Asians and Jews." Based on these claims, further genes for alcohol resistance were found.

"'We know that alcoholism is hereditary,' said Cindy L. Ehlers, associate professor of neuropharmacology at the Scripps Research Institute and lead author of a later study that claimed to document this genetic resistance to alcoholism by looking more broadly beyond the 'Jews and Asians' in 2002. 'But we only have very limited information on what is inherited, and almost no information on what genes might be involved except in the case of alcohol metabolizing enzymes.'"[4] The gene that this group discovered is at the ADH2*3 allele. Commentary on this finding notes that a related genetic pattern seems to be the reason for the absence of alcoholism among the "Jews": "'We would predict that the frequency of ADH2*3 will be lower in the alcoholics than in the non-alcoholics,' David W. Crabb, professor of medicine, biochemistry and molecular biology, and chair of the Department of Medicine at Indiana University Medical Center[,] observed. 'Similar findings have been obtained with individuals with another high-activity ADH allele, ADH2*2, that is found in Asians and Jews.'"[5] You can notice how a small group of "Ashkenazic Jewish" college students has become the "Jews." The problem with all of these findings is that they make assumptions about the constitution of "populations" from the genetic makeup of individuals or families. They then extrapolate a general genetic key for the resistance to alcoholism from that small sample (as if "resistance" were a behavioral reflex of that gene).

The idea that "my genes made me do it (or not do it)" remains the mantra for understanding alcoholism as an addiction. I (among many others) was and am not convinced that alcoholism fulfills the necessary definition to be understood as a disease, or indeed that dependence on alcohol has a single cause, certainly not solely a genetic one. But to reverse the argument and argue that there is a protective genetic component that shields a group such as the "Jews" is a rather odd extension of the medical argument into explaining resistance. This was a commonplace of nineteenth-century medicine, when the question was asked in 1854, for example, "To what agent or agents are the Jews indebted for their reported exemption from cholera?"[6] Such questions revealed themselves even in the time to be specious, as it turns out that Jews developed cholera just as frequently as anyone else.[7] While suspicion fed on "their intermarriage, the race being pure," as having "some influence in excluding extraneous sources of hereditary disease," the social context was also assumed.[8] What the British physicians had long known was that the Jews, now defined as members of an institution, the synagogue, quickly banded together to provide medical care for their co-religionists, a model that was advocated for all groups in London.[9] It is access to treatment and to preventative measures, or a question of reporting the incidents of disease, that creates the illusion of immunity.

Today the question of the genetic component to behavioral or social "ills" has reappeared with a vengeance. Contemporary medicine has even reintroduced the concept of race (which has never truly vanished) because of the politics of medical multiculturalism. The entire question of whether the "Jews" or the "Irish" or the "Native Americans" are appropriate designations for genetic pools or even comprehensible descriptors of statistical populations is again debated, but almost always as to the inclusion of a "race" as the site of illness—rarely because of its exclusion. The concomitant question of whether behavior always is genetically determined seems to be a central part of this new fascination with race. Yet as nineteenth-century physicians well knew, once the concept of "race" is used in medicine, it can be used to "explain" virtually anything.

Even in studies where a nongenetic explanation for the Jews' relationship to alcohol is sought, the result is completely determined by how the term "Jews" is used as a descriptor. Thus, one recent study in the United Kingdom on Jews, alcohol, and depression used self-reporting to define the "Jews" and discovered that "Jews were found to have less favorable beliefs about alcohol and drank less than Protestants."[10] In contrast, a study in Israel found that "Arabs tend to favor restrictive attitudes toward alcohol control measures in comparison with Jews."[11] Indeed, if you move from "Jew" to "Israeli" (but still defined as "Jewish"), there is the assumption that "a worrisome prevalence of non-ritual alcohol use among Israelis ... reinforced the position that the phenomenon of drinking is liable to develop into an important social and public health problem in the State of Israel."[12] The "cure" for this problem is seen as rooted in individual character traits, not in any type of group response.[13] Clearly, these are very different ideas of who a "Jew" is. Indeed, recently a survey of the literature on Jews and drinking dismissed the claim of a Jewish (no matter how defined) immunity to alcoholism in general as an unfounded assumption.[14]

The debate about Jews and alcohol seems to be one about the immunity of the Jews to alcoholism. The reality is that this assumption (and the social practice that it may or may not lead to) is part of the process of modernization that leads to the social integration of Jews into Western social practices and mores.[15] What I am interested in is the assumption that an excess of alcohol leads to the lack of decorum and that to become a part of the modern world, Jews in German-speaking lands had to establish within their religious practice the same nature of public decorum as was imagined among their Protestant neighbors. If one can trace this to a single point of origin, it is to the public letter that Moses Mendelssohn wrote to the Swiss preacher Johann Caspar Lavater in 1769 in which he countered Lavater's demand that he either refute the truths of Christianity or convert. Mendelssohn's careful answer stresses the need for a sense of decorum in public debate, which cannot take place under such demands. His Enlightened friends, such as Gotthold Ephraim Lessing, seemed to agree, since Lessing's *Nathan the Wise*, who captures Lessing's image of Mendelssohn, is a model of public decorousness. Indeed, Mendelssohn's defense of Judaism in his *Jerusalem* (1783) does not make it into a "rational" religion, as some later claimed, but into a decorous one.

We can begin with the general argument of the Enlightenment as applied to a wide range of intra-Jewish ritual practices from circumcision to burial as being barbaric and indecorous. All of these critiques seem even today to be comprehensible given our assumptions about the coherence of German Protestant society and the ritual practices of the Jews today. That the indecorous consumption of alcohol—*shiker ist a Yid*—is condemned as part of those aspects of ritual practice that had to be amended or abandoned strikes us, given our contemporary presumption of Jewish immunity to alcohol, as bizarre. But it is not more bizarre or any different than any of the other critiques of Jewish religious practices as revealing the inner nature of the Jews and their need for "civic betterment." Indeed, if we apply Norbert Elias's claims in his *Civilizing Process* (1939), the Jews become aware of the "threshold of embarrassment" concerning alcohol when they are forced to see themselves at the "threshold of repugnance." The "social pressure for self-control" becomes part of the idea of *Bildung* in German culture.[16] Jewish ritual comes in the age of Enlightenment to be the antithesis of the rational, as the Comaroffs noted: "ritual has long been a mark, in Western social thought, of all that separates rational modernity from the culture(s) of tradition. Whether as magic or mystery, as pseudoscience or social sacrament, it conjures up the very inverse of practical reason."[17] The very definition of practical reason is Protestant thought and practice in the German Enlightenment.

In April 1790 Paul Jakob Bruns (1743–1814), in an essay in the *Berlinische Monatschrift*, addressed the question of whether the Jews should abandon the holiday of Purim, the holiday celebrating the rescue of the Persian Jews by Esther from the machinations of Haman.[18] Bruns was one of the most notable Bible scholars of his day; at the time he wrote this essay, he was an historian, theologian, professor of Oriental literature, and librarian of the University at Helmstädt. After that university was closed in 1810, he taught for over three decades at Halle. In his essay of 1790, Bruns deplores the very act that rescues the Jews of Persia: the joy expressed by the Jews in the routing and destruction of their enemies is unseemly, as the act does not reflect "great deeds or persons that showed bravery and power for the improvement of their fatherland" (378). Rather the Jews are weak and whiney, mourn their own fate by wearing mourning before anything occurs, and then kill innocent people in vengeance. Indeed, the very act of Esther is not an act of great "expression of the soul" but rather is done grudgingly, showing the inherently weak character of the Jews. At the center of this tale, Bruns writes, is the desire for vengeance on the part of the Jews against their oppressors.[19] All this shows, Bruns stresses, is how alienated the Jews were from the Persians among whom they lived and how the Jews desired the destruction of their Persian enemies. Just so that his readers get the point, he notes that the Jews imagine today their treatment by the Christians being so revenged if only through the memory of their defeat of the Persians.

Bruns's argument centers on the character of the Jews as reflected in the story of Purim and the application of that tale to the world of eighteenth-century Jewry. He acknowledges that the Jews are in the midst of reform but that they should strongly look at the expression of the celebration of Purim, as it reveals the innate incompatibility of Jewish ritual with German sensibility. His reference is to the model evoked in Christian Wilhelm von Dohm's plan for the "Civic Improvement of the Jews," published in 1781–1783 in response to the request to Mendelssohn from the Jewish community of Strasbourg for a defense of the Jews in light of French attacks on them. Jews must transform themselves to become citizens of the state. They must reject or reform practices that are understood as inimical to that goal. This is very much in contrast to the views of other contemporaries such as the liberal educational reformer Wilhelm von Humboldt who, following John Locke, saw an inherent right to citizenship no matter what one's religious practices. Mendelssohn and most Jewish followers of the Enlightenment agreed with Dohm's position.

Bruns comments on the disorder among children in the synagogue who drown out the name of Haman with wood clappers as a sign of the lack of proper decorum. Central to his argument about the lack of decorum is the "exaggeration of gluttony (*fressen*) and drunkenness (*saufen*)" that accompanies the holiday (380). The terms, and their linkage with the Purim "comedies" that are played as part of the celebration, point to the notion that Jews are a nation that is lacking public decorum. Indeed, "Christians have disgust and disrespect for the entire nation [of the Jews]." But even "the philosophers among the Jews" are exasperated by these extravagances (380).

Bruns's source, if he has one that is greater than the word-of-mouth "common wisdom" of his time, may well have been texts such as Johann Jakob Schudt's early eighteenth-century accounts of Jewish holidays and beliefs.[20] There he begins his account of Purim with a condemnation of the "haughtiness and insolence" of the Jews at this time, who spend their time with "gaming, gluttony (*fressen*) and inebriation (*saufen*)" (308). The Jews of Frankfurt, for example, "riot, eat and drink and undertake all sorts of amusements" (314). They attend Purim plays that are little better than "shit" (*Mist*). This is a blanket condemnation of the festivities that are seen as a form of extravagance violating accepted order.

Here we have the view that Jewish ritual, especially the sanctioning of what Mikhail Bakhtin (1895–1975) calls "carnival," the reversal of all roles, is at the heart of the anxiety of Protestants in seeing the Jews as a version of the world answered by the rise of Protestantism. Martin Luther, in his infamous *On Jews and their Lies* (1543), noted that "the Jews alone might fill their bellies and feast on the world's joys.... For such a mode of life Muhammad promises his Saracens. In that respect he is a genuine Jew, and the Jews are genuine Saracens according to this interpretation."[21] Here may well be the first "modern," if knee-jerk, parallel between Jews and Muslims in terms of their relationship to the material world. Luther, who was no enemy of fleshliness, sees a differentiation between the hollowness of non-believers and the healthy corporality of the true believer. In this context, the Jew and the Muslim are interchangeable. Within Protestant thought, such notions of a lack of decorum had been traditionally associated with the Catholic celebrations of carnival at the time of the Reformation and beyond. Catholics are no better in this manner than Jews or Muslims.

Carnival represented a sanctioned rebellion within ritual not only against the structures of religious order and practice but also, from a Protestant point of view in the eighteenth century, against the order of the State, which the State must take seriously. In the second edition of his *Problemy poetiki Dostoevskogo* (*Problems of Dostoevskii's Poetics*), published in 1963, Bakhtin described the essence of the carnival: "It could be said (with certain reservations, of course) that a person of the Middle Ages lived, as it were, two lives: one that was the official life, monolithically serious and gloomy, subjugated to a strict hierarchical order, full of terror, dogmatism, reverence and piety; the other was the life of the carnival square, free and unrestricted, full of ambivalent laughter, blasphemy, the profanation of everything sacred, full of debasing and obscenities, familiar contact with everyone and everything. Both these lives were legitimate, but separated by strict temporal boundaries."[22] In Bruns's view, this temporality was the feast of Purim, and the force by which it was fueled was alcohol. While Bakhtin's view of the medieval peasant was his own fantasy, one can argue that this was certainly the lived experience of ghetto Jews and that Purim was a central part of that second order of life that allowed them to function within the limitations of the Jewish community and the boundaries of the ghetto. The actions in the synagogue at Purim place all into question: collective ridicule of officialdom, inversion of hierarchy within the community, violations of decorum and proportion, and celebration of bodily excess were part of the very structure that upheld order by allowing it to be flaunted on one day of the year. Even the sanctuary was not spared: the fool's sermon was preached from the pulpit. During Purim, this extended to the ability to violate all of the conventions of Jewish law from the overindulgence in drink to transvestitism. Indeed, the rabbis held that if one damaged another's property while intoxicated on Purim, one was not compelled to repair it.

Bruns's suggestion is to simply stop celebrating the holiday. It is a secular celebration, which is not prescribed by the Mosaic Law. He stresses this point, which was the rationale for the continuance of many Jewish rituals (including circumcision) among the Enlightenment Jews. He concludes with a simple threat—if the Jews do not stop such celebrations, the state authorities will. Order must prevail. No excess within ritual can be tolerated, as it undermines the very nature of the State by mocking it as no more in control of the Jews than were the Persians.

David Friedländer (1750–1834), perhaps the most radical thinker among the Jewish Enlightenment figures of his time, counters Bruns's suggestion almost immediately.[23] In a powerful polemic, he takes on Bruns's argument point by point, always circling back to the question of decorum. He begins by asking how one can observe the mote in one's neighbor's eye while ignoring the beam in one's own. "Helpful" criticism of the Jews and their rituals in the light of Dohm's earlier position now seems to have a negative, destructive tone in which the "narration of the religious prejudices of strange followers of other religions" (563) reflects a pleasure at their "comic" nature. At least, the argument seems to go, we Christians are not so silly as to do such things. Friedländer stresses early in his presentation the difference in the development of *Bildung* (here, acculturation) among the Jews of Prussia, Austria, France, and Poland, noting that most of the "Jews" whom Bruns addresses could not even read his essay (565). Those who could read it had already fulfilled the moral expectations of his views. The Jews of Prussia, among whom Friedländer counts himself, are the most sensitive to such views and had already modified their ritual practice, "even though there may be many Jewish children in Prussia who use the clapper at Purim and many adults who drink to excess (*berauschet*) on this day" (566). Given Friedländer's desire to strip Jewish practice of most ritual, as in his suggestions for the radical reform of the Kassel Jewish community a decade later show, this state of affairs still needed to be tended to.

Friedländer stresses in accord with Bruns that the true reward for such alterations in religious practice is the improvement of the entire community rather than the improvement of the individual. Yet he argues that such charges as made by Bruns do not necessarily lead to the acquisition of *Bildung* among the Jews but rather reflect the entrenched, pre-Enlightenment views of the nature of the Jewish character. Thus, the Jews had been "accused of violating their oaths, of being too attached to Palestine, or being pygmy-like in their stature, or having the advantage of not dueling on the Sabbath" (568). Such accusations are simply the reinforcing of stereotypes that do not need reinforcing, but countering.

Friedländer puts Bruns's views of Purim into this category. He stresses that Bruns's reading of the moral implications of the tale of Esther is simply wrong. The bloodthirstiness of the Jews, the nasty, whining, cringing nature of their character, is simply, according to Friedländer, not to be found in the Book of Esther (Megillah). To this end, Friedländer's quotes from Luther's translation of the Book of Esther (569) as well as contemporary Protestant readings of it by theologians such as Johann Gottfried Eichhorn, the founder of the "Higher" Criticism of the "Old" Testament (571). He counters that the celebration of Purim is a necessary part of the ritual practices of the Jews as it is not detrimental to the "common man" (573). He can work on the feast day and need only spend an extra hour in the evening listening to the text of the Book of Esther being read aloud in synagogue. Bruns's central point, that this text is understood not as a historical record of the rescue of the Jews of Persia but as a desired overpowering of the Christian states in which they now live, is dismissed by Friedländer in a most remarkable manner.

Friedländer argues that he is not all in favor of retaining the misuse of the festival of Purim, especially the excess of drinking and eating (*Schwelgen*), for what the Jews in the synagogues think about when they hear the Book of Esther read is not the overcoming of Haman or the possible application of such a coup d'état to contemporary states but the "feast (*Schmauß*) that awaits them and that remedies the fast day that had occurred; he stamps with his feet when he hears the name of Haman, because his fathers had done so" (575). In Prussia, such "immoralities were being lost and the rough edges [of the Jews] smoothed" (575). "Even if in Berlin the clapper has not completely disappeared, the Purim comedies, the drunkenness, and other excesses of an excessive happiness ... either never existed or have been long abandoned. At least I have ... neither seen nor heard about such things" (576). Indeed, the tradition of the lack of decorum and the interruption of the somber ritual of prayer in connection with Purim come to be seen as a hallmark of the ritual practices of the medieval German-Jewish world by Reformers such as Leopold Zunz.[24]

Friedländer charges his readers to abandon the generalities about the Jews and their lack of decorum and the threats that such a lack implies to the society in which they live. It is the duty of the "stronger," he notes, "to extend an arm to the weaker and say 'let us be friends'" (576). This is not achieved by Bruns's exaggerated carping that demands that the Jews alter their religious practices.[25] Indeed, it only exacerbates the hatred of the Jews by stressing the corrupt nature of the manner by which the Jews worship and act.

Such a position is very much in line with the general tenor of the time in terms of decorum. Two years earlier, in 1788, Adolf Freiherr von Knigge published his guide to social interaction, without a doubt the single most important statement of the Enlightenment concept of decorum.[26] He warns (and I quote a contemporary British translation) that "nothing can be more disgusting to a sensible man, than the sight of a rational being depriving himself of the use of his intellects by too copious draughts of that exhilarating beverage" (2:106). The sober Enlightened man has the duty "not to indulge them in their excesses, how pleasing so ever the shape maybe in which they appear, but to shew as far as prudence permits that you have an unconquerable aversion against them, and to be particularly careful never to join in smutty discourses" (1:139). The description would fit Bruns's and other earlier descriptions of the Jews at Purim, with the excess of alcohol and the lewd Purim plays. But Knigge's discussion of social intercourse with the Jews focused obsessively on Jews and money, Jews and trade, and Jews and haggling.[27]

This is typical for the Enlightenment. Montesquieu in *De l'esprit des lois* (1748) as well as David Hume in his essay "Of National Characters" (1748) agree with him about the public nature of the Jews.[28] Each, however, has his own explanation: Montesquieu believed that it rests on the "nature" of the Jews; Hume, on their political context. Knigge's image of the Jew is an Enlightenment one that perpetuates in different rhetorical guise the notion of an essential Jewish sensibility. But in the third edition of 1794, Knigge notes that he is not speaking about those "who have (perhaps not for their own happiness) transformed themselves to follow the morals of Christians." That is, he is not speaking of those Jews who have begun to transform themselves into "Germans." For these Jews, Knigge complains, Christian sins and foolishness replace the simplicity and moral rigor of their own beliefs. Here there is a sense that such Jews fall victim to the drunkenness associated with civil society, with debauchery, and with the lifestyle of the Christian fop.

Yet within Friedländer's argument is the double sense that such rituals, such as drunkenness, if not the misreading of the Book of Esther, had existed and had been eliminated, at least among the most Enlightened of the Jews, those of Germany. The lack of sobriety of the Eastern Jews was still in need of strenuous reform, as Friedländer notes in 1816, when he was consulted by Malziewsky, bishop of Kujawia, at the point when the Prussian government decided to improve the situation of the Polish Jews. (He published his report in 1819, with a title echoing that of Dohm's earlier tractate on German Jews: *On the Civic Improvement of the Jews of Poland.*) German Jews had become decorous and had abandoned crude practices that only masked the true religious significance of the celebration. Jews in Germany were not drunkards, at least not in religious rituals that formed the public face of Jewish practice.

Friedländer was, of course, quite right that in his and the public's perception, Enlightened Jews were no longer drinking to excess. No less an authority on public decorum than the Königsberg philosopher Immanuel Kant (1724–1804) recognized this. In 1798, sitting down at the age of seventy-four to revise his lectures on "anthropology," originally from the winter semester 1772–1773 but repeated as late as 1790–1791, Kant added,

> Women, ministers, and Jews do not get drunk, as a rule, at least they
> carefully avoid all appearance of it, because their civic position is weak
> and they need to be reserved. Their outward worth is based merely on
> the belief of others in their chastity, piousness and separatistic lore. All
> separatists, that is, those who subject themselves not only to the general
> laws of the country but also to a special sectarian law, are exposed through
> their eccentricity and alleged chosenness to the attention and criticism of
> the community, and thus cannot relax their self-control, for intoxication,
> which deprives one of cautiousness, would be a scandal for them.[29]

This is an addition to the first published version of his text in 1798. Kant summarized the assumptions that underpinned Friedländer's discussion of

Bruns and his defense of the decorum of the German Jews. It is interesting that in his further presentation of the Jews in his *Anthropology*, he stresses, as does Knigge and all of the earlier Enlighteners, their nature as merchants and hagglers, with a focus on the "Jews in Poland."[30]

It is only in his discussion of Western Jews that Kant specifically returns to the question of decorum. Kant had already stressed, as Hannah Arendt noted, that inherent to the very notion of history is the idea of progress, and that while freedom and culture are usually the end products of such progress, "only once, almost in passing, in a parenthesis, does Kant state that it is the question of bringing about 'the highest end intended for man and that is sociability' [*Geselligkeit*]."[31] If history is to aim toward culture, freedom, and sociability, so too must the Jews, as they must become a people once again "in" history. Jews cannot afford to be visible in the public sphere as Jews, a point already made by Moses Mendelssohn in his insistence that Jews learn to speak the language of the nation where they dwelt. But the distinction here between public and private, with religious rite and practice being a private matter (as espoused by Mendelssohn), quickly shows itself to be specious. Here they have ceased to act "like savages," who according to his views on madness in his lectures have no control over their consumption of alcohol: "The wildest peoples, as soon as they get to know strong drink, become desirous for it. People, who are indifferent to strong drink, very early succeed in rejecting this tendency."[32] Jewish "drunkenness" in terms of the eighteenth-century debate is an aspect of religious practice and does not directly impact on the public sphere in most cases. It is, however, seen as a reflection of inherent differences in religious practice that demand reform if Jews are to be seen as acceptable citizens in the public sphere—for all that the Jews do is pointless ritual. By Kant's day, the inebriation of the German Jews had given way to the notion of Jewish sobriety in the use of alcohol. It is hypocritical, for as with women and ministers of the cloth, it does not come from inner conviction but as a response to external forces. This change is one that is imagined as a process that took place in the late eighteenth century and—at least for Jewish thinkers such as Friedländer—was still not complete among Eastern Jews.[33]

The view, by the way, that Eastern Jews are prone to higher rates of alcoholism becomes a standard view in the course of the late nineteenth century, when eugenists in the United States, such as Emma Transeau, object to the presence of Eastern European Jews, a force in "the alcoholization of the immigrants" that will lead to American degeneration.[34] The common wisdom of the physicians by the turn of the twentieth century follows Kant. The British physician James Samuelson, in 1880, stated that "they [the Jews] are a small community; and their partial isolation from other religious denominations has a tendency to make them more careful of their morals."[35] Maurice Fishberg, the leading American exponent of Jewish public health at the turn of the twentieth century, argues, following Kant, that Jews have a much lower rate of alcoholism because they are subject to external social forces. This fitted nicely with his notion that "in their old home in Russia, the Jews abhor a drunkard; they name him with converts and outcasts. To have a drunkard in the family means difficulty in contracting suitable marriages for the children. The Jew knows that it does not pay to be drunk. Having lived for centuries under the ceaseless ban of abuse and persecution in the European Ghettoes, he has found it advantageous to his well bring always to be sober."[36] Yet Norman Kerr, at much the same time, advocated a genetic explanation: "This extraordinary people has, amid wondrous vicissitudes, preserved a variety of distinctive characteristics; and I cannot help thinking that some inherited racial power of control as well as some inherited racial insusceptibility to narcotism, strengthened and confirmed by the practice of various hygienic habits, has been the main reason for their superior temperance."[37] Or is it only, following the model set by Knigge, that when "the increased intercourse with non-Jews by the removal of social barriers" occurs, there is "an increase of alcoholism among Jews"?[38] Or, as Fishberg noted in New York at the turn of the century, "[A]lcoholism is decidedly increasing among the Jews in New York, particularly in the younger generation, who are adapting the habits and customs of life of their gentile neighbors."[39]

As Jews enter more and more into the public sphere, the question of who is the drunk becomes contested. In Izak Goller's 1931 Purim play, the king of the Persians, Ahasuerus, introduces himself with the following monologue:

> You can tell
> I'm a King of might,
> Drunk as a lord
> From morn till night!
> Princes a hundred
> And twenty seven
> Conquered have I

And sent to Heaven!
Gallons of Beer
I reckon as naught;
Whiskey I quaft
By pint and quart.[40]

Medicine too catches up. By 1944, Robert Bales, in his Harvard dissertation and subsequent publication, holds up the Eastern Jews as the model immigrant community when it comes to alcohol use.[41] They have become the epitome of "moderate, integrated, family based drinking," as opposed to Protestants who, if they drank, were much more likely to become alcoholics than Jews. If Kant's argument about Jewish moderation is based on the conscious anxiety of Jewish visibility, Bales accepts this, seeing alcoholism as the result of "anxiety and repression," both of which he finds (in 1944!) much less prominent among Jews. One can add that among Eastern European Jews, at least according to Maurice Samuels in 1943, it was the Russians who were "stupid, perhaps, and earthy, given to drink and occasional wife-beating, but essentially good-natured."[42] Everyone invents his or her own drunks.

Here, the adoption of this model becomes part of the way that Jewish, multicultural writers see the Jewish past. The American poet Jerome Rothenberg (1931–) provides his fantasy of a Polish pogrom in the 1930s in a poem published in 1974:

getting dead drunk he bled his jewish
barber with a shaky hand
or hiding from the cossacks still shouted
to the man who hid him
"take off your cap you jewish cunt"
a Radziwill can keep a boy's face
in a pail of water can make him
drink & puke then laugh at their women
forced to sit in trees crowing like
cocks would shower them with bullets
watch them fall & run but always
throw them coins or kiss another
Radziwill while mumbling
"beloved brother go to hell!"[43]

Rosenberg's poem places drunkenness firmly within the character of the Pole—here, not the Polish peasant but the Polish nobility. For this Jewish poet, the pogrom is itself a result of this lack of decorum.

The view that religious practice during Purim seems to preclude excess, at least in Germany, is established by the beginning of the nineteenth century. By 1857, an anonymous monologue appeared in the Jewish periodical *Jeschurun*. Edited by the leading Orthodox thinker of the nineteenth century, the Frankfurt neo-Orthodox Rabbi Samson Raphael Hirsch (1808–1888), this periodical represented a newly articulated voice that provided a critique of reform. Aimed at a "family" readership, it sought to inculcate Jews with a sense of the value of traditional beliefs and rituals in light of the pressure to efface Jewish difference through the elimination of Jewish ritual practices. For Hirsch, human difference, established as a necessity after the Flood, is a prophylaxis against another collapse of civilization. Entitled "A Speech by a Sober Drunk in a Meeting of Drunken Sober Men, Held at the Great Marketplace between the Rhine and the Oder on Purim, 5617," the author (perhaps Hirsch himself) nostalgically evokes the lost world of Purim,[44] bemoaning the fact the Jews have abandoned the celebration of a holiday that had meant so much to Jews in their grandfather's time, when they were cut off from the rest of the world by official policy. It was during Purim that "houses filled with shouts," that the "masked masses filled the streets" (377). When the non-Jews jealously asked what was occurring, they were told that it was the "Jews' carnival" (377). All of this nostalgia for a lost, freer past is told as a monologue by a sober inebriate "looking into the drunken-sober eyes" of his audience. Purim becomes in this view the lost place for Jewish joyfulness—not excess.

The author continues with the proverb, "Fever is not an illness; Purim is not a holiday" (378). That is, in its usual meaning, Purim is to be understood not as a day of festivity but as a sign for an act of remembrance and insight. He begins what amounts to a classical proverb sermon in Protestant style (using a proverb instead of a Biblical citation as its text) by dismissing the literal meaning of the proverb: "I could simply say, if I wanted to be dismissive, that with fever there is a powerful thirst that needs to be stilled by cool water; with Purim there a power[ful] desire for cool wine" (378). This evocation of inebriation is immediately dismissed as superficial, for his intent is to stress the underlying "fantasies" that are Purim, when one is led into "the beautiful world of happy lack of concern and careless joy." This is the world of Purim as he sees it. "Fever" thus removes one from the cares of every day and provides a fantasy for the individual in the hallucinations of fever. As with one surviving a great storm, Purim is the blue sky that appears on the horizon when the storm has passed (379).

The author, to clarify the need for Purim, marshals all of the power of metaphors for survival and respite. For, in the author's mind, his audience of mid-nineteenth-century Jews, such dangers as represented by the tale of Esther seemed to have passed. The fever has gone, and "we now have forgotten the doctor who had given us the healing China-drink" (380). Not alcohol but tea has cured the "fever" that represented the dangers confronted by the Jews. Tea, by the mid-nineteenth century, had become the bourgeois drink that was seen as both healthful and relaxing. The Jews have forgotten the dangers of the past and are now "beguiled drunks, drunk from a few moments of long desired peace" (381). Today inebriation is being lulled by the belief that all danger for the Jews has passed. But, the preacher warns, "clouds mar the future of the Jews. The German climate with its pleasant spring temperatures could not unify itself and already dark storm clouds are to be seen in the heavens" (381). The lost revolution of 1848 and the striving for a "greater German unification" marked the beginning of a possible age of danger for the Jews that would parallel the threat of Persia to "destroy all Jews and everything Jewish" (381). What those now drunken on the sense of relief from threat need to remember is the lesson taught by Mordecai, who never shied from being Jewish and confronting the enemies of the Jews. This is the new lesson of Purim.

By 1857 Purim had been separated from notions of drunkenness, at least in terms of German self-representation, even in neo-Orthodox circles. The evil associated with inebriation, however, has maintained itself and become part of the metaphoric critique of exactly those who have accepted the inherent lesson taught by Enlighteners such as David Friedländer. These new drunks are those inebriated by their sense of freedom as promised by the Enlightenment ideal of the equality of man in the light of uniform public behavior. In 1887, *Jeschurun* provided another reading of Purim in which the political implications for the present were also made clear.[45] That Jews, happy and well integrated into a state, can be at risk for life and limb at the moment they feel the displeasure of the mighty, is taken as a warning about the state of the Jews in Germany. But no word about drunkenness or inebriation, as metaphor or as "fact," is part of the world of Purim evoked in 1887. Purim has been stripped of any such associations.

Indeed, by the close of the nineteenth century, Purim seems to have acquired two completely acceptable functions in the cultural memory of the Jews. First, it is seen as a celebration that marks a watershed in Jewish history. Thus, Heinrich Graetz and Moritz Steinschneider both write historical accounts of Purim without any mention of excess except in terms of its function in earlier Jewish ritual.[46] *The Jewish Encyclopedia*, which catalogues the beliefs of the turn of the twentieth century, cites Steinschneider that "while Jews have always been noted for abstemiousness in the use of intoxicants, drunkenness was licensed, so to speak, on Purim, to comply with the command which seemed to lie in the Biblical term 'mishteh' (drink) applied to Purim… It is not, surprising that all kinds of merry-making, often verging on frivolity, have been indulged in on Purim, so that among the masses it has become a general rule that 'on Purim everything is allowed.'"[47] Alcohol use becomes something of the past, even in the accounts of Purim translated into German from Yiddish classical writers such as Jizchak Peretz. His tale, entitled "Drunk Every Day, Sober on Purim," plays in a distant Jewish past as imagined by "modern" Jews.[48]

Second, a newly reconstituted Purim becomes a central focus for early Zionist accounts of anti-Semitic activity and, equally important, Zionist meetings to counter such actions. The Zionist newspaper *Die Welt* has a regular column from its founding in 1898 recording such "Purim" activities. Among those who spoke (in 1900) at such a meeting in Dresden was Martin Buber, whose later tales of the world of Hasidic Jewry were to be stripped of both magic and excess.[49] He contributed to *Die Welt* "A Purim Prologue" in 1901. There he writes of "a happy, modest feast," a "feast of joy and color," and "a feast of warm handshakes"[50] (this is a poem, and my selection from Buber's rather long and mechanically rhymed text is adequate to give a flavor of the material without attempting to copy its poetics). Purim is a festival of "folk-joy," the "joy of the freed," which points to the celebration of Passover and the rescue of the Jews from Egypt. Purim is the model for the Zionist dream of liberation from persecution. He mocks the recent German–National appropriation of Purim as the fulfillment of the Enlightenment promise of acculturation. He writes his prologue in response to the colonization of Purim in 1901 as a German national holiday, "German-Jewish Day" (*Deutsche Judentag*). Suggested by the historian

Martin Philippson, chairman of the *Deutsch-Israelitische Gemeindebund* (German-Israelite Congregational Organization), as well as of the *Verein zur Förderung der Wissenschaft des Judenthums*, which was founded largely through his efforts in 1902, and of the *Verband der Deutschen Juden* (Organization of German Jews), the *Deutsche Judentag* was to reclaim Purim from any association with non-German images of excess.[51] Such Purim celebrations, without excess and alcohol awareness, are mocked by the Zionist Max Jungmann as a type of pathetic "Purim play." He further mocks the German claim that such celebrations are intended to show the Germanness of the Jews. This is underlined when the speaker in Jungmann's comic monologue is especially offended when someone responds to such claims of the decorousness of German Jewry in Yiddish![52] In all cases, Purim's celebratory nature seems to fall within accepted standards of decorum.

With all of the Jewish deemphasis on drunkenness and the lack of decorum, the image of the inebriated Jew within still haunts the vision of Christian anti-Semites at this moment. Oscar Panizza's (1853–1921) often quoted "The Operated Jew" of 1893 presents the tale of a Jew, Itzig Faitel Stern, who has his body transformed by cosmetic surgery and his manners and speech by education. At his wedding to a non-Jew, he becomes totally inebriated, all of his manners vanish, and his body reasserts its "essential" Jewish nature to reveal the misshapen Jew within. It is the consumption of alcohol that is the key to his undoing. The Jew avoids alcohol here, in an uncomfortable evocation of Kant, because it would reveal his true nature to an unsuspecting Gentile world. This is the rhetoric of the anti-Semite, whose work echoes the worst excess of the beginning of political anti-Semitism in Germany and is not taken seriously except as a sign of anti-Semitic excess, as the German philosopher Mynona (Salomo Friedländer) notes in his 1922 parody "The Operated Goy."[53]

Yet at this point any question of the association of *Western*, acculturated Jews with intoxication can no longer be made within legitimate medical science. Hugo Hoppe, in his standard study of the diseases of the Jew with an emphasis on alcoholism, states the commonplace that "moderation finds its most evident expression in the statistical fact that alcoholism is as good as unknown among the Jews. In the great army of drinkers, who inhabited our hospitals, our sanatoria for alcoholics, our mad houses, our prisons and jails, one rarely finds a Jew. Delirium tremens, acute alcohol poisoning, suicide as a result of drink is unheard of among the Jews."[54] Given the commonplace that Jews had a much higher rate of mental illness, which was supposed to predispose one to drink, it is clear, at least to Hoppe, that Jewish immunity to alcoholism had to have an inherited rather than cultural cause. This "fact" arises just as any ritual association with alcohol vanishes in the public discussion of Purim in Germany. Absolved of the charge of lack of decorum, the Jews are simultaneously blessed with the health and sanity awarded by moderation. In an age in which alcoholism was seen as one of the major sources of social conflict and physical degeneration, this is not a small gift. But it is a socially determined one, not one inherent to any biological definition of the "Jews" that could have any valence today.

One can add that among Orthodox Jews, the question of Purim and alcohol has reappeared as part of the American concern with drugs and the lack of social decorum among youth. Moshe Werzberger, a practicing internist in Brooklyn, New York, and former chairman of emergency medicine at Brookdale University Hospital, commented recently,

> As I was driving on Shabbos, rushing an intoxicated, unresponsive
> teenager who was vomiting blood to the ER, the absurdity of the situa-
> tion was painfully evident to me. Here was a young student who together
> with some friends at an Oneg Shabbos had, without any second thought,
> drunk himself to the point of endangering his life. Yet, on Purim we al-
> low our children unrestricted access to alcohol, endangering their lives.
>
> An unresponsive, intoxicated patient requires approximately nine
> hours to return to sobriety. During this time of stupor, lethargy, and
> diminished reflexes, the patient is in danger. He may lose control of his
> airway, vomit, choke, and heaven forbid die. He may have a seizure, or
> suffer an irregular heartbeat. If someone is used to drinking alcohol on
> a regular basis it is possible for him to attain much higher alcohol levels,
> which can cause him to lapse into a coma, or even to die from direct
> alcohol poisoning.
>
> It is time to reevaluate our community's use of alcohol. Clearly we are
> drinking much more than our parent's generation, and our children are
> drinking more than us. This is the age of "At Risk Children." Doesn't
> anyone see the obvious correlation between the profuse alcohol con-
> sumption among our youth and the unprecedented number of children
> using illegal and dangerous drugs? ...

As Jews, we were given the gift of a Torah way of life. Noach's son Shem was blessed because of his dignified behavior when his father became intoxicated. Cham, however was cursed due to his improper response to the situation. Jews until now had an admirable reputation for sobriety. The Torah teaches us how to elevate the use of alcohol through the commandments; such as kiddush on shabbos, the four cups at the seder, wedding ceremonies, and circumcisions. This is the proper setting for the use of alcohol.

One of the commandments of Purim is to drink. But how much need one drink to fulfill his obligation, is there a limit? How could it be that God requires us to endanger our lives, and the lives of others in order to fulfill our obligation on Purim? According to the Halacha the proper way to celebrate on Purim is as follows. The commandment of drinking is only fulfilled with wine. Therefore, beer and liquor should not be drunk at all on Purim. Furthermore, this commandment only applies at the daytime Purim meal. Any amount of wine, which will cause the person to become intoxicated and behave in an improper manner, should not be drunk on Purim.[55]

While clothed in the rhetoric of the "war on drugs," the author equates alcohol and cocaine consumption; this view is not very far from that of the Enlightenment critics of Purim and the Jewish excess.

Islam, as it abjures alcohol and drugs, seems to be beyond the concerns of Jewish abstinence. We shall see, however, that the greater question of decorum presents itself over and over in the discourse of multiculturalism. It is present in the very inception of the concept of "ethnic" culture around the figure of the Jew in the theoretical discussions of the late nineteenth and early twentieth centuries. Moreover, it underlies the meaning attached to the construction of the Jew, as evidenced in the debate about ethnicity and the multicultural that arises at the beginning of the twentieth century and shapes our present fantasies of Jewish difference.

THREE

JEWS AND THE CONSTITUTION OF THE MULTICULTURAL ETHNIC

Multiculturalism is a linked set of concepts that originated in Europe and then flourished in the United States, from where it acquired global resonance during the twentieth century. It is, as we have noted, a multiculturalism with two seemingly distinct models: one a model of the hybrid, of the "Golden" or "New Man," of the merging of differences to form a world that incorporates the best qualities of the cultures that contribute to it. This model is usually linked to images of Diaspora cultures, cultures in transition, cultures in conflict, and then cultures in amicable resolution. The alternative model is one of "cultural diversity," of cultures existing parallel to one another, each maintaining its integrity in light of the pressures of acculturation into a dominant model. This is "cultural pluralism," to use the phrase coined in 1915 by Horace Kallen (1882–1974). The American historian David Hollinger, noting the case of Horace Kallen, has gestured toward a notion that the very idea of cultural pluralism in the twentieth century may well have evolved out of the Jewish experience in America.[1] I hope to show in this volume that both models of multiculturalism used and use the "Jew" as the litmus test for the possibility, necessity, and danger of the multicultural, and that this continues until today.

At the end of the nineteenth century, the redefinition of the Jew as a member of a culture in response to biological theories of Jewish difference is pivotal in shaping the very notion of the multicultural. This is not to say that such philosophical or sociological views of Jewish culture or ethnicity are bereft of biological modeling and metaphors. Indeed, when one examines them closely, the biological imperative seems to be a permanent part of any discussion of difference. Yet the transformation of the image of the "Jews" from a religious category to an ethnic or cultural one is central to the constitution of multiculturalism. The "religious" definition of the Jew as perceived in the Western, Christian world constitutes an exclusionary definition of the Jew. Thus, in this model, the "Jew" is a follower of a different and lesser religious tradition than Christianity. "Religion" may be defined in the form of religious rituals, as we have seen in chapter 2, but it may also be reduced to those images traditionally associated with the "Jews," such as the Jew as an economic factor, which may have nothing at all to do with Jewish ritual or belief. What underlies this model is the powerful belief that even conversion will not change the innate nature of the "Jew." This image of the immutability of the Jewish mind rests on a biological assumption of innate Jewish difference.[2]

Yet it is imperative to comprehend that among Jews, the move into modernity, from seventeenth-century Holland to nineteenth-century Germany, means replacing the stereotypes associated with "religion" with qualities that were associated with the "ethnic." This seemed to free the "Jews" from the taint of a Jewish "mind" and "language" and to open all avenues of modernity to them. Thus traditional Judaism had not given much value to the production of a secular culture for a secular world, since religious practice defined every aspect of their world. This is not to say that individual Jews did not contribute to high culture in Europe as early as the troubadours of the Middle Ages, but they were always caught between religious belief and secular activity. With the socialization of Jews into the world beyond ritual practice, such cultural activities became important to their multiple self-definitions as Jews and as members of a greater society. It also served as proof that the claims of a biological or racial definition of Jewish difference could be countered by the cultural activities of Jews in arenas quite different than those circumscribed by the stereotypes of the Jew as well as Jewish religious practices.

In this chapter, I want to examine a series of European and American "theories" of cultural difference from the late nineteenth century to the early twentieth century in which the "Jews" come to be the litmus tests for cultural flexibility or difference. Out of these discussions developed both the notion of hybridity as well as cultural pluralism as the models for multiculturalism in the course of the twentieth century. Given the general view in Europe that the "Jews" constituted a clearly definable entity, separate from and perhaps indelibly different than all other groups, this should not surprise us. What does surprise is the function of such difference in defining how cultures interact and how "being Jewish" is rethought.

Certainly the most evident starting place is Georg Simmel's (1858–1918) theory of the "stranger."[3] Simmel's theories place his view of culture firmly against that of late nineteenth-century Comtean positivism in sociology as well as the dominant view of the interpretative "sciences" (*Geisteswissenschaften*), such as history, of the time that saw all events as unique. Simmel's generalizations about human nature are philosophical and sociological models of "types" such as the "stranger." By constructing such "types," Simmel was clearly answering the stereotyping of anti-Semitic rhetoric by presenting "scientific" models of difference that explained Jewish difference but which were not limited to the "Jews." His views transcended the limitation of a positivistic description of social "reality" as well as the notion that each moment of human history was unique and unable to be the basis for general laws of human behavior.

Appearing as an appendix to his general textbook of sociology in 1908, Simmel's theory of the "stranger" reflects the standpoint of an acculturated "Jewish" scholar, marginal to the Berlin academic establishment, who sees difference in terms of position and time.[4] The "stranger" is, to use Simmel's often quoted view, "the person who comes today and stays tomorrow" (37). It is not the confrontation with difference alone that defines being a stranger but also the sense of rootedness implied in the potential of the stranger to be separate whether that separateness exists in experience or not. "He is, so to speak, the potential wanderer: although he has not moved on, he has not quite overcome the freedom of coming and going. He is fixed within a particular spatial group, or within a group whose boundaries are similar to spatial boundaries. But his position in this group is determined, essentially, by the fact that he has not belonged to it from the beginning, that he imports qualities into it, which do not and cannot stem from the group itself" (37). Now it is clear that this is the image that resonates throughout the nineteenth-century debates about the role and nature of the Jews in Germany. It was most clearly articulated in the confrontation between the "Prussian" historian Heinrich von Treitschke (1834–1896) and the German-Jewish nationalist philosopher Hermann Cohen (1842–1918) in the so-called Anti-Semitism debate of the 1880s about the ability and desirability of Jewish assimilation. But Simmel generalizes about the nature of difference based

on this model rooted in his belief in a Jewish "type." This type, however, imports modes of behavior into the society into which she or he enters as well as internalizing existing models. Thus, the older model of decorum used to define the behavior of the Jew is no longer sufficient to define the stranger. You may know all of the rules, you may follow all of the rules, and yet you still remain a "stranger."

For Simmel, the stranger's difference stems from his self-definition, not from the imposition of notions of difference upon him. But the category into which the greater society places the stranger is one generated by their need to categorize and limit: "The stranger, like the poor and like sundry 'inner enemies,' is an element of the group itself. His position as a full-fledged member involves both being outside it and confronting it" (37–38). In a real sense, Simmel's stranger is a continuation of Hegel's master-slave dialectic of self-consciousness in *The Phenomenology of Mind* (1807), at least as read in the late nineteenth century.[5] In this reading, the slave is necessary to define the master, but the master is necessary to define the slave. Neither can exist without the other, and both feel an obligation to maintain the other's role. What is clear for the master's role is also present in that of the slave: the need to maintain a system that preserves the stability of their self-definitions. Thus the "stranger" is a role in society that must exist in order to define the "native."

Yet Simmel makes sure that the "slave" is not limited by his own self-consciousness. Simmel's stranger has the potential for greater creativity as he is not "radically committed to the unique ingredients and peculiar tendencies of the group" (39). The strength and weakness of the stranger lie in his or her separateness from and presence proximate to the group. Codes of behavior are thus observed from the outside; they may become malleable if judged inappropriate or insufficient. Creativity and innovation comprise the litmus test for the "stranger," and this manifests itself within the accepted categories of the world in which the stranger now finds him or herself.

When we see how this argument works in regard to Simmel's examples, it is clear that his idea of difference resounds in the figure of the Jew in quite a more complex manner. Central is Simmel's concept of individual identity being rooted in a network of social affiliation. Actually, he suggested that there are two types of such networks. The first, and here we can place his view of the Jews, is "organic," relying on a traditional understanding of identity within the group. The "rational" network is that which the individual develops over time and will, most probably, extend beyond the "organic." This is based on individual needs rather than group identification.

The stranger's relationship to the group is, according to Simmel, like that of the lover. The assumption is that the beloved is inherently unique and it is only with time that the erotic blinders are lifted and we see our partner in terms of shared human traits. This is the "possibility of commonness" and lies in the newly restated view, present in liberal Protestant thinkers in Berlin such as the theologian Adolf Harnack (1851–1930), that the relationship between Christian and Jew or at least Christianity and Judaism is one of a special but "rational" (in Simmel's terms) network. Like lovers, the Jew and the Christian are bound together inexorably, each now blind to the other's communality, focused only on their difference.

The place that Simmel (and indeed all of our commentators) locates the difference of the Jews is in the sphere of the economic, not the "cultural." In his *Philosophy of Money* (1900), Simmel had offered an alternative to Marxist theories of labor. In the essay on the "stranger," the Jew is evoked as a "natural" example, as the debate about the role of the Jews in constituting (or deforming) capitalism was an ongoing one:

> Once an economy is somehow closed the land is divided up, and handi-crafts are established that satisfy the demand for them, the trader, too, can find his existence. For in trade, which alone makes possible unlimited combinations, intelligence always finds expansions and new territories, an achievement which is very difficult to attain for the original producer with his lesser mobility and his dependence upon a circle of customers that can be increased only slowly. Trade can always absorb more people than primary production; it is, therefore, the sphere indicated for the stranger, who intrudes as a supernumerary, so to speak, into a group in which the economic positions are actually occupied—the classical example is the history of European Jews. The stranger is by nature no "owner of soil"—soil not only in the physical, but also in the figurative sense of a life-substance which is fixed, if not in a point in space, at least in an ideal point of the social environment. Although in more intimate relations, he may develop all kinds of charm and significance, as long as he is considered a stranger in the eyes of the other, he is not an "owner of soil." (38)

The Jew is thus always in a secondary role to the production of culture in a society. Beyond Johann Gottfried Herder's (1744–1803) Romantic notion of the rootedness of any culture in its "Volk," such views relegate the "stranger," here defined as the Jew, to a marginal position. This position is the result of the "nature" of the indigenous society and its existing organic network of relationship. The Jews, assuming these roles and excelling in them, reinforce it.

Over time, the stereotypes of difference become qualities of the Other:

> As a group member, rather, he is near and far at the same time, as is characteristic of relations founded only on generally human commonness. But between nearness and distance, there arises a specific tension when the consciousness that only the quite general is common, stresses that which is not common. In the case of the person who is a stranger to the country, the city, the race, etc., however, this non-common element is once more nothing individual, but merely the strangeness of origin, which is or could be common to many strangers. For this reason, strangers are not really conceived as individuals, but as strangers of a particular type: the element of distance is no less general in regard to them than the element of nearness.
>
> This form is the basis of such a special case, for instance, as the tax levied in Frankfort and elsewhere upon medieval Jews. Whereas the Beede [tax] paid by the Christian citizen changed with the changes of his fortune, it was fixed once and for all for every single Jew. This fixity rested on the fact that the Jew had his social position as a Jew, not as the individual bearer of certain objective contents. Every other citizen was the owner of a particular amount of property, and his tax followed its fluctuations. But the Jew as a taxpayer was, in the first place, a Jew, and thus his tax situation had an invariable element. This same position appears most strongly, of course, once even these individual characterizations (limited though they were by rigid invariance) are omitted, and all strangers pay an altogether equal head-tax. (41–42)

The "Jews" as taxpayers become a single conceptual category, a network from which there is no escape. But they are bound to the world of Christian Europe from which they are defined as an "economic entity" rather than as a cultural or "ethnic" one. The "Jew" becomes the definition of the "stranger."

The power of the association between the "stranger" and the "Jew," present in its original formulation, has echoes in modern theoretical presentations of Jewish history. Zygmunt Bauman resuscitated the idea of the "stranger" in his work on the sociology of alienation and the Holocaust, *Modernity and the Holocaust* (1989), as part of his desire to "dehistoricize" the Holocaust. For Gabriel Josipovici, Jewishness itself is the condition of going and resting. Israel is thus but one more stage in the life of the "stranger," not an answer to it.[6] All Jews are nomads—and contemporary multicultural theory has turned all people into nomads: "groups of people or subgroups . . . move into new spaces or territory and become part of or integral to that space or society. Over a time . . . the group in question may become identified with that social space."[7] Or, indeed, it may not. What was a "Jewish problem" in contemporary multicultural theory becomes the human condition, just as Simmel forecast.

Simmel provides a few clues in this representation of cultural difference as to how he understands the Jew in Western European (and by extension American) culture. He is much more open in a private letter written a decade earlier to a Zionist in Russia. Simmel rejected the Zionist project of political if not cultural separation, as he believed that the Jews were already so deeply fused with their Christian neighbors that, at least in Europe, a new people has arisen out of the hybridization. What is central for Simmel is that he defines the trace elements of Jewishness as an aspect of the blood of all "people of culture" ("Blut aller Kulturvölker"). (Ironically Otto Weininger, arch-Jewish self-hater and suicide, did much the same thing in his *Sex and Character* [1903] when he juxtaposed a "Jewish" mind-set with a "Germanic" one—and did not limit the former to Jews.)[8] Here, biology trumps all, but the metaphor that Simmel employs is that of the lovers entwined and unable to be parted. This takes place as the Jews enter into European culture and both partners are at the end in a "cultural embrace" ("feste Kulturumarmung").[9]

Many Jewish thinkers of the time wholeheartedly agreed with Simmel's assumptions and felt themselves in what came to be called the "German-Jewish symbiosis." As a result, some of the radical Zionists of the day felt that German Jews could never become truly Jewish. During World War I, a young Zionist leader, G. Wollstein, argued that German Jews should only be permitted to marry Eastern Jews and should be forbidden any access to the Hebrew-language (read: Zionist) journals of the day, for their Hebrew words only masked their German sensibility.[10] This is but the other side of the coin from those who assumed that the Jewish mind-set was inalterable and that the German qualities perceived in German Jewry were merely a superficial surface that disguised but did not change their Jewishness.

In his explanation in 1922 (written before 1914) of what constituted "ethnicity," the German sociologist Max Weber (1864–1920) claimed "the belief in group affinity, regardless of whether it has any objective foundation, can have important consequences especially for the formation of a political community" (56).[11] For Weber, the barriers to integration were clear: the refusal to marry outside the group (part of the "ritual regulation of life") and the refusal to communicate in a common language (and thus avoid having a shared cultural experience). These qualities inherently reinforce ethnic difference and are absolute barriers. He recognizes that anything can be seen as constituting the symbolic language of difference: "the styles of beard and hairdo, clothes, food and eating habits, division of labor between the sexes, and all kind of other visible differences can, in a given case, give rise to repulsion and contempt" (54). Here the image of the stereotypical Jew that will surface in his understanding of *Ancient Judaism* (1917–1920) shapes the constituent parts of ethnicity (especially, as we shall discuss, in the light of Werner Sombart's [1863–1941] discussion of Jewish difference).[12] One can add to this statement that this is equally true in constituting a cultural community rather than a political one. Non-Jews have regularly constituted the image and nature of the "Jew" as seen from their perspectives and needs (as Jean-Paul Sartre admirably illustrated half a century later in his *Anti-Semite and Jew*).[13]

Weber was writing at this moment his essays on *Ancient Judaism* in order to understand the contemporary "character" of the Jews.[14] Weber opens them with a restatement of the "problem" of the Jews, which can "best be understood in comparison with the problem of the Indian caste order. Sociologically speaking the Jews were a pariah people ('ein Pariavolk'), which means, as we know from India, that they were a guest people who were ritually separated, formally or de facto, from their surroundings."[15] Equally, they followed different codes of conduct, which were often seen by the host as antithetical to their own. This is quite different from Simmel, who saw the "Jewish" code of behavior as inherently linked to their role in the Diaspora. For Weber, the Jews constitute a foreign code of behavior. Later, in his *Sociology of Religion*, Weber clarifies his definition with the

Jews clearly in mind. "In our usage, 'pariah people' denotes a distinctive hereditary social group lacking autonomous political organization and characterized by prohibitions against commensality and intermarriage originally founded upon magical, tabooistic, and ritual injunctions."[16] Such prohibitions are not part of a dialectic in a Diaspora setting but are brought with the Jews as part of their common cultural inheritance. Note that Weber's categories of difference deal with "biological" processes such as marriage that distinguish the pariah people from their "hosts."

The notion of the Jews as a pariah people is one much older than Weber. Indeed, the opera composer Giacomo Meyerbeer's brother, the playwriter and librettist Michael Beer (1800–1833), wrote a drama entitled *The Pariah* in 1826 placing the burning question of whether Jews could be trusted to serve in the military (and thus be "real" citizens) into the "exotic" framework of an ancient "Hindoo" state.[17] No question of marriage or reproduction is possible here. This anxiety of hybridity already haunts the Enlightment image of the Jews even in Lessing's paradigmatic drama of Jewish emancipation, *Nathan the Wise* (1779), where the religiously different protagonists turn out to be siblings and therefore cannot marry. While Beer was advocating the integration of the Jews into the body politic as citizens, a century later Weber saw the refusal of the Jews to integrate as the basis of their creativity. This is a two-edged sword, as we shall see, but also a permanent sign of their self-imposed social (and by extension biological) isolation. One of the ironies is that for Weber, one of the hallmarks of the Jews as a pariah people is their lack of art. in terms of not only the traditionally evoked Biblical prohibition against graven images but also the "foreign" nature of the musical world of the Jews. It is Cain who is the "tribal father of the … musician" (28, 35). Or perhaps there existed among the Jews "a guest people of musicians, the descendants of Jubal" (196; this is one of the nineteenth-century theories of the origins of the "Gypsies" [Sinti and Roma]: they were seen, by scholars such as George Borrow in his *The Zincali, or an Account of the Gypsies in Spain* [1841], to have been a wandering tribe of itinerant Indian musicians who entered into the Western Diaspora as entertainers). If the Jews had a musical tradition, it was one very different than that demanded by the aesthetics of the West. Their music was a "means of evoking ecstacy" (97), not of creating an aesthetics of beauty. For Weber, the "creativity" of the Jews is a reflex of their pariah position, and it articulates itself primarily in economic terms.

Having grasped this salient definition of Jewish ethnicity, Weber returned to his classic study of the rise of capitalism, *The Protestant Ethic and the Spirit of Capitalism* (1905/1920), where he bracketed the Jews of the present to the Jews of the past: "The Jews stood on the side of the politically and speculatively oriented adventurous capitalism; their ethos was, in a word, that of pariah capitalism. But Puritanism carried the ethos of the rational organization of capital and labor. It took over from the Jewish ethic only what was adapted to this purpose."[18] Jewish engagement with economy, for Max Weber, maintained a direct link to the older Jewish model of pariah economy even in the world of modern capitalism (39). For Weber, the interior world inhabited by the Jews remained marginal, and this reflects the mental status of the Jew as pariah. Such a mind-set is inherently different from that of "modern man," for the Jews are not naïve enough to attribute worldly success to God's blessing. Their worldly success is the result of their ancient code that "acts toward strangers were allowed which were forbidden toward a brother" (271; this is a common formulation of the late nineteenth century which centered around the spurious claim that Jews at Yom Kippur are able to revoke all worldly contracts. This calumny resulted in a series of major court cases for libel at the time).[19] This preference for the group seems to be inherent to the way the Jews imagine the world and is only heightened by their oppression. In no way does he see the Jews as "embracing" and being "embraced" by modernity as they maintain this code. They are not engaged by labor and its organization, which he sees as a sign of the modern (186). His concern is that they remain always one remove from modernity in the separateness. Even modern capitalism (and here he is answering Werner Sombart quite directly) is only "Jewish" by association. Theirs was a "pariah capitalism," not the real thing.

Werner Sombart had defined the Jews as the point of departure for the development of modernity—and he did not like the modern. Yet Weber and Sombart shared a notion of the intractability of Jewish qualities. Their views remain on a plane very different from those of Simmel, who sees the mutuality between Jewish self-isolation (hardly a reality in Simmel's case or Simmel's world) and the stereotypical image of the Jew. Werner Sombart argued in *The Jews and Modern Capitalism* (1911) that the Jew is inherently immutable. His example is that of the United States and the claim of Jewish transformation in the New World by German-Jewish immigrants such as Franz Boas, who authored at the same time a detailed report for Congress on the "Changes in Bodily Form of Descendants of Immigrants."[20] Sombart's notion of the immutable does not contradict his image of Jewish mimicry; for him, the Jew represents immutable mutability:

> The driving power in Jewish adaptability is of course the idea of a purpose, or a goal, as the end of all things. Once the Jew has made up his mind what line he will follow, the rest is comparatively easy, and his mobility only makes his success more sure. How mobile the Jew can be is positively astounding. He is able to give himself the personal appearance he most desires. . . . The best illustrations may be drawn from the United States, where the Jew of the second or third-generation is with difficulty distinguished from the non-Jew. You can tell the German after no matter how many generations; so with the Irish, the Swede, the Slav. But the Jew, in so far as his racial features allow it, has been successful in imitating the Yankee type, especially in regard to outward marks such as clothing, bearing, and the peculiar method of hairdressing.[21]

The Jew is thus the litmus test of whether what is labeled deep or inherent cultural differences can be transformed or could only be disguised. Thus, even the acceptances of codes of decorum were no guarantee of "real" rather than feigned transformation. This was at a point, of course, where Jews in Western Europe had so totally transformed themselves that they questioned their own authenticity as Jews and were generating models of Jewish cultural identity that demanded an identifiable Jewish culture—and, one can add, not a Jewish economic model. But it was also the moment of the presence, from the Russian pogroms of the 1880s through the displacements of World War I, of extraordinary numbers of Eastern (read: unacculturated) Jews in Western Europe, Great Britain, and the United States. These Jews seemed to fulfill all of the categories that Weber and Sombart feared to be present in the "Jews."

By the early twentieth century, many secular Western European Jews felt that even though the Jews had changed to fulfill the expectations of their Christian neighbors, no changes would eliminate the anti-Semitism of the world in which they found themselves. Their own anxiety had been increased by the displacement of Eastern Jews, but these fears seemed to have been countered by a sense of common cultural or political goals. Neo-Orthodoxy had warned in the course of the nineteenth century about the effacement of Jewish difference as a response to the pressures for civil emancipation. The German neo-Orthodox thinker Samson Raphael Hirsch (1808–1888), who played a role in chapter 2, evoked the multiplicity of continents and peoples and cultures after the Flood that guaranteed that mankind would never again fall into the degeneracy (in which "all flesh had perverted its way on the earth") that prompted God's destruction. Hirsch sees diversity, and one can add Jewish difference, as a necessity, planned into the structure of human experience by God who commanded: "'As for you, be fruitful and multiply; swarm on the earth and multiply on it' ... God gave a special covenant, a special dispensation, to the different climates and countries. . . . It would accordingly be a description of a diversity and infinite variety of human races, and moreover 'on the earth' and by the earth, under the influences of the various lands. ... Noachian mankind is given the mission to spread over the whole world, and under the most diverse conditions and influences of climate and physical nature of the countries, to become Men and develop the one common real characteristic of Man: a diversity and a multiplicity that appeared to us in the above connection as God's new plan for the education of mankind, to avoid the necessity for any fresh total catastrophe. The diversity is to balance the deficiency and so pave the way to progress to the goal."[22] For Hirsch, this divine plan for human diversity, a plan seen in the spectrum of the rainbow that appeared after the Flood, was the answer to the pull of the German-Jewish reformers for a homogeneous German identity into which Jewish identity could be subsumed. But this did not mean, as we saw in the previous chapter, that Hirsch wished to distance himself from the moral claims made by the aesthetics of classical German high culture. A devotee of German high culture, especially Schiller and Goethe, Hirsch advocated *Torah im derekh eretz*, the coexistence of religious learning and secular culture, as could be seen in his extraordinary monologue on Purim. Even neo-Orthodoxy acknowledged the cultural claims of the Haskalah.

By 1914, a generation of secular German Jews had begun to think about whether their role in German culture was so poisoned that whatever they did, they would always be seen as marginal. In March 1912, a young German Zionist, Moritz Goldstein, published "The German-Jewish Parnassus" in the leading right-wing aesthetic journal of the day, and claimed, "We Jews are administering the spiritual property of a nation which denies our right and our ability to do so."[23] In the essay, he castigated Jews who "are completely unaware, who continue to take part in German cultural activities, who pretend and persuade themselves that they are not recognized." Goldstein advocated the creation of a self-conscious Jewish culture in Germany. A Jewish culture as opposed to a universal (read: European) culture had been earlier dismissed by German Zionists as an impossibility. Two years earlier Franz Oppenheimer had claimed, "We are collectively German by culture ... because we have the fortune to belong to cultural communities that stand in the forefront of nations. ...We cannot be Jewish by culture (*Kulturjuden*) because the Jewish culture, as it has been preserved from the Middle Ages in the ghettoes of the East, stands infinitely lower than modern cultures which our [Western] nations bear. We can neither regress nor do we want to."[24] How could Jews "fall back" into a Jewish culture, however defined, without showing that they never truly belonged within the world of Western high culture at all? But did they really belong or had they covered themselves with a veneer of culture that overlaid their pariah mentality?

It was to be in the United States that the question of whether a Jewish culture could exist within a society that claimed to be open to diversity of populations was to be most clearly articulated. American society in the late nineteenth century was self-consciously a Diaspora society with its overt focus on "foreign" immigration. Charles W. Chesnutt (1858–1932) commented in 1900 of the fantasy "that the future American race will consist of a harmonious fusion of the various European elements which now make up our heterogeneous population" (17). As an African American, he knew from his own experience that such a model excluded him and his world from the new hybridity—on "racial" and "social" grounds. The African American's role in American culture was analogous to that of the "Jew" in European culture. They were the essential Other against which the potential integration of all other groups could be measured. The reality, as we shall see, is that American popular culture by 1900 was already becoming a hybrid in which African-American elements were to dominate. Yet from his perspective, the Jews were one of the "various European elements which now make up our heterogeneous population." African Americans seemed in the mind of the theoreticians of ethnicity to be beyond cultural integration, but the Jews, seen at the time as racially "black," might serve as proof that the multicultural system works even at its assumed limits.

Americans, especially acculturated Jews, who desired a model that would extend the "fusion" model beyond the realm of race used the Jews as their example of that group that could be integrated in spite of their image of self-isolation and cultural separation. In 1915, the Jewish Harvard-educated philosopher and Zionist Horace Kallen strongly advocated "a diversity of cultures, especially those carried by ethno-racial groups," while his non-Jewish friend Randolph Bourne argued for cosmopolitanism marked by the dynamic interaction of precisely those groups.[25] In both cases, the "Jews" were seen as a test case for the potential of cultural integration. For Kallen, the Jews presented both the most recent case but also a special case in the American context. The Jews are more like the "homogeneous" first settlers of the British colonies than other recent groups. They are "in flight from persecution and disaster; in search of economic opportunity, liberty of conscience, civic rights" (71). They came from "lands of sojourn where they have been for ages treated as foreigners" and with the sole desire to become "completely incorporated into the body politic" (86).[26] Yet they are (with a side look at Hegel) "of all self-conscious peoples ... the most self-conscious." Jews are, for Kallen in 1915, "the most eagerly American of the immigrant groups [and] the most autonomous and self-conscious in spirit and culture" (87). The Jews can serve as the model for a cultural pluralism (one of the dominant threads in contemporary multiculturalism) that respects the totality of group experience and thus demands autonomy.

Yet Kallen is careful to place the Jew as a strand in the plurality of cultures within some common cultural norms. His version of the stranger too imagines peoples in constant mobility. "This mobility reinforces the use of English—for a lingua franca, intelligible everywhere, becomes indispensable—by immigrants" (75). This first generation—and here he answers those who define the Jews solely within the economic model—shows "economic eagerness, the greed of the unfed." This is not a "Jewish" quality but one of all "immigrants" (87). Even this group must reach for the cultural brass ring. English is "the language of the upper and dominant class, the vehicle and symbol of culture" (81). Its media such as "the facility of communications and the motion-picture"—never mind baseball—shape "like-mindedness" (81). Kallen thinks of this as a coping mechanism in the first generation and as a space into which the second generation (which "devotes itself feverishly to the attainment of similarity" [79]) comfortably exists. Even in this moment, "mixed marriage" is less likely because even the second generation's "primary ethnic differences" remain dominant (81).

The Jews (and here he speaks of the Eastern, Yiddish-speaking Jew, not his German Jewish co-religionists) are the best example of diversity within difference. He quotes H. G. Wells about the "Jewish quarter in New York [as] a city within a city" (87; a view echoed at more or less the same moment by Henry James in much less complimentary terms).[27] The Lower East Side is "far autonomous in spirit and self-consciousness in culture" (a phrase he repeats). It has a broad range of ideologies and institutions well beyond those of the synagogue, of Judaism as a religious practice. It is in the new demands of a Jewish culture that now functions in an American (read: English-language) context that Kallen sees the model for cultural pluralism. For Kallen, high culture is certainly part of the mix. This culture of the Jews in New York has "its artists, its literati, its press, its literature, its theater," as well as religious and social institutions (87). His view (like Theodor Herzl's) postulates a fantasy of Switzerland, multilingual and multiethnic, as a model, but with bilingualism as an inherent aspect of the new American scene. He sees the "melting pot" model of hybridity (which I shall discuss in the next chapter) as effacing cultural difference, so that "Jews . . . in order to cease being Jews . . . would have to cease to be" (91). His argument borrows the notion of an inherent quality of Jewishness that, unlike that model evoked by Sombart, could and will be destroyed by a transformation of the Jewish merely into "Americans." This very potential for the collapse of a self-conscious Jewish identity argues against Weber's model of the pariah people and its immutable nature as revealed in the economic sphere.

Randolph S. Bourne (1886–1918), on the other hand, in 1916 saw the multicultural as a cosmopolitanism that frees the "native born American" from the lethargy of his own culture: "It is not uncommon for the eager Anglo-Saxon who goes to a vivid American university today to find his true friends not among his own race but among acclimatized German or Austrian, the acclimatized Jew .... In them he finds the cosmopolitan note. In these youths, foreign-born or the children of foreign-born parents, he is likely to find many of his old inbred morbid problems washed away" (103).[28] Here the claim is for a healthy revitalization of American culture through the admixture of other cultures, including the "healthy Jew." Like Kallen's warning of what will happen if Jewish particularism (however defined) vanishes, Bourne complains bitterly of "the Jew who has lost the Jewish fire and become a mere elementary, grasping animal" in becoming the mere shadow of himself in the New World (99). Here Bourne falls back into the economic model that Kallen dismisses as a quality of first-generation immigrants. His view is not far from that of the French "philo-Semite" Anatole Leroy-Beaulieu (1842–1912), who in 1893 complained that "the de-judaised Jews are, in too many case[s], lacking in moral feeling."[29] Now in America it is the acculturated Jew who has lost his specificity as a Jew. Cultural pluralism was the means by which Jewish cultural degeneration could be prevented.

This anxiety of the Jew becoming "American" and thus falling back into the model of the *Homo economus* has an interesting cultural representation in the work of Franz Kafka. On 29 September 1912 Kafka's best friend, Max Brod, notes in his diary, "Kafka in ecstasy, writing all night. A novel set in America."[30] By 6 October Kafka sits Brod down and reads him "The Judgment" and "The Stoker," the first chapter of the novel fragment that would posthumously bear Max Brod's title *Amerika* when it is published in 1927. This novel mirrors the muckraking model of some of his American and German contemporaries in its ironic reversal of expectations of the Jew as *Homo economus*. Written in "ecstasy," it harks back to the lost draft of a novel he wrote in 1911 but also a juvenile novel of the two brothers, which he destroyed because it was too "literary." The new novel reflects the model of the idealistic novels of economic success, quite reversing the "rags-to-riches" life of the classic Dickensian or Horatio Alger (1834–1899) protagonist. Such novels are the basis for Kafka's subtle parody of the Jew in America. From Alger's first novel, *Ragged Dick* (1867), this new genre of dime novels known as the "city story" heroicized the young street urchins living in poverty among large, urban centers such as New York, Boston, and Philadelphia.[31] With uncommon courage and moral fortitude, Alger's youths struggle against adversity to achieve great wealth and acclaim. Kafka's sense of America with its social reversal in spite of a superficial cultural integration is already a theme in the novels of the American muckrakers, so named by Theodore Roosevelt because they, like the Man with the Muckrake in *Pilgrim's Progress*, who looked down at the filth and ignored the celestial crown, exposed and attempted to correct graft and corruption in both government and business. For German readers the novels of Upton Sinclair (1878–1968) such as *The Jungle* (1906), about Lithuanian immigrants caught up in the horror of the Chicago stockyards, was an essential anti-Alger tale of America. This novel of the exploitation and death of recent immigrants in Chicago inspired both George Bernard Shaw and Bertolt Brecht. In

addition to Sinclair, writers whose image of America counters the claims
of cultural pluralism were Lincoln Steffens and Ida Tarbell, whose major
works, *The Shame of the Cities* and *History of the Standard Oil Company*
respectively, appeared in 1901.

As I mentioned, the posthumous title, *Amerika*, is Max Brod's; today the
novel is called *The Man Who Disappeared*, after one of Kafka's draft titles for
the novel. The latter title points to precisely the anti-Alger trajectory of the
protagonist. The sixteen-year-old Karl Rossmann is packed off to America
because of sexual misadventure with a thirty-five-year-old housemaid, who
seduced him and then gave birth to his child. He is expelled by his parents,
who send him to an uncle in America to spare them the stigma of illegiti-
macy. He arrives in New York City, and this frames the opening chapter
with its confrontation with authority on board. Indeed, the first thing that
Karl Rossmann sees is the Statue of Liberty: "the sword in her hand seemed
only to just have been raised aloft, and the unchained winds blew about
her form."[32] This odd reworking of the lost early novel of America is an
answer to the "usual stuff," to Karl May's America of Saxon trappers and
Indians, to Alger's ever-cheerful newspaper boys. Here, even the West has
a prophetic force only as seen through the eyes of the European "stranger."
Informed by Kafka's reading of Charles Dickens's reformist novels such as
Oliver Twist and Flaubert, it is very much in line with the interests of the
American "muckrakers" whose portrait of immigrants in the new American
Diaspora is a picture of exploitation and collapse. It is an ironic reversal
of the myth of America as the "Golden Land" in the Yiddish theater of
Eastern Europe (and America) that had also become part of his image of
America. It is a world in which Rossmann spirals ever downward, losing his
connection to his uncle's bourgeois world of business, then getting a job as
an elevator operator, then as a common workman. His is a continuous tale
of expulsion and degradation, first from the ship with his relationship with
the stoker, then with his uncle's business allies, then with the head cook and
head waiter at the hotel where he is employed.

Rossmann's social and economic collapse is paralleled by precisely that
transformation which would have promised success in multilingual Prague
or New York. Being a German speaker in Prague is no more a promise of
intellectual or economic success than speaking English in America. There
Rossmann learns the "native" language and thus becomes an American: "At
first the English content of his early conversations with his uncle had been

confined to hello and goodbye.... The first time Karl recited an American poem to his uncle one evening—the subject was a conflagration—it made him quite somber with satisfaction."[33] Unlike many of the other "foreigners" in the novel, Rossmann truly learns English well. It becomes an asset when he seeks employment at the Hotel Occidental: "'You speak German and good English, that's perfectly adequate. 'But all my English I've learned in just two and a half months in America,' Karl said.... 'That says everything about you,' said the Head Cook. 'When I think of the trouble I had learning English.'"[34] Being transformed into an "American" through speaking English is not sufficient. Rossmann remains on his downward trajectory. The path of *Homo economus* in the New World is not toward success but toward destruction.

Only the fragmentary account of the "Open Air Theater of Oklahoma" seems to promise, as Kafka tells Brod, that all will be magically forgiven and that the wanderer will be returned to home and family. But when he is employed to work there, he is called by his nickname, "Negro," and is introduced as "Negro, a secondary school boy from Europe."[35] This moment in the novel provides one further insight into the aspects of the experienced world that he incorporates into his novel, for the question that dominated the image of the Jew in Kafka's Prague was "Are the Jews white?" Writing to Milena Jesenská in 1920, Kafka can comment quite literarily "naturally for your father there's no difference between your husband and myself [both of them Jews]; there's no doubt about it, to the European we both have the same Negro face."[36] But when the non-Jewish writer Jesenská herself turns, in 1938, to write about the persecution of the Jews and other minority peoples of Central Europe by the Germans, she writes about them metaphorically as "the Negroes of Europe." Social transformation by learning languages does not change the manner by which someone like Rossmann is seen. Kafka's self-awareness of how the body can betray is written into the hype of the confidence men who run the "great Theater of Oklahoma." No promise is made here, only the inevitable final downward spiral into oblivion.

By the 1920s it is the German-trained Robert E. Park (1864–1944), the founder of the "Chicago school" of urban sociology, who has "Americanized" Simmel's "stranger" as the "marginal man." His work returns to an American specificity evoked by Chesnutt some two decades before. The center of his concern is indeed "race" in an American sense, that is, the "race" of the African American.[37] Park, however, returns to read Simmel, "himself a Jew," as the ultimate form of "cultural hybrid, a man living and sharing intimately in the cultural life and traditions of two distinct people; never quite willing to break, even if he were permitted to do so, with his past and his traditions, and not quite accepted, because of racial prejudice, in the new society in which he ought to find a place" (165). For Park, "the emancipated Jew was, and is, historically and typically the marginal man, the first cosmopolite and citizen of the world." He is the "city man," a "trader" of "keen intellectual interest," sophisticated, idealistic, and without a sense of history (165). He is suspended between "the warm security of the ghetto" and the "cold freedom of the outer world." (This is his characterization of the American [German-] Jewish novelist and critic Ludwig Lewisohn's [1882–1955] autobiography *Up Stream* [1923].) He struggles with "conflicted loyalties." (Here, his example is the German poet Heinrich Heine.) He becomes pathological, suffering from "spiritual distress," and "his mind lack[s] integrity which is based on conviction" (166). By the time we come to Park, the ground has shifted. We are speaking no longer of the *Homo economus* but of the artist. The Jew has moved from beyond culture to being defined by his role in culture (if here in a pathological manner as alienated from society).

Park's concept of "marginal man" is popularized by his student Everett Stonequist in *The Marginal Man* (1937). In his introduction, Parks again evokes the stranger as having developed a distinctive personality that enables him to have "the wider horizon, the keener intelligence, the more detached and rational viewpoint." He is best exemplified, as Parks writes, by "the Jew, particularly the Jew who has emerged from the provincialism of the ghetto, has everywhere and always been the most civilized of creatures."[38] Here civilization is the goal of the stranger, and it is the civilization of high culture that the Jew represents in Park's fantasy of the multicultural world.

Multiculturalism focuses from this point on the role of the Jew in high culture. Yet the specter of *Homo economus* never vanishes. It becomes part of the figure of the Jew within the fantasies of Jewish "multicultural" writers such as in Abraham Cahan's (1860–1951) *The Rise of David Levinsky* (1917) or Michael Gold's (1893–1967) *Jews without Money* (1930). They are parallel to Kafka's *Amerika* in their bleak image of the moral or economic collapse of the Jewish immigrant in America. These texts are multicultural in that they focus on Jews being integrated for good or for ill into Horace Kallen's and Robert Park's America. The function of the Jews as a litmus test for the multicultural never vanishes, even among self-consciously multicultural non-Jewish writers in the twenty-first century, as we shall see later in this book. By then, the economic question becomes defined by the success of the Jews in the Diaspora and is seen as the factor that makes the Jews the most successful of the minorities in Western culture—and thus not part of the world of multiculturalism at all. This is the fate that other minorities in the Western Diaspora simultaneously desire and fear.

FOUR

JEWS, MULTICULTURALISM, AND ISRAEL ZANGWILL'S "MELTING POT"

As early as Shakespeare, the stereotypical Jew is denied any special relationship to Western (read: civilized and civilizing) music. The "Jew" in *The Merchant of Venice* is devoid of any moral and therefore aesthetic sensibility.[1] As Shylock says,

> Lock up my doors; and when you hear the drum
> And the vile squealing of the wry-neck'd fife,
> Clamber not you up to the casements then,
> Nor thrust your head into the public street
> To gaze on Christian fools with varnish'd faces,
> But stop my house's ears, I mean my casements:
> Let not the sound of shallow foppery enter
> My sober house. (*Merchant of Venice* II, v)

But just so that we do not miss the message, Lorenzo says to Shylock's daughter that her father is insensible to music:

> The man that hath no music in himself,
> Nor is not moved with concord of sweet sounds,
> Is fit for treasons, stratagems and spoils;
> The motions of his spirit are dull as night
> And his affections dark as Erebus:
> Let no such man be trusted. Mark the music. (V, i.)

"Mark the music" is the key to one powerful image of the stereotyped Jew that is part of English as well as European culture. To be civilized, the Jews had to learn to love the music of their world, to identify with and participate in a high culture beyond the Shakespearean fantasy of Jewish incomprehensibility and the myth of the noise of the synagogue and the *Judenschule* (Jew's school). This was accepting music as part of the decorous world of high culture that improved the human being.

In the eighteenth century, Moses Mendelssohn and the German-Jewish Enlightenment argued that Jewish transformation into citizens of a national state would enable Jews to be both Germans and Jews. Unlike the liberals of his time, such as Wilhelm von Humboldt, who demanded the extension of civic emancipation to the Jews without any qualification on the basis that all human beings shared these rights, the Haskalah (Enlightenment) model demanded observable change. For Germany, one of the "changes" demanded of the Jews was that they so alter their "Jewish" *mentality* that they begin to experience the ethical dimensions attributed to high culture (*Bildung*), dimensions from which they were felt to have excluded themselves because of their religious beliefs rather than their innate incapacity.[2] Music, especially the music of modern high culture, what is today called "classical" as opposed to popular music, becomes one of the places that such transformation is seen to take place. "Music" may indeed "hath charms to soothe the savage breast, / To soften rocks, or bend a knotted oak," as William Congreve (1670–1729) observed in *The Mourning Bride* (I, 1), but the "Jew" was capable of neither comprehending nor producing such an effect.

Certainly for the nineteenth century, the formulation that most strongly resonated was in Richard Wagner's 1850 essay, "Judaism [i.e., Jewry] in Music." This essay, widely reprinted at the close of the century, summarized nineteenth-century anti-Semitic images of the Jewish lack of any innate musicality:

> [O]ur modern arts had likewise become a portion of this culture, and
> among them more particularly that art which is just the very easiest to
> learn—the art of music, and indeed that Music which, severed from her
> sister arts, had been lifted by the force and stress of grandest geniuses
> to a stage in her universal faculty of Expression where either, in new
> conjunction with the other arts, she might speak aloud the most sub-
> lime, or, in persistent separation from them, she could also speak at will

the deepest bathos of the trivial. Naturally, what the cultured Jew had to speak, in his aforesaid situation, could be nothing but the trivial and indifferent, because his whole artistic bent was in sooth a mere luxurious, needless thing.... (88)

The Jew has never had an Art of his own, hence never a Life of art-enabling import (*ein Leben von kunstfähigem Gehalte*): an import, a universally applicable, a human import, not even to-day does it offer to the searcher, but merely a peculiar method of expression.... . Now the only musical expression offered to the Jew tone-setter by his native Folk, is the ceremonial music of their Jehova-rites: the Synagogue is the solitary fountain whence the Jew can draw art-motives at once popular and intelligible to himself. (90)[3]

It is into this world that Jews of the early nineteenth century, such as Giacomo Meyerbeer (born Jakob Liebmann Beer; 1791–1864), against whom Wagner fulminated in his essay, entered to show that they too could and did contribute to European high culture. Jews, however defined, could show that they had the sensibility and sensitivity to be full-fledged members of a world of ethics and aesthetics. Yet the more that they actually did so, the more anti-Semitic stereotypes held that they were incapable of contributing anything of value. In the end, they were inhibited by their Jewishness from comprehending the true nature of "classical" music.

In 1850 in London, Robert Knox, accused grave robber and medical hack, sat down and wrote the first systematic anthropology of the Jews in English. His 1850 *The Races of Men* picked up this thread when he observed that "the real Jew has no ear for music."[4] Knox was not merely paralleling Wagner. Both were perpetuating a view well known from the early modern period, as Shakespeare's Shylock illustrates. Benjamin Disraeli, novelist and politician manqué, had countered that view in his novel *Coningsby* (1844) in which Sidonie, the embodiment of all that is positive among the Jews, forcefully declares that "musical Europe is ours!" for every time a Christian listens to a Gioacchino Rossini[5] (1792–1868) or a Meyerbeer or is "thrilled into raptures at the notes of an aria by a [Giuditta] Pasta [1798–1865] or a [Giulia] Grisi [1811–1869], little do they suspect that they are offering their homage to 'the sweet singers of Israel!'" The Jews are endowed "with the almost exclusive privilege of MUSIC."[6] What is vital in reading Disraeli as against Wagner and Knox is that Disraeli stresses the Jew's preeminence in the music of European high culture, of the opera and the concert stage. Neither synagogue liturgy nor Jewish themes, but the most innovative high culture of the music of the day defines Jewish preeminence.[7]

For Disraeli's contemporary George Eliot, at least in her *Daniel Deronda* (1876), this is a "natural gift." Daniel "had not only one of those thrilling boy voices which seem to bring an idyllic heaven and earth before our eyes, but a fine musical instinct."[8] This natural instinct is very much in line with Eliot's sense that musicality is the litmus test for true nobility. In her much earlier 1854 translation of Ludwig Feuerbach's *Essence of Christianity*, we read, "If thou hast not sensibility, no feeling for music, thou perceivest in the finest music nothing more than in the wind that whistles by thy ear, or than in the brook which rushes past thy feet. What, then, is it which acts on thee when thou art affected by melody? ... Feeling speaks only to feeling.... . Music is a monologue of emotion."[9] Given Feuerbach's dismissal of Judaism as not a religion at all, but a gastronomic cult, using this model of sensibility to create Eliot's image of "Jewish" nature contains an ironic turn. Yet it is clear that the ability to both undertake and appreciate music makes her characters (and the Victorian image of the Jew) more humane.

In general, the notion that the Jew could not command the realm of high musical culture is undermined in the popular mind by the presence of "Jewish" performers (rather than composers) during the course of the late nineteenth century. Francis Galton's view of "hereditary genius" in 1869 includes only one Jewish "genius," and that is the poet Heinrich Heine, documenting Galton's interest in the "mental peculiarities of different races."[10] No musicians at all make the grade. But twenty years later Joseph Jacobs, the Australian anthropologist who wrote extensively on Jews and race in Victorian London, commented in 1889 that in "Grove's *Dictionary of Music* [there is] a far larger proportion of executants than composers.... [There is] clear evidence of general musical ability among Jews."[11] In his statistical survey of Jewish professions, he commented that the fact "that a Jew obtained one of the fifty scholarships at the new Royal College of Music, whereas one in five hundred would represent a proper proportion, seems to confirm the popular impression of the Jewish love and aptitude for music, and this may be further confirmed by the fact that of the six musical knights in England no less than three are of Jewish blood."[12] He later lists the musical "geniuses" of "Jewish blood," enumerating the three knighted composers, Julius Benedict (1804–1885), Michael Costa (1810–1884), and the famed composer of "Onward, Christian Soldiers" (1871) and the Savoy operas' Arthur Sullivan (1844–1900),[13] but places most of his emphasis on performers such as the violinists Joseph Joachim and Hermann Cohen.[14]

The rationale behind such a claim is not merely that there are more Jewish performers than composers (Disraeli can easily pair them), but rather that the nature of music seems to be divided between the "creators" and the "interpreters." The latter fulfill the anti-Semites' expectation of "mere Jewish mimicry," while philo-Semites ascribed "genius" to such interpreters. Georg Simmel, in his often quoted essay on the "Stranger" (1908), which was also quoted in chapter 3, put this in terms of the general economy: "Trade [here we can read: performance] can always absorb more people than primary production [here we can read: composition]; it is, therefore, the sphere indicated for the stranger, who intrudes as a supernumerary, so to speak, into a group in which the economic positions are actually occupied—the classical example is the history of European Jews. The stranger is by nature no 'owner of soil'—soil not only in the physical, but also in the figurative sense of a life substance which is fixed, if not in a point in space, at least in an ideal point of the social environment. [This would be the notion of the inherent creativity of the 'rooted' composer that Wagner represents.] Although in more intimate relations, he may develop all kinds of charm and significance, as long as he is considered a stranger in the eyes of the other, he is not an 'owner of soil.'"[15] The Jew had to show that he was not merely in trade but also a creative genius.

This debate rages among Jews on the Continent. Heinrich Berl picks up on the question of the originality of the Jews in music in a series of essays in Martin Buber's *The Jew* and then in a published collection of these essays in 1926.[16] Berl argues, against Max Brod's concept of Jewish music as well as his strong espousal of Gustav Mahler's work, that Jews reflect an "Asian" relationship to music because of their inherent psychology.[17] Music for them is form, not content. It is best exemplified by the rise of "New" music that dominates modernity from Georges Bizet (1838–1875; a "half Jew" in whom the Jewish half dominates [69]) to Gustav Mahler and Arnold Schönberg. Jews are a "form creating people," not a "cultural people" (86). They had already shown this in their own musical tradition of the liturgy, which infiltrates their attempts to write modern music as early as Meyerbeer.[18] This could not be transformed into Western classical music (87). Thus, they created modern music (Mahler and Schönberg) that lacks any melodic quality since the Jews lack the melodic which is the "sense of space" in music. As a people without "space," this impacts on their musical creativity. Berl's views echo the general principles of Wagner's son-in-law Houston Stewart Chamberlain's understanding of Germanic music in his 1899 anti-Semitic polemic against the Jews.[19]

Jewish virtuosi show similar qualities to composers. They may have genius in invention but are not creative as performers as they cannot make music truly sensual (84). The audience is enraptured by their playing because they are actors who transmute music into the visual world of appearances. Music, Berl stresses, is not visual: "it does not paint, it sings" (189). The Jewish performer, however, can only perform, not inhabit, the work of art. Berl's example is the Prague-born pianist Ignaz Moscheles (1794–1870), the teacher of Felix Mendelssohn-Bartholdy and great opponent of Franz Liszt.

A number of Jewish contemporaries strike out against Berl's rigid position. Arno Nadel argued that there is no "Jewish" music beyond the liturgical.[20] He denies the existence of any secular Jewish music except in the most recent attempts to evoke "Jewishness" in Western musical forms. Alfred Einstein's image of "Jews in Music" moves from the complex interaction between Jewish and non-Jewish musicians in Europe from the early modern period to the figures of the Jew on the musical stage, as in Eugen d'Albert's *Golem*.[21] He argues that there is little specifically "Jewish" among either the composers or, he adds, the characters. Berl's views are answered in part by the Prague musicologist Paul Nettl (1889–1972), who dismisses the underpinnings of Berl's so-called phenomenological analysis and replaces the view of a "Jewish" music with the notion that Jews adapt the music of the worlds they inhabit quite well to their own liturgical and cultural needs.[22] Whether Jews occupy high culture and "have" music is central to this debate. Do they mimic, do they borrow, and have they an inherent musical ability that is different from the Western underpinnings of musical creativity?

One can note here that a number of anti-Semites of the late nineteenth century answer the hypothetical question "Do we not have many notable figures among the Jews?"[23] In challenging the assumption that Jews have greater facility for music, Theodor Fritsch, perhaps the most widely read of these polemicists, answers that when any Jewish performer shows a modicum of talent, the Jewish press and Jewish agents immediately make him or her world famous. In a later account of "Jewish Statistics," his list of the "Jews in the Musical World" concludes with Hermann Wolff, the concert manager.[24] Simultaneously, Fritsch bemoans the fact that this emphasis on Jewish virtuosity signifies the disappearance of the German performer from the stage.

In the debate about Jewish cultural competency, it is usually the violinist, more than anyone else, who represents Jewish musical accomplishment at the close of the nineteenth century. Prior to Wagner, when we think of the nineteenth century and the rise of the violin virtuoso, it is Niccolò Paganini (1782–1840) who dominates the public's imagination as the essential violinist. He played so extraordinarily that he was said to have been aligned with the Devil (as, of course, was also said of the Jews).[25] This emphasis changes by the end of the nineteenth century. A "Jewish" cast to the image of the violinist begins in the generation of Johannes Brahms's friend Joseph Joachim (1831–1907), the son of a Jewish merchant family, who was not only the première violinist of his age but also a composer and conductor. By the 1930s, the role of the Jew as a major contributor to or destroyer of high culture focuses to no little extent on his (and they are virtually all men) ability to play the violin. The violin player as the exemplary figure of Jewish participation in high art is a reflex of the age of the multicultural.

At the end of the nineteenth century, societies to combat anti-Semitism arose. Central to their mission was to "prove" that Jews were as good if not better citizens than non-Jews, as the anti-Semites had made the argument that Jews were an inherent evil in Western society. Books were published to show that Jews did not dominate the "criminal classes," that they took part in civic obligations such as the military, and that they were a positive force in society. Especially after the accession to power of the Nazis in 1933, a spate of books and pamphlets appeared to chronicle the contributions of "Jews" (often very loosely defined) to Western high culture,[26] as if such proof answered the Nazis' claims of the overrepresentation of the Jews in high culture and their baneful effect on it. High culture, more than any other realm, became the place for this debate as it was widely accepted that the exposure to high culture improved the moral quality of individuals and of the society as a whole. Theater, music, art, and literature were inherently ennobling, unless—and here the anti-Semites' voice rang out—practiced by the Jews who used such claims of individual and civic improvement to poison the society in which they lived through undermining true (read: German) culture.[27]

The Russian cellist Gdal Saleski (1888–1967) published a comprehensive catalogue of Jewish musicians in 1927, *Famous Musicians of a Wandering*

Race, as a direct answer to the Wagnerian claim of Jewish musical parasit-ism.[28] It is basically a catalogue of composers, conductors, and instrumen-talists. Saleski stresses that he is not interested in a religious or political definition of the Jew but "purely a racial one" (vii). He argues through his biographical catalogue that "Jewish musicians have undoubtedly contrib-uted their mite to the world's music" (viii). They have done so, however, as human beings, not as Jews: "in the realm of music there are no artifi-cial racial and religious divisions. In this realm there reigns only talent and genius," which Jews show in great abundance. Saleski's views are quick-ly translated into popular form. In the mid-1930s, the Anti-Defamation League of B'nai Brith published a series of pamphlets under the title of the Fireside Discussion Group. (The echo of Franklin Roosevelt's "fireside chats" is unmistakable.) One, published in 1936 but typical of a wide range of such texts from the 1890s to the 1950s, is on *Jews in Music*. "Jews have taken an even greater place," this pamphlet claims, as interpreters of music and instrumentalists than they have as composers. It has been estimated that out of every twelve musical artists, vocalists, violinists and conductors, eight are descendants of the people of Israel"[29] (3). Of the seven pages of this pamphlet, two full pages are devoted to violinists. "Violin virtuosity has become almost synonymous with Jewish musical genius." Saleski, in *Famous Musicians*, lists seventy-three violinists who have achieved recognition: prominent among them are Leopold Auer, Mischa Elman, Jascha Heifetz, Fritz Kreisler, Yehudi Menuhin, Erika Morini, Max Rosen, Toscha Seidel, and Efrem Zimbalist. And thus on for two pages with the biographies of Elman, Zimbalist, and Kreisler ("the greatest violinist who ever lived"),[30] and ending with the then nineteen-year-old Menuhin. In Saleski's own work, the section on violinists is by far the longest. Jews make an important contribution to Western culture as violinists, even if their own "relation-ship" to being Jewish is truly tenuous. But the link between musical high culture and Jewish identity, so strongly denied until the close of the nine-teenth century, had become an intrinsic part of the self-definition of Central European Jewry.

The myth about being Jewish as an incomprehensible mental construct that leads to creative antagonism is answered in the early twentieth century by myths about music of necessity leading to other forms of creativity. Both seek to answer why Jewish "genius" arises. One views the scientific creativity of the Jews as stemming from their imposed position marginal to established science

(*Wissenschaft*); the other sees their musicality as a key factor central to their lives as educated citizens (*Bildungsbürgertum*) and as Jews.

Theodor Herzl writes in January 1898 that in 1895, "during the last two months of my residence in Paris I wrote the book *The Jewish State*.... I do not recollect ever having written anything in such an elevated frame of mind as that book.... I worked at it every day until I was completely exhausted; my only relaxation in the evening consisted of listening to Wagner's music, especially to *Tannhäuser*, an opera I went to every time it was performed. Only on the evenings when there was no performance at the Opera did I feel doubts about the correctness of my ideas."[31] The Phantom of the Opéra is in point of fact the centrality of musical culture for the definition of Jewish creativity. Herzl imagined a Jewish state, first in Argentina, and then in Palestine, with a side trip to Uganda, where European culture would dominate—a world imagined to look like Switzerland or the Austro-Hungarian Empire without the nationalist conflicts and bound together by Jewish identity and Western high culture. Thus the languages of that Jewish state would be the languages of Diaspora Jewry—with the exception of Yiddish, which was not a "real" language because, in Herzl's view, it did not have a real national culture.

Shortly thereafter in Britain and the United States, this question was being answered in Israel Zangwill's (1864–1926) extraordinarily popular play *The Melting Pot* (published 1909).[32] Here the question of high culture and specifically to the violin is raised in relationship to notions of cultural hybridity.[33] The debates about in what sphere the Jews could be imagined as functioning within modernity was answered: it was the sphere of high culture.

Zangwill's play was the hit of New York's 1908 theatrical season.[34] The "melting pot" comes to be *the* image of the excision of national difference through cultural as well as biological transformation.[35] It is the public face of what Theodore Roosevelt, who loved the play, saw as the opposition "against all hyphenated Americanism and all hyphenated Americans," as he wrote in a letter to the German-Jewish psychologist Hugo Münsterberg.[36] High culture for Zangwill and his contemporaries is a defining space for such transformation. One should note that while Ralph Waldo Emerson had earlier used the term "smelting pot" for the same idea, the Anglo-Jewish Zangwill provided a European fantasy of the role of culture in defining the Jews in the West. What is compelling is that Zangwill uses music to represent the universal. Music, here the music of high culture, also represents the natural, and at the turn of the twentieth century, the biological implications of the "natural" are crucial. The Jews "evolve" from the culture of the ghetto to high culture, and the development is the measure of social adaptability to the concept of *Bildung*.

The protagonist of Zangwill's play, the young violinist David Quixano, has survived as the sole member of his immediate family the Kishinev pogrom of Easter 1903. (The family name is taken from Amy Levy's 1888 novel *Reuben Sachs*, which deals with many of the same issues of acculturation.) While wounded in his left shoulder, his psychological trauma comes to be part of the defining quality of his character. The wound makes his playing the violin difficult, and his desire is to become a composer. The audience is introduced into the composite world of Jewish and European cultures, which shape his world through the stage depiction of the living room of his uncle, a piano teacher and conductor, at the very beginning of the drama: "On the left wall, in the upper corner of which is a music-stand, are bookshelves of large mouldering Hebrew books, and over them is hung a Mizrach, or Hebrew picture, to show it is the east wall. Other pictures round the room include Wagner, Columbus, Lincoln, and 'Jews at the wailing place'" (2, 49). This is the collage of the past and present, with the future also lurking in the icons of America—but it is Wagner who represents high musical culture for Zangwill, writing as he does in a world consumed, as George Bernard Shaw noted, by British Wagnerism, the epitome of *modern* (not classical; read: stuffy) musical high culture, indeed almost a religion in itself. But it is a musical religion that is accepted by left-leaning thinkers such as Shaw in spite of Wagner's "having [made the Jew] at that time ... the whipping boy for all modern humanity."[37] The fact that Jews, both in Germany and the United Kingdom, were just as fanatical followers of Wagner seemed to prove the transcendental quality of high culture, at least the Bayreuth version. The seemingly intrinsic relationship between the Jews and musical high culture is a trope in Anglo-Jewish writing of the day. In 1895, in B. L. Farjeon's novel *Aaron the Jew*, the Jewish character Mr. Moss the pawnbroker hums "the Jewel song in 'Faust,'" not because he is a musician but because "the instincts of his race ... had welded the divine art into his soul."[38] Indeed, like some contemporary purists, Moss detests any opera sung in English and loves only those presented in Italian (171). Thus Anglo-Jewry accepted Robert Browning's (1812–1889) view in his "Charles Avison," "There is no truer truth obtainable / By Man than comes of music."

Into this world of Jewish high culture comes Vera Revendal, the revolutionary daughter of Russian nobles, who has escaped Siberia and fled to England. (Zangwill evokes Oscar Wilde's first play, *Vera, or The Nihilists*, a melodrama about Russian revolutionaries, published in 1880.) She is shocked that the young violinist whose playing she had admired turns out to be a Jew: "A Jew! That wonderful boy a Jew… . But then so was David the shepherd youth with his harp and his psalms, the sweet singer in Israel. [She surveys the room and its contents with interest. The windows rattle once or twice in the rising wind. The light gets gradually less. She picks up the huge Hebrew tome on the piano and puts it down with a slight smile as if overwhelmed by the weight of alien antiquity. Then she goes over to the desk and picks up the printed music.] Mendelssohn's Concerto, Tartini's Sonata in G Minor, Bach's Chaconne…. [She looks up at the book-rack.] 'History of the American Commonwealth,' 'Cyclopedia of History,' 'History of the Jews'—he seems very fond of history. Ah, there's Shelley and Tennyson. [With surprise] Nietzsche next to the Bible? No Russian books apparently" (2:18–19). The musical canon is "universal," as is the literary canon, but the absence of Russian books (or music) illustrates how even this claim on universality of art (and beauty and truth) has political dimensions, for David's traumatic experience in Russia leaves him haunted by the face of the Russian officer who permitted the massacre.

David's uncle, Mendel, has brought him (and his grandmother) from Russia. He may well be the boy's savior but he is not his teacher, as he points out to Vera. David's musical talent is "natural": "He [David] is self-taught. In the Russian Pale he was a wonder-child. Poor David! He always looked forward to coming to America; he imagined I was a famous musician over here. He found me conducting in a cheap theatre—a converted beer-hall" (2:22–23). Like Recha in G. E. Lessing's Enlightenment paean to *Nathan the Wise*, David has learnt from the "Book of Nature," not those of men. Musical ability is usually seen as learned; David's musical ability is "natural," coming from his intrinsic humanity. Even his physiognomy points to his natural superiority: "He is a sunny, handsome youth of the finest Russo-Jewish type. He speaks with a slight German accent" (2:27). The accent here is evocative of belonging to the high culture of music. Here again, one can quote Shaw in the preface to the German edition of his work on Wagner: "And if I cannot love the typical modern German, I can at least pity and understand him. His worst fault is that he cannot see that it is possible to have too much of a good thing. Being convinced that duty, industry, education, loyalty, patriotism and respectability are good things (and I am magnanimous enough to admit that they are not altogether bad things when taken in strict moderation at the right time and in the right place), he indulges in them on all occasions shamelessly and excessively."[39] This idealization of the German is part of what makes him and his accent the mark of high culture in Zangwill's drama. That the flawed language of the immigrants mirrored the assumption of their inability to be truly of the culture is generally the case. Zangwill's friend (and later opponent over the question of a Jewish national state) H. G. Wells commented on the integrated, "high caste" colonial subject that "the Hindoo who is at pains to learn and use English encounters something like hatred disguised in a facetious form. He will certainly read little about himself that is not grossly contemptuous to reward him for his labor."[40] In Zangwill's fictive universe, speaking with a German accent, as we shall see, is proof of belonging to a liberal, high culture.

It is this "natural man" who is not only a brilliant violinist—of the Russo-Jewish type—but also a composer manqué, whose "New World Symphony" will reflect the merger of all of the groups of wanderers entering America into the "New Man."

> America is God's Crucible, the great Melting-Pot where all the races of
> Europe are melting and re-forming! Here you stand, good folk, think I,
> when I see them at Ellis Island, here you stand [Graphically illustrating it
> on the table] in your fifty groups, with your fifty languages and histo-
> ries, and your fifty blood hatreds and rivalries. But you won't be long
> like that, brothers, for these are the fires of God you've come to—these
> are the fires of God. A fig for your feuds and vendettas! Germans and
> Frenchmen, Irishmen and Englishmen, Jews and Russians—into the
> Crucible with you all! God is making the American. (2:33)

Their common language will be English but will also be music, spoken with a "slight German accent." As he notes in a Nietzschean mode, "[T]he real American has not yet arrived. He is only in the Crucible, I tell you—he will be the fusion of all races, perhaps the coming superman. Ah, what a glorious Finale for my symphony—if I can only write it" (2:34). This is the Jew as Zarathustra—not as odd an image as we imagine today given the obsession of early Zionists with Nietzsche and Nietzschean rhetoric.[41] When David does write it, "[T]he immigrants will not understand my music with their brains or their ears, but with their hearts and their souls" (2:142). Music transcends the limits of human speech, and becomes the place where truth and beauty and the American way reside. It is a new music, the "Sinfonia Americana," a music that has never been present before, as the philo–Semitic German conductor Pappelmeister (who, to signal his true function in high culture, speaks with a stage German accent) observes,

PAPPELMEISTER [Sublimely unconscious] Ach so-so-SO! Das ist etwas neues! [His umbrella begins to beat time, moving more and more vigorously, till at last he is conducting elaborately, stretching out his left palm for pianissimo passages, and raising it vigorously for forte, with every now and then an exclamation.] Wunderschön! … pianissimo!— now the flutes! Clarinets! Ach, ergötzlich … bassoons and drums! … Fortissimo! … Kolossal! … Kolossal! (2:77)

The new music is the new world of hybridity, of the melting pot, but its musical language is that of high culture, perhaps that of Charles Ives's "Variations on America" from 1891 or Antonin Dvorak's "Symphony No. 9, opus 95, from the New World" (1893). Such music exists in Zangwill's world.

But the claim on hybridity as the new form of music grows out of its nature as a biological force that lends itself to the improvement of all things. Here hybridity is the conquering of past hates and stereotypes that enables the lovers to join and become the potential parents of a new America. The melodramatic point of the play is reached when David recognizes Vera's nobleman father as the officer who enabled the violent peasants to kill his family. She then breaks with her father and his tradition completely: "David, I come to you, and I say in the words of Ruth, thy people shall be my people and thy God my God! [She stretches out her hands to DAVID.]" (2:154). But David is overwhelmed by images of the past ('There is a river of blood between us." [2:155]) and flees from her, only to be reconciled at the close of the drama at the performance of his symphony.

VERA - What else can I do? Shall the shadow of Kishineff hang over all your years to come? Shall I kiss you and leave blood upon your lips, cling to you and be pushed away by all those cold, dead hands?

DAVID - [Taking both her hands] Yes, cling to me, despite them all, cling
        to me till all these ghosts are exorcised, cling to me till our love
        triumphs over death. Kiss me, kiss me now.

VERA - [Resisting, drawing back] I dare not! It will make you remember.

DAVID - It will make me forget. Kiss me. [There is a pause of hesitation,
        filled up by the Cathedral music from "Faust" surging up soft-
        ly from below.] (2:183)

The past is obliterated in the sounds of Charles Gounod's *Faust* (1859), and
very specifically the religious evocation of a high culture with its Christian
roots, for the cathedral music from Act 4 echoes the guilt felt by Marguerite,
spurred on by the hidden Méphistophélès, who reminds her what she has
done in killing her child. The music is the *Dies Irae*, accompanied on the
organ, and it heralds her doom. It is the antithesis of the promise of the
elimination of guilt and trauma in Zangwill's final scene of intermarriage.
Rather, it echoes the joint abdication of Vera and David of the prejudices
of the "Old World" for the (mis-) alliances of the New. It is the fulfilment
of Wordsworth's sob about the "the still, sad music of humanity" in his
Romantic "Lines Completed a Few Miles above Tintern Abbey."

    Zangwill himself married a non-Jewish woman, Edith Chaplin Ayrton,
who came from a notable British liberal family (and who had a Jewish step-
mother).[42] He broke with a number of his closest friends such as Salomon
Schechter over this step. He stressed as late as 1924 that "my wife has the
same Jewish ideal as those which you credit me.... . Judaism is spiritual and
you appear," he writes in a letter, "to make it racial."[43] "Intermarriage," he
writes in the 1914 appendix to *The Melting Pot*, "wherever social intimacy,
will follow, even when the parties stand in opposite religious camps."[44] But
this is possible only through true cultural transformation and biological
changes, following a Lamarckian model of the inheritance of acquired characteristics, as he writes in 1900: "as Jews do, in the civilized community of
Europe and America[,] take on the characteristics of their environment and
become one with it, their isolation by [refusing] intermarriage is a mere bad
habit."[45] Remember that Max Nordau rationalized his own relationship to a
non-Jewish Danish woman (Anna) who had borne him a child (Maxa) a year
before their marriage. In his memoirs, which were rewritten and partially
compiled by his widow after his death, Nordau had no objection to mixed
marriages "in German society, which is still dominated by anti-Semitism.

His own marriage—which was in no way diminished in relationship to race and religion—permitted him to recognize that a mixed marriage could be harmonious, but elsewhere, such as in Germany, he saw such cases as unsuccessful."[46] Nordau's own ambiguity (and/or that of his non-Jewish widow) saw the problems resulting from mixed marriages as existing exclusively in German society, with its powerful image of the primitive nature of the Eastern Jew unable to be integrated into "real" German high culture. For Zangwill, his "America" is the site where such transformations can take place.

The marriage of David and Vera, like the mix of cultures in his symphony, will give birth to a "New Man," but is he the "New Hebraic Man"? In a letter of 12 November 1861, the Polish-Jewish sociologist Ludwig Gumplowicz wrote about civil emancipation to his friend, the Galician-Jewish nationalist Philipp Mansch:

> *Civil marriage!* My reply: that is supposed to be part of our striv-
> ing—that has to come. You have read the motion of the Commission for
> Religion—decided by Smolka. You are finding that 'religion is no ob-
> stacle to matrimony!' ... Give me your word that we shall marry the most
> beautiful Christian girls—alias *shikses*—in case that motion becomes
> law! I am joking and yet the matter is no joke. The day is not far where
> even this last wall of separation is bound to fall—and we are compelled
> to take leave from this shadow of our nationality which is long decayed
> but which for centuries keeps creeping after us like a vampire, sucks our
> blood and destroys our vitality.[47]

Gumplowicz's first point for the regeneration of the Jews, the means by which the final goal, intermarriage, can be accomplished, is the "acceptance of the language of the people among whom one lives." One of the languages that Jews had to master was that of music, but how could they do this without actually entering into physical relationships that showed that they were accepted as human beings able to comprehend the higher nature attributed to culture? Otto von Bismarck coined the phrase that one had to join the German stallion to the Jewish mare to improve both groups. The very notion of crossbreeding answered the charge of inbreeding lodged in the biological literature of the time against the Jews. What would the Jew now bring to the mix? Given the stereotypes of the time, certainly not physical strength but intellectual and cultural superiority. Even though Max Nordau prophesied the creation of the "New Muscle Jew" at the turn of the twentieth century, it is the Jewish violinist who captures the stage in Zangwill's image of the New Hebraic Man. It is high culture, not body culture, that will allow the Jew to be raised to the same level as everyone else.

Jewish hybridity, even with Bismarck's ironic comment, is not seen as advantageous in nineteenth-century Europe, for it is argued that rather than bringing something positive into the mix, it brings the negative, corrupting qualities associated with the Jew. Certainly a major literary representation of this trope is to be found in William Thackeray's *Vanity Fair*, which was as much a part of the German as of the Anglophone canon in the nineteenth century.[48] In the very first chapter, we are introduced to a Miss Schwartz, "the rich woolly-haired mulatto from St. Kitts," who goes "in downright hysterics" when Amelia Sedley and Becky Sharp leave school (8). She is depicted as neither very bright nor very talented. She retains her "primitive" love of ornament: "her favorite amber-coloured satin with turquoise bracelets, countless rings, flowers, feathers, and all sorts of tags and gimcracks, about as elegantly decorated as a she chimney-sweep on May-day" (200). This hysterical type is a *hybrid*, as her German name, which means "black," suggests. But her patrimony is not German, but Jewish: "Her father was a German Jew—a slave-owner they say—connected with the Cannibal Islands in some way or another," who has died and left his children a large inheritance (194). In the novel she is anomalous, an exotic whose sexuality is written on her body. Even her wealth does not cancel this out. Thus, George Osborne rejects a potentially lucrative match with her, exclaiming, "Marry that mulatto woman? … I don't like the colour, sir. Ask the black that sweeps opposite Fleet Market, sir. *I'm* not going to marry a Hottentot Venus" (204). The reference to the Hottentot Venus evokes the body of the African woman and her "primitive sexuality." But this figure represents a literary reworking of the hybrid's atavism. It also evokes the German Jews' supposed willingness, even eagerness, to cross racial lines for their own purpose.

Yet Zangwill does not wish this image to remain disconnected from the actual experience of the Jews that haunts the background of the drama. He provides documentation for his drama. Much like the historical dramatists of the 1960s, such as Rolf Hochhuth, he feels that since he is making a claim on the validity of this experience for the future, he must underpin it with the claim of an authentic experience. One of the numerous appendices recounts the life of

Daniel Melsa, a young Russo-Jewish violinist who has carried audiences
by storm in Berlin, Paris and London, and who had arranged to go to
America last November. The following extract from an interview in the
Jewish Chronicle of January 24, 1913, shows the curious coincidence
between his beginnings and David Quixano's: "Melsa is not yet twenty
years of age, but he looks somewhat older. He is of slight build and has
a sad expression, which increased to almost a painful degree when recounting some of his past experiences. He seems singularly devoid of any
affectation, while modesty is obviously the keynote of his nature. After
some persuasion, Melsa put aside his reticence, and, complying with the
request, outlined briefly his career, the early part of which, he said, was
overshadowed by a great tragedy. He was born in Warsaw, and, at the age
of three, his parents moved to Lodz, where shortly after a private tutor
was engaged for him. 'Although I exhibited a passion for music quite
early, I did not receive any lessons on the subject till my seventh birthday,
but before that my father obtained a cheap violin for me upon which I
was soon able to play simple melodies by ear.' By chance a well-known
professor of the town heard him play, and so impressed was he with the
talent exhibited by the boy that he advised the father to have him educated. Acting upon this advice, as far as limited means allowed, tutors were
engaged, and so much progress did he make that at the age of nine he was
admitted to the local Conservatorium of Professor Grudzinski, where
he remained two years. It was at the age of eleven that a great calamity
overtook the family, his father and sister falling victims to the pogroms.
'It was in June of 1905, at the time of the pogroms, when one afternoon
my father, accompanied by my little sister, ventured out into the street,
from which they never returned. They were both killed,' he added sadly,
'by Cossacks. A week later I found my sister in a Christian churchyard
riddled with bullets, but I have not been able to trace the remains of my
father, who must have been buried in some out-of-the-way place. During
this awful period my mother and myself lived in imminent danger of our
lives, and it was only the recollection of my playing that saved us also
falling a prey to the vodka-besodden Cossacks.'" (2:194–95)

Melsa's life, so very evocative of the protagonist's, is framed by Zangwill's
understanding that his life shows the transcendent ability of the Jews to
survive even the innate inhospitability of Russia through the vehicle of high

culture. Writing after the Dreyfus affair convinced many European Jews of the failure of the Enlightenment project, Europe and America remain the sites where Jewish life is not only possible but also where Jews will be transformed into a healthier and more creative New Hebraic Man. Neither Germany nor German high culture is condemned; rather, it is praised for its liberal culture of inclusion, and its role in creating and perpetuating "classical" music is evoked as proof, in spite of Wagner's reputation as an anti-Semite and the Bayreuth circle's support of political anti-Semitism. Zangwill sees the "East" as the source of an implacable anti-Semitism, which is inherently rooted in the "despotism" of states such as Russia. In contrast, a melting pot is only possible in terms of biological and cultural hybridity in "America and the other free Western nations such as England, Argentina, and Brazil."[49] The life of Melsa provides the final bit of proof linking Zangwill's fantasy of the transformation of the Jews within the world of high culture. His is the living "Sinfonia Americana" that is the melting pot.

The extraordinary success of Zangwill's play (and its afterlife in popular comedies such as Anne Nichols's *Abie's Irish Rose* [1922]) shaped the discourse about the relationship between the notion of a multicultural society and the Jews. Zangwill's legacy is not only the melting pot but also the metaphor of a musical high culture as testing place for the role of the Jews in modernity. In his 1915 essay, the American Zionist and philosopher Horace Kallen's coined the concept of "cultural pluralism" as an answer to the melting pot. He concludes his essay with the desire that the component cultures function "as in an orchestra, every type of instrument has its specific timbre and tonality, founded in its substance and form: as every type has its appropriate theme and melody in the whole symphony, so in society each ethnic group is the natural instrument, its spirit and culture are its theme and melody and the harmony and dissonances and discords of them all make the symphony of civilization, with this difference: a musical symphony is written before it is played; in the symphony of civilization the playing is the writing, so that there is nothing so fixed and inevitable about its progressions as in music, so that within the limits set by nature they may vary at will, and the range and variety of the harmonies may become wider and richer and more beautiful."[50] This is clearly aimed by Kallen against "Zangwill [who is] at best the obverse of Dickens, at worst he is a Jew making a special plea" (75). Kallen's evocation of the various instruments leads us to ask whether the Jew is indeed the violin in the symphony of cultural pluralism. Whether this is the case or not, it is the symphony orchestra, not the klezmer band, or even Irving Berlin's "Alexander's Ragtime Band" (1911), that is the image for Jews engaged in debates about multiculturalism at the turn of the twentieth century.

The theme of the "American symphony" as the ultimate expression of "the melting pot" comes to be a signature of the integration of Jews into American music. In 1924, Paul Whiteman asked George Gershwin (born George Gershovitz; 1898–1937) to write a "jazz-influenced concert piece" for his concert jazz band. In his autobiography, Gershwin speaks about the inspiration for the "Rhapsody in Blue" on a train journey to Boston:

> It was on the train, with its steely rhythms, its rattly-bang, that is so often so stimulating to a composer—I frequently hear music in the very heart of the noise.... And there I suddenly heard, and even saw on paper—the complete construction of the Rhapsody, from beginning to end. No new themes came to me, but I worked on the thematic material already in my mind and tried to conceive the composition as a whole. I heard it as a sort of musical kaleidoscope of America, of our vast melting pot, of our unduplicated national pep, of our blues, our metropolitan madness. By the time I reached Boston I had a definite plot of the piece, as distinguished from its actual substance.[51]

Jazz was made culturally acceptable by Whiteman and Gershwin—they moved it from the dance halls to the concert hall. "There had been so much talk about the limitations of jazz.... Jazz, they said, had to be in strict time. It had to cling to dance rhythms. I resolved, if possible, to kill the misconception with one sturdy blow.... I had no set plan, no structure to which my music must conform. The Rhapsody, you see, began as a purpose, not a plan."[52] The new melting pot was the merger of African-American music (with a touch of klezmer) with the cultural world of the concert hall. This is the tradition of the Jewish entry into a new form of musical high culture.

We should remember that the American perspective at the beginning of the twentieth century retains its hope for some type of authentic Jewish presence within a multicultural world, so very different than the failed symphony that Gershom Scholem postulates in his open 1964 letter, in which he argued that "the Jews attempted a dialogue with the Germans, starting from all possible points of view and situations, demandingly, imploringly, and entreatingly, servile and defiant ... and today, when the symphony is over, the time may be ripe for studying their motifs and for attempting a critique of their tones.[53] By 1964 the German symphony may well have been over in his estimation, fulfilling a prophecy about the failure of a Jewish culture in Germany made in the nineteenth century. Yet it continues to echo.

FIVE

FRANZ KAFKA'S DIET
An Answer to Hybridity

The claim that the Jews had to transform themselves became one of the hardiest tropes of that literature which doubts the benefit of such transformation. The transformation of the Jewish body was desirable but inherently impossible because the results were imagined as catastrophic. The model for Franz Kafka (1883–1924) at the fringes of the Austro-Hungarian Empire at the beginning of the twentieth century was that of religious conversion, at least for those Jews who remained in the European Diaspora. Unlike Israel Zangwill's "American" dissolution of religious belief into ethnic toleration, Kafka knew that the older European option of religious conversion did not lead to any resolution. As we saw in chapter 2, neither did the myth of transformation through immigration to the New World. By the end of the nineteenth century, the very notion of conversion from Judaism to Christianity was considered in European intellectual circles as impossible as converting from one race to another. Throughout Kafka's writing, such transformation is always an impossible wish: the rider who merges with his horse in his fantasy of America, "Desire to Become an Indian" (1913); Gregor Samsa's horrid transformation into a giant vermin in "The Metamorphosis" (1915); and the incomplete and pathetic metamorphosis of ape into man in Kafka's "Report to an Academy," first published in Martin Buber's journal *The Jew* in November 1919. What is lost or (partially) gained in all of these cases is the code of decorum by which the characters function in the world of "civilized behavior." Certainly the tale of Karl Rossmann in Kafka's *Amerika: The Man Who Disappeared* (1912) showed that the transformation of religion to ethnicity was as much a dead end as any other form of metamorphosis. The world of liberating high culture is parodied in the fragment about the "great Theater of Oklahoma" that Max Brod uses to close his restructuring of the novel when it is finally published. No promise about spiritual transformation is made there, only the inevitable final downward spiral into oblivion of the immigrant in a hostile world. Indeed, Kafka's use of the "theater" as the place to resolve all of the personal and moral dilemmas of his protagonist is a strong parodic echo of Goethe's use of that cultural institution in his *Wilhelm Meister* novels of education, except of course here the theater will reveal itself not as a "happy end" but as a confidence trick. *Bildung* will not rescue anyone.

The theme that high culture cannot save the Jew echoes in Kafka's major work that represents "transformation." Once transformed in "The Metamorphosis," the traveling salesman Gregor Samsa sinks into a decline that is marked by his loss of human epistemology by forgetting the rules of decorum. He comes to represent the world with the cultural and social limitations of a bug:[1] "As Gregor Samsa awoke one morning from uneasy dreams he found himself transformed in his bed into a gigantic insect."[2] The loss of connection with codes of decorum defines his transformation into a gigantic insect, which seems to forget the social rules by which the Samsa family lives. Ironically, it is the appreciation (or lack of it) of musical high culture that charts Gregor's transformation. Again, it is the violinist and her instrument that mark high culture in this parody of Jewish life in Kafka's Prague. Music is something that Samsa, before his transformation, cannot appreciate: "With his sister alone had he remained intimate, and it was a secret plan of his that she, who loved music, unlike himself, and could play movingly on the violin, should be sent to study at the Conservatorium.... [This] was often mentioned in the talks he had with his sister, but always merely as a beautiful dream which could never come true." (111).[3] Music is the gift he will give to his sister, a gift not appreciated by his parents, but which shows that even though he does not enjoy music, he understands the social capital that it represents in his world.

Once transformed, Gregor can no longer function as the breadwinner in the family, a role that he has assumed and that he imagines gave him power as well as obligations. Now, an unemployed gigantic insect, he imagines the sister's violin playing as both a potential source of income to replace that which he has lost and also a sign of the social environment that he has now lost:

On that very evening—during the whole of his time there Gregor could not remember ever having heard the violin—the sound of violin-playing came from the kitchen. The lodgers had already finished their supper, the one in the middle had brought out a newspaper and had given the other two a page apiece, and now they were leaning back at ease, reading and smoking. When the violin began to play, they pricked up their ears, got to their feet, and went on tiptoe to the hall door, where they stood huddled together.... "Is the violin-playing disturbing you, gentlemen? It can be stopped at once." "On the contrary," said the middle lodger, "could not Fräulein Samsa come and play in this room, beside us... ?" (129)

Once all gather in the living room, the gigantic insect hypnotically wanders out of his room, suddenly attracted by the beauty of his sister's violin playing: "Gregor's sister began to play; the father and mother, from either side, intently watched the movements of her hands. Gregor, attracted by the playing, ventured to move forward until his head was actually inside the living room. He felt hardly any surprise at his growing lack of wonder about consideration for the others; there had been a time when he prided himself on being considerate" (130). This lack of decorum terrifies her as well as the new borders, who promptly move out.

Gregor has begun to become different in the way that he sees the world, losing even the internal language of decorum but gaining the instinctual attraction of the magic associated with music (not of high culture): "Was he an animal, that music had such an effect upon him? He felt as if the way were opening before him to the unknown nourishment he craved. He was determined to push forward till he reached his sister, to pull at her skirt and so let her know that she was to come into his room with her violin, for no one here appreciated her playing as he would appreciate it" (130–31).[4] The sound of the violin in this ironic reversal of associations becomes the sign, not of high culture, but of the elemental, instinctual drive. The German proverb observes, "Wen verführet die Begier, der verkehrt sich in ein Tier" (Whom desire seduces, acts like an animal). Here the sister reappears with the power of Orpheus to free Eurydice from underworld, or so Gregor hopes. But we know how both tales end.

But it is the violinist who captures the attention of Samsa's world. On 18 December 1911, Kafka, overwhelmed by the Yiddish traveling theater that has descended upon Prague (and enamored with the actresses who act in it), attends a version of Joseph Lateiner's *Davids Geige* (*David's Violin*). He provides a summary and commentary in his diaries: "The disinherited son, a good violinist, returns home a rich man, as I used to dream of doing in my early days at the Gymnasium. But first, disguised as a beggar, his feet bound in rags like a snow shoveler, he tests his relatives who have never left home: his poor, honest daughter, his rich brother who will not give his son in marriage to his poor cousin and who despite his age himself wants to marry a young woman. He reveals himself later on by tearing open a Prince Albert under which, on a diagonal sash, hang decorations from all the princes of Europe. By violin playing and singing he turns all the relatives and their hangers-on into good people and straightens out their affairs." Music provides access to wealth—as Gregor Samsa hopes to see with his sister's talent, but it is also one of young Franz's dreams. Music for Lateiner frees the world from its ills. Kafka can no longer believe that this happens so easily. Indeed, he has the rich uncle in *Amerika*, seeing Karl Rossmann's passion for music, offer him the chance to take violin lessons. Karl does not take up the offer. Indeed, violin playing is one of the things that Kafka, ill and desperate in 1922, regrets having abandoned, like Hebrew, marriage, and his own dwelling (23 January 1922). The violin signals the failure of transformation, not its success.

The transformation into a bug had been a theme in Kafka's sense of his own body. He had dreamt of himself as a huge bug, saw bugs in perfectly clean hotel rooms, and now would capture the anxiety of transformation from human into bug. He had sketched such a reverse transition from ape into human in one of his tales for Martin Buber, mirroring the ironic path that European Jews had taken since the Enlightenment. (Were they now truly "human" or merely a simulacrum of what humans imagined themselves to be?) Now the question is posed, as with Joseph K.'s sudden transformation into an accused in Kafka's rump novel *The Trial*, was is the transformation of a human being into an insect truly a change of status? The ape becomes "human," that is, he acquires a human manner of seeing the world with his acquisition of language. But he remains marked by sexual passion for his "kind." In the end, all he had acquired are the rules of decorum, which his new mate does not share.

All these transformations reflect both Jewish and anti-Semitic accusations against Jewish assimilation: Jews will never become true Germans; their Germanness is a mere sham. The more they try to change, the more they reveal themselves as fundamentally defective. Jews see and represent the world differently than Germans; their sexuality, their bodies, remain as different as the bug's or the ape's.

No healthy assimilation is possible, not even in the fantasy world of Kafka's texts. Even the French historian Anatole Leroy-Beaulieu (1842–1912), a member of the French Academy and a staunch defender of the Jews at the time of the Dreyfus affair, noted that irony is the weapon by which "the baptized Jew takes vengeance upon the God of the Christians and upon their social system, for the disgrace of compulsory baptism."[5] Kafka is aware not only that conversion is impossible but also that marrying outside the "race" can lead to ghastly results. This can be seen in his understanding of the particular nature of the *Mischling*, the offspring of race mixing between Jew and non-Jew.[6] The *Mischling* had a special status in the culture of the period, for the *Mischling* magnified the most egregious aspects of both "races." These children of Jews and non-Jews, these *Mischlinge*, are Jews, but in heightened form, bearing all the stigmata of degeneration that exist in incestuous or inbred families. Like the sign of congenital circumcision, the mark of the decay of the Jew is present even (or especially) in the *Mischling*: "The children of such marriages [between Jews and non-Jews,] … even though they are so very beautiful and so very talented, seem to lack a psychological balance that is provided by pure racial stock. We find all too often intellectually or morally unbalanced individuals, who decay ethically or end in suicide or madness."[7] There is no place one can hide; there is no means of becoming invisible. The *Mischling* is the end product of the process of Jewish degeneration that produces children who reveal the hidden racial difference of the Jews, their "Blackness."[8]

The model of the *Mischling*, however, comes to represent the "essential" nature of the Jew in racist culture of the twentieth century. In Josefa Berens-Totenohl's best-selling novel of the Third Reich, she describes the Jew as "a *Mischling* in blood and home, in language and promise, in thinking and acting. No one really knew him."[9] His physiognomy likewise gives him away; his eyes and his hair color reveal that he does not belong. Even the dogs of the farm know that, barking at his approach. The fin de siècle literary Jew is no longer "pure" in anything, not even racially. The Jew now provokes the anxiety associated with the boundary-crossing *Mischling*. This *Mischling* is manifestly, ineradicably different.

Nowhere is this anxiety more powerful at the turn of the twentieth century than in Kafka's Prague. In 1909 Max Warwar published a biting feuilleton on the front page of the Zionist periodical, *Self-Defense* (*Selbstwehr*), a periodical of which Kafka was a fervent reader and sometime correspondent. Warwar bemoans the "flight from the type," the anxiety of Jews about their own bodies as signs of their inherent difference.[10] "There are reportedly Jews," writes Warwar, "who stand for hours before the mirror and like vain women observe their exterior with jealousy and distaste, complaining against nature that had so irrationally formed them in light of the laws of their development. These Jews feel their profile as a band of shame, and suffer for they have not learned to experience what is there as beautiful." These male Jews are like women, but women who are constantly unhappy with what nature has provided them in the way of beauty. They are ashamed of their own "type." This "type," of course, according to the Zionist Warwar, is a pure type, but these Jews act as if their bodies represented a mixed type. Some try to escape their bodies through conversion, by "crawling to the cross," but the conversion fails, and they do not acquire any respect for their "external being" from the "other" through conversion. Conversion is no escape from race, as it is only the desire to appear like the "other," in Warwar's term, that motivates their false conversions. What they wish to escape is the "Jewish type," being a "true, black-haired Jew." It is blackness that marks the Jews as different in Prague. Blackness, for Warwar, is a sign of the pure type, a sign of inherent difference. These "black Jews," seen by Warwar in the singer's self-representation in the *Song of Songs*, can be beautiful: "For the soul even of the blackest of Jews can be as pure as gold." And it is indeed the blackness of the Jew that should be the erotic center of their attraction: "Perhaps it is this very fire that burns in the eyes of Jewish men and women, that extends an inescapable attraction to all that come close to it. And the blacker such a type is, the more demonic and darker the fires burn in the eyes, and the more intimate the magic that such a Jew can exude." Warwar sees, however, that this is precisely not the case in contemporary Prague. There the sexual attraction to such a "type" is felt only by "Christians, Teutons, and Romans," not by Jews. And this attraction leads then to crossing racial boundaries, and the creation of mixed racial types. In this argument, Jews must remain true to their own "type," to their own body, and to their cultural difference as "Orientals."[11]

In this ideological construct, the Jews as "Oriental" are as marked by the color of their skins, by their yellowness or their blackness, as Africans. In addition to their moral, psychological, and physiological failings, all inscribed so that they can be read by the physician, the *Mischling* is pro- verbially creative. This is a negative quality of the Jew that has its roots in the nineteenth-century discussion about the relationship between ge- nius and madness. Creativity was understood by physicians such as Cesare Lombroso as early as mid-century as a symptom pointing to some form of underlying degenerative pathology. This labeled the creativity of writers (such as Heinrich Heine) as a sign of their pathology, and this pathological nature was embodied in the writer's use of language. The Jew's creativity is in the Jewish use of the German language.[12] But they cannot become too like Aryan Christians, for then they are inauthentic: "If the Jew differs from us, so much the better; he is the more likely to bring a little variety into the flat monotony of modern civilization. I am rather inclined to find fault with these sons of Shem—as I find fault with the Orientals who adopt our customs—for resembling and copying us too closely."[13] The inauthenticity of the Western Jew, copying "us" too closely, is the inauthenticity of the convert, whether a religious convert or a cultural convert. Jews have the "remarkable faculty of taking on a new skin, without at bottom ceasing to be a Jew,"[14] for Leroy-Beaulieu knows where the "real" Jew lies—it is in the East, where the essence of the Jew is revealed and cannot be masked by conversion: "There seems to be something of the reptile in him [the Eastern Jew], something sinuous and crawling, something slimy and clammy, of which not even the educated Israelite has always been able to rid himself.... This is a quality that transforms him again ... into an Oriental; it is a racial feature, an inherent vice, not always to be washed away by the water and salt of baptism."[15] And it is the voice that reveals the Jew even after his seeming transformation into a "Frenchman": "The metamorphosis was often too sudden to be complete.... A glance, a word, a gesture, all of a sudden lays bare the old Jew at the bottom."[16] It is the face and the voice that reveal the hidden Jew.

In Kafka's world, hybridity is not a solution, neither for Kafka as a writer nor for him as a person. Earlier options of cultural and biological integration are also seemingly closed to him. Visiting Meran in April 1920, his visibility as a Jew becomes even more evident to him. There, his very language reveals him as a Jew to the "Germans" in a way that is most telling for a writer.[17] In this same account, he rails against the baptized Jew and the *Mischling*: "What horrid Jewish energies live on close to bursting inside a baptized Jew, only to be modulated in the Christian children of a Christian mother!"[18] Here, the promise of eventual integration into an ideal society, as the Christian child of a Christian mother, is the result of the process of the physical transformation of the Jew. The intermediate stage of this transformation is the baptized Jew. This baptized Jew represents in Kafka's vocabulary of images the status of the Westernized, acculturated, perhaps even assimilated Jews, whose only hope is in the eventual total physical acceptance of their offspring who have become physically identical with the Germans (but not the Czechs). As Ernst Lissauer observed in 1912,

> The Jews are in an intermediary stage. The emancipation of the Jews is
> but a hundred years hence; it began only a hundred years ago and is not
> yet completed. These hundred years is but a very short span of time.
> Our poorly educated sense of history often allows Jews and Non-Jews to
> forget that the Jews were in the Diaspora for 1700 years, under extraor-
> dinary pressure and need, and that the effects of such an extended time
> cannot be eradicated in a century. When we tabulate these figures, the
> "Jewish Question" acquires quite a different image. One can thus see
> that the Jews still possess many of the characteristics that come from the
> Ghetto and that awake the hate of the Non-Jew, but also that on the other
> hand many of these characteristics have been lost, as assimilation has
> been relatively successful.[19]

Among the markers of difference that seem not to have been lost but only repressed, in the fantasies of Western Jews, is the inability of the Jew to command the language of high culture. And Jews who speak differently look different. Kafka meets a Jewish goldsmith from Krakow who had been long in America, and whose "German was disturbed by an English pronunciation and English expressions; his English was so strong that his Yiddish was given a rest." And this traveler looked different: "He had long, curly hair, only occasionally ran his fingers through it, very bright eyes, a gently curving nose, hollows in his cheeks, a suit of American cut, a frayed shirt, falling socks."[20] Here is what the Eastern Jew becomes when he attempts to transform himself—an individual without language, without culture, marked by the physiognomy of the Jew.

Yet Kafka is himself that Eastern Jew. Kafka's grandfathers had been village Jews in rural Bohemia who primarily spoke Yiddish, the language of Central European Jewry; his father spoke Czech, but when he moved to Prague opted to identify with the German-speaking community and raised his son as German speaking. As the language philosopher and Prague Jew Fritz Mauthner wrote in his 1918 memoirs, "I had to consider not only German but also Czech and Hebrew, as the languages of my 'forefathers' … I had the corpses of three languages to drag around with me…. As a Jew in a bilingual country, just as I possessed no proper native language, I also had no native religion, as the son of a religionless Jewish family."[21] What changed over time was not only their language but also the very meaning that the covenant with God had for them. "And there is a relationship between all this and Jewishness, or more precisely between young Jews and their Jewishness, with the fearful inner predicament of these generations. Psychoanalysis lays stress on the father-complex, and many find the concept intellectually fruitful. In this case I prefer another version, where the issue revolves not around the innocent father but around the father's Jewishness. Mostly young Jews who started to write in German," Kafka writes in June 1921 to Max Brod, "wanted to get away from their Jewishness, usually with their father's consent (the vagueness of it was what made it outrageous). They want to get away, but their hind legs still stuck to the fathers' Jewishness, while the forelegs found not firm ground. And the resulting despair served as their inspiration."[22] They flailed about in a cultural world that they shaped self-consciously from the outside, but to which they felt they could never truly belong. Kafka sees this using a biological model. His father's family, the Kafkas, at least in Franz's account, were brutal, tyrannical, and uncultured. Indeed, he credited his becoming a vegetarian in 1909 and his lacking musicality to them: "Unmusicality is not as clearly a misfortune as you say—in the first place it isn't for me: I inherited it from my predecessors (my paternal grandfather was a butcher in a village near Strakonitz; I have to not eat as much meat as he butchered) and it gives me something to hold on to; being related means a lot to me."[23] When Max Brod takes Kafka to the première of Gustav Mahler's seventh symphony, conducted by Mahler in Prague on 19 September 1908, Kafka (then thirty-five) cannot comprehend what he is hearing. He feels himself unable to deal with the complexity of such huge works. Also clear is Kafka's discomfort at the situation Brod has forced him into—he must suffer the incomprehensible so as not to offend his friend.

Food, musicality, and decorum—the world of the unacceptable and that which defines true acceptability. Music is for Kafka a sign of the perils of hybridity and transformation, as we have seen in "The Metamorphosis," where Gregor's growing inability to eat anything but the food that is deemed by him appropriate to his bug-like state measures his transformation as surely as his newly discovered love of music. In the very late tale "Josephine the Singer, or the Mouse Folk," Kafka provides a commentary on the assumption that the Jewish voice at the fin de siècle was a sign of illness and disease. It is linked with another assumption, that the food consumed by the Jews, read in the time as a prophylactic against food-borne disease, was also a sign of the impossibility of their integration into society. Kafka's "conversion" to vegetarianism is seen by him as a true transformation. "He compared vegetarians with the early Christians, persecuted everywhere, everywhere laughed at, and frequenting dirty haunts. 'What is meant by its nature for the highest and the best, spreads among the lowly people.'"[24] Kafka sees his eating habits as being linked to who he is, to his sense of self, but also to a marginal world.

For if you are what you listen to, you are also what you eat. The intense debate in the nineteenth century about *Schächten* or *shehitah*, the Jewish ritual slaughter of animals for human consumption, is closely associated with arguments about decorum and health.[25] The most widely read fin de siècle work on public health in German was by Ferdinand Hueppe, who held the chair of hygiene in Prague beginning in 1889. His discussion of animal slaughter begins with a diatribe against ritual slaughter.[26] For him, slaughter must occur so as not to violate "our moral feelings." Animals should be anesthetized or at least stunned before slaughter. "From the ethical standpoint *shehitah* must be halted, because it is the crudest and most disgusting method…. [I]n *shehitah* the cramps as the animal bleeds to death are so horrible, so that any feeling human being, who has once seen it must turn from such primitive and disgusting techniques with abhorrence." Hueppe argues that the hygienic claim that meat that has been bled is healthier is false; indeed, "such meat is of lower quality." *Shehitah* is insupportable in "our climate and cultural conditions." Only the Jews, who belong in a foreign space and have a different culture, would advocate such a procedure. Thus, the charges of cruelty, brutality, and indifference to suffering are lodged against the Jews in light of their ritual practice of *shehitah*.

The societal response to the ritual slaughter of animals by Jews is itself brutal and direct.[27] The anticruelty forces in Europe and America teamed up closely with the anti-Semites, who saw everything associated with the Jews as an abomination, to label this form of slaughter cruel and barbaric. In Germany as early as the first Congress for the Protection of Animals (1860), there was a strong attack on ritual slaughter. This was in the light of contemporary views such as that of Arthur Schopenhauer, who saw in the Jews' refusal to use "humane" methods of slaughter such as "chloroform" a sign of their "unnatural separation" of human beings from the animal world that he attributed to the spirit of Judaism.[28] Such attacks were always accompanied by comments linking animal slaughter with other forms of Jewish "brutality." In 1885, the attack on ritual slaughter in Great Britain led Robert Fowler, the lord mayor of London, to comment that the obsession with this Jewish practice recalled the ritual murder accusations from the time of Chaucer.[29] In the 1883 meeting of the Congress for the Protection of Animals in Vienna, the argument was made that the protection of ritual slaughter, or at least its lack of condemnation, was a sign that the Jews controlled the political process in Europe. By 1892, a law against ritual slaughter was passed in Saxony. And by 1897, there was a clear link between such attacks and the antivivisection movement, as the cruelest physicians were reputed to be Jews.[30]

Indeed, Karl Liebknecht denounced the right-wing attacks on ritual slaughter on the floor of the Reichstag on 24 April 1899 as a further attempt to attack the Jews, and a colleague of his in the same debate simply labeled these attacks "anti-Semitic desires." Liberal newspapers such as the *Berliner Tageblatt* in 1893 called those campaigning against ritual slaughter "pure anti-Semites." *Die Nation* in 1894 observed that "the cry against the so-called *Schächten* belongs to the best loved sport of the modern persecutor of the Jews."[31] It is no accident that the most repulsive anti-Semitic film of the Third Reich, Fritz Hippler's *The Eternal Jew* (1940), concludes with a scene of ritual slaughter as conclusive evidence of the Jew's inhumanity.[32]

An argument has been made that after the Holocaust, the focus on ritual slaughter in Germany (and the rest of Europe) moved from the rhetoric of anti-Semitism to that of animal rights.[33] In point of fact, these two views were and remain linked. The Nazi view was that Jewish ritual practices revealed that the Jews were inherently inhumane; the focus on animal rights (above those of human beings as members of a religious community) argues that anyone (including the Jews) who would violate the explicit rights of an animal is inhumane. Talal Asad has noted that "for a long time now the law has been concerned to penalize 'unjustifiable' pain and distress in animal[s]." Today, he sees a shift toward the "normalization" of "desirable conduct," which is merely another way of defining "decorum."[34] Creating a claim of the rights of animals to avoid pain (and death) as equivalent to those of human beings trying to fulfill their ritual obligations strikes me as a continuation of the older position clothed in new, more p.c. rhetoric. The claim is that Jews violate inalienable rights, those of animals, to further their "outmoded" or "cruel" practices. These "rights" are merely a reflection of nineteenth-century secular debates about nature, begun by Jeremy Bentham, which ignored any and all theological claims. On 15 January 2002, the Constitutional Court in Karlsruhe dismissed a suit advocating a ban on ritual slaughter in Germany. On Friday, 17 May 2002, the members of the German Bundestag, the lower house of parliament, voted 543–19 to amend that nation's constitution to include rights for animals. This was echoed by a two-thirds affirmation in the Bundesrat, the upper chamber. The proposed law amended Article 20a of the German Basic Law. That section is concerned with requiring the state to protect human dignity and now reads, "The state takes responsibility for protecting the natural foundations of life and animals in the interest of future generations." This echoed the inclusion of animal rights in the constitutions of three of the new German states (*Neue Bundesländer*) as well as the city-state of Berlin. Shortly thereafter, an advertisement supported by the most vociferous antivivisection organization, *Der Bundesverband Menschen für Tierrechte*, as well as members of the Constitutional Court appeared in a number of German papers asking for support for a court case to ban the ritual slaughter of animals as a violation of their newly acquired civil rights. The ritual slaughter of animals is regularly defined, even in this day of a heightened awareness of Islam, as a function of the Jewish community.

Ironically, the boom in the sale of kosher food (which only means ritually supervised) in the United States today has much the same "hygienic" rationale. As one hot dog maker's advertisement has it, kosher food answers to a higher authority—but it also carries with it the promise of better eating. "What kosher-certifying enhances today is 'economic vigor.' Out of a market of $500 billion, U.S. food manufacturers sell more than $170 billion worth of kosher-certified products each year.... Whenever a company takes a food line kosher it sees a jump in its market share. And for Nestlé or Nabisco or Best Foods or General Mills, even a fraction of a percentage point may translate into millions of dollars."[35] Kosher has become interchangeable with "organic" and is therefore deemed healthy—a claim that anyone raised on traditional Eastern European cooking will be happy to correct.[36] Ritual slaughter as a sign of Jewish cruelty disappears as a problem in this context. Perhaps this will be an answer to the uniqueness of ritual slaughter for Muslims and Jews in a future Europe?

Could halal become the next "organic" for Europeans? Certainly at the moment, as Olivier Roy notes, there is a greater demand for "Western" food to be made from halal meat than for the rejection of "McDonald's" for traditional (whatever that might mean) food.[37] The general tendency in diasporic communities is to want access to the "modern" fast-food culture. This has created a "natural" alliance between old adversaries such as Muslims and Hindus and new adversaries such as Jews and Muslims. In nation-states where such coalitions are not desirable or necessary, there has been a general condemnation of fast food as a sign of the West. As one neofundamentalist leader stated in Pakistan, "This is forbidden—the Kentucky chicken and the McDonald burger is forbidden for Muslims. There are people present here who can make such foods, which are better than this McDonald burger and Kentucky chicken. Why should we allow from abroad these things?"[38] Such attitudes seem still to be marginal to the Western experience, which may over time reject McDonald's but through the rhetoric of "health" or "antiglobalization."

In 2002, the Meat and Livestock Commission in the United Kingdom advocated that British farmers diversify into the thriving halal meat sector as Muslim families in Britain consume 20 percent of the lamb and mutton eaten while being only about 5 percent of the population.[39] In addition, the market for halal Christmas turkeys, perhaps the ultimate multicultural animal, has exploded in the United Kingdom.[40] The turkeys are prepared Tandoori-style, without, I am sure, the traditional Brussels sprouts. Can ritual be given new meanings within a diasporic community without being reduced to "kosher-style" or "halal-style" as Hasidic mysticism has been reduced to Madonna wearing a bracelet amulet? Fareena Alam asks whether Islam in Britain should always be reduced to "beards, scarves and halal meat." She bemoans this reduction to the "ethical vagaries of ritually slaughtered meat."[41] For Muslims, an alternative to the tradition of sacrificing a ram on Eid al-Adha (Feast of the Sacrifice) has been created on a Web site where one can sacrifice virtual rams. That is a direct response to charges of "inhumanness" lodged against Islamic religious practices both within and without the Muslim community. Can that be a further sign of alternative practices developing within Islam? Thus, Kafka's world of food and music is recuperated in the twenty-first century; but in this adaptation may, as with the curse of the violin player, lay further problems in the confrontation with modernity. Is not the claim of high culture (and the decorum of the table) that its consumption makes people better and more moral? Are they not both worlds in which the claims of difference are claims of not just inferiority but also of inhumanness? Food and music are often paired in Western culture, nowhere more than in the world of Jews and Muslims in the Western Diaspora.

Recently in France Odile Bonnivard offered an "identity" soup to coalesce French nativist sentiment against Jews and Muslims. Shouting "we are all pig eaters!" her group (supported by Jacques Le Pen's National Front) distributed "pig soup" to the poor on the streets of Paris, Strasbourg, and Nice. Halal and kosher foods were denounced as defining the distance of the Jews and Muslims from "European civilization and Christian culture." "Slices of oily sausages [are handed out] as flags bearing the French fleur-de-lis fluttered overhead."[42] Thus food remains a visceral mark of difference in secular Europe.

SIX

ALBERT EINSTEIN'S VIOLIN
Jews, Music, and the Performance of Identity

Who are the three most famous Jewish violinists of the twentieth century? Ask any member of the generation who grew up after World War II in the United States, and the answer is easy: Jascha Heifetz (1900–1987), without question; Jack Benny (1894–1974), the Jewish comic of radio, film, and concert hall fame; and, of course, Albert Einstein (1879–1955). Why is this of any interest?

The role of music, especially of the violin, was a central aspect of Albert Einstein's life and, more important, of his public persona. But it is, as we have seen, also an emblem of the successful or unsuccessful integration of the Jews into Western high culture during the twentieth century. It is certainly part of our contemporary image of Einstein that links both the personal and historical meanings. In Richard Powers' brilliant novel of 2003, *The Time of Our Singing*, Einstein as a musician haunts the pages of this extraordinary chronicle of twentieth-century American life at the color bar. He first appears in the 1930s as "a white-maned old New Jersey violinist in a moth-eaten sweater, who spoke German with David [the German-Jewish protagonist] and frightened Ruth [his African-American wife] with incomprehensible jokes." It is he who first recognizes the extraordinary gift of their son and insists that the boy have "the strongest musical education possible." Money should be no object: "[T]hey didn't dare oppose a man who'd rooted out the bizarre secret of time, buried since time's beginning. Einstein was Einstein," David thought, "however Gypsy-like his violin playing."[1] This Einstein—the violin player—stands at the periphery of this brilliant novel of race relations and music in the American twentieth century. He embodies both abstract notions of the physicist's world and the persecution of the Jews of Europe. David Strom is in America, where he is still haunted that "his appointment in the Physics Department at Columbia ... would certainly be taken away by anti-Semitism, anti-intellectualism, rising randomness, or the inevitable return of the Nazis" (9). This sense of a specific moment of alienation links Jewish identity, and Einstein recurs at a stream-of-consciousness moment after David and his sons are confronted by an American anti-Semite: "[David] shepherds the boys through the crowd, out onto the street and their next public humiliation, talking as he walks. 'I told him what Einstein says. Minkowski. 'Jewish physics.' Time backward and time forward: Both are always. The universe does not make a difference between the two; only we do'" (355). With all the power that radiates from the image of Einstein, Powers does have it wrong: it is not the exoticism of the "gypsy violinist" that Einstein's violin embodied but the calculus of European high culture, of Bach and Mozart, who also stand at the very heart of his novel.

Now thinking about Einstein and music, one could make an argument that Einstein's relationship to music reflected the inner mathematical nature of music itself, for from Pythagoras to Helmholtz, an ever greater understanding of the relationship between music and mathematics had been evolving. Even Newton saw music as one of the spaces in which numbers provided insight into the aesthetic.[2] Yet Einstein sensed that the relationship was more complex. "Music," Einstein wrote to Paul Plaut in October 1928, "does not influence research work, but both are nourished by the same sort of longing, and they complement each other in the release they offer."[3] Music is part of his emotional world. Here I want to make a rather more concrete argument about the meanings attached to the image of Einstein's violin—that in the course of the twentieth century, playing "serious music" on the violin was the intersection of the image of the Jew and the rewards and status of European high culture.[4] That intersection provided Einstein with a means of thinking about himself simultaneously as a Jew (in his time) and as a universal human being with claims on all high culture.

Born in 1879 in Ulm, Germany, Einstein (why should he have been an exception?) took violin lessons from the age of five to fourteen. Rebelling against the rote pedagogy of his teachers, he once threw a chair at one of his teachers and drove her from the family house.[5] His studies with Herr Schmied were not much more productive, as for him "music did not go beyond the mechanical aspect."[6] Only after he stopped studying was he dazzled to discover at thirteen Mozart's sonatas. As he observed, "[L]ove is a better teacher than a sense of duty."[7] For the aged Einstein, "Mozart's music is so pure and beautiful that I see it as a reflection of the inner beauty of the universe."[8] Later in life, in an interview given to the *Saturday Evening Post* on 26 October 1929, he claimed that had he not become a scientist, he would have become a musician: "I live my daydreams in music."[9]

Ironically, something similar happened with his religious instruction. His father, according to Einstein's son-in-law, Rudolf Kayser, in 1930, was "proud that Jewish rites were not practiced in his home."[10] When the family moved to Munich in 1880, things shifted ever so slightly. Albert at six was eventually enrolled in a Catholic *Volksschule*, and his family asked an unnamed relative to give Albert some instruction in Judaism as an antidote to his exposure to Catholicism. This moved the very young Einstein to an awareness of "being Jewish," which had an ethical dimension, as his sister Maja wrote many decades later: "He heard about divine will and works pleasing to God, about a way of life pleasing to God—without these teachings having been integrated into a specific dogma. Nevertheless, he was so fervent in his religious prescriptions that, on his own, he observed religious prescriptions in every detail. For example, he ate no pork. This he did for reasons of conscience, not because his family had set such an example."[11] He enthusiastically studied the psalms with Heinrich Friedmann, his religion instructor at the Luitpold Gymnasium. Being Jewish through ritual is parallel to the discovery of Mozart as it is a world beyond that which he found in his mundane existence. Both set him apart. Ritual was abandoned when the young Einstein discovered "science" by reading popular scientific texts such as the pamphlet series on popular science edited by Aaron Bernstein, a particular favorite of liberal Jews of the time as it was very much in line with their idea of Judaism as a rational religion built upon scientific principles and beliefs.[12] He chose not to be bar mitzvah'ed at thirteen, abandoning any sense of a Jewish identity rooted in ritual practice; but as much as he distanced himself from religious practice, he never overtly refused to acknowledge his identity as a Jew.[13] Rote music and rote religion seemed to Einstein pointless. Yet Mozart and music remained as part of the German (and Jewish) high culture that permeated his world and family life as much as did his Jewish identity, an identity beyond religion.

Thus in 1920 Einstein's first biographer recorded Einstein's view of his sense of religion. Einstein told him in a series of interviews that "he learned simultaneously the teachings of the Jewish as well as the Catholic Church; and he had extracted from them that which was common and conducive to a strengthening of faith, and not what conflicted."[14] But the author also linked belief systems and music: "Signs of love of music showed themselves very early. He sought out little songs in praise of God, and used to sing them to himself in the pious seclusion that he preserved even with respect to his parents. Music, Nature, and God became intermingled in him in a complex of feeling, moral unity, the trace of which never vanished."[15] Jewish practice and identity as being not that of the Christian majority; Mozart and the violin being signs of belonging to high culture as a Jew.

Being Jewish is both indelible and a question of mind-set; on this, both Jews and anti-Semites of the time agree. It is the human that moves all of us equally, but experience that shapes our sense of self, as Einstein comments in 1949: "By the mere existence of his stomach, everyone is condemned to participate in [the] chase [of life]. Moreover, it was possible to satisfy the stomach by such participation, but not man insofar as he is a thinking and feeling being. As the first way out, there was religion, which is implanted into every child by way of the traditional education machine. Thus I became— despite the fact that I was the son of entirely irreligious (Jewish) parents—to a deep religiosity."[16] Raised in a nonobservant family, he had, according to his own words, "longed for a religious life and for religious instruction."[17] After his youthful experience with Protestant liberalism in the person of Jost Winteler, his host father in Switzerland, Einstein confronted the anti-Semitism of Germany, which, as with many secular Jews of his generation including Theodor Herzl, transformed him into a self-conscious Jew. This took place in Berlin, where, according to an essay by Einstein published in the *Jüdische Rundschau* in 1921 (and echoed in later comments in 1929), "So long as I lived in Switzerland, I did not become aware of my Jewishness.... This changed as soon as I took up residency in Berlin [in 1914].... I saw how anti-Semitism prevented Jews from pursuing orderly studies, and how they struggled to secure a livelihood."[18] It was anti-Semitism, specifically the anti-Semitism present in the university and directed, according to Einstein, against "Eastern-born Jews in Germany, who were continually exposed to provocation."[19] But this anti-Semitism was the force through which "we can preserve ourselves as a race: at least that is what I believe."[20] Einstein's interest in religious practice waned as he became a teenager; a commitment to high culture and a Jewish identity (now seen as reactive) remained intact in the world of heightened German anti-Semitism.

The association with Jews who did not merely define themselves in terms of the negative image of the anti-Semite shaped Einstein's sense of Jewish identity. It was not an identity rooted in religious belief but, like Sigmund Freud's claim of an intellectual and emotional tie, a tie to "the pursuit of knowledge for its own sake, an almost fanatical love of justice and the desire for personal independence—these are the features of the Jewish tradition which make me thank my lucky stars that I belong to it."[21] This retrospective view in Einstein's autobiography (*Mein Weltbild*) quite parallels his coauthor Sigmund Freud's view in 1926 (the year that he first met Einstein) that being Jewish is sharing "many obscure emotional forces, which were the more powerful the less they could be expressed in words, as well as a clear consciousness of inner identity, the safe privacy of a common mental construction.... Because I was a Jew I found myself free from many prejudices which restricted others in the use of their intellect; and as a Jew I was prepared to join the Opposition and to do without agreement of the 'compact majority.'"[22] This accorded him, according to his own account, the ability to react against the claims of the majority and pioneer new ways of understanding human beings. For Einstein as well as Freud (and other Jews of the time), this is an inborn quality transmitted through a gene for creativity. Its analogy is the strong belief, shared by Einstein and Freud, that through such a transmission, Jews "were as naturally prone to civility as Gentiles were to violence."[23] "Genius" and "decorum" are linked through Jewish experience and its inheritance. This view is the theory of Jewish creativity in 1919 by Thorstein Veblen, the American sociologist for whom Jewish "skeptical animus" trumps Gentile "conventional verities."[24]

As we have noted, the creativity of the Jewish scientists (pace Veblen) seems to come from their imposed position marginal to established science (*Wissenschaft*). This is the position that Georg Simmel defines as that of the "stranger," but it carries with it the danger of being stereotyped as a "genius." Jewish musicality becomes, on the contrary, a key factor central to their lives as educated citizens (*Bildungsbürgertum*). Linking these is Einstein's relationship to music. Charlie Chaplin tells an anecdote in his autobiography of a conversation with Einstein's wife, Elsa, in which she told Chaplin that Einstein suddenly stated at breakfast, "'I have a wonderful

idea.' And after drinking his coffee, he went to the piano and started playing. Now and again he would stop, making a few notes, then repeat, 'I have
a wonderful idea.' She told me he continued playing the piano and making
notes."[25] Two weeks later, he appeared from his study with his completed
theory of relativity. (Note that this anecdote confuses the wives or the dates
or both—its intention is not to establish a fact, but to perpetuate an image.)

Such tales of creative reverie evoke other moments of intense creativity
such as the story told of Isaac Newton, who turned to a dinner companion
after an intense conversation to ask whether Newton had actually eaten dinner while they were talking. As Steven Shapin has amply illustrated, such
myths recount our collective sense of the nature of genius as inherently distanced from the pace of "normal" life.[26]

There is a specifically Jewish twist to Einstein's piano playing in Chaplin's
tale. (The Fireside Discussion group from the 1930s, which we discussed in
chapter 4, notes that "among pianists also, Jews do not lag behind. They fill
the concert halls as do their colleagues with the violins.")[27] Remember how
Theodor Herzl evokes "Wagner's music, especially … *Tannhäuser*," as his
inspiration for the writing of *The Jewish State*.[28] It was Herzl whom Einstein
admired more than anyone, according to Isaiah Berlin, for shouting "'at the
top of his voice' that only the establishment of a national home in Palestine
can cure [the] evil [of anti-Semitism]."[29] Herzl imagined a Jewish state with
Western cultural values, as did Einstein.

It is the violin and the world of Western culture that shape Einstein's
private life. As a young man, he uses the violin as a tool of seduction and is
very successful at it. Indeed, so aware is he of the erotic aspect of his musical
life that he comes to prefer older women who "do not … threaten impres-
sionable hearts."[30] His playing was passionate, and his contemporaries felt
that it revealed "the delicate realm of his intense emotional life."[31] Indeed,
in one competition a local school inspector stresses the exceptional quality of Einstein's "emotional performance" of a Beethoven sonata.[32] His best
friend at the Zurich Polytechnic is Michele Besso, with whom from the very
first semester he made music each Saturday afternoon.[33] In Zurich he also
regularly plays Bach, Mozart, and Handel with Adolf Hurwitz, a professor
at the Zurich Polytechnic, and his daughter Lisbeth. Einstein's first wife,
Mileva, is the fourth in the quartet; the musical experience is part of their
shared life.[34] Einstein, unlike Herzl, plays Bach, Hayden, and Mozart; he is
lukewarm about Beethoven, and Wagner is beyond any discussion.[35] In 1912

Einstein met the physicist Paul Ehrenfest, who became his closest friend. Their friendship was certainly centered about their common scientific interests, but they also played piano and violin duets whenever they were together.[36] He imagined that their music generated as much excitement as their science.

In Prague, during the unhappy seventeen months of 1911–1912 when he held a chair in theoretical physics at the German-language university in Prague, he would regularly attend the very Jewish salon of Berta Fanta, the first woman university graduate in Prague. There he met Franz Kafka and Kafka's friends Hugo Bergman, later the librarian of the Hebrew University, and Max Brod, the novelist, as well as philosophers such as Erich Kahler and Hans Kohn. After a strenuous evening of debate at the salon, members of the circle (certainly not including Kafka) would play chamber music, with Bergman conducting.[37] There he also befriended the amateur violinist Moritz Winternitz, a specialist for archaeology and an expert in Sanskrit because his cousin was a music teacher and joined them in playing trios. It was in Prague that Einstein was first aware of a positive sense of Jewish identity, even though he did not then publicly subscribe to it. Prague exposed Einstein to self-consciously Jewish (and modern) thinkers such as Martin Buber. Not that Buber's sense that science could never be a path to moral and ethical truth as it was rooted in the material world had any impact on Einstein at all. But it was here that the link between a new Jewish culture and European high culture was reified for Einstein by people who thought that they were truly and necessarily compatible.

Einstein does understand that "music" is culturally determined in a way that he assumes science is not.[38] When he discussed music with the Bengali poet and Nobel Prize winner Rabindranath Tagore at his summer house in Caputh, Germany, on 14 July 1930, Einstein puzzled about the cultural conventions surrounding Western music:

TAGORE – It is difficult to analyze the effect of eastern and western music on our minds. I am deeply moved by the western music; I feel that it is great, that it is vast in its structure and grand in its composition. Our own music touches me more deeply by its fundamental lyrical appeal. European music is epic in character; it has a broad background and is Gothic in its structure.

EINSTEIN - This is a question we Europeans cannot properly answer, we are so used to our own music. We want to know whether our own music is a conventional or a fundamental human feeling, whether to feel consonance and dissonance is natural, or a convention, which we accept.

TAGORE - Somehow the piano confounds me. The violin pleases me much more.[39]

As it clearly pleased Einstein, even though his playing skills seem to have eroded. In the late 1920s, the violinist Walter Friedrich noted, "Einstein's bowing was that of a lumberjack."[40] But it is the music world that Einstein's violin evokes, a universal claim which resonated even more strongly among Jews in the 1930s who again were denied by anti-Semites a valid place within the world of Western music.

By the 1920s, Einstein was regularly asked to do musical benefits (are there physics benefits?) for Jewish causes. In Berlin he was involved with the *Hilfsverein*, the organization devoted to aiding Eastern European Jews (not Mischa Elman or any of the other Russian violinists with a worldwide reputation, needless to say).[41] There is a photograph of him in January 1930 playing at a welfare benefit for the youth department of the Jewish community in Berlin, his head covered with a *yarmulke*, seated in front of the bimah at the "Neue Synagoge" in the Oranienburgerstrasse, playing his violin.[42] Einstein played the second movement of J. S. Bach's "Adagio in B-minor for Two Violins" with the violist Alfred Lewandowski. Lewandowski's father was Louis Lewandowski (1821–1894), one of the greatest Jewish liturgical composers of his age. When in 1864 the Oranienburgerstrasse synagogue was built, the elder Lewandowski was offered the opportunity of creating an entire new service with organ accompaniment—a task never before undertaken. The culmination of his career came in 1882 with the publication of his magnum opus, *Todah W'Simrah* (*Thanks and Song*), a setting of the entire liturgical cycle for four-part choir, cantor, and organ. Classically trained, he brought the power of German high culture into the synagogue, where in 1930 Einstein and his son played works by the ultimate Protestant composer, J. S. Bach.

God may not have dwelt exclusively in playing Bach in the synagogue. Five months later, in April 1930, Einstein attended a performance of the Berlin Philharmonic conducted by Bruno Walter playing Bach, Beethoven, and Brahms. The soloist was the very young Yehudi Menuhin. After the concert Einstein held him and told him, "Now I know that there is a God in Heaven."[43] Not only Einstein but God is a violinist! This was a belief certainly shared by Einstein and his close friend, the conductor Erich Kleiber.[44]

Einstein had understood that Jewish acculturation had not brought about the Enlightenment promise. Einstein defines being Jewish as an indelible mark: "Not necessarily. Actually it is a very difficult thing to even define a Jew. The closest that I can come to describing it is to ask you to visualize a snail. A snail that you see at the ocean consists of the body that is snuggled inside of the house, which it always carries around with it. But let's picture what would happen if we lifted the shell off of the snail. Would we not still describe the unprotected body as a snail? In just the same way, a Jew who sheds his faith along the way, or who even picks up a different one, is still a Jew."[45] Being Jewish meant transcending the internalization of the anti-Semite's image while never abandoning the moral significance of German high culture. Einstein stated that "we must first of all educate ourselves out of ... the slave mentality which [anti-Semitism] betokens. We must have more dignity, more independence, in our own ranks. Only when we have the courage to regard ourselves as a nation, only when we respect ourselves, can we win the respect of others; or rather the respect of others will then come of itself."[46] Anti-Semitism assumed that Jews could never share the cultural patrimony of the Germans; that when they attempted to do so, from Felix Mendelssohn-Bartholdy's resurrection of Bach to Jewish violinists like Menuhin, they could only simulate truly understanding. Einstein assumed that high culture was universal (even if it was culturally bounded) because he knew that Jews like himself were part of the human race and that all humans are moved by music.

On 30 January 1933, Hitler became chancellor of Germany. The flight of German Jewry began with a trickle. Yet when German Jews moved to Palestine in the 1930s, they founded *Musikvereine*.[47] In January 1933, Einstein found himself in Pasadena, California, working at the Carnegie Observatories and teaching at Cal Tech. He kept his silence about Hitler's takeover, not wanting to exacerbate the Nazis' ill feeling toward the Jews. He spent his time in scientific discussion with friends and playing Mozart quartets on his violin.[48] Resigning from the Prussian Academy of Science, he finally gave a newspaper interview in March 1933 in which he was asked about his citizenship. He concluded his answer by noting, "Humanity is more important than national citizenship."[49] It is humanity that responds to high culture, not Germans or indeed Jews. In the spring of 1933 Einstein found himself back in Europe, not in Switzerland but in Belgium. He had befriended the Belgian King Albert and Queen Elizabeth in 1929. In May 1933, he visited the royal palace to play string quartets with the queen.[50] In Princeton, New Jersey, Einstein relied on music as one of his connections to his European and thus also to his Jewish identity. Dorothy Commins tells of the summer of 1946, when Einstein recognized her on Mercer Street as a pianist and asked whether they could play together. He showed up that evening at eight o'clock with Bach, Corelli, and some Dutch folk melodies. They played the "Bach Concerto in D Minor" over and over again because Einstein simply "loved the piece."[51] Today, Einstein's violin stand (if not his violin) is to be seen in the museum of the Historical Society of Princeton in Bainbridge House, 158 Nassau Street, a strangely silent place devoid of music.

It is central to Einstein's understanding of Zionism that he never sees it purely as a political program. He recognizes, as do many of his contemporaries, including his acquaintance Franz Kafka, that "however much the Jews adapted themselves, in language, manners, to a large extent even in the forms of religion, to the European peoples among whom they lived, the feeling of strangeness between them and their hosts never vanished. This is the ultimate cause of anti-Semitism."[52] Any Jewish state had to be linked to a sense of Jewish cultural renewal. In 1933 Einstein wrote, "It is not enough for us to play a part as individuals in the cultural development of the human race; we must also attempt tasks which only nations as a whole can perform. Only so can the Jews regain social health.... Palestine is not primarily a place of refuge for the Jews of eastern Europe, but the embodiment of the reawakening of the corporate spirit of the entire Jewish nation."[53] Thus, as Isaiah Berlin noted, Einstein's Zionism is close to the "unpolitical cultural nationalism of Ahad Ha-am: what Einstein was advocating was, in essence, the creation of a social and spiritual center."[54] But one can add to that a center that incorporated European high cultural norms and traditions rather than abandoning them. On the twenty-fifth anniversary of the founding of the Hebrew University, Einstein told a reporter for the *New York Times* that "the support for cultural life is of primary concern to the Jewish people. We would not be in existence today as a people without this continued activity in learning."[55] And we can add high culture. Ahad Ha-am wrote in 1894 that one strives for a "Judaism, which shall have as its focal point the ideal of our nation's unity, its renascence, and its free development through the expression of universal human values in the terms of its own distinctive spirit."[56] For this, he advocated having a Jewish culture that was equal in status and value to all other national cultures. For him, as a writer, it was the book that encompassed the new Jewish culture. But there are other small objects, such as the violin, that seemed to demand being seen as transcending all national cultures, even that of the Jews.

Highly portable instruments of high culture were part of the ideology of the modern Jewish Diaspora. As the Anglo-Jewish advice columnist Irma Kurtz commented, "Why are Jews violinists? You can pick it up and run";[57] and Einstein was certainly part of that world even while in Germany (or Switzerland or Prague). But this is only partially a joke—high cultural activities that were not language dependent became one of the most important factors in maintaining a continuity of identity for German Jews "in exile." They were portable in the sense that they were ubiquitous in those lands where Jews found themselves and formed a link to their own understanding of themselves as participants in a world culture. This was even more important after 1933, when Nazi official policy limited Jewish performers in the official state cultural organization called the *Kulturbund* to the performance of "Jewish" or foreign classical music. Only such public performances by Jews were permitted. Bach and Mozart were "aryanized" in Germany; they continued to be played by German Jews such as Einstein as part of their patrimony. Understanding Einstein as a Jew does not mean seeking after his religious identity in its narrowest terms. It was in the Jewish cultural and political life of the twentieth century that he saw himself. Each image of Einstein with a violin is thus an affirmation of his role in both Jewish and world culture. Music has meanings beyond those we usually register. And Einstein as a Jew and a violinist provides an elegant case study for such meanings. Indeed, his is that generation that had begun to doubt the totality of the Enlightenment promise—but music, that force that seemed to provide a dialogue beyond the political, remained a shared value. Gershom Scholem's view in the 1960s that "the symphony is over" was never true for Albert Einstein.[58]

SEVEN

WHOSE BODY IS IT ANYWAY?
Hermaphrodites, Gays, and Jews
in N. O. Body's Germany

"N. O. Body" is a most appropriate pseudonym for Karl M. Baer (1885–1956) to have used when he sat down to pen his autobiography, which appeared in 1907,[1] for being "nobody" was his way of seeing his body. It was doubly alienated (he writes "nobody" in English rather than German), as it was male as well as female, Jewish as well as German. This is how he imagined his immediate past life raised as a woman, Martha Baer, in a Jewish family in Imperial Germany. But it is "nobody" that Odysseus tricks the Cyclops into answering when asked who has harmed him—"Who has hurt you?" "Nobody," the blinded giant responds. In his autobiography, written only a year after he is legally able to change his sex assignment from female to male, Baer is simultaneously the clever trickster but also the damaged giant. His autobiography is a document of transformation, but of a physical one understood in the rhetoric of late nineteenth-century biological and racial science, for N. O. Body is also the signature under a sign asking for "an educated, desperate young man willing to make a last experiment with his life" that Theodor Herzl has his protagonist read in the paradigmatic Zionist novel of 1902, *Altneuland* (Old New Land). Our protagonist stops being Martha Baer and becomes Karl M. Baer, with Martha still lurking in the middle initial. He is, in an odd way, the "real" Gregor Samsa—a person who awakens one day in a body not her own.

On its surface Baer's autobiography is a remarkable fin de siècle document of "hermaphrodism," as the Berlin sexologist Magnus Hirschfeld

(1868–1935) notes in his epilogue (109ff.).[2] Its subject suffered from false gender assignment because of the apparent ambiguity of his genitalia as an infant. He was registered and treated as a female child rather than a male child, an error of assignment that became evident only at puberty. He was a "pseudohermaphrodite," to use the terminology of the day, as his body was hormonally and psychologically gendered male, even though his genitalia seemed at first glance ambiguous. Sex was defined by the appearance of the body and was dimorphic: there were men, and there were women. Anyone who was neither or both was seen as pathological.

The central argument of the autobiography is expressed on its opening page: "one may raise a healthy boy in as womanish a manner as one wishes, and a female creature in as mannish; never will this cause their senses to remain forever reversed" (7–8). No confusion about gender can exist except, as is the case here, through the fuzzy ineptitude of the physician who at Baer's birth in 1885 (not 1884, as in the text) stated that "on superficial inspection, the shape has a feminine appearance, ergo we have a girl before us" (9). But the autobiography shows that this was never the case. Baer was always a male, even when treated as a female. As Hirschfeld notes in his epilogue, "The sex of a person lies more in his mind than in his body" (110). For Baer, there was no ambiguity in his sense of discomfort as a woman caused by the outward appearance of his genitalia. His desires were male—from the games he wished to play to the women with whom he fell in love. But he had been assigned the gender role of a woman, which made his masculine desire seem perverse to him. The argument of the autobiography is that male children, however raised or treated, remain masculine in their intrinsic identity. This was very much against the tendency of the time and, again, against the practice of the late twentieth century.[3] Today this sounds extraordinarily prescient.

After the 1960s gender reassignment surgery of children with "ambiguous genitalia" followed the view of scientists such as the Johns Hopkins psychologist John Money, who argued that it was culture, not nature, that defined gender.[4] It became usual to alter the external genitalia of babies with ambiguous sexuality to the female because of its greater surgical simplicity. These children were treated with hormones and raised as females. Over the past decade, a substantial literature argues that Baer and Hirschfeld were right and Money was wrong. Gender is imprinted in the psyche as well as on the body; "anatomy is not destiny." The primary case used by Money as his proof of the successful raising of a boy as a girl was that of David Reimer (known in popular culture as the case of John and Joan). He was one of two identical twins, whose botched circumcision in 1967 led to the amputation of his penis at eight months and his being raised as a girl. Money announced this as proof that culture was the sole determinant of gender. At twenty-five, Reimer demanded to have his sexual identity as a man reconstituted. He had always felt himself to be male, even in his culturally and hormonally reinforced role as a woman. By the early twenty-first century, he had become a media darling, appearing on *Oprah*. In May 2004, he committed suicide at the age of thirty-eight.[5] His death was read as proof of how wrong Money was.

Reimer's life rebutted, as the first major reassessment of the case noted, the primary assumptions that everyone is psychosexually neutral at birth and that all healthy psychosexual development is dependent upon the appearance of the genitals.[6] This view, espoused by Money, argued from a set of assumptions based on the existence of hermaphrodites. He assumed that they were ungendered at birth. But who are these undifferentiated hermaphrodites? Do they not have a gendered identity from the very beginning of their lives? But is not their understanding of the meaning of gender also shaped by the historical world in which they are born? Certainly this was the case for the world of the five-year-old "Martha" (Karl) Baer, who, like Reimer, much preferred the games and toys of boys to those of girls even though the world treated him as it would a little girl.

The publication of Baer's autobiography in Germany is part of a fixation in the late nineteenth and early twentieth centuries with this surprisingly malleable category of the "hermaphrodite." The "freakish" body, the body whose physiology did not reflect societal norms, has always fascinated European culture. From Petronius' representation in his *Satyricon* of hermaphrodites in first-century Rome to Velazquez's dwarf center stage in the Spanish court portrait of *Las Meninas* (1656) to the fantasies about sexual desire in Victor Hugo's *Hunchback of Notre Dame* (1831), Europeans have stressed physical difference as a manner of defining the ever changing boundaries of the "normal" and "healthy" body. Central to all of these representations was the need to "see" the physical difference of the body. Difference had to be physical, even if the fascination was with the unseeable (and, in these terms, unknowable) aspects of what makes human beings different. Thus, ruminating about sexual desire and practices, such as homosexuality, which was in the process of becoming the subject of the medical gaze in the nineteenth century, did not have the same empirical claim as observing physical difference, such as that of the hermaphrodite.

In the late nineteenth century, there was an explosion of autobiographical accounts of sexual difference that attempted to translate a fascination with behavioral or social aspects of sexual difference into physiological terms. One of the central metaphors for this difference was that of the "hermaphrodite." Virtually all of these attempts were cast as part of a new "medical" (or "forensic") attempt to understand the psyche of "perversion." Homosexuals could only be judged by their acts; there seemed to be no way of "seeing" their difference in contrast to the healthy, normal body. How could one identify the homosexual? Could he (and, at this point, the pervert was always male) be as visible as the hermaphrodite? In a medical model, the homosexual was inherently different from the healthy heterosexual, but was this difference an intrinsic one or could anyone be or become homosexual?

In the 1860s the German lawyer Karl Ulrichs provided an alternative model for a nonjudgmental account of "uranism," or homosexuality.[7] He hoped this would free the homosexual from the moral and/or medical taint that accompanied any representation of "perverse" sexual attraction and/or activity in the evolving medical model. He sought to defuse the legal status of the homosexual as sexual criminal while avoiding the medicalization of homosexuality as a perversion. One can add that liberals such as Richard Kraft-Ebing, in his 1886 *Psychopathia Sexualis*, also wished to free the homosexual from the charges of criminal sexual activity or moral depravity by medicalizing homosexuality and thus providing therapy rather than prison as the alternative. Ulrichs's argument was that the homosexual (and his references are exclusively to male same-sex desire and activity) was a "third sex," a natural alternative to the "two" sexes, male and female.

By the end of the nineteenth century, physicians such as Magnus Hirschfeld applied the model of the third sex and sought a biological rather than a theoretical model. Of special interest to Hirschfeld were thus the "intermediate cases" of sexuality, the model for which was the hermaphrodite, who according to these accounts was both female and male and thus neither male nor female.

Hirschfeld and the sexologists of the 1890s found it necessary to turn to the broader medical audience as well as the broader public with case material to prove their argument. While Michel Foucault had to excavate his famous mid-nineteenth-century case of the French hermaphrodite Herculine

Barbin from the Parisian archives of the Department of Public Health, it is much less difficult to find analogous cases of sexual difference in Germany after the 1890s.[8] This literature explodes in the medical literature of the day, and it quickly seeps into general public discourse.[9] Thus the autobiographical literature on homosexuality, cast in the model of the "third sex," uses the hermaphrodite as its concrete analogy for German consumption. Thus the pioneer (and long-lived) sexologist Havelock Ellis published the first volume of his studies on sexuality collaboratively with the writer John Addington Symonds (1840–1893) in Germany in 1896.[10] Symonds's autobiographical account of "this question of Greek love in modern life" was the core of this work, which was published only the next year in Great Britain to the horror of his friends. Among other texts Ellis included is a detailed summary of "Ulrichs's views" on homosexuality as an appendix to the German original (and anonymously in subsequent English editions).

By 1900 there were hundreds of autobiographical accounts of sexual "anomalies," including hermaphrodism, available in the technical literature, and some in the more popular literature. Magnus Hirschfeld's volume on *Berlin's Third Sex*, with massive citations from autobiographies, appeared as volume 3 in the original urban sociological series of *Metropolitan Documents*, widely sold in German bookstores prior to World War I.[11] "M. Baer" contributed a volume on *The International Trafficking in Girls*, an area of expertise that she developed as a journalist, to the series in 1908. This series, edited by Hans Ostwald, formed the basis for much of the urban sociological studies of social groups in the 1910s and beyond. Most, like the Hirschfeld and the Ellis volumes, cut and pasted these into "scientific" discourses about sexual difference as firsthand "proofs" of the nature of sexual difference. Indeed, Hirschfeld even discussed the case of Baer, although anonymously, in an essay published in 1906.[12] Here, the hermaphrodite always served as the model for sexual difference. The "third sex" was like the hermaphrodite in that it was to be found in nature.

This notion that the hermaphrodite can serve as the model for an understanding of male homosexuality is not merely an idiosyncrasy of the turn of the twentieth century. Michel Foucault writes in his *History of Sexuality* that "homosexuality appeared as one of the forms of sexuality when it was transposed from the practice of sodomy into a kind of interior androgyny, a hermaphrodism of the soul. The sodomite had been a temporary aberration;

the homosexual was now a species."[13] This takes place in the 1890s, the world in which Karl Baer lived.

As a literary trope, the modern notion of hermaphrodism as metaphor for the impermanence of sexual dimorphism takes place at the same time. In 1891 we find a "magic seed" in Archibald Ganter and Fergus Redmond's novel (and then a remarkably successful play) *A Florida Enchantment* that transforms the protagonist and her servant into men. But Victorian and early twentieth-century erotica often turned on the confusion of sexual roles, whether in the form of androgynous characters or transvestism. Thus, in *"Frank" and I*, the reader discovers that the "female" lover of a young man turns out to be male; and in *Miss High-Heels*, the hero, Dennis Evelyn Beryl, is transformed by his sister into a woman. Such purposeful sexual confusion is also at the core of Agatha Christie's early novel *The Man in the Brown Suit* (1924). It is, of course, only in 1928 with Virginia Woolf's *Orlando* that the full promise of the metaphor of hermaphrodism for the instability of sexual identity is played out.[14] After that, it becomes a commonplace in the literature of the twentieth century.

In Germany, as in the rest of Europe, there was a steady stream of medical studies interested in hermaphrodism throughout the nineteenth century. But it is with Magnus Hirschfeld's work in the 1890s that the *model* character of homosexuality was stressed in such studies.[15] By then, the hermaphrodite had become, not only a model for, but also the etiology of, homosexuality. At the beginning of the twentieth century, Hirschfield published a long series of essays by Franz von Neugebauer (1856–1914) in his *Yearbook of Sexual Intermediate Stages* in the 1900s.[16]

Neugebauer was the most important commentator on the biological nature of hermaphrodism within Hirschfeld's model during this period. He argued that all children were born "bisexual" and that homosexuality was an inherent quality of brain development. But he was also convinced that women who appeared to be male were less likely to have truly bisexual characteristics than a man who desired to appear as a woman. (The rationale is clear: why would a high-status individual such as a male desire to be a low-status individual such as a woman? There is a social advantage to the latter, but never to the former.) A gynecologist in Warsaw and chief of staff at the Evangelical Hospital there, Neugebauer had systematically collected "930 observations of hermaphrodism in human beings; 38 of these were cases which had come under my own observation, and the rest I found dispersed in ancient and modern literature."[17] In his work, he rethought the nosology of hermaphrodism. However, following Hirschfeld's model, he also understood the social consequences of such biological categorization. He clearly links hermaphrodism and homosexuality, as does Baer's image of the childhood sexual exploration and his young adult sense that he might be a lesbian: "It occurred to me alone, that I perhaps felt in that way" (64). As Neugebauer argued, this is not an unusual sense of sexual confusion:

> The male or female character of the genetic sense of pseudohermaphrodites depends very often on the sort of environment in which they are brought up, that is to say, upon whether they are educated as boys or girls; it must be set down entirely to the influence of suggestion if a male hermaphrodite, owing to mistaken sex brought up as a girl, afterwards shows a feminine genetic sense, seeks to attract men and betrays perverse homosexual inclinations, and if when the mistake in sex is discovered he energetically opposes every attempt to make him abandon girls' petticoats, their way of life, and his feminine predilections and occupations, and if he declines to assume male attire and change his social position, and appear in future as a man. Such homosexual inclinations acquired by suggestion have in some cases been only temporary, and the male, though brought up by mistake as a female, has, sooner or later, recognized his virility, and has not hesitated to demand his social and sexual rights sometimes somewhat abruptly. There have been instances in which a male person, recognizing that his true sexual position had been misunderstood, has adopted male attire without consulting anyone, and without giving notice of the fact to the magistrate or any other authority; one such person found a mistress whom he put in the family way, and only demanded the adjustment of his social position on the evidence of that pregnancy—an incontestable proof of his manhood. In other cases the genetic sense with homosexual desire has persisted during the whole life of an hermaphrodite, whose true sex has been misunderstood; there have even been instances in which hermaphrodites of the male sex brought up as girls, have, then, too late, their true sex has been recognized, with all possible insistence demanded castration.

But this can lead to a sense of alienation if one does not resolve the question of sexual identity:

The consciousness of being neither man nor woman, the constant and shameful fear that the malformation, though concealed with the utmost care, may some day betray itself and leave the sufferer to be the scorn and derision of those about him, are perpetually upsetting the mental balance and psychotic repose of the unfortunate pseudohermaphrodite, who racks his brain demanding why he should be so afflicted, and seeking some way out of his miserable social position. Not daring to confide in anyone the poor hybrid passes his days and nights dwelling upon his lot; feeling excluded from the society of either men or women he cultivates solitude and avoids intimacy of any kind with anyone; he passes his nights in agony and tears; his health gives way, and he becomes suspicious, distrustful, shy, savage, irritable, irascible, vindictive, violent, and impulsive to an extent that may drive him to crime, or he becomes moody, apathetic, and melancholy, till at last he ends his days in self-destruction.

In Imperial Berlin, male cross-dressers could be arrested just because they appeared different. In Weimar Germany, such cross-dressers (not necessarily homosexuals or hermaphrodites) were given identity cards to allow them to present themselves in public. Such a social danger of mis-seeing haunted the world in which Baer grew up. What would happen if one looked inappropriate for one's sex?

On December 2, 1891, a gendarme arrested a young girl of 19 on the platform of the railway station at Pilsen, on the suspicion of being a man disguised as a woman. It was in vain that the prisoner showed her personal papers, in which she was described as Marie Karfiol, born on such a day, at such place, and of such parents. In spite of her protestations, she was taken to the mayor's court, where medical evidence proved that there had been an error of sex, and that Marie K. was a male hypospadiac. She then admitted that at the time of her birth there had been some difficulty in determining her sex, but she had been brought up as a girl. At the time of her puberty suspicions as to the real state of the case had led to her being taken to see the mayor of her village and the priest; but no further action had been taken. Later on she abandoned herself to her fate, being ashamed to speak to anyone of her doubts. Her pretty hair was cut off and she was dressed in men's clothes; but in her novel attire she had a very timid and wild appearance.

Thus the anxiety focused on the feminized appearance of the male. This runs like a red thread through Baer's autobiography. His female schoolmates will not play with him because their teachers call him a boy; equally telling is the fact that "street urchins also shouted 'Norbert' after me": he was seen as "something odd" in public (38). When the older Baer loses his passport on a trip to Hungary as a newspaper correspondent, the police see "her" as a disguised man, which is "very suspicious" (86). It is only the fact that a passerby recognizes her from her portrait in a woman's magazine that rescues Baer. Being seen as different on the street was dangerous, especially if the assumption was that you were a feminized man.

Cesare Taruffi's classic monograph on hermaphrodism, originally published in Italian in 1902, appeared in 1903 in Germany. Here the notion that Hirschfeld had stressed—of the hermaphrodite as model case—was spelled out in explicit detail. The model is always the feminization of the male as an answer to sexual dimorphism and sexual identity. Baer's life as he accounts it after his transformation is that of a feminized man, not that of a mannish woman. "Feminization" is here to be understood both in its general, cultural sense and in its very specifically medical sense. "Feminization," or the existence of the "feminized man," is a form of "external pseudo-hermaphrodism."[18] It is not true hermaphrodism, but rather the sharing of external, secondary sexual characteristics, such as the shape of the body or the tone of the voice. The concept begins in the middle of the nineteenth century with the introduction of the term "infemminsce," to feminize, to describe the supposed results of the castration of the male.[19] By the 1870s, the term is used to describe the *feminisme* of the male through the effects of other diseases, such as tuberculosis.[20] Here is Baer's fantasy that the dropping of his voice was a sign of tuberculosis, as "consumptives are often hoarse" (41). One can see him reading in the medical (or popular medical) literature of the day looking for a pathology that would explain his growing masculinization. He "coughed, suffered from backaches," and "in [his] lively imagination thought [he] felt all the symptoms mentioned in the book" (41). Indeed, he later used a feigned case of "consumption" to return home from his first job as an apprentice in a banking house, "as my lungs had become weak" (56). But what he was doing was simply reversing the model: diseases such as tuberculosis feminized men according to the literature of the time, precisely the problem from which he actually suffered. He has a need to see his state as an expression of a somatic pathology, but one that could be treated.

"Feminization" was the direct result of actual castration or the physiological equivalent, such as intensely debilitating illness. It reshaped the body.

Baer's autobiography is remarkable as much for its mode masking its subject's identity as it is for its candor. But Baer does something unique. He redefines his ancestry as "French" in order to explain his social difference:

> Our lineage is not German. Our forefathers came from France. My family is very old and proud of its family tree, whose beginnings reach back as far as the sixteenth century. For generations however, the descendants of this old family had moved up to the heights of existence, only to soon descend to the middling life of small shopkeepers. (13)

"French" was also understood in Baer's time as a racial category as well as a political one. Thus the archracist French Count Joseph Arthur de Gobineau (1816–1882), widely read in Germany, argued the inherent superiority of the "Aryans" (Germans) over the "Celts" (French). Being "French" in Germany is a racial label that is mirrored in the body: "Our outward appearance alone is enough to easily distinguish us from the other inhabitants of Bergheim: black or brown eyes, brown wavy hair, and sharply defined southern European features are seldom found among the Saxons and Franconians of those mountain valleys" (14). These "French" bodies seem to be just as visible as the odd masculine body of the hermaphrodite.

Baer's French "mask" is transparent, but it is also unnecessary as there is no reason in the argument of his autobiography for his identity to be anything but that of a hermaphrodite. It is the "somber gray [that] hung over our path through life" (10). Yet there was clearly a need to stress another category of difference that also affected his understanding of his own body. As Hermann Simon has brilliantly shown in his detective work that identified Baer as the author of N. O. Body's autobiography, Baer was not only a Jew but also able to create a meaningful life for himself as an officer of the Berlin lodges of the Jewish fraternal organization of the B'nai B'rith (Brothers of the Circumcision; 113–36). That group seemed to have demanded neither educational certification nor birth records, as Baer fears at the end of his account. His absence of any formal education as a male meant that his social role was truly damaged. He stresses this himself. It was sufficient for them that he was a member of the Jewish community.

It is also the case that being Jewish and living uncomfortably as a woman have evident parallels in Baer's self, at least in 1907. The volume is prefaced by an anonymous poem:

> Over my childhood
> Hung a threatening fist.
> All my peaceful pleasures
> Were shrouded in a mist.
> The wounds this left were deep,
> Like a dagger, stabbing me,
> I could forget them, or dream them away....
> But healed—they never shall be. (7)

As the reader's introduction to the struggles of Martha to learn to be a young woman, this poem reflects the author's sense of a trauma beyond healing; repression perhaps, but reconstitution never. Baer borrows (and very slightly adapts) the text from the published work of his Zionist friend Theodor Zlocisti's *About the Path Home: Verses of a Jew* (*Vom Heimweg. Verse eines Juden*; 1903).[21] There the lines clearly refer to the actual author's Jewish identity in the Diaspora. The transformation of the politics of German-Jewish identity into the politics of sexual identity leaves the "wound" unstated. Perhaps both indeed are present. The notion that one is raised a "German" but is in fact a "Jew" seems to be a reality in the world in which N. O. Body lived. As a Zionist, he acknowledges the impossibility (or at least the difficulty) of being a "German" while being a "Jew." Identity is fixed; no cultural forces can reshape it. The essential identity will eventually out. Jews remain Jews no matter what their upbringing, just as a man remains a man even though raised as a woman.

Baer becomes "French" rather than Jewish in his account in 1907 because the sexual implications of being Jewish are clear to him. Just as he transforms all of the Jewish holidays and practices into "Catholic" ones in his account of his early life, as Simon shows, so too does he desire to transform his Jewish body into a French one. (Being Catholic in late nineteenth-century Berlin at the time of the *Kulturkampf* against the Vatican was almost as exotic as being Jewish.) That the Jew was an anomalous sexual case was part of his world. For Baer and for the world in which he lived at the beginning of the twentieth century, the "damaged" genitalia of the male Jew, damaged through circumcision (though there is a debate as to the sources addressing this) whether circumcision can be inherited after generations—meant that the male Jew is already neither truly male nor actually female. He becomes, to use Ulrichs's coinage, "a third sex."

It is clear that the model that Ulrichs employed to characterize the homosexual as beyond the dimorphism of traditional sexual identity is analogous to the basic argument that Theodor Herzl used to establish Zionism. If the Jews were inherently "Oriental," the basic argument in the Berlin anti-Semitism struggle of the 1880s, then the Jews should recognize their "Oriental" nature, leave Europe, and return to Palestine. It is not a blemish but a recognition of their natural state. Being different in both cases is transformed from a pathological and stigmatizing identity to a positive one. Jews are Jews first and foremost; they may appear to be Germans, but their essential Oriental nature can only be repressed, never destroyed.

It is in the physiology of the male Jew that the myth of Jewish sexual difference is located. Circumcision, however, is not a powerful enough myth; the world of European anti-Semitism creates the notion that male Jews menstruate. Menstruation is the sign of womanhood in Baer's autobiography. It is "a dark matter," as it had to do with "sexuality, and because one was then an adult." All of the girls in Baer's school "were 'it' already," so Baer too "arrived at school one morning, beaming. 'It' was there" (50). This "lie" continued for "ten years, in many countries and among strange customs, and it caused me many a worry" (50). Doubly so, for had Baer read further into nineteenth-century medical literature on the topic of male menstruation, by writers such as F. A. Forel and W. D. Halliburton, he would have found a fascination with male menstruation with regard to the problem of hermaphrodism as a sign of bisexuality as prominent in the nineteenth century.[22] Paul Albrecht in Hamburg argued for the existence of "male menstruation," which was periodic and which mimicked the menstrual cycle of the female through the release of white corpuscles into the urine.[23] The sexologist Paul Näcke provided a detailed discussion of the question of "male menstruation" and its relationship to the problem of male periodicity.[24] Näcke cited, among others, our old friend Havelock Ellis, who had been collecting material on this question for years. Certainly the best known advocate of this view in the 1890s was Sigmund Freud. His belief in male periodicity rested on the work of his friend and collaborator Wilhelm Fliess. Fliess's published work on this topic made it the subject of popular medical interest.[25] With the rise of modern sexology at the close of the nineteenth century, especially in the writings of Magnus Hirschfeld, male menstruation came to hold a very special place in the "proofs" for the continuum between male and female sexuality.[26] The hermaphrodite, the male who was believed to menstruate, became a central focus of Hirschfeld's work. But all of this new "science" that used the existence of male menstruation still drew on the image of the marginality of those males who menstruated and thus pointed toward a much more ancient tradition.

The idea of male menstruation is part of a Christian tradition of seeing the Jew as inherently, biologically different. From the late fourth-century *Adversus Judaeos* (*Against the Jews*) of the early church father Saint John Chrysostom through the work of Thomas Cantipratanus, the thirteenth-century anatomist, the abnormal and abhorrent body of the Jew marked the implacable difference of Jewish males. The argument was that male Jews menstruated as a mark of the "Father's curse," their pathological difference.[27] This view continued throughout the Middle Ages until the early modern period. The view that attributed to the Jews diseases for which the "sole cure was Christian blood" reappeared again as part of the blood libel accusations in the late nineteenth century.[28] It was raised again at the turn of the twentieth century in a powerfully written pamphlet by the professor of Hebrew at the University in St. Petersburg, Daniel Chwolson, as one of the rationales used to justify the blood libel that Jews killed Christian children (or virgins) to cure themselves. Chwolson notes that it was used to "cure the diseases believed to be specifically those of the Jews," such as male menstruation.[29] This version of the blood accusation ties the meaning of the form of the circumcised genitalia to the Jew's diseased nature.

These older charges about Jewish male menstruation, of Jewish hermaphrodism, reappear with their reprinting in the nineteenth century.[30] By the end of the nineteenth century, the archracist Theodor Fritsch—whose *Anti-Semite's Catechism*, first published in 1887, was the encyclopedia of German anti-Semitism—saw the sexuality of the Jew as inherently different from that of the German: "The Jew has a different sexuality than the Teuton; he will and cannot understand it. And if he attempts to understand it, then the destruction of the German soul can result."[31] The hidden sign that the Jewish man is neither male nor female is his menstruation. The implicit charge of pathological bisexuality, of hermaphrodism, had traditionally been lodged against the Jewish male. (Male Jews are like women

because, among other things, they both menstruate as a sign of their pathological difference.)

But Baer was a Jewish girl who did not menstruate but had to maintain
the fantasy that he did. Was he, as he presumed in his first real job, merely an
"anemic and poorly developed" girl, for whom "menstruation did not begin
before the twenties" (64)? Or was he truly different? The question of ritual
cleanliness during and after menstruation, the identification of his body as
the antithesis of the menstruating Jewish male—here, the female who does
not menstruate—is clarified only when he comes to understand his body as
that of a healthy, Jewish male, who does not menstruate. Masculinity will
out. The resolution of Baer's conflict comes through a physician who recognizes him as a man and urges him to comprehend his desire for a woman as
"a natural feeling" (99). All ambiguities are resolved—Baer claims—and the
state resolved his question of identity by reassigning him as a man. He trains
his new male body through exercise and sport. He becomes a "real" man except for "a slight furrow left behind from tight lacing." That mark remains
written on the body. No circumcision marked Baer's new male body, but the
scar of his role as a woman. Yet the world into which he remade himself was
the world of a growing anti-Semitism in which the appearance of the Jew on
the street was as "clearly" marked as that of the woman. Indeed, the closing
of the public clinic for cosmetic surgery in Nazi Germany (in 1933) and the
introduction of the Yellow Star (in 1942; 1939 in Poland) both were aimed at
making the invisible visible, as the fabled ability to recognize Jews at a glance
turned out to be an anti-Semitic fantasy. Baer ends his life in Israel after his
flight to Palestine from Germany in 1938. By then, Germany was obsessed
more by Jews than the ambiguity of gender.

EIGHT

THE FANATIC
Philip Roth and Hanif Kureishi Confront Success

As Jews attempted to enter into the multicultural world of high culture in the course of the nineteenth century, the idea of Jewish economic success retained a sinister tinge.[1] Even many Jews saw worldly success as the force that alienated the Jews from their own culture and identity.[2] Had not groups on the left and the right from the 1890s onward warned about the collapse of a Jewish culture or indeed its transmutation into an empty copy of the world in which the Jews of Europe lived? The Jew whose identity was defined by "business" became the antithetical image of the cultured Jew. Social transformation in the Western Diaspora became a mark of cultural collapse. No symphony would be produced by such acculturated Jews, only the desiccated products of capitalistic social Darwinism.

Such a dichotomy between success and art was equally present in America—Israel Zangwill's potential paradise for Jewish hybridity—but a hybridity that would result in a new American high culture, a "New World Symphony," not Jewish economic success (though Zangwill actually promises economic success for his protagonist in *The Melting Pot* when he has him offered the first violin chair in an orchestra). Jews in the world of American multicultural letters were depicted almost always within a "naturalist" mode. Jewish poverty was more interesting than Jewish economic success. Success seemed to be tied to a loss of identity and (if Abraham Cahan's *The Rise of David Levinsky* [1917] is to be believed) moral values.[3]

Economic success in this world was always part of a world of transformation. In some cases, it marked leaving the world of a Jewish religious identity for that of a Jewish ethnic identity, as in Samson Raphaelson's short

story and play, *Day of Atonement*, as well as in Alan Crosland's 1927 film made from the latter, *The Jazz Singer*.[4] There, ritual represented the religious (and the musical) past now seemingly traded in for a world of lower inherent cultural and therefore moral value. American popular culture and jazz were just that, even though it is in popular culture (think of Irving Berlin) that the Jews truly entered into the multicultural arena of America. That a fictive cantor's son might be confronted with a choice between his Carnegie Hall solo violin debut and singing in synagogue on Yom Kippur is a highly unlikely scenario as these would not have been seen as "alternatives" in the quite the same manner.

The question of Jewish "success" continues to be raised in the 1940s by Budd Schulberg in *What Makes Sammy Run* (1941) and Saul Bellow in his *Dangling Man* (1944).[5] In 1951 Oscar Handlin, in his *The Uprooted*, began to imagine a world in which the experience of the immigrant—and Handlin was himself the son of Jewish immigrants—posed the test case for the result of the immigrant experience, and that is alienation: "the immigrant's alienation was more complete, more continuous, and more persistent. Understanding of the reactions in that exposed state may throw light on the problems of all those whom the modern world somehow uproots."[6] Georg Simmel's stranger, "the person who comes today and stays tomorrow," becomes the prototype for American Jews as the "immigrants were American history," according to Handlin. In 1950 the American-Jewish sociologist David Riesman published what comes to be the definite study of American conformity, *The Lonely Crowd*.[7] The result of the "melting pot" seems not to be creativity but alienation. The Jew is the businessman destroyed by the system, Arthur Miller's Willy Loman in *Death of a Salesman* (1949), not the composer of the new American symphony. Willy Loman is in no way explicitly "Jewish," for the critique of the destructive forces of capital and competition has transformed the "Jewish" experience of the false promise of success into the American experience of failure.

In 1959 Philip Roth published a collection of short stories that fixed his reputation as perhaps the most radical critic of Jewish success, but with a twist. *Goodbye, Columbus* was an immediate "hit" in that it seemed to capture the conflicts of American Jewry (and other "ethnic" groups) in the era of good feeling that was the age of Eisenhower.[8] Philip Roth, who claimed to be most influenced by his reading of Franz Kafka, presents a world in which transformation is by definition a failure of will and identity. Many of the stories of *Goodbye, Columbus* (the title is taken from the final line in a record of the Ohio State sports' season during which the brother of the protagonist's love interest played basketball) are versions of Kafka's tales of failed metamorphosis. The notion of transformation of the "stranger" into the citizen is set in the title story (earlier published in the *Paris Review*) when the protagonist Neil Klugman (*nomen est omen*: the smart one) makes an ironic pass at the woman who fascinates him at the country club.[9] She asks him to hold her glasses as she dives into the pool. A poor boy from Newark working in a public library, Klugman is attracted to Brenda Patimkin, the nouveau riche daughter of a bathroom fixture manufacturer, as a sort of water sprite.[10] She is perfect in every way. Her perfection reveals itself on their first date after she is finished playing tennis to having been a constructed part of the world of Jewish transformation:

> 'I don't like to be up close, unless I'm sure she won't return it.'
> 'Why?'
> 'My nose.'
> 'What?'
> 'I'm afraid of my nose. I had it bobbed.'
> 'What?'
> 'I had my nose fixed.'
> 'What was the matter with it?'
> 'It was bumpy.'
> 'A lot?'
> 'No,' she said, 'I was pretty. Now I'm prettier. My brother's having his
>   fixed in the fall.'
> 'Does he want to be prettier?'
> She didn't answer. (12)

This becomes an ironic motif in the tale—Neil constantly asks Brenda whether she wants to have something else "fixed." This is Roth's image of a supposedly malleable Jewish identity in 1959.

Physical transformation becomes, ironically, associated with the non-Jewish face in Roth's novel *American Pastoral* (1997), his paean to American life during the Vietnam War and the pain caused by becoming American. There he has Dawn Levov, the non-Jewish wife of his Jewish protagonist "Swede" Levov, see aesthetic surgery as a cure for her soul.[11] Her Jewish doctor, Shelly Salzman, comments, "You don't know how many women come to me who've been through a terrible trauma and they want to talk about something or other, and what turns out to be on their mind is just this, plastic surgery. The emotional and psychological implications can turn out to be something" (353). After the face-lift in Switzerland, Swede falls into commonplaces about its effect: "Erased all that suffering. He gave her back her face" (298). And his wife writes to her Swiss aesthetic surgeon, "I feel it's taken me these twelve months to recover [from] the surgery. I believe, as you said, that my system was more beaten down than I had realized. Now it is as if I have been given a new life. Both from within and from the outside. When I meet old friends I have not seen for a while they are puzzled as to what happened to me. I don't tell them" (188). Passing as middle-class non-Jews, the model for Jews in the 1960s, becomes the model for the aging non-Jewish woman in the 1990s.

In *Goodbye, Columbus*, Brenda's father, whose largesse enables the family to live in a seeming paradise—with refrigerators full of ripe fruit, like the Garden of Eden, and tennis lessons and nose jobs—still has the family "nose." "Brenda's old nose fitted him well. There was a bump in it, all right; up at the bridge it seemed as though a small eight-sided diamond had been squeezed under the skin. I knew Mr. Patimkin would never bother to have that stone cut from his face, and would yet, with joy and pride, no doubt, had paid to have Brenda's diamond removed and dropped down some toilet in Fifth Avenue Hospital" (26). The theme of toilets as the origin of the Patimkins' fortune is an ongoing pun. Here they enable the surgery and the flushing of the "eight-sided diamond." The "eight-sided diamond" is the flaw that is seen as "Jewish" in a world where physical accultura-tion is defined by activities such as tennis, Ohio State basketball (but not at City College), or table tennis. It is a world in which middle-class sports, not the consumption of alcohol, marks the web of social interactions at the country club. The Patimkin home has a basement bar fully stocked with "bacchanalian paraphernalia." Yet Patimkin was a man "who himself does not drink, who, in fact, gets a fishy look from his wife when every several months he takes a shot of schnapps before dinner" (38). The twenty-three bottles of Jack Daniels in the bar represent what the middle class should indulge in. What remains of the Jewish social network is the deep suspicion about drunkenness and the attendant lack of decorum. The appropriation of an appropriate body of the etiquette of middle-class life is a sign of the successful struggle for an appropriate identity.[12] Jews in this world do not look like Jews, yet they do not drink like non-Jews are supposed to (pace Rabbit's wife in John Updike's *Rabbit, Run* [1960]). The Jews are an abstinent people—*shicker ist a goy*.

The country club world of the Patimkins is far distanced from the world of Neil's aunt Gladys and her husband. He lives with them and finds her just as unacceptable in her stifling world of surrogate mothering as he eventually finds the moral (and economic) world of the suburbs. For his aunt, "the [Patimkins] couldn't be real Jews ... since when do Jewish people live in Short Hills?" (53). But it is not the place that has transformed them; they have been transformed into the place: "the old Jews like my grandparents had struggled and died, and their offspring had struggled and prospered, and moved further and further west, towards the edge of Newark, then out of it, and up the slope of the Orange Mountains, until they reached the crest and started down the other side, pouring into Gentile territory" (82). There they were transformed, losing a specific religious identity (no one is sure whether they are Orthodox or Reformed or Conservative—but all are sure that they are Jewish [81]). What they gained was a sense of ethnic identity, and that also needed to be transformed.

But what is the authenticity that Roth postulates as an identity for the Jews? If there is any in this world, it is in the "small colored boy" (29) who enters the sanctuary (or tomb) of the library searching for "the heart section. Ain't you got no heart section" (31). In the "art" section ("he had the thickest sort of southern Negro dialect"), there is indeed the "heart of the matter."[13] There (suspected of all sorts of illegal acts by the other librarians), he discovers a volume of Gauguin. He is captivated by the volume and returns over and over to sit and be overwhelmed by the images of a world that he now can imagine. His physiognomy is unchanged: "he was very black and shiny, and the flesh of his lips did not so much appear to be a different color as it looked to be unfinished and awaiting another coat" (33). What is changed is his way of seeing the world. Neil manipulates the records so that the book stays on the shelf. Eventually, the boy stops coming and the book is checked out by another patron: "What had probably happened was that he'd given up on the library and gone back to playing Willie Mays in the streets. He was better off, I thought. No sense carrying dreams of Tahiti in your head, if you can't afford the fare" (110). In a sense, that is the motto of the conclusion of the novella: Brenda leaves Neil and returns to the arms of her family, returns to the middle-class life that she might not be able to have with him. Abandoned, he stares at the Harvard Library, having visited her in Boston, and imagines throwing a rock through the window. He does not: "I looked hard at the image of me, at the darkening of the glass, and then my gaze pushed through it, over the cool floor, to a broken wall of books, imperfectly shelved" (124).

The imperfection of the Patimkin nose is the parallel to the imperfection of art that gives the promise of some type of redemption, a redemption that Roth (and his readers) finds in his own texts. Redemption is to be found in art—not in kitchen sinks and bathroom fixtures (the Harvard Library "has Patimkin sinks in its rest rooms" [124]) and their spoils. It is in the act of writing that the "heart" lies. For Roth, the Jew as economic man has been replaced by the Jew (potentially) as cultural man. Social integration may destroy social values since deracinated Jews are too much like everyone else, but it also provides an opening to a world of culture that can redeem. Certainly that world is not to be found in Aunt Gladys's apartment in Newark or even in the library itself. It is to be found only in those books that inhabit the dusty or ill-kept shelves and how they impact on the individual.

Ted Hughes (1930–1998) evoked the image of the fanatic in the opening of his extraordinary poetic account of Sylvia Plath's deep desire to write:

> You were like a religious fanatic
> Without a god—unable to pray.
> You wanted to be a writer.
> Wanted to write? What was it within you
> Had to tell its tale?
> The story that has to be told
> Is the writer's God, who calls
> Out of sleep, inaudibly: 'Write.'[14]

Klugman's transformation into a writer lies ahead. But his is the future of the "fanatic" for art, the writer whose tale has to be told, not that of Brenda's suburban husband.

The crisis of conformity is at the heart of this story, but the promise is not that the protagonist will rot away in the Newark library, but that he will develop the "voice" that we hear in the narrative of the novella. He will become a fanatic, an artist—a "heartist." At the other end of the tale of transformation is Roth's account of "Eli, the Fanatic," certainly the most widely read of these stories by literary critics.[15] The tale is set in Woodenton, a suburban community only opened to Jews after the war. Eli Peck, a young lawyer, has been sent to "negotiate" with Leo Tzuref (= *tsorris*, trouble?), the Holocaust survivor who is the director of the "Yeshiva of Woodenton." Located in an old mansion, which is totally empty, it has "no books in the book shelves, no rugs on the floors, no draperies on the big casement windows" (231). It is the antithesis of the Patimkin mansion and the suburban houses here occupied by the other Jews. It is a place of study, a place of sanctuary. Yet the very notion of a Yeshiva evokes in the suburban Jews who send Eli Peck to demand its closure a world of fear. It is a place of "strange sounds" where there are "going to be a hundred little kids with little *yamalkahs* chanting their Hebrew lessons" (237). It evokes all of the images of a world that they have sought to flee. This is Woodenton, not "Brownsville," they complain (237).

The suburban Jews see the Jews at the Yeshiva as "goddam fanatics ... [since] this is the twentieth century" (239). Their image of Judaism is a "scientific" religion beyond reproach. One man drives his child all the way to "Scarsdale to learn Bible stories" and is appalled that she is frightened by the story of the binding of Isaac. "She gets nightmares from it, for God's sake! You call that religion" (256). They are "fanatics. Do they display common sense? Talking in a dead language, that makes sense? Making a big thing out of suffering, so you're oy-oy-oy all your life" (257). These are the Jews, as Peck writes Tzuref, who have had "to give up some of their more extreme practices in order not to threaten or offend the other" (242). Such transformations, Peck suggests, would have prevented the Holocaust.

The views of Jewish education espoused by Peck's neighbors are part of the general Enlightenment critique of Jewish institutional practices as deforming the Jewish soul. As early as Lazarus Bendavid's *Something on the Characteristics of the Jews* (1793), a general critique of Jewish institutions, especially the schools, became the central means of explaining the perceived negative character traits of European Jewry.[16] By the late nineteenth century, the widely read Jewish author Karl Emil Franzos, living in the outer reaches of the Austro-Hungarian Empire, in the Bukovina, deplored the impact of Jewish education of Jewish intellect and life. Franzos, the son of a German-speaking, highly acculturated Jewish physician, was the author of *From Half-Asia* (1876) and, most importantly, *The Jews of Barnow* (1877). These works were banned by the Austrian government, who saw them as revolutionary in their depiction of the poverty and ignorance of the Eastern

Provinces. What Franzos advocated was the complete acculturation of the Eastern Jews into a German-speaking, Western society. In the continuation of the "ethnographic" writing *From Half-Asia* in the 1880s, Franzos presented a study of "Child Prodigies in the Ghetto."[17] This literally undertakes to study a series of cases of child prodigies and presents them to us in mock-ethnographic form. It presents the Enlightenment view on the Jewish children who Peck finds at the school—at least as seen by his neighbors.

The centerpiece of Franzos's account is his visit with a number of local skeptics to the home of a not quite five-year-old prodigy, Ruben Grüner, in "Barnow," his pseudonymous town in Galicia. The child is "ugly and pale" (31). By two, he knows all of his prayers in Hebrew and can even read the language. By five he is a wonder, at least in this little town. He is seen by the "educated" in the town as a "sad figure, the living proof of what horrible training (*Dressur*) can do to a gifted child at the costs of his health and length of life" (33). The child is produced for the skeptical visitors and shows off his abilities—he has memorized the Torah and the commentaries and can answer complicated questions such as why God listened to Balaam's curse. His intelligence is indeed rote learning, and his "rationality" is merely the repetition of existing knowledge. The child appears "deathly pale and tortured" to the narrator and looks like he will not survive to the next summer. In that winter, the child dies of a high fever (47).

The result of the Talmudic training of his mind is his physical death. But, indeed, his spirit had been long dead, as Franzos had shown. Franzos speculates that the "incomparable material," the Jewish superior intelligence of these children, would have been otherwise better used in Berlin or Vienna—and to a greater reward! (48). Franzos's next child prodigy is a young man with a "pale, sharply profiled face" who aspires to become a magician, watches the "miracle rabbis," and learns all of their tricks by simply observing them. He does this through a "simple feat of memory" (57). Here the association between rote learning and the absence of virtue is made overtly, for the child-magician's stated intent is to dupe his victims and thus to have power over them.

With these cases, Franzos documents his view of the deforming power of Eastern European Jewish traditions on native high intelligence. He provides a summary of the reasons for the deformation and lack of true creativity on the part of these Jews. This begins with physical causes: the early marriages, which work against individual desire; "oriental physical laziness"; lack of exercise and physical work that "allows the race to decay physically"; the "one-sided emphasis on the intellect" as a means of earning one's daily bread; the early physical development of the Jews; and the use of educational traditions that stress memory ("With the messenger it is the musculature of the legs, with the wood cutter that of the arms that is overdeveloped, so too is it the brain of the Talmudist and the merchant" [59]). But this physical weakness is also the result of the centuries-long inheritance of mental gifts and dexterity. These prodigies are but the natural outgrowth of the complete living conditions of a people. They are neither intelligent in the Western sense nor can they be virtuous in the same way (59–60). This is exactly what Peck and his neighbors fear.

Peck and his Jewish neighbors are very uncomfortable with having these "visible Jews" in the neighborhood, especially the unnamed young assistant at the Yeshiva whose "black coat fell down below his ... knees.... [He wore a] round-topped, wide-brimmed Talmudic hat [and had a] ... beard ... [which] hid his neck and was so soft and thin it fluttered away" (235). It is this man who is the representative of the school in the town, and his visibility makes the local Jews uncomfortable.

Likewise, Tzuref seems empty, "a bald shaggy-browed man who looked as if he'd once been fat" (231). Initially, Eli Peck thinks that Tzuref's body is deformed. In the candlelight (the school has no electricity), he thinks, "[T]he crown of his head was missing!" But "Eli realized all he'd seen was a skullcap." Like Tzuref, the eighteen young students at the Yeshiva are Holocaust survivors, and they vanish as strangers approach.

Peck's suggestion for a compromise with the Yeshiva is that the assistant, whose clothing represents everything of the world that he has lost (as Tzuref tells Eli), simply wear "modern" clothing when he goes into town. This is his response to Tzuref's righteous claim that the law of man is "shame" if it demands the Yeshiva to be closed. For him, "the heart is law! God!" (246). Tzuref's accent may not be as strong as that of the young black in *Goodbye, Columbus*, but it is implied in that comment that he is a "D.P. German" (238). It is the heart of the matter again—but is it art?

Eli's obsession with this young man who is his own age moves him to bring him his own clothing and shoes. The assistant dons them and walks through the town, "walking up and down every street" to show that he is willing to sacrifice, it seems, his overt Jewish visibility (261). In exchange, the young man brings Eli his black gabardine and hat. And in a scene now often quoted, Eli dons the discarded clothing: "he smelled the color of blackness: a little stale, a little sour, a little old, but nothing that could overwhelm you" (264). He walks through the town and "had the strange notion that he was two people. Or that he was one person wearing two suits" (268). This moment of cultural cross-dressing does not come cheaply: the assistant is still recognizable as a Jew, with his beard and side-locks, and Eli is seen to have gone mad in his inappropriate disguise. The response of the town's inhabitants in seeing him so dressed is that he was having another nervous breakdown. And when he enters the hospital to see his newly born son, he is overwhelmed by the staff and tranquilized: "The drug calmed his soul, but did not touch it down where the blackness had reached" (276).

Roth's tale is often taken as an answer to the dilemma of the opening tale, the question of hollowness for which there seems to be redemption only in art, here the performance of identity. The Jew as successful citizen cannot confront the loss of the Holocaust because there are no longer any inner strengths within the community. All that is left is to become a simulacrum of that loss, just as Eli insists that the survivor don his green suit (a "J. Press" suit and not a "Brooks Brothers," as Peck's wife Miriam surmised [252]) and become a simulacrum of himself. The sole possibility is collapse, is despair in an existential manner.

Kafka's giant bug and his half-civilized ape find themselves in suburbia. Yet the promise of redemption, of transformation, remains. If we leave *Goodbye, Columbus* with the protagonist on his way back to Newark and the library, we know that there will be a second act; here, the birth of Peck's son provides an alternative ending. The story and his birth are set in May 1948, just when the State of Israel was declared. The epigram for the volume is a Yiddish proverb, "The heart is half a prophet," and the prophet may be Elijah, the prophet (1 Kings 21) taking on the Lord's mantle, zealous for the Lord and not Baal. But the transformation is half a one. Eli will not become a *baal tshuva*, one who returns to the fold, but he is part of a generation who sees the need for a resolution to the conflict between (public) "Jewish" and "American" identities. Certainly the notion of a "conversion" by merely dressing the part ironically reverses the function that cosmetic surgery has in creating "invisible Jews" in Roth's earlier account of Jewish success. The concept of *teshuvah* (return) had been read into contemporary Jewish thought by Martin Buber, whose work in the 1950s was "Jewish thought" in the United States. In *I and Thou*, Buber stressed the unmediated relationship between man and God. Unlike the claims made about the "hocus-pocus abracadabra stuff" going on at the Yeshiva, the experience that Eli has is unmediated. He has become one who is seeking God. In the rational world in which he lives, that constitutes a break with reality—as well it is—and he becomes the object of interest of the medical profession. This is the sort of conversion advocated by the Lubavitcher movement, which is not concerned about having Jews study for years the tradition but with having them fulfill the minimal ritual obligations of the faith. Putting on a *stremil* would be the metaphoric equivalent. Roth redeems the image of the "fanatic" by illustrating that the transformation can (and perhaps will) move in both directions—if only through the medium of art.

What Roth implies for Jewish cross-dressing Joseph Skibell's second novel, *The English Disease* (2003), charts. The title, a term that usually refers to melancholia, charts an account of the life and adventures of the American musicologist Charles Belski as he travels from the American Southwest to California to a tourist trip to Auschwitz and back.[18] Belski is an expert on the neurotically depressed Austrian-Jewish convert to Christianity Gustav Mahler, whose disease Belski also shares. In the novel he finds himself on the assimilated Jews' journey into the past. But the true transformation in the novel is not that of the Jewish protagonist but that of his non-Jewish wife, Isabelle, who comes to Judaism through "New Age" practices and eventual undertakes the arduous task of an Orthodox conversion. The narrator notes that the dress of the neo-Orthodox is "little more than a matter of sartorial affectation, the men barbaled in dark suits and Borsalinos, the women intentional dowds in amorphous skirts, turbans and snoods" (217). The protagonist sees this as "nothing more than a nostalgic game of dress-up, a sentimental post-Holocaust masquerade with everyone showing up as a fantasy version of his own grandfather!" (217–18). Yet in the conclusion of *The English Disease*, in which the couple is remarried in an Orthodox ceremony, Skibell presents an unambiguous sense of longing and fulfillment: "It's as though I were standing inside a perfectly formed circle of light, and an odd feeling wells up in my chest. I experience a kind of shattering in my heart, which, had I only been another person or myself at another time, I might have recognized as joy" (236). Skibell is able to capture the "American dilemma" of acculturation. Here the wife has become the "fanatic," and through her the protagonist, tested through an exposure to Auschwitz as tourism, can approach some type of recognition of loss.

There is an earlier pattern of seeing such "fanaticism" as a form of the return to the roots but purely in negative terms. Izak Goller, the Liverpool rabbi, novelist, and dramatist, describes such a conversion in his 1929 novel, *The Five Books of Mr. Moses*.[19] The title character, "[Moses] Moses, the English Jew, accustomed to the somewhat vapid formalism of the more pretentious synagogues of Anglo-Jewry, felt as he took in the scene before entering [in a *stiebel* near Brick Lane], the wonderful manner in which here the alien Jew was at home with his God" (16). He becomes a "Hebrew Master" and "a fanatic for all things Jewish. He grew a little beard and was rarely seen with uncovered head; every custom in Jewry, original or ghetto-wrought, was become dear to him" (17). The "fanatic," like Shylock, had been robbed of his daughter, who has fled his home to be with a non-Jew. He now turns to an Eastern European religious identity totally "foreign" to him for solace. But Goller's novel turns out to be a tale much in the model of Israel Zangwill: in the end the "bastard" grandchild of Mr. Moses, raised a Catholic, marries a Jewish war hero, and they put the conflicts of their families behind them.[20] (The father had converted to Catholicism from the Church of England parallel to Moses's conversion to Orthodoxy and abandoned Moses's pregnant daughter.) Indeed, the end of the novel sees the young couple walking away from the embittered old men, seeing their conflict as one of the past. The war hero not only earns the Victoria Cross but also was the son of a tailor whose sole desire was to be a poet (72). Their marriage was not at all a destruction of Jewish identity—any more than the marriage at the end of *The Melting Pot*. (One might add that like *The Melting Pot*, the novel has a life on the West End stage under the title *Cohen and Son* [1932].) Moses's "fanaticism" is matched by that of the man who seduced his daughter. He becomes a "Prince of the Church" whose goal is to convert the Jews. The marriage resolves the destructive "fanaticism" of this generation, for rather than being a violation of divine order, of religious law, it turns out to have been merely the transgression of a social taboo: "Jews, longer civilized and further-travelled than most other nations, have perhaps acquired taboos more than other nations. Taboos of health and of behaviour and of race preservation" (28). "Race preservation" is no longer necessary in this best of all liberal worlds. Thus, a return to Orthodox religious practice in 1929 England is a return to a world of taboos, not to a world of love and expiation.

Such contrasting notions of the fanatic provide a context for the debate about clothing, and manners, and decorum. Friedrich Nietzsche had contrasted the "freedom of spirit" to "fanaticism." For Nietzsche the fanatic is consumed by the desire to have and hold a single truth beyond anything. His free spirit is convinced that truthfulness itself is the only acceptable goal. "Truthfulness" becomes the operative category. Like Eli Peck, who is not completely convinced of the truthfulness of his mission and message when he first visits Tzuref, the free spirit questions each and every truth. The fanatic is self-righteous, a sign of weakness, as it precludes achieving "richness in personality." The free spirit, and here we may well wish to include the seemingly demented Eli Peck, is marked by a strength of self, which can achieve greatness through transformation.[21] However, we imagine that he will be "cured" of this through the psychotherapy advocated by his wife throughout the tale and the drugs that enable him to sink into oblivion at the end of the tale.

In 1997, half a century after *Goodbye, Columbus*, the Anglo-Pakistani-Indian and Muslim author Hanif Kureishi returned to the question of fanaticism and religious transformation in his short story "My Son, the Fanatic."[22] Kureishi, born in Kent, was raised in London and made his first mark as the author of the multicultural film *My Beautiful Laundrette* in 1984. Kureishi, in his autobiographical *My Ear at His Heart: Reading My Father* (2004), discusses his own background, the son of a would-be novelist, born a Muslim in India, who spends his life after the partition of India as a minor clerk in the new Pakistani Embassy in London.[23] He was "a Muslim who had left India in his early twenties and never returned [and who] made a religion at home out of library books, discontent and literary ambition" (11). Married to an "English" woman, whose parents run a small shop, his father's life in complex ways parallels Kureishi's own, except, as he notes, for his own success as a writer. Hanif Kureishi's children "ask me if they're Muslim and put their arms next to mine, to compare colours. They like to declare their Indianness to the other children at school, most of whom are from 'elsewhere'" (21–22). Kureishi lives in a multicultural world of hybrids, including himself and his children, where the "tradition" of being a Muslim is reduced to the superficial criterion of "colour."

According to Kureishi's construction of his own family's history, his father's father, a successful physician in India who becomes a colonel in the Indian Army medical corps, already comes from a lost Muslim world in

Poona that was equally "multicultural." The family there had "their own cricket team ... with other Hindu, Parsi, Christian and Jewish boys joining them occasionally" (33). His uncle, a celebrated journalist and cricket commentator, noted that in India 'they were friends with Hindus, Parsis, Anglo-Indians and Jews,' unlike in the world of contemporary Pakistan with its ever growing Muslim neofundamentalism (91). This past, especially the Indian past before partition, is a utopian lost world inhabited by men who could transcend, for good or for ill, the provincialism of religious fundamentalism. Kureishi's paternal grandfather, the colonel, sets a pattern. (His mother's family hardly appears in his account at all.) This grandfather, according to his father's account, is secular, drinks whiskey, and consorts with Parsi women; his grandmother prefers "to recite verses from the Koran" (66, 97). This is the world that Kureishi evokes when he imagines the history of his own family, but it is in the literary model of American-Jewish writing that Kureishi finds his doppelganger as an ethnic writer.

Kureishi sees Philip Roth as the central figure (along with Anton Chekhov) whose work shaped his own sense of being a writer. Unlike Chekhov, whose writing seems to be beyond time and place, it is Roth who defines the multicultural for him. "The immigrant family and its desire for integration and respectability, the self-obsessed son with unruly desires and a taste for goy girls, were right up my street. The belief in education and learning, the family's desire for their sons to be doctors and even artists—anything but not a failure—along with the son being amazed by the father's oddity, seemed immediately familiar to me" (160–61). Yet Roth represents something else: the ultimate triumph of the multicultural. "On this side of the Atlantic ... there would be a British-Asian literature, and that Asianness would come to permeate British life by way of its culture, as Jewishness had permeated American, and that it would become chic and then tired, making way for other ethnic groups" (160). It is of little surprise that Kureishi, whose further work will be dealt with in further detail later in this book, presents a rereading of Philip Roth's world of success, transformation, and fanaticism.

The story "My Son, the Fanatic" begins with Parvez, a Pakistani immigrant who had come to London twenty years earlier, wondering what had happened to his son Ali. His "room was becoming neat and ordered" (119). This is a new London, as John Clement Ball, quoting Homi Bhabha, notes concerning Kureishi's fragmentation of the new Commonwealth city of London into "its essentialist identities, and shown it to be a 'liminal

signifying space that is internally marked by the discourses of minorities
... and tense locations of cultural difference.'"[24] His son had thrown out
his "computer discs, video tapes, new books and fashionable clothes." This
upsets Parvez, as "he had bought him good suits, all the books he required
[for his education as an accountant,] and a computer." His room looks more
and more barren; even the pictures on the walls have vanished. Initially,
Parvez is convinced by his fellow cab drivers that Ali is taking drugs and
selling things to support his habit. And there is no change in his demeanor
to indicate any drug use. He even turns to a friend, the prostitute Bettina,
for advice. She advises him in a very serious voice about the signs and symptoms of drug use. But the only "drug use" going on is Parvez's ever greater
reliance on whiskey, against Islamic law, to fuel his inquiries about his son.

Eventually it becomes clear to Parvez that the physical changes in his
son, such as his growing a beard, are the clues to his transformation. He
prays five times a day; he ritually washes beforehand. His transformation
was into a religious tradition that Parvez had abandoned after his mistreat-
ment as a child at the hands of the mullahs in Lahore (123). In London, he
and his friends "made fun of the local mullahs walking around with their
caps and beards, thinking that they could tell people how to live, while their
eyes roved over the boys and girls in their care" (123). Kureishi's own father
"had talked about the childhood monotony of having to learn the Koran by
rote, and of being hit by sticks by the Moulvis [religious teachers]" (166). He
"wouldn't teach us about Islam, which we came to regard as pointless super-
stition. Once I gave him a Smoky Bacon crisp; as he swallowed I informed
him what it was, that the pig had entered his body. He rushed into the bathroom and emerged foaming at the mouth, having washed out his mouth with
soap" (108). The complexity of the repression of religious ritual and its om-
nipresence as a subtext in the lives of Muslims in the Diaspora parallels the
"lost" world of Jewish religious identity as reflected in Roth's world.

There is even a parallel in the reality of Jewish attitudes in Eastern
Europe to ritual, shaped by the Haskalah. Such attitudes are already present in Pakistan before partition. One commentator notes that during the
required "theology hour" at Aligarh University, the students either were
absent or "busied themselves writing humourous verse or drawing rude and
rough caricatures.... Our communal consciousness was ... far more secular than religious."[25] This was, of course, among the Muslim elite to which
Kureishi's family belonged. Kureishi's views on religion mirror the view

that "excessive devotion to religion is a form of narcissism, a barrier in fact, between oneself and the world, a convenient way of neglecting the individual and replacing him with God" (118). Religion and religious ritual have been abandoned in the Western Diaspora by Parvez's migrant generation as a sign of the world of poverty and cruelty from which they had escaped. This was typical of the Pakistani migrants of the 1960s, who "suffered an almost total lapse of religious observance; yet migration was not perceived as a threat to their heritage. It was possible to live on the margin of British society, avoiding any deeper involvement than work necessitated.... The migrant lived and worked in Britain on behalf of his family."[26] Kureishi's image of the Pakistani cab drivers and the network in which Parvez functions mirrors this experience, which is a substitute for the religious community. Kureishi sees the mosque in his own experience as not being the place of "music, stories or community, as I had in church as a child. I found ideology and fundamentalism, and young people holding extreme, irrational and violent views" (168). The world of childhood is the world of the (Anglican) religious community of his mother; Islam, especially after the 1989 fatwa against Salman Rushdie, "didn't seem compatible with any kind of combative imagination" (168). It is the space where irrationalism is the desire to separate oneself from the multicultural world of hybridity.

The conflict is now set between the father, whose desire is for the improvement of his son within the acculturated values of England, and his son's newly discovered Muslim neofundamentalism. In a scene of Oedipal dimensions the father, drinking "his usual whiskey and water" (124), generates his son's marked disapproval. The more his son winced at his consumption of alcohol, the more he drank, and the more "the waiter, wanting to please his friend, brought another glass of whiskey" (125). His son's comment is "don't you know that it's wrong to drink alcohol?" (124). Parvez confronts his son, shouting that he has not lived a wicked life; his son calmly retorts that he has not lived by the Koran. He has eaten pork and had indeed ordered his wife to cook it: "You're not in the village now, this is England. We have to fit in." Parvez also relishes fitting in. His son, on the other hand, sees his father as "too implicated in Western civilization" (125). For him the West is a place of sin and permissiveness; only jihad will cleanse it for the reward of paradise. This view is common among neofundamentalists who see that their status as a Muslim minority in the West must give way either to *hijra* (the return to Muslim lands) or to the conversion of the West to

Islam.[27] But it is not new. It is a rhetoric that comes out of colonial India (now Pakistan). In Maulana Ihtesam al Hasan Kandhalwi's *Muslim Degeneration and Its Only Remedy*, a text from the 1930s widely used in British *Deobandi* mosques, one can find similar views: "The Muslim youth ... affected and influenced by the so-called modern trends or the Western way of life take pleasure in laughing at the very ideals of Islam and openly criticize the sacred code of *Shariat* as being out of date and impractical.... The first and foremost thing to do is to change the aim of our life from material motives and acquisition of wealth to the propagation of ... Islam."[28] For Ali, it is the association between true prayer and sobriety that is the key, as it stands in the Koran: "O you who believe / Approach not prayers / With a mind intoxicated / Until you can understand / All that you say" (Surah 4:43).

Parvez is stymied: "I love England ... they let you do almost anything here" (126). And that is precisely where Ali locates the problem. His father "grovels" before the "whites" who think that they represent the best civilization in the world. Parvez ironically notes that Ali had never left England. But, of course, the virtual Ummah to which he now belongs transcends national boundaries and identities. As one British Muslim observed, "Living in a non-Muslim society, Muslims have to be careful of every step they take. They must be conscious of what they are doing at all times."[29] It is this heightened consciousness of difference that defines the experience of the son as opposed to that of the father.

Parvez begins to try and accommodate his son. He starts to grow a beard and sits down to speak with him further on a day when he is assured that his breath does not smell of whiskey—for the use of whiskey, perhaps even more than the consumption of pork, marks the Westernization of Parvez. Muslim neofundamentalism stresses the use of soft drinks, perhaps in the form of Mecca-Cola, as a sign of the struggle against the degeneracy of the West.[30] He urges his son to live life, something Ali rebuffs, noting the suffering of "our oppressed people" (129). One evening Parvez is driving Bettina home after her night on the street, and they pick up Ali. She "inadvertently" touches Parvez's shoulder while speaking to Ali, and Ali remonstrates with her that a prostitute has no business touching a Muslim. Bettina jumps out of the car in a "cold fury" and vanishes. At home later, Parvez bursts into Ali's room where he is praying, knocks him over, and hits him until "the boy's face was bloody" (131). Ali turns to his father and says "through his split lip: 'So who's the fanatic now'" (131).

For Kureishi in this story, the religious conflict is a conflict of generations.[31] The "success" of the father is seen by the son as failure. The process of "re-islamisation" here follows the pattern of the creation of a subculture within the world of Western poverty in which only the Islam preached within that culture is even seen as valid. The struggle for identity within Kureishi's fictive world is tied to the ironic notion of the "success" of Parvez as a taxi driver. In the economic world of London, his position is certainly not that of the Patimkins, but in one sense (in his desire that Ali become an accountant) reflects the moment in the world of the Patimkins or the Pecks before they achieve economic success and are able to move to the suburbs (or, in London, North). Such a Muslim youth culture does indeed exist today as a youth subculture of children who "do not speak the original language or attend the mosque, but do eat at McDonald's, wear baseball caps, buy expensive clothes, fully engage in consumerism and breed dogs at home."[32] Dogs, needless to say, are classed by Muslims as unclean animals. Except for that, they act just like the Patimkins and the Pecks.

Not madness but incomprehension reigns at the end of the story. Here we can return to another of Philip Roth's tales, "The Conversion of the Jews," where the young Ozzie torments his Hebrew school teacher, Rabbi Binder, with questions such as given that God could create the world, "why couldn't He let a woman have a baby without having intercourse" (128). The rabbi had argued for a human, historical Jesus, rather than a divine one. Ozzie repeats this to the point where "Rabbi Binder's hand flicked out at Ozzie's check.... Ozzie ducked and the palm caught him squarely on the nose. The blood came in a short, red spurt." Ozzie is overwhelmed, runs to the roof of the synagogue, and threatens to jump. Eventually he makes everyone get on their knees. This includes his mother, who had "hit Ozzie across the face with her hand" (131) for the same transgression—or rather for having angered the rabbi for the nth time with his questions. He makes all of those assembled below on the street swear, "God can do anything." Ozzie is exhausted and says, "You should never hit anybody about God" (144), before he leaps into the firemen's net.

Is it "God" or the seeking for truth that haunts these two tales? Certainly the role of the fanatic has been redefined in radical ways from the Jewish suburbs of the 1950s to the East End of London in the 1990s. Roth seems to gesture that the performance of identity that Eli Peck undertakes in his madness is a realization of that world lost by the Patimkins, by middle-class Jews who so need to pass that they turn themselves into a parody of the world into which they have entered. After the Shoah, such a transformation seems just as impossible as Kafka's ape becoming a man or Gregor Samsa finally learning to appreciate the violin. Kureishi presents the transformation of the son into a religious figure completely unlike that image of religiosity experienced in Pakistan, for there Islam is experienced, for good or for ill, within a national, ethnic, linguistic context. All of this has vanished in London and been replaced by an abstract, stripped-down version of a globalized, deterritorialized Islam. The parallels to the world of the middle-class Jew here are clear. Ali wishes for a world that has never existed; Peck imagines himself into that world that has (for him) vanished and reappeared.

For our present-day multicultural world, it is Kureishi's rewriting of Roth that seems to resonate for Anglo-Jewry. In 2005 Mike Leigh, prolific Anglo-Jewish filmmaker (*Secrets and Lies* and *Vera Drake*) returned to the world of the theater with his *Two Thousand Years* at London's National Theatre. This tale of a multigenerational Jewish family in Cricklewood, a northwest suburb, tells the tale of the turn toward religion of the youngest member of the family, Josh, a twenty-eight year old still living at home. His father Danny, a middle-class Anglo-Jewish dentist, and his mother, Rachel, a sabra born on a kibbutz, are shocked by their son's sudden turn to religion. "It's like having a Muslim in the house" is their feeling. The model for Leigh's Jewish world is not Roth and the shadow of the Holocaust but Kureishi and the new virtual Ummah. Both models live out notions of their own commitment to the truthful—and yet live in worlds where violence seems to be just below the surface. It is no surprise that Josh is portrayed in one scene putting on tefillin (phylacteries) and most of the viewers assume that he is "about to inject heroin into his arm."[33] Fanaticism and success are truly in the eye of the beholder.

NINE

"WE'RE NOT JEWS"
Imagining Jewish History and Jewish Bodies in Contemporary Non-Jewish Multicultural Literature

I. MULTICULTURALISM AND THE JEWS

By the end of the twentieth century, the multicultural retains its contours. The Jew is a fixed figure in the literary imagination that figures the multicultural universe. Both models, in highly attenuated form, can still be found. Both the hybrid and the cultural autonomous exist, interact, contradict, and defend the frontier of the multicultural, laying claim to its political power to include and exclude. In such a world, how do writers who self-consciously see themselves as multicultural members of clearly delineated groups (ethnic, social, religious) or see themselves as inherently hybrid of such groups imagine culturally defined minorities, such as the Jews?

There has been an explosion of studies on this topic, contrasting African-American images of the Jew and Jewish-American images of the black,[1] "African-American" being understood as an autonomous culture often adversarial to "mainstream" culture (defined as "white"). In writing about the transmutation of the "ethnic" in American culture during the twentieth century, David Hollinger has quite correctly noted that Jewish identity "receded in significance when all Americans of predominantly European stock were group[ed] together."[2] Jews became "white" after the Holocaust. But "white" here was always understood in terms of the antithesis to "blackness," to the racial difference of the African American. The significance was that "Jews were once widely thought of as a race, but are no longer" (38). Unless, one must add, they function in two "multicultural" realms: if they are juxtaposed, in the fantasy world of the multicultural text, to African Americans as the "most successful minority"; or if, in the multicultural competition for the prize as the most oppressed and victimized, they are defined in terms of the Holocaust. This multicultural theme seems to have its limits in stressing the boundaries between these two groups rather than the possibility of hybridity (to be found, for example, in the intertwined history of jazz and klezmer in the United States).[3]

But is multiculturalism solely an American "problem"? What groups count at the end of the twentieth and beginning of the twenty-first centuries as "multicultural"? What happens when this project is extended beyond the black-Jewish paradigm and beyond the borders of the United States? What happens, then, when other groups are brought into the discussion of multiculturalism? And what happens when it crosses national, even linguistic, boundaries? What happens when a writer self-consciously representing her or his work as the voice of a multicultural writer needs to define difference? The reception of these works is often very much in line with the self-definition of the author. The specific subject position of the text is seen as part of the fiction itself. Each multicultural text takes as one of its themes the creation of a multicultural voice in the novels, whether it is that of the narrator or of the protagonist. It labels itself as functioning on the imagined frontier of the multicultural.

In many of these multicultural texts the figure of the Jew, defined within the world of the fiction, is a key to the understanding of the very nature of the multicultural society represented in it. This figure takes on different contours based on the existing stereotypes of the Jew within each culture and each ethnic cohort. The core concepts that shape the image of the Jew are the age-old ones: the Jew as foreign and victim; the Jew as cosmopolitan and successful. It is how these concepts function in a multicultural context as expressed in the age-old fantasy about Jewish physical difference that is the subject of the present question.[4] Are Jews "inherently" different? That is, can there be a difference beyond history and culture that is inscribed on the body? The error inherent in this question is that it elides the fact that bodies both in fantasy and in reality themselves are historically constructed objects. Suffering and success shape the body as do hunger and affluence.

The fantasy about the uniqueness of the Jew's body, however, postulates that the difference of the body reflects an essential difference in the mind or soul. What happens when such tropes are used, if only ironically, in contemporary multicultural literature? To ask with Audre Lorde, can such texts dismantle the master's house, anti-Semitism, with the master's tools, irony?[5] For in the new multicultural world, instability is one of the major features that shapes notions of difference. Performance rather than identity is at the core of the new multiculturalism, even with its overt political gesture toward "minor literatures."

Each of the texts I am examining uses the Jew as a litmus test to define a particular multicultural world in terms of the physicality of the "Jew." They have a specific Western origin, having appeared in England, South Africa, the United States, and Germany. They also appeared at approximately the same time, at the end of the second millennium. It was (and is) a moment in Western literary culture when the issues of multiculturalism have become a central concern (pro or contra) to the writer as well as to the literary world. It is as much a question of what is written as what is published, now for a wider, even global audience.

All of these texts provide a sense of how the "Jews" can figure in the collective fantasies of other actually or potentially "successful" minorities. (This is in marked contrast to the case of the African-American writers' image of the Jews, from the fiction of Richard Wright to Spike Lee's 1990 *Mo' Better Blues*. Such images assume a world in which African Americans remain marginalized and subjected to discrimination.) Multiculturalism is also a space where the contrast between the "haves" and the "have nots" is played out. The more you can claim the status of victim, the stronger your case for primacy in this world in which "all animals are equal, but some are more equal than others." In the past decade, the "Jews" have been imagined as a successful minority. This perceived success came at exactly the time, as Peter Novick has noted, when the Shoah had become the touchstone for all histories of persecution and genocide.[6] Jewish-American writing has focused on the Shoah for the past forty years ever since Bernard Malamud, Philip Roth, and Saul Bellow inscribed this on the American literary consciousness. The centrality of this topic in defining the Jew in literature also has a literary dimension beyond Jewish-American writing. More than Anglo-Jewish or German-Jewish writing, Jewish-American culture is an example of how a successful multicultural presence in a national literature can be established.

From Saul Bellow to Stephen Spielberg, the introduction of Jewish subject matter by self-consciously Jewish cultural figures has made the representation of the Jew part of the mainstream of both American high and mass culture. These multicultural texts of the late 1990s and early 2000s represent how the image of the Jew figures in contemporary fantasies of a multicultural society partially in light of the success and power of Jewish–American writing, which by then had become mainstream American writing.

II. READING JEWISH DIFFERENCE

Islam figures greatly in the contemporary discourse about Jews and multiculturalism. In the Anglo-Pakistani-Indian novelist and screenwriter Hanif Kureishi's short story "We're Not Jews" (1997), the representation of the Jew within a multicultural context is given an exemplary formulation.[7] "We're Not Jews," retrospectively set in the 1960s, centers on a "mixed marriage" between an English woman and a Pakistani man. (This echoes in complex ways Kureishi's own account of his parent's marriage.)[8] One should note that sharia, Islamic law, does permit Muslim men to marry Jewish or Christian wives (and they may maintain their original faiths). This is permitted only in non-Muslim lands of the Diaspora.

At the beginning of the story, the woman has gone to school to complain about her son Azhar having been bullied by her neighbor's son. Confronted by her ex–Teddy boy neighbor and his bully son on the bus, Azhar's mother tries to ignore their taunts. As the child of an Englishwoman married to a Pakistani laborer with pretensions of becoming a writer, their son is torn between the two worlds of "England" and "Pakistan"; each has constructed the other. England in the Teddy boy's fantasy is the land of the white and the English. There is truly no black in their Union Jack.[9] Pakistan in the tale is defined by a new nationalism and its Muslim roots. Yvonne, Azhar's mother, may be English, but her class identity as even marginal to the working class puts her at the lowest common denominator of what is "English." Azhar's father had lived in China and India but had never actually been to Pakistan, as indeed had Kureishi's father. He is Pakistani only in the sense of belonging to an Urdu-speaking and Muslim cultural diaspora.

The child's confusion becomes manifest when his mother teaches him to answer "Little Billy's" bullying by denouncing him as "common." Class is defined by etiquette and shame.[10] The Teddy boy's response is "But we ain't as common as a slut who marries a darkie" (43). The extended family into which she has married is different but is still a full step above the most liminal figures in English society. "Mother always denied that they were 'like that.' She refused to allow the word 'immigrant' to be used about Father, since in her eyes it applied only to illiterate tiny men with downcast eyes and mismatched clothes" (45). Her choked response to being taunted: "Mother's lips were moving but her throat must have been dry; no words came, until she managed to say, 'We're not Jews'" (45). Big Billy, the bully's father, answered, "You no Yid, Yvonne. You us. But worse. Goin' with the Paki" (45). Who is the "Yid" in Kureishi's vocabulary of constructs? The "Yid" is even more pathetic than the victims of apartheid, as the father notes, "where people with white skins [who] were cruel to the black and brown people" who were considered inferior are the ultimate victims because they appear to be "white" but are really not. The Jew is the foreigner everywhere. Azhar had heard his father say "that there had been 'gassing' not long ago. Neighbour had slaughtered neighbour, and such evil hadn't died. Father would poke his finger at his wife, son and baby daughter, and state, 'We're in the front line'" (45). For his parents, the memory of the Shoah is written onto their own experience, and they thus understand how easily they too could become the victims of racial persecutions. They have the potential of becoming "Yids."

The Shoah defines a difference that is not merely victimhood but also an odd sort of Orientalism, that casting of the exotic East as the place from which those who are inherently unassimilable come. What the liminal characters share in the Diaspora is their "Oriental" fate, that of victims. This is reflected in Kureishi's own sense of the world in which he was raised. He asks in his autobiographical account of his and his father's life, "[W]hy did millions of ordinary people—the sort who lived on our street, us, even—commit the worst imaginable crimes? The fact that one race had attempted, literally, to physically exterminate another, was a shocking truth, almost unbelievable in terms of the other things we like to believe about ourselves: that we had achieved a certain level of civilization and control, that 'we,' the British, were superior, for instance, to the natives of India, a position preferable to the terrors of quality" (104–5). The Shoah becomes the litmus test for all horrors and "explains" British colonialism. "If everything was the fault of Hitler, and had been mended by the hero Churchill, what was there left today?" (104). Churchill, the last exponent of the colonial world, is the villain of the piece, equal to Hitler. "With the Holocaust in living memory—the man who cut my hair once showed me the number tattooed on his arm—a new form of racism emerged, this time directed against those in the former Empire, as though people couldn't live without racism, they really need to express their hate in this form" (105). The elision of the difference between Germany and England, between the murderous anti-Semitism of the Nazis and the destructive, yet never genocidal, experiences of the "English," evokes the Jews as the model for the Diaspora experiences of Muslims in Great Britain.

The marker for the difference in this world of vanishing colonialism is not only skin color but also language.[11] Just as Big Billy mangles spoken English, so too does Azhar's father, whose desire to become a writer is limited by his lack of a "sure grasp of the English language which was his, but not entirely, being 'Bombay variety, mish and mash.' Their neighbour, a retired schoolteacher, was kind enough to correct Father's spelling and grammar, suggesting that he sometimes used 'the right words in the wrong place, and vice versa'" (47). (Given Kureishi's account of his own father's ineffectual attempts to become a published writer, this seems to mirror his own sense of his command of English as a cultural tool.) The tale ends with the child listening to his father and his father's family shouting in Urdu during a cricket match on the radio. "He endeavoured to decipher the gist of it, laughing, as he always did, when the men laughed, and silently moving his lips without knowing what the words meant, whirling, all the while, in incomprehension" (50–51). Language confusion, exile, and cosmopolitanism are all qualities of the image of the Jew in the world of Kureishi's characters. To identify with them, however, means accepting the potential of a cosmopolitanism that is tainted by the failure of language as a marker of belonging. Yet Kureishi's image of the Jew's language tied closely to physicality.

The Jews are "illiterate tiny men with downcast eyes and mismatched clothes." This is a very "English" manner of seeing the Jews, and therefore is ascribed to Azhar's mother, whose prejudices are "English" even though (or because) she is married to a South Asian. The image she uses is analogous to one ironically employed by Julian Barnes in a description of one of his protagonist's Jewish friends:

> Toni far outclassed me in rootlessness. His parents were Polish Jews and, though we didn't actually know it for certain, we were practically sure

that they had escaped from the Warsaw ghetto at the very last minute. This gave Toni the flash foreign name of Barbarowski, two languages, three cultures, and a sense (he assured me) of atavistic wrench: in short, real class. He looked an exile, too: swarthy, bulbous-nosed, thick-lipped, disarmingly short, energetic and hairy; he even had to shave every day.[12]

After the Shoah, the "Yids'" physical state is a reflex, in the eyes of the character, of their history, but it is also written on their bodies. Kureishi evokes this early in the volume of short stories in which "We're Not Jews" appeared. In the title story, "Love in a Blue Time," he portrays the close friend of the protagonist as the son of "political refuges from Eastern Europe who'd suffered badly in the war, left their families, and lived in Britain since 1949.... Britain hadn't engaged them; they barely spoke the language. Meanwhile Jimmy fell in love with pop. When he played blues on his piano his parents had it locked in the garden shed.... He had remained as rootless as they had been, never even acquiring a permanent flat" (8). "Culture," that elusive "thing" so pursued by the South Asians in Kureishi's "We're Not Jews," is part of the inheritance of the "immigrant" from elsewhere.

Kureishi's operative concept of the "immigrant" is close to that of the "stranger," who is, to paraphrase the Berlin sociologist Georg Simmel, one who comes and then stays and stays and stays.[13] The Jewish immigrants who haunted the East End of London had set the pattern in the 1960s in Great Britain. But even more so, those immigrants who had escaped or survived the Nazi Holocaust marked for the British sensibility the outcast invited for a short time who becomes a permanent part of the society. Even these immigrants, it turns out, have access to high culture. Azhar, Kureishi's narrator, needs to feel that he is English in spite of (or because of) the class system. While his parents are stuck in their world of difference, he is not. He can become a real writer (like Kureishi himself) and move into an intellectual world of the 1990s where the multicultural is prized. He is not merely a "Yid" whose difference transcends all class difference. Yet one also has to note that British law (the Race Relations Act of 1976) also makes this distinction. Jews are a "racial / ethnic" group and therefore are protected against discrimination; Muslims are neither an ethnicity nor a "race." Sikhs, in 1983, petitioned the House of Lords and were declared an "ethnic group." This reflects, of course, the feeling that anti-Semitism, given the Holocaust, is an absolute evil—even if biological categories such as "race" have to be applied to "protect" Jews. In the United States, on the contrary, as David Hollinger observes, Jews are no longer considered as a race but as white.

How true this remains can be seen in 2001. After racial riots in the North of England during the spring of 2001, where South Asians and members of the white-only British National Party clashed, reporters were driven from a South Asian housing estate with the shouts of "Jews," followed by a "barrage of unprintable remarks about Jews." In the end, in this world of Diaspora Islam, all non–South Asians are "Jews."[14]

III. KAFKA AS A SOUTH AFRICAN

How complex such multicultural discourses about the Jews are can be seen in another text published at more or less the same time as Kureishi's short story. Achmat Dangor's novella "Kafka's Curse" is set in South Africa before the election of 1994.[15] The theme, like that of Philip Roth's *The Human Stain* (2000), is passing, specifically a "colored" man passing as "white" by becoming a "Jew." It is a text rooted in the ideology of a specific multicultural Diaspora, that of South Africa under apartheid, where Dangor was born in 1948. He was a member of the black cultural group Black Thoughts and banned for six years in the 1970s. He notes, "In addition to those inexplicable inner urges to tell stories, I was influenced by my upbringing in a staunch, if not dogmatically 'fundamental' Muslim environment. In addition to the conventional Western school, I attended 'madressa' (Islamic school) each day."[16] One might add that the school was most probably full of the most intense anti-Jewish rhetoric given the fact that he attended it during the height of the Arab campaign against Israel, a campaign in which the full armament of anti-Jewish images were used. Dangor uses and undermines these images in his representation of the Jew.

Dangor's novella is his literary fantasy of the meaning of multiculturalism projected back into the world of apartheid. The protagonist of the tale, Omar Khan, changes his name to Oscar Kahn because he was able to pass as "white": "I was fair, and why not, my grandmother was Dutch. This oppressive country had next-to-Nazis in government, yet had a place, a begrudged place but a place nevertheless, for Jews. Can you believe it? For that eternally persecuted race? Because they were white" (23). Azhar's mother, in Kureishi's world, does not regard the "Yid" as truly white. The Jews of South Africa become "white" only after the beginning of the twentieth century. Before that, they are labeled as "colored," as they seem to be in Kureishi's world. They become white because they become a successful minority and have the economic clout to demand being labeled as "white."[17]

In South Africa, as in Great Britain, there is a set of images of the Jew that shapes Dangor's representation. Kureishi represents the "Yid" only from the perspective of the outsider. The "Yid" is the projection of all that is said about the South Asian. In Dangor's world, the Jew is a trickster always cheating the non-Jew; he "may always be known to a farmer by the shape of his nose, the many rings on his fingers, and by the tongue being too large for his mouth."[18] The physiognomy reflects his character. This comment was made in a piece early in the twentieth century in the Anglophone *Cape Punch* about the "Boereverneuker," the Jew who cheats the Boer, himself a stereotyped figure. It had changed little by the 1980s. Here Jew and Boer, cheat and victim, are seen as separate from the Anglophone writers/ readers who are, from their perspective, clearly superior to both in terms of their command of the language of power. The image of the Jew's "tongue being too large for his mouth" is a trope found in European science of the day. Its reflection on the inability of the Jew to command the language of the culture—and still be able to cheat the Boer—takes on a specific local coloration as seen from the perspective of Anglophone hegemonic claims on "real culture."

Jews are a race apart, like the Boers and, by extension, the blacks. Even Jews who do not "look Jewish," who look "white," will eventually reveal their inner nature in their appearance. They look "white," for "as yet the stress of trade had not awakened the ancestral greed, which would one day dominate his blood and modify his physiognomy."[19] At that point the Jew becomes a "Peruvian," an odd, turn-of-the-twentieth-century term for Jewish traders in South Africa (a "Peruvian" perhaps because of his non-Western, non-white exoticism that puts the Jew on the very margins of the known world). And the "Peruvian," the Jew who "looked worth no more than the clothes in which he stood," was "still muttering in Yiddish" (51). Language marks the difference of the Jew from the Boer and the Anglo. Here is the reflection of Kureishi's image, now placed in a society in which multiculturalism ignores the "colored" inhabitants of the society and focuses only on the nuances of what can be defined as "white."

And yet there is the constant anxiety about Jewish superiority in South Africa, given the history of the South African gold fields and diamond mining. Here the myth of Jewish "hyperintelligence" that haunts the medical and psychological literature of the nineteenth century takes on its South African specificity. The Jew wins over the non-Jew "due to his shrewdness and wit" (73). This is the playwright Stephen Black's phrase in the context of a fin de siècle representation of the Jew as a successful entrepreneur. Given the central role of the mercantile system in defining success in South Africa among the British, the questionable position of the merchant is projected onto the Jews, who are shown to have no "class" but to be shrewd and therefore successful. True success, it is implied, comes with having both culture (language) and money—and Jewish characters can never have this.

The Jews may appear to acculturate themselves, but the acculturation is only superficial. They are malleable when conditions permit them to be. They then appear to "merge into the political life of the country, without abandoning their own racial loyalty" (70). Even when they put on the mask of culture, they remain racially "Jews" and are therefore different under the clothes they put on or the language they seem to acquire. Put them to the test—such as the litmus test of war—and they will reveal themselves as merely Jews in all of their racial identity.

The very term "Jews" has a South African dimension evoked only in passing by Dangor, for while there are some Sephardic Jews and some Central European Jews in this story, South Africa evidences a uniformity of the term "Jew" in terms of its social history that parallels the cohesive representation of the Jew in Afrikaans and Anglophone non-Jewish culture of South Africa. The greatest majority of Jews who came to South Africa were Lithuanian Jews (*Litvaks*) whose language was Yiddish. The language politics of South Africa during the early twentieth century presented two languages of power, Afrikaans and English. No other language would be acceptable, and what these two languages had in common was their alphabet.

In the Cape Colony in 1902, an Immigration Restriction Act was passed in order to limit the immigration of people from the Indian subcontinent. Only "Europeans" were to be given the privilege of immigration to South Africa. "Europeans" were defined by the alphabet of the language they spoke. Yiddish, needless to say, was not accepted as a "European" language. Since only languages written in the same alphabet as Afrikaans and English were "white," Hebrew became "colored." The "Hebrews" entered into the world of southern Africa with its overwhelming black population not as members of the privileged, hegemonic race—as "white"—but as a marginal race, as "colored." This view was, of course, very much in line with late nineteenth-century racial theory in Europe. Houston Stewart Chamberlain, Wagner's son-in-law and the most widely read popular racial theorist of the day in all of Europe, argued that the Jews were a mongrel race for having mixed with blacks in their Alexandrian exile, and this fact could be read on their physiognomy.

The urban environment gave the Jews both more visibility and more protection. Falling on the "wrong side" of the color bar during the colonial period (eventually leading to the institution of apartheid) could have been fatal for Jewish cultural and political aspirations. There would have been no hiding in the protective environs of the city. Thus, Jews lobbied against the categorization of the Cape immigration bill and had Yiddish reclassified as a "European" language. And yet the Cape censuses continued to differentiate between "Europeans" and "Hebrews."

Dangor's protagonist, Oscar Kahn, defines his "whiteness" by moving into a white neighborhood. He left the Indian township of Lenasia, moved to a Johannesburg suburb, passed as a Jew, and married Anna Wallace, who was of impeccable British ancestry. Kahn suffers from their anti-Semitism. "Anna's mother hated me. I think she suspected even my Jewishness. Prejudice has unerring instincts" (32). For Anna's friends, he is a sexual object but not a potential husband because of his visible difference: Oscar is "all brown bread and honey! Good enough for bed ... but to marry?" (11). Marriage and reproduction and the difficulty of passing are at the heart of this tale. Her friends know that he is different: "Are you Indian?" "No, the Kahn here is a good old Jewish name" (31). *Nomen est omen*, but how does one become "Jewish"?

Oscar is eventually employed as an architect by a Jewish architect. Meyer Lewis employs him, trains him, and slowly makes him over into an image of himself: "In my dreams I often slit Meyer's bulbous throat and danced with naked feet in the pools of his hot blood.... I began to hate his hybrid South African Yiddisher tongue, his sharp contemptuous eyes.... Meyer was short and stocky" (24–25). Language and physicality define the "real" Jew in the tale. Meyer, like Oscar, is a successful Jew. Yet he is still marked by his linguistic and physical difference. He is a successful version of Kureishi's "illiterate tiny men with downcast eyes and mismatched clothes."

When Oscar buys a house in a white-only suburb, it is a house marked in an odd way by his "Jewishness." When he courted Anna, she would watch him masturbate: "[Anna] was not surprised that I was circumcised; a Jewish custom after all" (31). Muslim men, like Jewish men, are physically different. This difference becomes the stain that mars the image of Oscar's house in the white suburb. It is a ninety-year-old house. Oscar insists that it cannot be altered in any way. It has an odd configuration. When you approach the front door, you are confronted by "a strange fountain that stood in the centre of the path leading to the front door, forcing people to confront the sorrowful sight of a castrated David, his drooping stone penis broken at the tip like a child's pee-pee. *It was an integral part of the house's nature*, Oscar said" (Emphasis in the original: 11). The fountain of the "young boyish David had water piped up through his foot and out his penis. The piping was made of metal and it rusted. Over time the rust coloured the water until he appeared to be peeing blood" (37). The ancient fantasy of male Jews bleeding regularly had been the origin of the idea of Jewish ritual murder from the early modern times to the present. Jewish men were believed to need Christian blood to "heal" their bloody discharge. This view persisted into the late nineteenth century.[20] It was raised again at the turn of the twentieth century in a powerfully written pamphlet by the professor of Hebrew at the University in St. Petersburg, D. Chwolson, as one of the rationales used to justify the blood libel. Chwolson notes that it was used to "cure the diseases believed to be specifically those of the Jews," such as male menstruation.[21] The house that Oscar occupies is a "Jewish" house with its bleeding David. While Oscar is circumcised, as a Muslim he is not condemned to bleed.

The earlier inhabitant of the house, a little boy called Simon, was embarrassed by the blood-peeing David, so he took a garden spade and "lopped David's penis off" (38). Again, in the Western image of the Jewish body, circumcision is a form of real or attenuated castration.[22] The power of the image of Jewish circumcision in the West is such that it actually elides any reference to the practice by other peoples, such as the Muslims. When Oscar buys the house, one of his first tasks is to repair the statue and have it working again. It begins to pee blood again. Oscar believes that he probably tore the new plastic tube when he inserted it. His daughters read it differently: "The girls blushed. The elder one said that David was peeing monthlies" (38). Dangor makes an association between the Jewish body, here clearly not a white body but a successful body nevertheless, and the mythmaking inherent in Western society about Jewish physical difference. It was just as present in the legends of Jewish difference in southern Africa a hundred years before as it was in the Muslim propaganda concerning the Jews in the 1970s and 1980s.

After Oscar dies, his children discover that his mistress, Elizabeth Marsden, is a sculptress "with a gift for pissing Davids. Young erotic Davids. Fashioned in our father's image" (115). Oscar has become "Jewish" even though it is this mistress who knows Oscar's secret. His mistress "was the only one who really saw that Oscar was not Oscar, smelled his bastard genes, the oily stench of his 'coolie' ancestry" (112). In becoming a Jew, he also becomes one whose success marks him as only superficially "white." Oscar's therapist, Amina Mandelstam, notes that "the name he took—Oscar—defined his personality" (47). It made him into a Jew. It also defined his body, as it did Amina's husband. Her husband was Jewish: "The cripple Jew was being questioned [about Oscar's death]. But there was no photo of him. I wonder what a cripple Jew looks like?" asks one of his relatives (103). The "Jew" is defined by his crippled (circumcised body), but it is also simultaneously the body of the Muslim man.

Hybridity is the centerpiece of this magical realist tale in which the protagonist eventually develops symptoms of an unknown disease, Kafka's curse, that transforms him virtually into a tree, breathing carbon dioxide and expelling oxygen. As with Kafka, as I have argued elsewhere, it is the fantasy of Jewish physical difference that defines the Jew, no matter whether he is "Jewish" or not.[23] Like Coleman Silk, the protagonist of Roth's *The Human Stain*, Oscar becomes a Jew and therefore adapts all of the perceived physical differences of the Jew, giving proof to Jean-Paul Sartre's claim that societies make their own Jews through the discourse of anti-Semitism. The society here, that of apartheid South Africa, roots its image of the Jew in the discourse of a false cosmopolitanism that is merely the world of the "Oriental," here again defined as the Eastern Jew, the *Litvak*, in a Western society. Dangor's image of apartheid South Africa evokes the world of Nazi Germany with all the anxiety about passing. Writing from a postapartheid perspective, Dangor can present the image of the Jew into which his protagonist has transformed himself in the most ironic manner. Yet it is also clear that this transformation, like that of Gregor Samsa, is a failure because of its very necessity.

IV. LONDON AND ITS JEWS

The multicultural views label the Jews as the ultimate victims because of their experience in the Shoah. And this is tied to their difference. Jewish difference is the inability to integrate into a society, to be able to claim true command over language, culture, and physical difference. Sadly, whether through ironic recapitulation or simple repetition, these images are the images that existed prior to the Shoah in Western culture. In Kureishi's world, the Jewish experience is the litmus test for essential difference. In Dangor's world, it is the key to a form of belonging. For Zadie Smith, it becomes something quite different and yet very much the same. Her brilliant first novel, *White Teeth* (2000), is perhaps the most complicated comic novel yet written on the multicultural frontier.[24] Born in northwest London in 1975, she is herself a product of multicultural London. She was born into a mixed-race family; her mother is from Jamaica, and her father is English. A graduate of Cambridge University in English, her first novel has been spectacularly successful. It won awards for Best Book and Best Female Newcomer at the BT Emma (Ethnic and Multicultural Media) Awards, the Guardian First Book Award, the Whitbread Prize for a first novel in 2000, the James Tait Black Memorial Prize for fiction in 2000, the W. H. Smith Book Award for New Talent, the Frankfurt eBook Award for Best Fiction Work Originally Published in 2000, and both the Commonwealth Writers First Book Award and Overall Commonwealth Writers Prize. The operative question that Smith asks in her satire of late twentieth-century England is how can one define "Englishness," and this is much the same project as that of Kureishi. How can one be different without being a victim? And can that difference be a positive rather than a negative quality?

Smith's novel presents a multigenerational account of the development of "Englishness." It begins with the older generation, Archie Jones, who is a working-class Englishman married to a black immigrant from Jamaica, and his friend Samad Iqbal, a Muslim from Bangladesh. They had been friends since they both served in the same tank with the British army in Romania in World War II. The twin sons of Samad (Magid and Millat) and Archie's daughter (Irie), who were all born in England, represent the second generation. All are "foreigners" there because of their visibility and in spite of their seeming hybridity:

This has been the century of strangers, brown, yellow, and white. This
has been the century of the great immigrant experiment. It is only this
late in the day that you can walk into a playground and find Isaac Leung
by the fish pond, Danny Rahman in the football cage, Quang O'Rourke
bouncing a basketball, and Irie Jones humming a tune. Children with
first and last names on a direct collision course. Names that secrete within them mass exodus, cramped boats and planes, cold arrivals, medical
checkups. It is only this late in the day, and possibly only in Willesden,
that you can find best friends Sita and Sharon, constantly mistaken for
each other because Sita is white (her mother liked the name) and Sharon
is Pakistani (her mother thought it best—less trouble). Yet, despite all the
mixing up, despite the fact that we have finally slipped into each other's
lives with reasonable comfort (like a man returning to his lover's bed
after a midnight walk), despite all this, it is still hard to admit that there
is no one more English than the Indian, no one more Indian than the
English. There are still young white men who are angry about that; who
will roll out at closing time into the poorly lit streets with a kitchen knife
wrapped in a tight fist.[25]

The new world of England is a world of hybrids, reflected in their very
names, but it is also a world still dominated by class, for, as we shall see, even
those labeled as "middle class," the Jews, do not really belong to the true
corridors of power in this world.

The economically successful hybrids are not Archie Jones and Samad
Iqbal but the Chalfens, upper middle class, liberal, and the very definition
of "English." "Marcus and Joyce, an aging hippie couple both dressed in
pseudo-Indian garb," are very outspoken at the meeting of parents in the
school attended by all of the children (110). They are successful: "the father is something of an eminent scientist and his mother is a horticulturist"
(252). They are the most "English" people we meet to this point in the
novel. Their Englishness is defined by their class status as well as by their
hippy clothing.

We are very slowly introduced to their son, Joshua Chalfen. At first sight
he is "pasty, practically anemic, curly-haired, and chubby" (226). He is very
white. But he is also revealed to be "Josh-with-the-Jewfro" (247). He is a Jew
if only by the very definition of his body. He too is a hybrid: "a cross pollina-
tion between a lapsed-Catholic horticulturist and an intellectual Jew" (258).

Being Jewish is being a misfit. Joshua is a "smart Jew," an outsider, who immediately identifies Irie as "one of his own" (247). His "own" is a collection of physical misfits with whom the very bright but very tall Irie seems to belong. She is more or less adopted into the Chalfen clan as a sign of their social commitment to racial equality. Liberal, English, and yet visibly different, Joshua and his parents are the cosmopolitan insider as outsider.

The Chalfens ironically interact only with those who have "good genes." And that is, by definition, the Chalfen family, "two scientists, one mathematician, three psychiatrists, and a young man working for the Labour Party." Success becomes the measure by which intelligence is judged. They rarely visit Joshua's maternal grandparents, the Connor clan, "who even now could not disguise their distaste for Joyce's Israelite love-match." Other than Irie, they have no friends (261). The Chalfens are not only hybrids but also "strangers" and "sojourners," no matter how they deny it: "the Chalfens were, after a fashion, immigrants too (third generation, by way of Germany and Poland, né Chalfenovsky).... To Irie, the Chalfens were more English than the English" (273). They are, of course, merely disguised "Orientals," Eastern Jews who appear to fit into this new English world better than most of the other "hybrids." From the very moment of civil emancipation in the eighteenth century, Jews are seen as having a natural mimicry as part of their difference. They can transform themselves into any nation or people. By doing this, they prove that they remain Jews.

Jewish difference is understood as a physical difference. As Joyce notes about her husband's appearance, "[T]hat's Dr. Solomon Chalfen, Marcus's grandfather. He was one of the few men who would listen to Freud.... The first time Marcus showed me that picture, I knew I wanted to marry him. I thought: if my Marcus looks like that at eighty I'll be a very lucky girl" (293). Physical difference trumps everything else. It is seen as palpable, even if it is defined as "beautiful." Joshua is the product of the assimilation of his father into England, represented by the Irish clan of the "Connors." Once you become English, you forfeit any right to be anything else but different:

> These days it feels to me like you make a devil's pact when you walk
> into this country. You hand over your passport at the check-in, you get
> stamped, you want to make a little money, get yourself started ... but
> you mean to go back! Who would want to stay? Cold, wet, miserable;
> terrible food, dreadful newspapers—who would want to stay? In a place

where you are never welcomed, only tolerated. Just tolerated. Like you are an animal finally housebroken. Who would want to stay? But you have made a devil's pact … it drags you in and suddenly you are unsuitable to return, your children are unrecognizable, you belong nowhere. (336)

They have become what Georg Simmel called a sojourner, who cannot belong and who cannot return. Joshua is one of these "sojourner" children who remain different, as his origin is in history, not in geography. His father has no nostalgia for Poland or Germany. He is English, but only from his own perspective and that of the other multicultural figures.

It is twentieth-century Jewish history, specifically the Shoah, that dominates the novel, not the history of Jamaica or the history of South Asia: "Because this is the other thing about immigrants (fugees, emigres, travelers): they cannot escape their history any more than you yourself can lose your shadow" (385). The plot, much too convoluted and funny to recapitulate, reveals that the mad Nazi doctor that Archie Jones and Samad Iqbal were to have captured in Romania, but whom Archie lets escape, is the mastermind behind Marcus Chalfen's plan to manufacture "FutureMouse," a genetically engineered mouse that will live forever. Joshua is seduced into sabotaging the experiment and releasing the mouse by the Keepers of the Eternal and Victorious Islamic Nation, an organization plagued by its "acronym problem"—KEVIN is hardly an alternative to British blandness. The line between the medical experiments at Auschwitz and the attempt to create a perfect human being today is shown to be clear. Marcus turns out to be the "natural" ally of the Nazi because of his emphasis on genetic inheritance and rationality. His actions can only be redeemed by his son, who is misled by sexual desire into opposing his father. At the conclusion of the novel, almost as an afterthought, Zadie Smith has Irie and Joshua marry, for "you can only avoid your fate for so long" (448). Yet Irie's daughter is the offspring of one of Samad's twins. In this play of multiculturalism, it seems that the family who most relied on "genetics" for its identity, the Chalfens, will remain without offspring. It is the old model that the hybrid is sterile. The utopian end to the novel sees the "FutureMouse" scampering away, proving that random hybridity is better than scientific planning but also showing that visibility is the key to defining difference.

The history of the Jews and the medical and eugenic experiments in the Third Reich frame the very definition of difference in Smith's novel. The common history of Archie and Samad is their experience fighting Fascism. The history of the struggle against the Nazis becomes background for the contemporary struggle against homogeneity. The Jews, the victims of the Nazis, become their (unwitting) accomplices at the end of the millennium. Joshua's rebellion against the scientific ideals that his father represented is his means of putting himself, no matter how misunderstood, on the right side of the issue. Yet he remains suspended between all of the groups, not smarter, not more cosmopolitan, not different from them. The transparency of his character shows that he exists more than most other characters in the light of a history, merely an Eastern European Jew not quite aware of his own limitation even though it is literally inscribed on his body.

This focus on the Jew as the background of modern hybrid multiculturalism is continued in Smith's second novel, *The Autograph Man* (2002), in which the protagonist is Alex-Li Tandem, a half-Jewish, half-Chinese autograph trader from the same area of North London where her first novel played.[26] (Here the name is the game: the tandem nature of the character exposes his multicultural identity.) Alex's best friend is Adam Jacobs, who is "a black Harlem Jew from the tribe of Judah" (4). In each of these "cases," hybridity leads not to the resolution of conflict but to its exacerbation. Both young men are inherently unhappy about their conflicted identities.

On the surface, Alex is after the elusive Garbo-like Kitty Alexander, the faded movie star whose signature he covets. And yet this serves as a mask for the revelation, through one of the secondary characters, that all of the puzzle pieces revealed are part of a cabalistic vision of the world and of God. Again, it is the Jew who is revealed to be at the core of the claims of the modern. Cabala, here in the version of Hollywood's newest fad, shows itself to be the key to the autographs so assiduously collected by the protagonist. They are indeed the shards of God. Jewish victimization, Jewish particularism, and Jewish differences define both London and New York in Smith's vision of the multicultural. In this novel the "multicultural" is reduced to the hybrid, as if only the children in *White Teeth* occupy Smith's new world.

Certainly the theme of a hybridity in which that which is Jewish vanishes into the historical mix haunts the recent multicultural novel in the United Kingdom. As a literary response to the fatwa lodged against him, Salman Rushdie published his *The Moor's Last Sigh*, which was on the Booker Prize short list for 1995 and won the Whitbread Book of the Year award for that year. It is a clear, multicultural answer to the fundamentalist claims of those who had condemned his earlier novel on Islam. It tells the history of the wealthy Zogoiby family as narrated by the ultimate Muslim-Jewish-Indian hybrid, Moraes Zogoiby, a young man from Bombay descended from Sultan Muhammad XI, the last Muslim ruler of Andalusia.[27] Deformed, aging prematurely because of Werner's syndrome, he is the pathological product of two worlds, of the Da Gamas' Christian and European ancestors and of the Zogoibys' Indian-Jewish family. He is "a jewholic-anonymous, a cathjew nut, a stewpot, a mongrel cur" (104). Intrinsic to the multiculturalism of this character, who encompasses and links both East and West, is the insularity and assimilation of the Cochin Jews, who vanish in the course of the novel into that new mix that is India. Rushdie's narrative evokes an ancient model of storytelling in which the Jews exist in the past but vanish as the storyteller moves toward the present.

Rushdie's approach presents interesting parallels and contradictions to Amitav Ghosh's *In an Antique Land* (1992) subtitled "History in the Guise of a Traveler's Tale."[28] Here we have the parallel tales of the present-day narrator, a Indian Hindu learning colloquial Arabic in an Egyptian fellaheen village (as Ghosh did in the 1960s), and of Abraham Ben Yiju, a prosperous Tunisian-Jewish merchant living in medieval India and his Indian servant/ slave Bomma. The details of the latter are extracted by the scholar-narrator from (actual) documents found in the Cairo Geniza (manuscript crypt) and published by Ghosh in *Subaltern Studies* as a historical essay.[29] Thus this book claims to be "non-fiction" while still using all of the conventions of modern fiction. Here the reader sees that the present experience of the Indian in Egypt and the medieval past of the Jew in India represent Ghosh's fantasy of the universality of the hybrid, multicultural world of today's London or New York (where the author now lives).

The present tale of the Indian scholar in Egypt replicates the tale of the Jewish merchant in India. Yet there are basic and real differences in Ghosh's imaginary construction of the past. Where the present world is one in which the Indian is quite separate from the world in which he lives, as a good anthropologist would deem to be, the medieval Jew in India not only trusts his Indian slave to represent him abroad but he marries a "native" whom it is imagined "converts" to Judaism (227). Their Jewish children return to Egypt to become judges (328). The Judaism of Ben Yiju, the medieval Jew, is seen by Ghosh as infused with Sufi mystical thought (263). Today's Egypt, at least in the world of the village where the protagonist lives, seems to be essentially Muslim. Yet by the end of the book we are shown that in today's Egypt it is impossible to distinguish between Jewish and Islamic practices and beliefs.

Religion, that force which is believed to divide, is revealed to be the place where hybridity dominates. The "holy men" honored today by the Egyptian villages turn out to be as likely to be Jewish "saints" as Muslim ones (329). Yet this underpinning of today's Muslim world in today's Egypt still makes the Hindu is as exotic as the Jew is imagined to be in medieval India. Ghosh projects his own status on to that of the medieval Jew, seeing his relationship with his Indian slave as a fantasy of his desired relationship with his Muslim neighbors.

India is, of course, seen through Hindu lenses by Ghosh and his protagonist. It is an India of cattle worship and the burning of widows (according to the narrator's ironic account of the Egyptian peasants' image of India) while circumcision, so vital to the self-definition of Islam and Judaism is seen as defining Egyptian "civilization" against Hindi "barbarism." Thus there is the odd exchange between an Egyptian peasant and the scholar protagonist:

> "Of course you have circumcision where you come from, just like we do? Isn't that so, mush kida?"
> I had long been dreading this line of questioning, knowing exactly where it would lead.
> "Some people do," I said. "And some people don't."
> "You mean," he said in rising disbelief, "there are some people in your country who are not circumcised?"
> In Arabic the word "circumcise" derives from a root that means "to purify": to say of someone that they are "uncircumcised" is more or less to call them impure.
> "Yes," I answered, "yes, many people in my country are 'impure.'" I had no alternative; I was trapped by language. (62–3)

But the claims about "purification" comes to reveal the innate "barbarism" of the Muslim in contrast to the Hindu: "The word 'to purify' makes a verbal equation between male circumcision and clitoridectomy, being the same in both cases, but the latter is an infinitely more dangerous operation, since it requires the complete excision of the clitoris. Clitoridectomy is, in fact, hideously painful and was declared illegal..." (203) The Western opposition to the various practices of clitoridectomy in Islam has been one of the defining moments in the twentieth century that distinguished "civilized" from the "uncivilized" behavior.[30] The civilized world is that of the Hindu; the hybrid world of the Egyptian remains beyond the pale of civilization, no matter how hybrid it seems.

Most recently, Vikram Seth's *Two Lives*[31] (2005) presents an autobiographical account of his "Shanti Uncle and Aunty Henny," with whom Seth lived when he came to London in 1969. Shanti was his grandfather's brother who studied dentistry in Germany and then married the daughter of his Berlin Jewish landlady after she came to England in 1939. This is a "true" story relying on in-depth interviews with the uncle and a treasure trove of letters written by his aunt. They have no children, and he assumes the role in this book of their spokesperson. What is striking is that much like the work of another "Indian" writer, Ruth Prawer Jhabvala, herself a Jewish immigrant in the colonial Diaspora, the Jewish immigrant experience in the Diaspora is subsumed to that of the Indian.[32] Indeed as Somini Sengupta notes in a review-article in *The New York Times*, Seth's book "can also be read as an Indian claim to World War II," if not, as seems the case, to the legacy of the Holocaust.[33] Where Jewish was, Indian is—even if the Indian embodied by Seth is the new hybrid, postmodern citizen of the world.

The black experience in the United Kingdom is often reduced to the experience of Caribbean blacks who arrive in a postwar Britain on the verge (it seems) of becoming a multicultural world. Their world is by definition already defined by cultural hybridity. In Andrea Levy's *Small Island* (2004), the world of Jamaica, the birthplace of the novelists' parents, already incorporates the "Jew."[34] The novel, winner of the Whitbread Book of the Year award as well as the Orange Prize for Fiction (2004), is set during and immediately after World War II as Caribbean blacks begin to settle in larger numbers in the United Kingdom. As with *White Teeth*, the war frames the action. It is the racism of the British in their response to all foreigners, but especially the Jews, that introduces racism as the central theme of the novel. The neighborhood, one character laments, is "overrun" by foreigners: "And as for the Jews. They moaned about Jews even after we knew what the poor beggars had been through. They were all right in their own country, Mr. Todd reasoned, but he wanted none of them down our street" (112). What we learn in a flashback is that the male protagonist, Gilbert Joseph, who fought for the "Mother Country" in the RAF during the war and whose tale of postwar life in London frames the novel, is appalled at being called an "anthropoid." "I looked to the dictionary to find the meaning of this word used by Hitler and his friends to describe Jews and coloured men. I got a punch in the head when the implication jumped from the page and struck me: 'resembling a human but primitive like an ape.' Two whacks I got. For I am a black man whose father was born a Jew" (129). And indeed, part of the background to Levy's construction of Gilbert Joseph's character is that his father was "a circumcised member of the Jewish faith" who converted to Christianity in the trenches of World War I when he literarily "shared a tin of fish with [Jesus] and lent him some writing paper" (130). His conversion branded him as an outcast whose co-religionists turned their backs on him: "I can know if a man is a Jew from his rear" (130). From the standpoint of his black wife, he is "nearly white," and she was "pleased to be parading around" with him (130). He has nine children; one of his sons is the protagonist.

Levy has the sacrifice of the family in their enthusiasm for the mother country be predicated on the anti-Semitism felt by his family in their own world, the world of white Jamaican Anglicanism: "The picture in the newspaper was of a German Jew. He wore a cloth star on a dirty coat. He walked along a street, hunched and humbled, while non-Jews eyed him with an expression of disgust Lester [his brother] and I knew too well from those Sunday services. With the fervour of a crusade my brother wanted to fight this war" (130–31). This belief in a struggle against racism empowers the figures in the novel, who are confronted, as the reader has already seen, by the day-to-day racism of the "small island" when they settle in London after the war. The Jews are in a complex way surrogates for this racism and literally, through the model of hybridity, become part of the struggle of the blacks in Levy's novel for recognition as full human beings.

They are also failures as opposed to the Afro-Caribbean characters. The image of the "hunched and humbled" Jew, like that in Kureishi's "illiterate tiny men with downcast eyes and mismatched clothes," signals those ground down by oppression. Thus, George Joseph's Jewish father is a failure at everything, having internalized the racism of his Jamaican world. When an aunt comes to reclaim her son, who was being raised with his family, the father's comforting words are "that he could now rest easy because he was certainly not Jewish" (198). His decline into drunkenness leaves it to his wife and family to successfully launch a bakery, which supplies money for the child to study. Indeed, George Joseph's powerful moral position in regard to the racism he finds in Britain and his self-reliance are the reflection of his mother's and not his father's response to racism. As with the Jewish father in *White Teeth*, in the end he is revealed to be a failure, and this failing is tied here to his Jewishness.

In the world of Muslim South Asian writers, hybridity is replaced by a sense of cultural diversity, but one that functions in relationship to a mythic past as well as to the present. Grittier than *White Teeth* is the world of London's East End represented in Monica Ali's *Brick Lane* (2003), one of the best-selling novels by and about South Asians that has appeared after 2000.[35] (It was short-listed for the Mann Booker Prize in 2003.) The novel chronicles the life of Nazneen from her birth in what is now Bangladesh to her life in the East End. It is a novel of education in which culture and sexuality are linked. The Jews too play an odd role in framing the quality of the multicultural world into which Nazneen eventually enters from her linguistic and cultural isolation. At the very beginning of the novel's image of London, a group of women living in a council flat [public housing] are depicted sitting about bemoaning the fact that one of them has gone to work: "'The husband is working but still she cannot fill her stomach. In Bangladesh one salary can feed twelve, but Jorina cannot fill her stomach.' 'Where is she going? To the garment factory?' 'Mixing with all sorts: Turkish, English, Jewish. All sorts. I am not old-fashion.... But if you mix with all these people, even if they are good people, you have to give up your culture to accept theirs. That's how it is'" (29). Here the Jew represents the danger of the multicultural world that will entice Muslims into leaving their faith and altering their identity. It is central to understand that the "Jews" here are part of the present, part of the danger that lurks beyond Brick Lane.

At the very end of the novel, this topic reappears. Nazneen's lover, Karim, is fomenting a crowd in Brick Lane to political action. Chanu, Nazneen's husband, hears him and tells her about the flux of immigrants in the East End, oblivious to his own exposure as a cuckold. He has failed at everything in London and is about to return to Bangladesh: "Do you know how many immigrant populations have been here before us? In the eighteenth century the French Protestants fled here, escaping Catholic persecution. They were silk weavers. They made good. One hundred years later, the Jews came. They thrived.... Which way is it going to go?" (463–64). There is no question, given the trajectory of the novel, that the children (and the wives) will adapt. It is only the fathers who fail. But here the Jews are an artifact of the past. They are not working the factories—this would be a sign of failure—they have moved on up to a better world, a more affluent one, perhaps that of *White Teeth*.

V. GERMANS AND JEWS—AND AMERICA

Multiculturalism in Germany, a country that imagined itself for much of the nineteenth century as a homogeneous society (with Simmel's "strangers" in its midst), is politically correct and very avant-garde. Of all the self-consciously "multicultural" writers in Germany, Thomas Meinecke is perhaps the most explicit in terms of the function that he sees the figure of the Jew playing in the modern, multicultural world. For Meinecke the Jew must be part of the multicultural mix. Born in 1955 in Hamburg and now living in a small town in Bavaria, Meinecke is the author of a series of novels that employ the notion of the hybrid as the ideal for the contemporary world. His first novel, the winner of the Heimito-von-Doderer prize for young novelists in 1997, was *The Church of John F. Kennedy* (1996), which chronicles a young German's car trip from New Orleans to Amish country. What is striking about this first novel, a novel of travel and education in the older model of Laurence Sterne and Jean Paul, is its extraordinary humor in dealing with the complex hybridity of American society. Meinecke places his protagonist into this mix by stressing the often forgotten role of the Germans in the American mix. He highlights this suppressed role by quoting throughout the novel passages from letters and diaries of nineteenth- and twentieth-century German immigrants to America. These authentic texts comment, like snapshots, on the world that the protagonist (and the author) visits at the end of the twentieth century. Jews figure throughout this novel as part of the mix that defines America.

In his novel *Tomboy* (1998), Meinecke addresses the question of the slipperiness of gender designations. (He had begun this already in his long novella *Wood* [*Holz*] of 1988, in which a Jewish bisexual figure is introduced as one of the central characters.) Employing the work of the American professor of Talmud, Daniel Boyarin, on masculinity and Jewish identity, the question of what makes a man a man centers on Boyarin's definition of the Jew. In addition, Meinecke introduces the figure of Judith Butler, Boyarin's colleague at the University of California, Berkeley, as one of his pivotal figures. Lesbian, Jewish, and a strong advocate of the notion that all gender is performative, Butler serves as the key to the novel's concern with the construction of gender identity. Rarely has multicultural theory been appropriated in such a direct way in modern fiction. Again, it is the Jew who serves as the fulcrum for Meinecke's observations about the flexibility of gender.

Meinecke's recent novel, *Bright Blue* (*Hellblau*; 2001), does much the same thing with ideas of ethnicity and multiculturalism as *Tomboy* undertook with gender. Again set in America, the novel deals with the question of how ethnicity and race are defined. His initial question relates to Mariah Carey, the pop singer: is she white or black? She has a black father and a white mother, but what is she actually? Society sees her as black, and yet she is a hybrid. In Meinecke's fiction, the question of race eventually focuses on the Jews. Boyarin and I serve as touchstones for this question. The Jewish body appears to define difference as much as does the "black" body of Mariah Carey.

What happens in a world defined by hybridity, in which all groups intermix with each other and yet maintain some sense of difference, to those groups that hold themselves apart? Meinecke picks up on the debate, outlined in chapter 7 of this book, about the genetic illness of the Jews. His protagonist and friends ruminate about the idiosyncrasies of the Orthodox Jews of Borough Park. One tells that researchers at the Johns Hopkins University had discovered the breast cancer gene, the result of "century old religious rules." What happens to such self-isolating groups, the character notes, is that their very isolation increases their risk of disease and eventual extinction. Jews, or even those bearing a Jewish name, come to bear the stigma of these illnesses. Indeed, in 1998, the Satamer Rabbi Joseph Eckstein ordered the dissolution of more than two hundred marriages because both partners carried the gene for the same genetically transmitted disease. "The majority of these," the character notes, "would not have originally voluntarily married one another."[36] Arranged marriages within the group "cause" genetic illness, and thus those who most want to avoid the "healthy" mixing of a hybrid culture are condemned to eventually vanish.

VI. MULTICULTURALISM IN THE USA—AND THE JEWS

Certainly the most striking recent literary representation of the anxiety about identification with the "Jews" in an American context (beyond African-American literature) is to be found in Gish Jen's novel *Mona in the Promised Land* (1996).[37] Jen ironically comments on the Chinese-American

construction of the acculturation of "Jews" and "Asians." Set in suburban Scarsdale in 1968, the novel chronicles the adolescence of a Chinese-
American woman whose family moves into a "Jewish" neighborhood in its
quest for upward social mobility. Their neighbors are "rich and Jewish":
"they're the New Jews, after all, a model minority and Great American
Success. They know they belong in the promised land" (3). The protagonist identifies strongly with the Jews in her peer group and sees her body
in terms of their own anxiety about their physical visibility. The Chinese
desire in this novel to become a "model minority" like the Jews. And this is
measured by their economic and cultural success.

One day she and her friends sit around and discuss aesthetic surgery.
"'Do Chinese have operations to make their noses bigger?' someone asks"
(92). Yes, Mona replies: "'She too envies the aquiline line ... in fact she
envies even their preoperative noses.' ... 'You can't mean like this schnozz
here?' somebody says, exhibiting his profile.... She nods politely." "And
your eyes too." She continues to explain that Chinese Americans often have
"operations to make single-fold eyelids into double-folds." In the course of
this discussion, Gish Jen supplies an ironic environmental explanation of
how and why "Oriental" eyes have their specific form, but concludes with
a comment by one of the Jewish boys about Mona's eyes: "You look like
straight out of Twilight Zone" (93). The exoticism of the "too small" nose
and the "too Oriental" eyes for the Jews is a clear marker of their sense of
their own difference.

It is no surprise in this world as seen from Gish Jen's perspective that
it is not Mona who gets the new nose or Western eyes: "Barbara Gugelstein
is sporting a fine new nose. Straight, this is, and most diminutive, not to
say painstakingly fashioned as a baby-grand tchotchke" (124). While Mona
"admires her friend's nostrils, which are a triumph of judiciousness and
taste," she herself is not moved to have aesthetic surgery. What Mona does
is to convert to Judaism! But, as one of the African-American characters
disparagingly comments, becoming a Jew in religion but not physically is
difficult in her world, for in order to be a "real" Jew "that nose of yours has
got to grow out so big you've got to sneeze in a dish towel" (137). Jewishness
means belonging to a visible outsider group. For Mona this has become an
insider group, which defines her sense of her own body. The role of aesthetic
surgery is to reshape the external visibility of that group. Yet, as the novel
shows, it is a sign of false acculturation. Barbara's nose job is faulty; it "runs

extraordinarily when she cries" (237). Jews with short noses remain marked as Jews in this seemingly hostile world, and the Chinese, such as Mona's physician sister, acculturate with the rise of multiculturalism by becoming "Asian American," a form of the alteration of identity without the alteration of the body. Happiness is becoming something else, something identifiable as "Asian" which is not too "Chinese."

Yet Jewish visibility does not simply remain as the sign of success. It is haunted by history. Early in the novel, Mona's mother tries to explain to her about the Japanese invasion of China when she announces that she has a Japanese boyfriend: "Are you sure? In school, they said the War was about putting the Jews in ovens" (15). For Mona, it is the Shoah that defines the past. Later in the novel the success of both the Chinese and the Jews is measured against those, such as the African Americans, who are shown to be in a permanently liminal position in American society. History fixes the positions of the Jews and the "wanna-be" Jews, such as Mona—just as in Senoçak's novel, Sascha Muchteschem, who I discussed in the opening chapter, is condemned on a talk show as a "Wannabe-German" (130). The more one wants to belong, the more the dominant society in these tales knows its own value and the "fact" of the protagonist's true difference. In complex ways, that is the moral of Gish Jen's account of the "Asians" as a "model minority" in the United States. Hybridity leads to assimilation and a loss of individual identity, even when a character such as Sascha Muchteschem actually has a dual cultural inheritance.

Fitting into American society means having the right kind of nose. In the fictional world representing the imaginary body of the American Jew, the retroussé "Oriental" nose comes to be an ideal. But for the Chinese American, according to Gish Jen's portrait, it is a sign of the new "Asian" identity. One nose *does* fit all. There, aesthetic surgery is a sign of middle-class rather than American identity, though one could argue that there is a fatal parallelism between these two ideas of imagining oneself as different. Thus, among Asian Americans in California, double eyelid surgery has become "the gift that parents offer their daughters when they graduate from high school or college."[38] This parallels the experience of Jewish Americans in the 1960s. For the Vietnamese and Koreans in America, aesthetic surgery becomes a means of defining identity as flexible rather than permanent. Hybridity means now reshaping the body to make it more American. Yet the end result is not an American body but an Asian-American body. The diasporic body remains marked as different and, just as "black" became "beautiful" in the 1960s, so too is Asian beautiful today.

This Asian-American take on the inclusion of the Jews into the new multicultural world has a flip side. While Gish Jen's world is that of the Chinese American in the 1960s, Chang-rae Lee's *Native Speaker* (1995) looks at a rising Korean-American urban culture in the 1990s.[39] Here the theme is replacement and displacement of language and culture. The Korean Americans are entering into the social and political arena in emulation of but also as a replacement of the "Jews." In a flashback the Korean-American protagonist Harry Park is shown working in his father's store on Madison Avenue in the 1980s. The other employees are all Korean natives. Indeed he is the only native speaker of English in the store, but he, to spite his father who wants him to quote Shakespeare to the customers, "grunted my best Korean to the other men." As a Korean speaker, he was invisible: "I could even catch a rich old woman whose tight strand of pearls pinched in the sags of her neck whispering to her friend right behind me: 'Oriental Jews'" (53). The Koreans have become the Jews in the sense of a commercially obsessed and isolated community that could never share the cultural values of the white middle class. But this sense is also present in those other immigrant groups that the Koreans have now displaced. Park's "WASP" boss in the "detective agency" that employs him as an undercover operative notes, "My pop owned three swell pubs but he died broke and drunk. The Jews squeezed him first, then the wops, then people like you. Am I sore? No way. It doesn't matter how much you have. You can own every fucking Laundromat or falafel cart in New York, but someone is always bigger than you" (46). The process of displacement seems natural, but, as with the experience with the "rich old woman," there is not a hint that power also devolves to the new groups. The politics of New York City are a surface politics of replacement and displacement, while the true power remains always in the hands of the establishment. Each group seems to envy the newcomer: "it's the Jew envious of the new Korean money" (260). The reality is that the envy creates a desire to protect the gains made by the earlier immigrants—especially the Jews. Park's own experience seems to be similar to that of the Jews. Is he not an "Oriental Jew"? His immigrant parents raised him in a city apartment above their store until there was enough money to move into the suburbs: "we silent partners of the bordering WASPs and Jews, never rubbing them except with a smile" (53). In the suburbs, they are different. They are si-lent, a stereotype of the "Oriental," but also a sign of the anxiety about claiming American culture. This silence marks Harry Park's relationship to the multicultural world and his envy of it: "I used to wish that I were more like my Jewish and Italian friends, or even the black kids who hung out in front of my father's stores; I was envious of how they'd speak so confidently, so jubilantly celebrate the fact with their hands and hips and tongues" (182). The Jews are part of the new multicultural America.

Park marries a Caucasian woman and they have a son, Mitt, who dies tragically in the novel. But Mitt, suspended between two worlds, a hybrid, is an outsider in the suburban world where the division between cultures is a powerful one: "the other kids would have more ammo against Mitt, they were all just Westchester white boys, some of them Jews. Maybe Mitt could say 'kike' (which he did once in the house until Lelia cracked him hard on the ass) or else pretty much nothing.... Because there isn't anything good to say to the average white boy to make him feel small" (243). But is it not the case that calling a Jew a "kike" does "make him feel small"? Is there not a difference, unstated by the protagonist, between all of the other whites in suburbia and the Jews? Is it that they try too hard to be white? Should they have remained isolated in their Jewish enclaves so ably satirized in Philip Roth's *Goodbye, Columbus* (1959)? There is a geographic boundary—in the novel, it is Connecticut—where the Koreans (like the Jews of an earlier day in Gish Jen's world) can escape back into a world populated by Koreans: "Maybe Connecticut Koreans are too distant, perhaps they have more mon-ey or class than other Koreans. They send the kids to private day schools and drive expensive 4X4s and they belong to country clubs that have no blacks and no Jews" (278). Here they emulate or perhaps parody the world of the WASPs, where no ugly word can harm them. But this world is paralleled in New York City by the neighborhood at Forty-first and Parsons, where the Korean community is "lodged in converted row apartments dating from the fifties, when the population was still Italian and Irish and Jewish. Now the signs are all in Korean" (315). It is language, which separates in this world as surely as the meanings attached to the body, that defines Gish Jen's Long Island. But in this multicultural world, it is a defining factor that is infinitely malleable and changeable. What defines difference here is the ability of the Jews to slide into language and become—at least in their fantasy—white and thus "real" Americans.

If Gish Jen's Long Island posits the Jews as an ironic norm of beauty ("Jewish is beautiful"), Oscar Hijuelos's novel of Havana, *A Simple Havana Melody (from When the World Was Good)*, presents a Cuban-American fantasy of the Jewish body.[40] It echoes the physical difference of the Jews and the impact of the Holocaust in a way more than slightly reminiscent of Achmat Dangor's novella "Kafka's Curse." Hijuelos was born in 1951 of Cuban parentage in New York City and has received the Pulitzer Prize and numerous other awards for earlier fiction that stressed the theme of Cuban culture seen through American eyes. The protagonist of this novel, Israel Levis, is a pious Catholic, "an individual, blessed by a Catholic God," who composes the hit song "Rosas Puras" in the 1930s. At the opening of the novel we see him having now returned to Havana, old and very ill, after the war: "On his arm seven numbers in green ink" (23). He has been in Buchenwald. How he got there is at the heart of this fiction.

In his own fantasy Levis had assumed that he, "a Cuban Catholic with a name like Israel Levis, was immune to the terrors descending upon the Jews of Europe" (37). Hijuelos stresses in the novel (following Jean-Paul Sartre's fantasy in the late 1940s) that anyone could be made into a Jew, and yet Levis is in complex ways already "Jewish" before he confronts Nazi racism in the 1940s. His name is redolent of his hidden nature, for though his family "had been for generations, quite irretrievably Catholic," he may well have had a "distant Catalan ancestor, who may or may not have had some Jewish blood" (49). He is Catholic in all senses, but that in Spanish or Cuban terms can also mean that he is multicultural. His "Jewish" ancestor (real or not) marks him as different. Yet the Jew in his lineage is much closer. After his father (and siblings) die, his mother, in a moment of madness, announces to him, "'My son, the idea has come to me that perhaps your father was a Jew. And that is why God has been acting so cruelly to us.' Then: 'We must make up for this with our prayers'" (81). The Jew is the victim, the one who is punished for having crucified Jesus, and who will be punished in all eternity.

It is not just Israel Levis's lineage that marks him as the hidden Jew but also, even more so, his body. Thin and emaciated when he returns to Cuba after the war, he was equally huge before the war. Indeed his nickname then was "El Gordo," the fat one, but most extraordinary about his body was the exaggerated size of his penis. Even when he was a small child, "the manifestation of his future virility [was such] that their housemaid, Florencia, when bathing him often remarked, 'What a wonder!'" (53). And yet, as he matures, his sexuality is extraordinarily compromised even though his body is highly sexualized. Attracted to men but obsessed with the singer Rita Valladrares, he can only "perform" with prostitutes. His ambiguous sexuality points to a reading of his physical size as an indicator of his difference. Only much later, when he moves to Paris in 1932 to escape Havana and his mother, does the huge Israel Levis find love and sexual satisfaction with a Jewish woman named Sarah Rubenstein. It is with her that he is for the first time fully sexual as a male.

Israel's stay in Paris brings him in direct conflict with the Nazis. While his music is "degenerate," it is also very popular (254). With the fall of France in the spring of 1940, suddenly Israel Levis, whose ancestry and body imply something "Jewish" in the Cuban context created by Oscar Hijuelos, is transformed into a Jew by the Nazis. He aids Sarah and her daughter in escaping from Paris, but he remains there ensconced at the Grand Hotel, which has become one of the Germans' headquarters. He goes to mass each day at Notre Dame, as a good Catholic should. He remains popular. He performs at parties, at one of which he meets the head of the Paris Gestapo, who speaks to him in Spanish, noting that he had heard him many years ago in Vienna (273). With the beginning of the terror against "foreign" Jews, his Cuban passport is seized. He is ordered to come to the Gestapo because of his evident "Jewish" name. It labels him as a Jew. But we the readers know that he is not one, whatever the multicultural references to his "Jewishness" have been in the novel to that point. The questioning quickly turns to the heart of the matter, to Levis's physical difference, to his penis. To this point, only its size has been revealed to the reader. At the Gestapo's inquisition, he is asked if he is circumcised: "It happened that with his birth his father, Doctor Leocadio Levis, had thought of the minor operation as a preventative against the possibility of cradle-borne infections" (275). His claim that he was not a Jew was dismissed: "The police were amused—how could any man with a name like Israel Levis be anything but a Jew, no matter what his protests?" (275). Even more so, his "Jewish" body reveals his true nature to them. He is to be placed on a train to the death camps, only to be "rescued" by the Gestapo general, who has him sent to Buchenwald, where he plays for the guards. There he has a special status, as he plays for the camp officers on a "grand Bosendorfer piano under an enormous chandelier and gilded ceiling" (37). Still, the horrors of the camp turn his huge body into a shell, a survivor.

The novel, a Cuban-American novel of Havana, becomes a novel of the Cuban as Holocaust survivor. The multicultural image of the Jew remains that of the ultimate victim. The Cuban history that marks him, such as the political despotism of the Cuban dictatorship of Gerardo Machado, is paralleled to the rise of the Nazis. The random murders in Havana that drive Levis to Paris foreshadow the street brawls and beatings of the Jews that he sees on a trip to Munich. The elision between the Cuban, seen through the eyes of the Cuban-American writer, and the Jew in the Shoah is as complete. For the American reader and writer, the Jew is a sign of the Holocaust. The Holocaust also defines the victim status of the protagonist. All of his difference is that of the Jew. The imaginary Jew is again a disguise for the multicultural experience of the victim. The Jew truly does not exist, except in the fantasy of the persecutors. Israel Levis takes on the mantle of the Jew in this American multicultural novel. His actual difference as a fat man, as a bisexual man, and as a creative genius is in the end defined by his difference as a Jew.

VII. LOOKING AT MULTICULTURALISM AGAIN

We began with Kureishi's identification of the Jew as marked to be permanently different. In the United Kingdom Kureishi saw, at least in his fantasy of the 1960s, a particularly good example of a culture in which the transition to a multicultural, perhaps even hybrid, society had begun from what had been perceived as a purely class-based society. The Jew at this point was the litmus test for immutability and difference. By the mid-twentieth century British Jews, as opposed to "immigrant" Jews, had made it into the highest reaches of the British class structure. Assimilation, even conversion, marked their path from Benjamin Disraeli to the Rothschilds. And yet they remained "foreign" even in their movement up the class ladder.

The multicultural writer seems able to observe the complexity of a world in which the "Jews" seem to be omnipresent. Whether in examining the problem of Diaspora, of acculturation, of hybridity, or of risk, the "Jews" become the touchstone for all of the pitfalls that present themselves to other cultural groups. The Jews are either the ultimate victim, because of the Shoah, or the worst case for assimilation, as in the image of the false success of those German and American Jews that we have seen. Contemporary "Jewish" multicultural writers, as we shall see, tend to amalgamate their image into that of the multicultural world in which the Jews are just one more culture in the multicultural salad bowl. Non-Jewish multicultural writers are torn between the image of the Jews as victims and as the most successful minority community. This is especially the case when they themselves are part of a group (such as the East Asians or South Asians) that seems to be repeating at least part of the paradigm by becoming successful in the Diaspora. Multiculturalism, as a brand label, seems to work best if (like naturalism) it focuses on economic liminality. In such cases the authenticity of the representation of the group as well as their image of the Jews is guaranteed to the reader by the claims by the writer (or the publisher) of the writer's ethnicity. In such claims of an authentic representation of the experiences or desires of the multicultural writer, the Jews are an odd case precisely because of the Shoah. Hegel could not understand why the Jews continued to exist as a people, while their contemporaries from the Babylonians to the Romans had vanished; so, too, it seems impossible to imagine the Jews as anything but a symbol for death and destruction after the Shoah. This contrasts in an often bizarre manner with the very notion of Jewish success. Thus the Shoah looms always in the background, signaling the inherent difference of the Jews from all other groups. This becomes sort of a form of Holocaust envy signaled by the attempt to place the experiences of such multicultural ethnic worlds as at risk from the same fate or indeed having had an analogous historical experience. The multicultural universe, as constructed from a self-consciously non-Jewish perspective, needs to have the Jew present for its own purposes.

TEN

ARE JEWS MULTICULTURAL ENOUGH?
Late Twentieth- and Early Twenty-First-Century Literary Multiculturalism as Seen from Jewish Perspectives

I. A NEW JEWISH WRITING?

It should be of little surprise that Jews today—with multiple national, cultural, linguistic, class, and gender identities—desire to imagine that what constitutes their own "Jewishness" is seemingly independent of anti- or philo-Semitic images. Yet it is very clear that today, at least within Jewish diasporic literary culture, those images are often framed by the debates about multiculturalism. And yet, as I have shown, by the end of the twentieth century the various global discourses about multiculturalism marginalize the "Jews" while often using the Jewish experience as one of the models for the multicultural.[1] This is even more the case in contemporary Germany, where the legacy of the Holocaust and the model of American Jewry have structured the very notion of a multicultural world. "Multi-kulti" is the newest buzzword providing a liberal fantasy for the "new Germany."[2] In that fantasy, the Jewish aspect is often reduced to nostalgia or liminality. The multicultural presence of Jews of all definitions in the new Germany is less visible than klezmer bands and 1930s Yiddish films. Yet there is a growing presence of German-language Jewish writers in Germany whose Jewish identity is part of their Russian identity. They became Jews by becoming German and thus are thought of as Russian. Indeed one of my students in Berlin, when I taught one of their books, was amazed that the author was, according to his own account, Jewish, since his Russian persona belied the student's image of what a "Jewish" writer could or should be.

No place is more appropriate for such thought experiments about the nature of identity in a utopian society than the world of contemporary writing. Among Jewish authors (a term that we still must define), there has been an anxiety about the meanings associated with place, for good or for ill, since the Holocaust. Theodor Adorno claimed in *Minima Moralia* that "dwelling, in the proper sense, is now impossible. The traditional residences we grew up in have grown intolerable ... the house is past ... it is part of morality not to be home in one's home."[3] Yet the claims of multiculturalism beginning with the early twentieth century are that this rupture would be healed. Certainly the claims of Zionism echoed that desire. The multicultural world has the special quality of creating the illusion of a complete world in which all of the various problems and identities would be able to be worked out— with utopian or catastrophic conclusions. The social results in these fictions may have little or no impact in the lived lives of the non-Jewish authors or that projection called the "Jews."

In this chapter, I shall examine examples of the contemporary rise of a multicultural discourse with all of its complexity within the fictional worlds of self-identified Jewish writers. "Multiculturalism" is that brave new world in which the real or perceived boundaries among peoples would be resolved. Contemporary multicultural theory echoes the earlier use of "race" in thinking about multiculturalism along the jagged boundary of "race" that frames contemporary literary studies and in which the Jews are simply dismissed as "white." They had become white in the Diaspora after the Holocaust and were thus able to take a place in the mainstream of American and European letters. Having become "white," they were quickly lumped with the forces of patriarchy and oppression by the new voices of multiculturalism. Their "whiteness" seems to deny them any presence in a world of hybridity defined by skin color as a key to cultural difference. Thus in Anita Desai's self-consciously ironic *Baumgartner's Bombay* (1988) the narrator observes that her German-Jewish protagonist exiled in post-partition India will always be different: "In Germany he had been dark — his darkness had marked him the Jew, *der Jude*, in India he was fair — and that marked him the *firanghi* [foreigner]." The difference of the Jew as outsider, indeed as pariah, seems to be doubly marked and indelible, no matter what his context. In the world of the South Asian, non-Jewish Diaspora (in which Desai writes and wrote) this is understood as a double alienation.[4]

Yet the multicultural is also the antithesis of hybridity in its idea of cultural pluralism. Horace Kallen's early view of the Jews as possessing primarily a cultural rather than national identity has shifted radically today, where among many non-Jewish multicultural writers the fantasy of a monolithic "Zionism" has become the enemy of the "multicultural." While multiculturalism can allow for, and indeed celebrate, the merging of cultures so as to eliminate boundaries, one of its strongest claims (in the new global culture that is both hybrid and multicultural) is its insistence that each of us has a "culture" in a reified ethnic or class sense. And often the word used is "race." Yet central to both models of multiculturalism is that "culture" is the basis for our identities. "Biological" difference, the difference explicit in the older and some of the present views of "race," can be displaced onto a symbolic, cultural level even while the word "race" is used. At the same moment, this "authentic" cultural heritage is commodified and thus made available for all consumers. Indeed, "authenticity has become the key term for post-modern reconstructions and 'renewals' of Jewish identity."[5] Simultaneously the recent discussions about "race" in medicine in chapter 2 are but the latest reappearance of a discredited but often evoked category of authenticity that attempts to replace cultural categories.

Self-identified Jewish writers today struggle with variations of both models of the multicultural—one in which things Jewish come to be interchangeable with all other qualities of all cultures and with the sense that "being Jewish" is simply analogous to all other ethnicities, religious practices, and secular beliefs. Indeed, the simple fact that being Jewish has no single common denominator (culturally, religiously, or politically) makes the very consensus of what is "Jewish" within the model of multiculturalism impossible to specify.

There is a powerful, newer literature across the world that desires to be multicultural, but in its own "Jewish" voice. It is the impossibility of defining this "voice" that is at the heart of the Jewish anxiety about all forms of multiculturalism in which the claim for authenticity is central. Recently Michael P. Kramer has attempted to provide a set of criteria to define

"Jewish" literature.[6] For him, Jewish literature is literature either written by Jews (however defined) or evidencing specific culture-based Jewish criteria. Such a literature can be written in what is agreed upon through consensus as a Jewish language, but as such it may well not deal with any Jewish questions or indeed even be written by a Jew (pace the Hebrew fiction of Anton Shammas). It may focus on the fantasies of Jewish characters or emerge from a fictional recounting of Jewish historical experience. It may thus be anti-iconic (Geoffrey Hartman), liturgical (Cynthia Ozick), therapeutic and prophetic (Leslie Fiedler), marked by laughter and trembling (Saul Bellow), or even marked by the absence of any common language, territory, or culture (Sacvan Bercovitch) (298). Variants of these views are and have been answered by or incorporated into the contemporary discussions of multiculturalisms and the Jews. Kramer, on the other hand, states that "to be considered a Jewish writer, in my view, one need not use a 'Jewish' language, or exhibit certain 'Jewish' literary characteristics, or address certain 'Jewish' subjects, or even know how to ask the 'Jewish' question. One need only be a writer of Jewish extraction, a member of the Jewish race" (290). Or, "We cannot escape race, not if we insist on a category called 'Jewish literature'" (313). "Race" seems to demand to be translated as ethnicity rather than biology, but it does have strong echoes of both the earlier use by Kallen and the more recent use in the discourse of multiculturalism. Kramer's article was followed by critical responses from other literary scholars in the field for whom the confusion between ethnicity and that horrid, dated, frightening category of "race" needed to be teased apart (322–49). Kramer clearly conflates and confuses "extract" and "race": whereas the former does not necessarily contain a biological sense, the latter does. And yet there is a heavy, meaningful, and nonreductive use of "race" within the claims of multiculturalisms, especially in the nonhybrid presentations of the multicultural. For all of its claims of culture as the basis for multiculturalism, the ghost of race haunts much of this literature.

The great answer to the idea of "race" remains that of "ethnicity." "Ethnicity," as W. Lloyd Warner and Paul Lunt noted in 1942, subsumes and is subsumed by other categories such as religion.[7] Lapsed (i.e., secular) American Irish Catholic writers such as James Farrell can simultaneously be all three in their writing. One can make an equivalent claim for James Farrell's contemporary, the Yiddish writer Sholem Asch. Here is the difference between the image of the Jew and the image of the Muslim in the West.

Olivier Roy notes, "The term 'Jewish' can also refer to non-believing and non-practicing persons. In this sense it is also an ethnic marker, closer to a racial category. But the symmetry [between Jew and Muslim] stops there. A Jew who has turned Catholic is often still perceived as a Jew (for example, Cardinal Lustiger in France), a Muslim turned Christian will be less easily dubbed a Muslim (for example, Carlos Menem, [Rudolf] Nuriyev)."[8] Can one, or will one, be able to speak of a Muslim (or a Turkish or a Pakistani) Diaspora writer as culturally hybrid between "Muslim" (or Turkish or Pakistani) and English (or German or French) cultures?

Kramer's seemingly tautological definition of the Jewish writer ("one need only be a Jew to write Jewish literature") is at the core of all Jewish engagement with modern multiculturalism. It subsumes without denying all of the other formal or content definitions of Hartman, Ozick, or Fiedler. More importantly, it refuses to acknowledge that in the United States and much of Europe after the Shoah, "Jewish" became primarily a religious rather than an ethnic label because of the abuse of "race" during the Holocaust. The image of the Jew as defined by religious identity (rather than political, ethnic, or cultural) was dominant. Today all meanings are again in play as part of the thought experiment that composes Jewish writing. Such problems seem to be of the nature of Diaspora identity—and indeed, from Georg Simmel to the present, one of the litmus tests of "ethnicity" is the question of assimilation (biographical, cultural, geographical, linguistic, and biological) into unfriendly and different worlds. But in the case of Jewish writing, this has always been the model. Indeed, multiculturalism in Israel follows precisely this trajectory.

Within modern Jewish writing, the multicultural adopts multiple, often contradictory stances. The problem of hybridity is ironically presented in the Jewish Francophone novelist and scriptwriter Philippe Blasband's short story "A True Exile" ("Une exil véritable").[9] Born in 1964 in Teheran to a Jewish family, he was educated in Brussels. His first book, a long and detailed autobiographical novel, won the Rossel prize in 1990. In this ironic monologue, we seem to have a similar set of expectations. The narrator, speaking to his friend who seems to be mired in a false nostalgia for a lost Iran, describes himself as having a Belgian father, a Belgian passport, and French as the mother tongue; he professes ignorance of most things Iranian. Yet he is, in his account, the perfect hybrid, the man between two worlds who has begun to integrate his Iranian ethnicity into his sense of Belgian identity. This

Belgian identity is clearly Walloon; it is French in all its aspects, and thus it masks the split that still haunts Belgian culture today, a split that equates ethnicity and language, for the choice of becoming truly Belgian means for him becoming French speaking rather than Flemish speaking. At the close of this monologue, he defines himself yet again as "not a bad Iranian, not much of an Iranian at all, neither truly Belgian, nor truly a Jew" (109). This is the fantasy of the Jew as "merely" part of the multicultural mix, a mix defined as Francophone and thus beyond the struggle for linguistic hegemony that is still modern Belgium. This ironic simplification seems to be possible only when an author like Blasband has also written a novel on the fate of a Jewish family who moves from Teheran to Brussels.[10] It reflects the old joke about a pitched battle between French and Flemish speakers in Belgium during the 1960s in which both sides are separated by the police, who order the Walloons to one side of the street and the Flemish to the other. A Jew walks up to a policeman and asks, "And where do we Belgians go?" The answer, in the discourse of contemporary multiculturalism, is "Any place you want, but not here."

Contemporary Jewish identity, at least that as self-defined by Jewish writers, provides an answer to the economic liminality ascribed to the multicultural—it is the role of the ultimate victim. David Biale, stressing the performativity of Jewish identity, stresses the irony in "the success of the American Jewish community in building a Holocaust museum on the Mall." It was "as if by transferring the European genocide to America" that American Jews could sustain the old image as "the chosen minority," yet "only a group securely part of the majority," Biale noted, "could institutionalize its history in this way."[11] The Jews are also an odd case precisely because of the Shoah. This is so very different from the tortured voices of the earlier generations of Jews living in multi-"racial," if not multicultural, environments. Thus the distanced and self-critical voice of Hanif Kureishi's "We're Not Jews" has a prefiguration within a Jewish context in the Nobel Prize–winning Nadine Gordimer's representation of two very different models of Jewish identity. Recoiling from the rhetoric of apartheid South Africa, she writes about the Eastern Jew in light of the Anglo-Jewish identity of her mother's family. No multiculturalism, Jewish or not, can rescue these Jews from their inherent difference from one another, a difference defined by the hierarchy not of multiculturalism but of apartheid. Cultural pluralism, as in the case of the father in Art Spiegelman's *Maus*, provides a worst case for identity among American Jews, that of being black, just as being Jewish is the worst case in the world of Kureishi's characters. In a short story reflecting an analogous situation in apartheid South Africa, Nadine Gordimer reflects that her mother saw her husband and his family as "ignorant and dirty ... you slept like animals around a stove, stinking of garlic, you bathed once a week. The children knew how it was to be unwashed. And whipped into anger, he knew the lowest category of all in her country, this country. 'You speak to me as if I was a kaffir.'"[12] Gordimer's historical vision of how Jews created, not a world of Jewish hybridity, but a hierarchy of cultural values often around categories of decorum has parallels in pre-Shoah American letters (in texts such as Michael Gold's *Jews without Money* [1930]).

Such a view contrasts in an often bizarre manner with the very notion of Jewish success but within a multicultural model of cultural pluralism for Jews and non-Jews alike. Here the "natives" can take on different meaning than being a "kaffir." One can evoke Mark Kurlansky's short story "The Unclean" (2000) about a Philadelphia rabbi whose congregation is now the "oldest working synagogue in the Americas" (93).[13] Exiled to the multicultural "island" (to the unnamed Curaçao's Mikvé Israel-Emanuel Synagogue), Berman is unhappy because of the paucity of kosher food, and he institutes a kosher slaughterhouse. His Sephardic congregation is amused. They had become quite multicultural, at least in their diet, since "there is nothing to eat [on the island] but pork and shrimp," but they humor him. When he institutes a ritual slaughter of chickens, there are no takers among his community or the local Ashkenazi community. But the local minister of health is delighted with the idea that he is selling "clean kosher chicken" (99). There is an attempt to create an industry for the island by exporting these "highly prized chickens" (110). The press of business means that the chickens are not actually ritually slaughtered, and the rabbi is so depressed by this failure that he decides to conform to the multicultural world of the island. At the end, he capitulates and eats a "fistful of large shrimp" and develops a major allergic reaction to the seafood. Thus the "specially prepared chickens" are retrospectively given a cultural explanation—the rabbi was allergic, and thus "Blade's island chickens were viewed ... now as something medicinal" (115). But in the end, no one would buy these special chickens but the local indigenous healers, the "obeah men ... who respected clean chickens. What's more, they paid better than Jews, and they did all the slaughtering themselves" (116). The ultimate American answer to Blasband's claim for integration—here it is the hybridization of Jewish identity and practice into the Afro-Caribbean cultures of the islands, which retain a partially Jewish flavor. Food, as in the world of Franz Kafka, remains one of the contested spaces for Jewish identity—now with the blessing of a new reading of "kosher" culture.

Thus, in an age of multiculturalism, when American Jewish writing has become "American" writing, many American Jewish novelists of an older generation have trouble with multiculturalism.[14] Philip Roth's novel of 2000, *The Human Stain*, takes on the political correctness of multiculturalism as one of its central themes, and Saul Bellow has had a constant struggle with multiculturalism over the past two decades. Remember the outrage to his comment "Who is the Tolstoy of the Zulus?" about whether there is an African culture?[15] Jews on the brave new frontier of multiculturalism seem always to be the subject of comparison. In the fantasy of the new multicultural author, they belong to a world of power but are also that world's most victimized group. This continuation of older images often makes it difficult for Jewish writers of older generations such as Bellow and Roth, sensing their distance from such representations, to imagine themselves as part of the multicultural universe. What remains of constant fascination is how many of the older motifs of Jewish difference, including images of the body and the language of the Jews, are internalized in this context. For younger self-identified Jewish writers, the spaces defined by multiculturalism become ones that they must necessarily inhabit to function as part of this new cultural world.

For the Israeli writer A. B. Yehoshua, the potential of a Jewish multiculturalism as including all cultures becomes the centerpiece of his novel *Mr. Mani* (1990). A multigenerational but also multicultural novel that centers on the Jews, the entire multicultural world of the Middle East comes to be Jewish. Jerusalem is its own multicultural universe in which the Jews reside as one of the peoples of the city. Even the Muslims are, in the last resort, merely Jews of a different stripe. He commented on the political implication of such a model of multicultural hybridity:

> For all its implausibility and lack of realism, the concept of the modern
> Canaanites will always serve as a fruitful challenge to Zionist Israel.
> When I wrote the "Fifth conversation" for *Mr. Mani*, we were in the first

difficult months of the Intifada, before we became inured to atrocity, and
every dead Palestinian child still caused us sleepless nights. At the time,
I recalled that at the beginning of Zionism, Ben Gurion and President
Ben Zvi came up with the peculiar notions that Yosef Mani [the "Isaac"
of the book's culminating "conversation"] propounds—that the Arabs
of the country were merely converted descendents of Jews who had remained devoted to the land after the destruction of the Second Temple.
And that perhaps due to their attachment to the land they gave up their
loyalty to the faith of their fathers. Yet now we torture our brothers of old
with the afflictions of the occupation.[16]

Such a view, in which each of the multicultural layers of the history and
material world of Jerusalem is revealed to be interrelated, he recounts in an
extraordinary passage, tracing a walk through the back alleys of the city that
closes the novel:

[B]y climbing Arditi's stairs you can get to Bechar and the Geneo's roof,
and then through their kitchen to the courtyard of the Greek patriarch,
for where, if you cut straight through the chapel, you need only open a
little gate to find yourself in She'altiel's salon. If She'altiel is home, you
may have a cup of coffee with him and ask his leave to proceed, but if he
is not, or if he is sleeping you need not turn back. Just tiptoe down his
little hallway without peeking into the bedroom and you will come to
five steps belonging to the staircase of an old building destroyed by the
Crusaders, which lead directly to the storeroom of Franco's greengro-
cery. Once there, you need only move some watermelon and sacks aside
and stoop a bit to enter the little synagogue of the Ribliners, where you
will find yourself behind the Holy Ark.[17]

This is Yehoshua's answer to not only the "neurotic" condition of exile but
also the complex relation between Jew and Muslim. It is a multicultural
world that fits into the "Jewish" world of contemporary Jerusalem.

Here the idea is that the Jews in their very hybridity are a microcosm
of the multicultural world. Jews are seen to be innately "multicultural,"
as containing within themselves the world. The Bulgarian-born, German-
speaking Nobel Prize winner Elias Canetti (1905–1994), writing about the
Mellah, the Jewish Quarter in Marrakech, in 1968,

walked past as slowly as possible and looked at the faces. Their het-
erogeneity was astonishing. There were faces that in other clothing I
would have taken for Arab. There were luminous old Rembrandt Jews.
There were Catholic priests of wily quietness and humility. There were
Wandering Jews whose restlessness was written in every lineament.
There were Frenchmen. There were Spaniards. There were ruddy-com-
plexioned Russians. There was one you felt like hailing as the patriarch
Abraham; he was haughtily addressing Napoleon, and a hot-tempered
know-it-all who looked like Goebbels was trying to butt in. I thought of
the transmigration of the souls. Perhaps, I wondered, every human soul
has to be a Jew once, and here they all are: none remembers what he was
before, and even when this is so clearly revealed in his features that I, a
foreigner, can recognize it, every one of these people still firmly believes
he stands in direct line of descent from the people of the Bible.[18]

The image of the Jew as the universal man—as the hybrid that encompasses
all humanity (including the Nazi)—is certainly the ultimate extension of a
model that sees Israel as the ultimate multicultural space. But both of these
"see" the multicultural nature of the Jew within a Muslim framework. The
Jew is the positive cosmopolitan; the world the Jew inhabits is the world of
Islam. In this seemingly monolithic world, a very specific geographic space
(Jerusalem, Marrakech), the Jew represents the ultimate in hybridity.

One can add that there is a position for the Jewish writer in a multicultural world where the writer's "Jewishness" becomes the literal equivalent of
"modern" or "Western." The voice of the "Jewish" writer in a sense lays claims
on the position of the "Western" world. No better example is the Anglophone
Jewish-Indian writer Nissim Ezekiel (1924–2004), whose work is peppered with
self-consciously Jewish references. Thus he sees himself as part of the multicultural setting of a specific place, Bombay (Mumbai), which he reads on one level
as a Christian space against which his Jewish identity is defined. For him, the
"other" culture to which he feels superior is that of the Muslim:

> I went to Roman Catholic school,
> A mugging Jew among the wolves.
> They told me I had killed the Christ,
> That year I won the scripture prize.
> A Muslim sportsman boxed my ears.[19]

The Jew is better at even Christian Scriptures than the Christian, but not quite as good at sports as the Muslim. But he fits into the seemingly self-conscious mix of Bombay. There the poetic voice experiences a Jewish wedding, with much the same ironic distance also employed by the poet in accounting his early education at a Christian school:

> Well, that's about all. I don't think there was much that struck me as solemn or beautiful. Mostly, we were amused, and so were the others. Who knows how much belief we had?
>
> Even the most orthodox, it was said, ate beef because it was cheaper, and some even risked their souls by relishing pork. The Sabbath was for betting and swearing and drinking.
>
> Nothing extravagant, mind you, all in a low key, and very decently kept in check. My father used to say, these orthodox chaps certainly know how to draw the line in their own crude way. He himself had drifted into the liberal creed but without much conviction, taking us all with him. My mother was very proud of being 'progressive.'[20]

There is a tone reminiscent of Franz Kafka and Philip Roth looking at the diversity of the Jews and their eating habits. Inconsistency seems to be a result of the acculturation of the Jews into "Indian" society. Yet they do eat beef, a food that is just as taboo in Hindu religious practice as pork is in Jewish and Muslim culture. The "fanaticism" of the Orthodox is perhaps admirable, but it is incompatible with Ezekiel's father's need to accommodate and still be Jewish.

The fulcrum of religious identity forms Ezekiel's sense of the Jewishness of the Jews. This has not transformed itself into an Indian-Jewish ethnicity, but rather maintains itself in parallel to the other groups with whom he interacts (Christians and Muslims), who are also defined by their religious identity. This comes forth in a powerful way in the conclusion to his very long set of poems "Latter-Day Psalms" written in 1978:

> The images are beautiful birds
> and colourful fish: they fly,
> they swim in my Jewish consciousness.
> God is a presence here
> and his people are real.

I see their sins. I hear
His anger.

Now I am through with
the Psalms; they are
part of my flesh.[21]

Poetry becomes the surrogate of religion for Ezekiel. His position is clearly
that of the "Jewish" poet, whose secularized sense of his own Jewish identity
is formed by the poetics of the Anglophone Bible. His position is that of a
Jew, and yet this position is easily transmuted into that of the "neutral" observer of the multicultural scene.

One long narrative, however, contrasts his own position with that of his
Muslim neighbor:

My Muslim neighbour's daughter,
getting on to nineteen
but not yet matriculate,
wears a *burkha* when she leaves for school
a hundred yards away.

They've tried and tried
to get her married off,
but three successive years
the girl has failed in English.

The poet agrees to tutor his neighbor's daughter, but notes that the girl
is the same age as his own daughter and they have not "tried to get *her* married off." The neighbor's daughter sheds her *burkha* during lessons and is
overtly flirty. She also takes his daughter home "one day"

and shows her pictures
in a certain kind of book.
My daughter tells my wife
who tells my mother
who tells me. I laugh it off.

The neighbor's daughter realizes that he knows about the book; she intimates that she has been molested, and the lessons stop:

> They probably decide I made advances,
> and almost hint as much
> to my poor mother, who's outraged.
> There's gratitude for you, she says,
> *That girl will never get a husband!*
> A month later she was married.
> Now she doesn't need that picture-book.[22]

For Ezekiel, the Muslim neighbor, still captured by an archaic and arcane religion, subverts what are "natural" desires and makes them obscene or pornographic. The "Jewish" voice here is that of the teacher. It is the force for modernity, as he mirrors in his image of his own daughter. The forced, arranged marriage may be an outlet for sexual desire, but the sense is that it is not a healthy outlet. Jewish ritual, in its own ineffectual manner, is better than the colonial claims of Christianity and the coarseness of Islam.

Jewish writing is no more or less difficult to define than those other national literatures in the various diasporas of colonialism, slavery, occupation, or domination. The difference is the obsessive concern with the Jews on the part of the cultural elites in Christianity (and its secular literature) as well as Islam. That is what makes such a mind experiment so very different for Jews engaged in the experiment of multiculturalism. This is also why modern Jewish writing adapts a multiple, often contradictory notion of the multicultural, depending on the location and self-definition of Jewish culture.

II. PRAGUE AND THE EAST AS PLACES OF NOSTALGIC INTIMIDATION

My own thought experiment has to do with what the appropriate spaces are for Jews to inhabit in this new multicultural world. What spaces in the world are defined as "multicultural" (in addition to Disneyland Paris)? For the mid-twentieth-century self-defined Jewish writer in the Diaspora, that space (*makom*, to use the Hebrew) has often been labeled "Prague" or the "East." The power of a "Jewish" space such as "Prague" has its roots at least in the late nineteenth century, but it reappears with a new power in the world of American Jewish writing of the 1980s, a trope looking for a world more dangerous than New York or Chicago. It is a world behind the "Iron

Curtain" with all of the ghosts of a Jewish cultural past. The East is often the counterpart as an imagined past to Israel as the space that defines the Jewish present or the future. What was imagined in the past as a religious experience (such as the world of Rabbi Judah Loew, the Maharal of Prague [1525–1609], the great Talmudic scholar whose name is associated with the creation of the Golem) comes to be translated into an ethnic experience. Works from the early twentieth century such as Franz Kafka's *The Castle* and Jiri Weil's *Mendelssohn on the Roof* stand as literary godfathers to this Jewish, multicultural Prague. Both Saul Bellow (*The Dean's December* [1982]) and Philip Roth (*The Prague Orgy* [1985]) placed the search for American Jewish authenticity in the present in this ghostlike, multicultural, and very Jewish Eastern Europe.[23]

Roth's Prague and Bellow's Bucharest are the mirror image of the Prague of those Soviet–era Czech-Jewish writers such as Lenka Reinerová. Her and their world ended with the Velvet Revolution after which young Western visitors discovered the hip Prague of the 1990s. Lenka Reinerová was an aged Jewish German-language writer living in Prague, the last branch of the socialist tree that leads through the high modernism of a cryp-to-Jewish Prague in writers such as Egon Erwin Kisch, Max Brod, Oskar Baum, and Hermann Ungar (about whom she writes). Born 17 May 1916 in Prague, she was a committed Communist writing for the *AIZ: Arbeiter-Illustrierten-Zeitung*, who did not see the Velvet Revolution as a necessarily liberating force. She still lives in Prague. An exile in Mexico during World War II, she was a returnee who formed a bridge between Stalinist Prague and Pankow. Her 1983 Soviet-era volume of short stories magically reap-peared in a reedited form in 1996.[24] Here she presented a "Prague" of pure nostalgia in which the Jewish aspects are encapsulated in her worry about what language she should use: "The German of my mother, the Czech of my father or the Hebrew of my ancestors?" (8). I presume she means her ancestors exiled in the land of Egypt, as Yiddish might well have been the language of her great-grandparents, but hardly Hebrew. In the last tale, added for the post–Velvet Revolution volume, she begins with a "Jewish joke," a Chassidic tale (223–24), politically jumping off the new function of Prague as the city of the Jews—or at least of Kafka, the new marketing icon for the new Jewish tourist in the East. It is the multiculturalism of a dead or at least defunct Hapsburg world in which the Jews (secular and religious, right and left, of Austria and Galicia) played multiple roles. Now they have become multicultural window dressing in an acceptable ethnic form. They are the aesthetic parallel to the carved Jews as marionettes—in at least three sizes—that one can buy outside the Jewish Cemetery in Prague. With their skullcaps, religious raiment, beards, and side locks, they look like religious figures but are in fact ethnic representations, no different from the Czech dolls dressed in their regional costumes.

After the collapse of the Cold War, the East, in the classic contours of Prague, appears in the work of Benjamin Stein. In his first novel, *Das Alphabet des Juda Liva* (*The Alphabet of Juda Liva*), published in 1995, the response to ideas of Jewishness and narrative space is overt.[25] Stein was born in 1970 in East Berlin and now lives in Berlin and Munich. He has won a number of fellowships, including the prized Alfred-Doeblin Fellowship of the Academy of the Arts. His novel is seemingly shaped by the discourse of Latin American magical realism. It moves, through the creation of a Jewish narrator, from contemporary Berlin (after reunification) to late medieval Prague. The frame is that the protagonist hires a storyteller to come on a weekly basis and provide his wife with an ongoing tale. It is storytelling in a Jewish vein, which is at the center of this tale. The language of this novel seems to be shaped by the vocabulary of the Cabala, indeed so much so that, following the model of many "Jewish" works of contemporary German fiction, it concludes with a glossary of terms for its evidently non-Jewish audience. Here the authenticity of the fictive topography seems to be guaranteed by the authenticity of the language of the narration.

But the "Jewishness" of this voice is suspect specifically because it makes such demands on the very idea of authenticity. Stein's novel stands in a narrative tradition of the German Democratic Republic (GDR), which is being continued here, with a massive dose of Jewish mysticism. Beginning with Johannes Bobrowski's brilliant and original *Levins Mühle* (*Levin's Mill*; 1964), written by an avowed Lutheran writer in the GDR, it continues through the first "Jewish" novel in the GDR, that is, a novel with a Jewish protagonist written by a Jewish writer, Jurek Becker's *Jakob der Lügner* (*Jacob the Liar*; 1969). This is the first GDR novel set in the East, in an unnamed Nazi ghetto, and populated by Jews of all social, religious, and cultural backgrounds. It is, however, not a book (and then a film) cast in the heroic mode of anti-Fascist literature, but a serious attempt to look at the complex interactions of the Jews in the ghetto in light of the inevitable possibility of death and destruction. In both of these texts, we have complex narrative strands that demand the presence of a palpable "Jewish" voice in the text. What makes the voice "Jewish" is its claim to stand in a narrative tradition of a folkloric, Yiddish narrative, such as that of Sholem Aleichem. Indeed, it is the musical *Fiddler on the Roof* in its Walter Felsenstein version at the East Berlin Komische Oper, which has stood midwife to this novel as much as anything else.

Stein's novel, with its magical movements between levels of narrative, uses a self-combusting narrator who moves from contemporary Berlin to medieval Prague through his tale. He picks up these GDR traditions of representing a Jewish discourse. But the physicality of the narrator also picks up on the image of the Jewish body and of the smart Jew, for like the protagonist of Becker's novel, the narrator (not Jakob) is the smart Jew, insightful into the past and knowledgeable about the present. But Stein's narrator is also physically marked as the Jew of the anti-Semite's nightmares. He is described by the narrator as "neglectedly bearded and bow-legged" ("verwahrlost bärtig und O-beinig"; 11) when we are first introduced to him. Again, it is the physicality of the Jew that marks his difference and is used in the novel to delineate Jewish particularity.

Stein's novel uses in a more complex narrative form the idea of an internal Jewish narrative form taken from Cabala, but it reveals itself to be a German literary response to the world. Here it is Prague that is the antithesis of Germany. The space of nonauthenticity is Germany; that of authenticity for Jewish discourse remains Prague. It would seem that the antithesis between modernity and the past, between Berlin and Prague, escapes the "American" curse. Thus the Prague that Stein's novel represents is that of not only *Der Golem* (both Gustav Meyrink's 1915 novel and Paul Wegener's 1920 film) but also the American recapitulation of this theme in the 1980s of the notion of Prague as the Jewish space of experience, as seen from the world of American Jewish letters. The authenticity of Prague is a place of Jewish trial. This is certainly the case in Stein's novel, even with its movement into the Middle Ages as a contrast to the Berlin of postreunification Germany.

Esther Dischereit's *When My Golem Revealed Himself to Me* (*als mir mein golem öffnete*; 1996) presents a self-consciously West German appropriation of the myth of the Golem as a means of creating a secular Jewish space.[26] Dischereit was born in 1952 in West Germany of a Jewish mother and a non-Jewish father, and has stressed her "mixed" background as a means of both identifying and being identified as Jewish and yet in no way being so accepted by the German-Jewish community. In this thematic volume of poetry with a strong narrative strand (quite unusual for Dischereit), the underlying dimension of the "Golem" as the figure representing the "East" is quite different from that of Stein. Here there is a powerful attempt to integrate the past into the contemporary experience of a Jewish identity. The Golem serves her as a muse:

> I sat
> before your door
> as
> my golem
> revealed
> took me
> aside
> and canceled
> the lines
> now you sweep
> dust
> from your door. (5)

Dischereit's multicultural perspective is that of a secular Jew appropriating a discourse from German culture (and not necessarily German-Jewish culture) to provide a "Jewish" subject for her poetry. Here the Golem is the survivor, like the Jewish voice in the text:

> I saw the flowers
> growing in Dachau
> it is the most beautiful photo
> of my daughter. (7)

The Golem is the dust from the past now present:

> I was
> Born a golem ...
> And hang me
> On the word
> And aleph
> We have remained dead. (6)

It is the dust of the lost and the dead:

> We want a bit Aleph
> and want to break matzo
> play mother, great-grandfather
> whom we have not seen ... (9)

The importance here is that the Golem does not exist in a distanced Prague but in the daily experience of the German Jew after reunification.

For Stein, multiculturalism is the contrastive world of the ancient (and Jewish) city of Prague with the unstable world of a vanished East Germany that could become the place for a new Jewish world or a new Nazi one. Dischereit focuses her eye on the Golem as part of the contemporary multicultural world of the new Berlin Republic, the Federal Republic of Germany. The function of the Golem as the link between past and present with a place in both worlds is central to one of the most important "Jewish" books written in the United States at the new millennium, Michael Chabon, *The Amazing Adventures of Kavalier and Clay* (2000).[27] Chabon was born in Washington, D.C., in 1963 of a Jewish Russian-Polish and Lithuanian family. But he was raised in Columbia, Maryland, "which," according to an interview with him in *The Jerusalem Report*, "during the late 60s was this kind of planned quasi-utopian, multiracial interfaith suburb located between Baltimore and Washington. That much of this world was Jewish went without saying, even for a boy growing up in a deliberately multicultural environment. That the brash new universe of American comic books would, like the movies or Tin Pan Alley before it, prove no less Jewish, one could discern not only from the names of the people listed on their mastheads, but from the distinctive and often peculiar conventions they embraced."[28] The multicultural aspects were clear; the Jewish aspects submerged in this multicultural world of the garden cities around Washington, much less so. He attended the writing program at University of California, Irvine, when his master's thesis, a story about sexual and intellectual coming of age, became the best-selling novel *The Mysteries of Pittsburgh* (1988). He is the author of a number of best-selling novels, one of which (his 1995 novel, *Wonder Boys*, about a frustrated professor) was adapted by Hollywood into a film starring Michael Douglas and Robert Downey Jr. He is very much a self-identified Jew. Chabon considers his Jewish identity more cultural than religious, although the two often seem to overlap. "Part of what makes Jewishness so unique and special is that it is very difficult to separate out the cultural from the religious, the ethnic from the liturgical," he said. "It's one big blur, and that is part of what has made Jews so puzzling to others over the years. Unfortunately, at many moments throughout history, that puzzlement has turned quite ugly."[29]

With his novel of 2000, he returns to a multicultural presentation of a Jewish world that incorporates the Holocaust and two places of Jewish testing: Prague and New York. Each is "multicultural," as each presents groups in conflict: the Germans occupy Prague, and the German-American Bund haunts New York. Only in America, however, are these conflicts resolved in terms of the creation of a new American culture.

Prague is very much a literary construction. Chabon very clearly evokes Franz Kafka as he presents the tale. In the back story to the comic book *The Escapist*, which the protagonist Josef Kavalier and his cousin Sam Clay develop, Chabon actually evokes Kafka's description of the Statue of Liberty with "her sword raised in defiance to the tyrants of the world."[30] Kafka's novel *Amerika* begins with the vision of the Statue of Liberty ... the sword in her hand seemed only just to have been raised aloft."[31] Kafka's world of faulty transformations, of changes that end in disaster, is different from that of Chabon. Kafka is not convinced that there is a magical world of transformation with any positive outcome. Chabon believes that this might be possible—in the end, it is the American dream of the integration of the Jew that creates a new American culture.

Chabon begins the novel with a flashback, an interview with the aged Sam Clay speaking about the origin of *The Escapist*. His greatest influence was the escape artist Harry Houdini, he stated, and Houdini's "first magic act, you know ... was called 'Metamorphosis.' ... It was also a question of transformation" (3). But of course that story was "like all of his best fabulations, [as it] rang true" (3). He had had very little interest in Houdini and the trick of metamorphosis, which manifested itself in the transformation of the rescued Czech Jew, Josef Kavalier, into an American icon; for it was his cousin, the young Czech Jew who believed that "Jews were merely one of the numerous ethnic minorities making up the young nation of which Joseph was proud to be a son" (24–25), who had obsessed about Houdini and the art of escape. In Chabon's novel, Kavalier must rescue the Golem from Himmler's Nazis occupying Prague. The Golem has ceased being the magical figure that rescues the Jews. Chabon answers here a model evoked by the works of Cynthia Ozick, whose female "Golem" haunts her work as early as the 1970s.[32] The Golem is the object of succor, not the heroic figure. At the end, he becomes part of America.

Sam Clay, Kavalier's cousin, may not have dreamt of Houdini as a boy, but he "dreamed the usual Brooklyn dreams of flight and transformation and escape" by becoming a figure in high culture, "a major American novelist" (4). Likewise, Josef's younger brother Thomas Masaryk Kavalier, who eventually drowns on his way to America, has a "musical chromosome of his mother's family" (28). He is able to write operas at ten. Indeed, he had begun an "opera *Houdini*, set in fabulous Chicago" (28). The Jewish entrepreneur Sheldon P. Anapol, seller of jokes and cheap novels, and eventually the publisher of *The Escapist*, "as a young man ... had played the violin well enough to hope for a musical career" (80). The irony of this all is that it is in popular culture, in the creation of the comic book, that he manages to fulfill his desire to entire into the American cultural mainstream. High culture vanishes, is destroyed or abandoned, and what remains is the Jewish contribution to a new America, that of popular culture.

The protagonist Josef Kavalier's Jewish boyhood in Prague focuses on an apprenticeship as a magician and escapist under the tutelage of Bernard Kornblum. Like many "Jewish" novels from the nineteenth century, such as those of Eugène Sue, there is the incorporation of a mystery and a society that protect the "Jews" or, as in the anti-Semitic *Protocols of the Elders of Zion*, rule the non-Jewish world. Here it is a world of parody in which theatrical magicians are the guardians of the Jews. Kornblum belongs to a secret circle, which has guarded the clay body of the Golem of Prague since the sixteenth century, when it had been animated to save the Jews of Prague. But this is not a league of true magicians but merely stage magicians. Their technical artifice is equivalent to the status of transformation in the novel. No surreal, magical world of transformation as in Kafka's "The Metamorphosis" dominates. Indeed, to prevent its confiscation by the Nazis, the Golem is disguised as a huge human corpse and shipped out of Czechoslovakia. Joe is smuggled out inside the same coffin and manages to travel across Asia and the Pacific to America. No magic; only illusion.

Only at the very end of the novel, after Joe reappears to reclaim his wife and son from Sam, does the Golem suddenly reappear one day. Joe had used his time hiding from the world to create what was clearly the first illustrated novel, thousands of panels long, about Joe Golem, "a wayward, unnatural child … that sacrificed itself to save and redeem the lamp lit world whose safety had been entrusted to it" (577). Done in black and white, it prefigures Art Spiegelman's *Maus* as that text to capture the experience of the Holocaust as a commix and, like Spiegelman's work, is a work of personal healing: "— telling this story—was helping heal him" (577). It is very Jewish, as Sam notes, having looked at it: "You have an awful lot of Jewish stuff in here" (585). The "Jewish stuff" now surfaces. Present in the very invention of the comics four decades before, in a subliminal way as the Jewish publisher did not wish it to be present, it now explodes into high culture.

Suddenly the "real" Golem appeared, delivered by a courier in his huge box, at the suburban home now occupied in suburban bliss by Sam Clay, his wife (Joe's former lover), and Joe's son. It has traveled from Prague to Vilnius and from there over time and space to New York. When the extraordinarily heavy crate is opened, "the entire box was filled, to a depth of about seven inches, with a fine powder, pigeon-grey and opalescent, that Joe recognized from boyhood excursions as the silty bed of the Moldau." This is the mud from which the Golem had been made by the Maharal. When Joe had helped rescue the Golem (and himself) from Prague, it was still recognizably in the shape of a huge human being. It had degraded when, it was assumed, it was removed from "the river that had mothered it" (611). And then it was as light as a feather, as it was without a soul: "This is nothing. This is … just an empty jar" (62). Now it is heavy and turned back to clay, and Joe "wonder[ed] at what point the soul of the Golem had reentered its body, of if possibly there could be more than one lost soul in all that dust, weighing it down so heavily" (612). The lost souls of the Holocaust reappear in America as the heritage of these new American Jews. The tradition of the Golem is transferred to the next generation with Joe's/Sammy's son. America is now the ultimate multicultural space—in both the good and bad sense. For the "Jews," there is both success and victimization. The novel, itself a cultural artifact of American Jewish cultural confrontation with the multicultural, presents the Jewish Diaspora experiences as multicultural and cross-cultural.

The notion of Jewish success as the creation of mass culture, the comic book, out of the horrors of the Holocaust fairly well summarizes the conflicts within any notion of Jewish cultural identity in contemporary American Jewish fiction. Is the novel but a new comic book? As of February 2004, Chabon is now writing *The Escapist* comic books for the mass market

(Dark Horse Comics); maybe we should ask if the novel is not the precursor to the comic in its American and multicultural definitions—from *manga* to the Mexican and Italian illustrated novels. Here the medium is the message. The ethnic Golem no longer represents the multicultural but the comics. He has become American.

Chabon's next novel, *The Final Solution*, published in 2005, is a further exploration of the Holocaust, now in the context of an unnamed Sherlock Holmes's Sussex of the 1940s.[33] Holmes, ancient but still keeping his bees in his retirement, seeks to uncover the motivation for the theft of a parrot from a mute child brought to England on one of the rescue trains from Germany. Here too the Holocaust is the point of the meeting of cultures, for as in his earlier novel its conflict takes place beyond the bounds of Nazi Germany, where, at the time in which the novel plays, success is assured. The fascination with the boy's parrot is that it has memorized endless streams of seemingly meaningless numbers. It is suspected that these are Swiss bank accounts. At the very close of the novel, the child speaks for the first time and the reader learns that the numbers are those of trains—one assumes the trains taking Jews to the death camps. And then the parrot "flew up into the rafters of the station roof, where, in flawless mockery of the voice of a woman whom none of them would ever meet or see again, it began, very sweetly, to sing" (127). High culture, now the remembered voice of the child's mother, survives even the Holocaust.

Certainly the most striking novel by a "new" Jewish writer that moves the confrontation with the notion of the multicultural into another "Jewish" realm is Jonathan Safran Foer, *Everything Is Illuminated* (2003). Set in the contemporary Ukraine, the novel focuses on the Ukraine figures of multiple generations who since the collapse of the USSR have become of necessity multicultural, in that they now deal with Jewish tourists from throughout the world seeking their roots in the fragments of the post-Shoah world. Jonathan Safran Foer was born in 1977 and attended Princeton University, where he won the Freshman, Sophomore, Junior, and Senior Creative Writing Thesis prizes after studying with Joyce Carol Oates. After graduation he worked at a number of jobs, including as a morgue assistant, receptionist, math tutor, ghostwriter, and archivist. He was awarded the Zoetrope: All Story Fiction Prize in 2000 and has had stories appear in hip publications such as *The Paris Review* and *Conjunctions*.

In 1999 he went to the Ukraine, hoping to find the woman who saved his grandfather from the Nazis. Finding very little factual material on the trip, he created a mind experiment around his experience of the multicultural commodification of the Holocaust tourist experience, which resulted in the uncovering of one of the hidden horrors of the Holocaust buried deeply in the family who served as his guides. The novel captures the multiple discourses in ever improving English—that ultimate multicultural language. Both the Jews of the past and more so, in a more comic mode, of the Ukrainians of the present such as Alex Perchov, his young Ukrainian translator, speak accented English. Alex who initially writes/speaks in a comically inflected (multicultural) English sees his English improve radically as he learns about his grandfather's activities in the Shoah.[34] The playing with levels of linguistic competence, of local knowledge, of globalized and commodified tourism, and of a multiple Diaspora perspective of the successful American now on the search for the victims in his family provide a radical view of the limits of such a multicultural thought experiment. Thus the protagonist writes about the inherent hybridity in memory of all aspects of Jewish life, past and present, of all of the stories of the Jews in the Diaspora:

> We are talking now, Jonathan, together, and not apart. We are with each other, working on the same story, and I am certain that you can also feel it. Do you know that I am the Gypsy girl and you are Safran, and that I am Kolker and you are Brod, and that I am your grandmother and you are Grandfather, and that I am Alex and you are you, and that I am you and you are me? Do you not comprehend that we can bring each other safety and peace? (214)

After the complicity of his family in the Shoah is revealed, Alex writes,

> Grandfather interrogates me about you every day. He desires to know if you forgive him for the things he told you about the war, and about Herschel. (You could alter it, Jonathan. For him, not for me. Your novel is now verging on the war. It is possible.) He is not a bad person. He is a good person, alive in a bad time. Do you remember when he said this … ? Everything is the way it is because everything was the way it was. Sometimes I feel ensnared in this, as if no matter what I do, what will come has already been fixed…. Grandfather is not a bad person,

> Jonathan. Everyone performs bad actions. I do. Father does. Even you
> do. A bad person is someone who does not lament his bad actions.
> Grandfather is now dying because of his. I beseech you to forgive us, and
> to make us better than we are. Make us good. (45)

All stories are intermingled in a world of cultural pluralism that, in the end, through the actions of the Holocaust, becomes a hybrid of joint experiences or memories in the history of the semimythical shtetl Trachimbrod, which lies along the River Brod. For the novel functions also on a rather magical realist level in the imagined reconstruction of the shtetl from which the narrative voice, also called Jonathan Safran Foer, imagines his family coming. Indeed the very use of this device of magical realism points the novel clearly in the direction of literary multiculturalism. Needless to say, the novel quickly won the National Jewish Book Award.

The image that the East is a place of testing gives way in contemporary Jewish writing to the odd combination of Holocaust tourism and Jewish self-loathing. One comes to the East as part of a mass of visitors experiencing the material world left after the Shoah. Indeed, the Anglo-Jewish writer (and comedian) David Baddiel has his novel of "German" (read: German-Jewish) internship on the Isle of Man during the war, *The Secret Purposes* (2004), end with a chapter in which the German-Jewish protagonist goes with his "hybrid" daughter (born of a non-Jewish mother) to Auschwitz as part of an organized "Holocaust education" tour.[35] The recent British fascination with the Holocaust (and in Baddiel's case with his own family, which had escaped from Königsberg) stems to no little degree from the American Jewish model. There, one comes from one's own convoluted sense of a Jewish identity shaped by the American experience and the intense presence of the Holocaust in that world. The claim that there is a "new" Jewish writing within American multiculturalism is documented in Paul Zakrzewski's anthology *Lost Tribe* (2003).[36] Zakrzewski's texts are heavily oriented toward a "new" Jewish reading of Eastern Europe and the legacy of the Holocaust as part of a multicultural world as presented in Foer's work. Indeed, Foer's novel is present in a summary version in the anthology. The status of the successful minority coupled with that of the perennial victim is central to any understanding of the multicultural voices in this volume. Thus, in Ellen Umansky's "How to Make It to the Promised Land," children in a middle-class Jewish summer camp are forced to reenact the Holocaust (following the model of the Holocaust Museum in Washington, D.C.). Often the Holocaust is evoked to provide a true "multicultural dimension" to a Jewish life, as in Michael Lowenthal's tale "Ordinary Pain," in which a bar mitzvah boy, appropriately named Larry Blank, becomes a local celebrity when he concocts an account of his grandfather's heroic death in Buchenwald. Gabriel Brownstein's "Bachelor Party" is in a sense the opposite tale. It is the fantasy of expiation of a German woman who has sex with him to free herself and her father from the ghosts of their Nazi past.

One can find analogous texts in Aimee Bender's "Dreaming in Polish," which uses the Holocaust and Holocaust tourism to define a Jewish identity in America; and Tova Mirvis's "A Poland, a Lithuania, a Galicia," which sees the desire for a fundamental Orthodox religious identity as the absolutely antithesis of American multicultural Jewish education. The discourse about Eastern Europe, if one remove in Israel, comes to frame an understanding of the Jew in the American multicultural framework.

Here we can contrast another recent Jewish voice about the East, Adam Biro's *Two Jews on a Train* (*Deux juifs voyagent dans un train: une autobiographie* [1998]). Here, too, present and past narratives are intermingled, with the Holocaust as the link. Here, too, there is a protagonist bearing the name of the author: "When his students asked the wonder-rabbi of Budapest, Adam Biro ben Mordechai, if he was happy."[37] Biro's magical book plays on the worlds of the Jews in France—survivors, North African Jews, modern secular Jews, and religious Jews. But there is not a world beyond the multicultural worlds of Biro's narrated Jews. When these Jews touch the worlds in which they exist, it is only to reify their own existence as Jews. Francophone multiculturalism in this voice may use all of the literary and narrative devices that Foer employs, but it does not postulate a world in which the Jew is but one player—and that virtually as a catalyst for the insight of another.

But we have to understand that the creation of Foer's Ukraine is part of an American multicultural voice. In an interview he noted, "When I am in the shower I might sing like Eminem or Radiohead or something that's contemporary on the radio." The interviewer quickly asks, "Will you sing [Eminem's] 'White America' for me?" and Foer answers, "Well, I'm a little hoarse."[38] Eminem's 2002 paean to post-9/11 America demands a hybridity of all contradictory cultures:

I never would have dreamed in a million years id see
so many mutha fuckin people who feel like me
Who share the same views
And the same exact beliefs
Its like a fuckin army marchin in back of me
So many lives i touch,
So much anger aimed at no particular direction
Just sprays and sprays[39]

All America becomes "White America" in the world of the white rapper. It is the ultimate hybridity to be found in the new, hip-hop multiculturalism.

Carol Eisenberg, writing in *Newsday* in 2004, comments on this new multiculturalism that is particular to American Jews of Foer's generation: "Theirs is a generation, after all, reared largely in the American suburbs without firsthand knowledge of privation or persecution—and for whom hip-hop is often more familiar than Hebrew. They have watched with fascination, and not a little envy, as one ethnic group after another has rediscovered its own particularity now that Americans have come to embrace multiculturalism." The new Jewish multiculturalisms in America focus on the permanence of a Jewish ethnicity in specific ways: "[Some] pass around books by a new generation of self-consciously Jewish writers like Jonathan Safran Foer, Myla Goldberg, and Gary Shteyngart, who explore sex, religion and even the Holocaust in fresh and often outrageous ways. Some assert newfound ethnic pride by wearing edgy and sometimes explicit slogans such as "Yo Semite" and chortling over *Heeb* magazine's homage to the big-hipped, big-nosed appeal of 'the Jewess.' Young, Hip and 'Jewcy' A generation weaned on irony and multiculturalism defines what it means to be ..."[40] Cool means multicultural, but with Foer it is a borrowed, constructed multicultural resulting from a failed, real-life attempt to connect with the past as exemplified in the Ukraine: the construction of "good" Ukrainians who learn the value of English, America, and thus expose the murderers perpetrated against the Jews in their own family; and the literary past of the "cool" world of a magical realist Jewish world now lost through the very actions of these non-Jews. Parallel is the less successful evocation of a lost Vienna through devices pioneered by W. G. Sebald's *The Emigrants* in Dara Horn's prize-winning novel *In the Image*.[41] Or in the classic model of the ex-pat novel of the 1930s (pace Somerset Maugham) such as Arthur

Philip's *Prague*, in which the blond, blue-eyed character Scott Price turns out to be the American Jew from Los Angeles.[42] Here all of the "Americans" exemplify the inherently but unrecognizable multiculturalism inherent in this view of America. Here this lost world is more *Fiddler on the Roof* than Sholem Asch and not that far from the Prague of Chabon or Stein.

For Jonathan Safran Foer, the Holocaust and Eastern Europe at present stand as the set piece and the commodification of "Jewish," contemporary Holocaust tourism. This shapes this multiperspectival novel. Another one of the "cool" Jewish multicultural writers already tabulated writes in quite a different voice. It is the most extraordinary variant on the Jewish "émigré" novel, much like the turn-of-the-twentieth-century novels of Abraham Cahan (*Yekl*) and Sholom Asch (*East River*) merged with Henry Miller's acid sense of American multiculturalism in his *Tropic of Capricorn*. Gary Shteyngart, a Russian Jew whose family immigrated to New York City in 1978 when he was six, turned his "American Jewish" experience into his first novel *The Russian Debutante's Handbook* (2002).[43] His account stresses the impossibility of integration. His protagonist, the Russian Jew Vladimir Girshkin, is employed (in a Henry Miller sort of manner) in an office dealing with immigrants, the Emma Lazarus Immigrant Absorption Society no less, a position that his middle-class professional parents find well below his potential. (Lazarus wrote the poem "The New Colossus," which is inscribed on the base of the Statue of Liberty: "Give me your tired, your poor / Your huddled masses yearning to breathe free / The wretched refuse of your teeming shore....") Each week is a different "cultural week" at the Emma Lazarus Society where the "wretched refuse" have claim on attention. We see "Chinese Week" with "tea and a stuffed panda.... Although Vladimir was taught to foster multiculturalism, he looked blankly into the sneering faces of his countrymen, stamping his way through their mountains of documents" (65). The ironic claim for the Russians (read: Jews) is that they have *kulturni*, high culture, unlike the other immigrants: "Vladimir [hoped] his childhood excursions to the Kirov ballet and the Hermitage had made him *kulturni* enough" (70).

While his parents have integrated themselves into suburban America (in their own fantasy), Vladimir never can. America is a multicultural hell called Brooklyn, according to one Russian character: "A studio apartment. Spanish people everywhere. Oh, the plight of the poor. Maybe a few Greeks who hired him to blow up their diners for insurance purposes" (20). America

is a place from which to escape—where else but to Eastern Europe, perhaps
to "Prava? Vladimir perked up. The Paris of the 90s? The stomping ground
of America's artistic elite? The SoHo of Eastern Europe?" (20). In Prague
he comes across a world of American Jews, exemplified by the "writer Perry
Cohen" from Iowa. In Prague, that most Jewish of cities, now the city of
Kafka—whose visage has become the logo for Prague tourism—Cohen
"discovers" himself. Prague is the place where there is a hotel where "Kafka
took an important crap in 1921.... See the plaque by the door" (279). But
Vladimir is not impressed with Cohen's seemingly tortured acknowledgement of his new Jewish identity: "in the end what determines your fate is the
size of your trust fund, the slope of your nose, the quality of your accent. At
least his daddy wasn't accusing him of *walking* like a Jew" (207–8). Prague is
the "waiting room to the West" (267), where mindless violence defines daily
life, where identity is one of the objects available for exchange.

Eventually Vladimir, nose, walk, and all, winds up being aware that
Prague has become the new multicultural city, with Cohen now typical of
its inhabitants. It is a city where you could have "a kale-and-cabbage lunch
at the new Hare Krishna joint, or head for the Nouveau where they drank
Turkish coffees and became awake and animated, played footsie to the quick
time Dixieland jazz" (308). Prague is populated with young Americans from
the Midwest and comes slowly to take on the qualities of a simulacrum of
that world.

The protagonist remains too Russian (and therefore too Jewish) for a
multicultural America, even a multicultural America transplanted into the
"East." His mother had noted that unlike American Jews, his difference is
written on his body: "Look at how your feet are spread apart. Look how
you walk from side to side. Like an old Jew from the shtetl.... How can a
woman love a man who walks like a Jew" (44). His mother endeavors to walk
like a "normal" American: "You, too, could walk like a gentile. You had to
keep your chin in the air. The spine straight. Then the feet would follow"
(46). But Vladimir never quite learns this lesson. He is unable to transform
himself into a "gentile," even in the world of Prague.

Vladimir's autonomy as a Russian Jew separates him from all other
groups, each of which is also defined as physically different. His adventures
in New York City as well as those in Central Europe, where he becomes
the "American Jew" for the Russian Mafia, illustrate a sense of never really belonging. Prague is the "New, Proved & Euro-Ready Prava" (324).

Vladimir remains what he is—an incomplete hybrid, neither Jew nor Russian nor even, with his mother's tutelage, an American, a Gentile. Yet one thing does define him—that is the Holocaust as a space, a place. He travels to Auschwitz in a convoy of (German) BMWs taking Cohen and his Prague acquaintances to "confront" their virtual past. Vladimir's family had been spared the Holocaust because his grandmother had negotiated a move from the Ukraine to Leningrad before the Germans came. There at Auschwitz, for the "rootless" Vladimir, "if he possessed even the trace of doubt of an agnostic, now would be the time to mumble what he remembered of the Mourner's Kaddish. But with Hebrew school resolving the last enigmas of the empty heaven above, Vladimir could only smile and remember the feisty Grandma he once knew as a child" (405). Again, the Enlightenment image of Jewish education as destructive is evoked to acknowledge Vladimir's "ethnic" (or, in Soviet terms, "national") identity as a Jew, even at Auschwitz. Only when he attempts to leave the new Russia with his criminal collaborators from the Russian Mafia and is confronted at the airport with the violence of the new world does he moan: "'Oh, my poor people,' said Vladimir suddenly as the violence commenced. Why had he said this? He shook his head. Stupid heritage. Dumb multicultural Jew" (446). In the end, the "multicultural" returns to define Vladimir's humanity, a humanity put into question, as in Henry Miller's world, but never quite abandoned. And the name for this compassion is "multiculturalism." The novel's last line, imagining the America of Vladimir's imagined son, living in Cleveland, "the most ignominious parts of the earth" (451), is utopian: "An American in America. That's Vladimir Girshkin's son" (452).

The Russian Debutante's Handbook is in many ways the exemplary antimulticultural novel in its evocation of the multicultural. Yet at the end biological hybridity marks the goal of the new Jewish writer. To become an American, one must—here the theme is one from the nineteenth century—physically merge with America. Thus one can stop walking like a Jew. His literary antecedents were to be found as much in the Russian tradition of Ivan Goncharov's *Oblamov* as in the North American immigrant novel such as Mordecai Richler's *The Apprenticeship of Duddy Kravitz* (1959). Shteyngart felt himself isolated in his new multicultural America and captured that sense of failure in what has turned out to be a very successful novel. When Shteyngart (like his protagonist Vladimir Girshkin) actually returns to Russia, he seems pleased that his accent is seen not as American

but Jewish. "After I'm in Russia for a while, I lose it."[44] The mark of his hybridity, his accent, vanishes, and he becomes neither American nor Jew, just
another Russian, like Blasband's Belgian. The brave new frontier of multiculturalism uses Jewish difference, but in ways often in contrast to those
of Jewish writers who feel that their cultural success is as "mainstream"
authors and not as marginal voices. And yet, of course, to accomplish this,
they have to be more multicultural than the self-proclaimed multicultural
authors. They must fit in everywhere by not fitting in anywhere. This is,
then, the transition to their transformation. This "cool" Jewish multiculturalism in America certainly has its analogies elsewhere.

Elena Lappin, born in Moscow in 1954, lives in London and published
her first volume of short stories in 1999, followed by a comic novel *The Nose*
(2001) that picks up on a number of the threads about Jewish multiculturalism in her tale "Black Train."[45] Prague returns as a place of testing the new
Anglo-Jewish "cool" multiculturalism. (It is in odd ways in the work of
her brother, the Berlin-based German-Jewish enfant terrible, novelist, and
short story writer Maxim Biller, born in Prague in 1960.)[46] Staged at the
moment of the Warsaw Block invasion in 1968, "Black Train" begins with
the narrator's mother, a famed Czech actress, deep in a drunken sleep "in
full view of a large melancholy party" (19) when Olina, a young friend of the
narrator, points out that she is sitting "in a small brown puddle of her own
making." It was Olina "who first informed her parents that my mother was
asleep in a pool of liquid shit" (22). The family is forced by circumstances
and embarrassment to immigrate to Canada via Vienna. Canada is for the
father of this family a place of deep depression, of sitting at home weep-
ing, "his face buried in a large Czech dictionary." (This is so very different
from the multicultural fantasy of Canada in Mordecai Richler's brilliant
Solomon Gursky Was Here [1989], where Jews form part of the hybridity that
makes for an authentic, "native" Canadian. Richler's career began with his
novel of the Inuit, *The Incomparable Atuk* [1963]. In *Solomon Gursky Was
Here*, Jews and indigenous peoples merge into the "New Canadian Jew";
24.) The young narrator in Lappin's tale, barely a teenager in Prague, becomes a "Happy-go-lucky Canadian girl" (25) who falls in love with "Jimmy
D'Angelo from Valhalla, New York" (25). She loved him because he was
inherently different from her émigré family. (Her family is unnamed as
Jewish throughout the tale.) "He never worried about my past. Couldn't
read my father's dark poetry" (25). And yet of course he is as equally

multicultural: he saw her mother as not much different from his own, called Lucia (and speaking with a "funny accent"; 25); thus, Anna Kitrlík becomes Anna D'Angelo. Jimmy is a plumber in Westchester, and they move into a well-established, working-class world when suddenly, after the Velvet Revolution, Olina abandons her husband and children in Prague to run off to Westchester with "a man named Jack Cohen, a fucking Jew," according to her abandoned husband. She shows up in the next suburb, wealthy and overwhelmed. She had been seduced by his wealth and his intense sexuality. Visiting her friend, she is overwhelmed by the distance to her past. Jack needs Jimmy's talents in their Frank Lloyd Wright–designed houses, as the sewer pipers are backed up. When Jimmy visits later that week, he investigates the blockage and the odd connections, unstopping them, "which caused a powerful jet of shit to cascade down those designer pipers straight into the kitchen sink and beyond. Jimmy said that when he came downstairs, he found Olina sobbing, her white jeans and mini top dripping with ugly black and brown droplets" (36). The narrator is about to call her mother in Ottawa to tell her the tale but rather tells her psychologist, in the form of a dream about a tornado that lifts both their and Olina's cars up into the air and drops them onto a "distant neighbor's lawn." The last line reads, "Dr. Brousand tells me to hang on to that image until I have learned the names of all those trees, in English" (37). St. Augustine noted long ago that we are born between piss and shit; multiculturalism, in this feminist view of competing worlds, seems to agree.

The fecal moment that begins and closes the tale frames the very notion of what multiculturalism can be. Anne Michaels used this device to present the inhumanity of the Holocaust in the opening of her debut novel, *Fugitive Pieces* (1996), set initially in German-occupied Greece and then in a multicultural Toronto. For Lappin, it is a sign of "not fitting" in either one of the societies, of shame being the indicator of lack of integration. Shame, here connected with language and accent, marks the multiculturalisms of the Jew. In this tale, it appears to be like all other multiculturalisms—the need to integrate into the Diaspora setting over generations. And yet the factor of the catalyst, of Jack Cohen's seduction of Olina only because he wants a Czech bride as a prize, forms the impossibility of any true multiculturalism for a Jew. Only conflicts can result, conflicts that are framed by the very bodily function that defines shame in this world. Cohen is the new Jew in America to which he belongs but in which he desires the old: "Jack had a weakness for Czech women and had finally 'settled' on Olina, telling her how wonderful she was and how wasted in Prague and in her hopeless marriage. And now he wanted children (he was almost fifty, never married)" (33). It is the true impossible of the multicultural except as an appropriation of the exotic that we find in these Jewish writers' dystopia of multiculturalism.

III. BECOMING A JEW BY BECOMING A GERMAN: THE NEWEST JEWISH WRITING FROM THE "EAST"

The recent mass relocation of Jews from the former Soviet Union to the new Berlin Republic provides us with a unique set of literary examples of multicultural thought experiments about being an Eastern European Jew.[47] If the testing of Jewishness in a literary Prague (Michael Chabon, *The Amazing Adventures of Kavalier and Clay* [2000]) or the Ukraine (Jonathan Safran Foer, *Everything Is Illuminated* [2003]) reveals the contours of a constructed Jewish ethnic identity as claimed by the contemporary American Jewish writers, the Russian immigrants to Germany take a quite different tack. In the Berlin Republic, with its official (if recent) designation of the "Jews" as a state-sanctified religious community, there is little virtue in the multicultural shibboleth of "hybridity" or even of "cultural pluralism" among these new Jews.[48] Being "Jewish" is much more closely defined. If anything, these new German Jews, mainly from the former Soviet Union, perpetuate an ethnic identity for the Jews (in the older vocabulary, a "national" identity as inscribed on their passports). The value of such an identity is that it is malleable in their focus on transforming themselves into Jews in Germany. Indeed, in such cases they believe that they can become Jewish by becoming German. It is given that 85 percent of Jews (however defined) in the Federal Republic of Germany are from the former Soviet Union—some 120,000 Jews have immigrated to Germany since 1989. Some returned to their homelands; some moved to other destinations. At the moment, the total number of Jews in Germany hovers at slightly more than 100,000. Many of the "Russian Jews" (an estimate has it as high as 80 percent) are not "Jewish" by Orthodox Jewish standards, that is, they neither have a Jewish mother (and grandmother) nor have they undergone Orthodox conversion.[49] It is clear from these statistics that a large number have not joined the official, state-sanctioned Jewish community. The transformation of such "Soviet Jews" into Germans is reflected in the literary products of these new Jews in Germany for whom the central question is their integration into a new Germany—a Germany, one may add, with very different expectations for the literary representation of the Jew.

The center of the literary work that has recently appeared from this growing minority of Jews in Germany is, for the most part, on the contemporary world, not on a mythopoesis of the past. We can begin with Anna Sokhrina, who however so far has solely published in Russian about her German "multicultural" experiences. She is at present a bit older (around fifty) than the first generation of German-language Russian-Jewish writers but has pretty damning, insightful, and intelligent things to say about the Jewish communities in Germany with their fantasies about homogeneous Jewish identity. In a Germany so extraordinarily multicultural, the presence of such Russian and Ukrainian Jews seems to be but a blip on the "multi-kulti" (ironic German shorthand for a politically acceptable "multiculturalism") horizon. In the end, they are labeled as "Jewish." This formed the rationale for their privileged immigration after February 1991 to a reunited Germany as *Kontingentflüchtlinge* (quota refugees). One might note that before 1991, this category encompassed primarily the Vietnamese boat people and a few officials from the Albanian embassy. Being "Jewish" is very vaguely defined under this category: those who, according to their papers (*Personenstandsurkunde*), are of a "Jewish nationality" (*jüdischer Nationalität*) or have at least one "Jewish" parent.[50] Thus an internal Soviet passport, which used the label "Jewish" as a "nationality," would guarantee one admission, or having a parent who had such a passport would guarantee a child admission under these categories. As it had been disadvantageous to have such a label in the USSR (and other Communist countries), many "Jews" transformed themselves into "Russians" (or other Soviet nationalities) and had to draw on their parents' national identity to lodge a claim of being "Jewish" for the German authorities. Jewish authorities in Germany were confronted with "Jews" who did not fulfill any religious definition of Jewish identity, never mind the official Orthodox one. It is this tension that echoes in much of the new literature written by "Russian" Jews.

Becoming Jewish means becoming German or at least becoming Jewish in the sense of a German-Jewish sensibility. Sokhrina observes in a recent novel a fictive confrontation with Jewish official functionaries who wanted to figure out whether she (or her literary surrogate) was really "Jewish": "I swear by the lord Jesus Christ that I am Jewish," her protagonist says in the coolest, multicultural way.[51] Not religion but "national" identity is the Russian model for the Jew; it is a model that allows for such Jews to be Russian Orthodox or atheists. This collides with the German understanding of the "Jew" as defined (like Catholics and Protestants—the other two confessions that have state sanction) by religious practice, ritual, or at least knowledge. (With the Holocaust as involuntary exile, and destruction as the formative historical experience, not voluntary immigration and the desire for transformation into a German.) The irony of such a definition points toward a new "Jewish" identity—being Jewish as belonging to a category labeled as "Jewish" by the State, without, however, any demand that such a label has any religious or even ethnic content. The "Russian Jews" now in Germany function in a universe where a model of multiculturalism values only cultural pluralism. But the "Jewish culture" in this equation is understood in Germany as defined solely in terms of a rather rigid notion of a Jewish post-Holocaust religious identity.

The centrality of this definition can be seen in the work of one of the youngest Jewish writers from Russia who has debuted in Germany. Lena Gorelik's autobiographical novel recounts her journey to Germany and her acclimatization as a Jew in Germany after her family moved there from the USSR in 1992.[52] Born in Leningrad in 1981, she creates a protagonist who mirrors her imaginary image of the new Germany which she entered at the age of eleven. She spends an early chapter depicting her protagonist's somewhat older brother's struggle for a Jewish identity once he comes to Germany. He is sequentially a Buddhist, a Jew for Jesus, and an Orthodox Jew. All are answers to what Gorelik labels the struggle of Russian-Jewish emigrants, without any religious identity whatsoever, for some type of orientation in the new Germany. "He is an emigrant, who is seeking after a spiritual home" (41). His Jewish orthodoxy is a phase through which he passes, including keeping the laws of kashruth and going to Israel to learn Hebrew. Hebrew is the litmus test for a Jewish religious identity in Germany. The Hebrew classes at the Jewish Center in Berlin are offered in Russian. But it is not a secular Jewish identity that he seeks in Israel, but a religious one that transforms his body. When he reappears in Berlin, his grandmother's response to his newly acquired long beard is that such a man would never find a bride! But once he develops an interest in a left-wing fellow student who decries religion, his religious fervor lapses. She is succeeded by a nice Russian-Jewish immigrant, whose only flaw is that she believes in

Jesus. Gorelik notes in an aside that this struggle for a religious identity is not a German anomaly. In the United States, many Russian Jews become Scientologists (45). Religious identity as a Jew is here truly a performance that is rooted in the struggle for a new Western identity.

"Religious" identity defines the Jew, but the ability of the "Jew" to be understood as part of "German" culture retains an older and still valid association, for the "Jew" must speak German. Unlike writers such as Sokhrina, who write for a Russian-language readership in the former USSR and the Russian cultural Diaspora, to have a claim on a Jewish identity in Germany, one must write in German—for in Germany, as in the United States, the role of non-English writers writing about the Diaspora experience in their indigenous language is always suspect. For whom are they writing? Why are they not addressing "me," the German- or English-language reader? The very notion of an "American" or a "German" literature rejects works written in German in America or in English in Germany. (The debate about the status of Spanish-language writing in the United States or Turkish-language writing in Germany is equally fraught.) Thus "religious" identity is paired with the ability to function bilingually. Thus the "Russian-Jewish writer" serves as a figure mediating between two cultures: a "real" one of the reader's experience, and a fictive one, given the claim of authenticity, of the world reflected in the writer's representation of his or her experience of the "East" or of the Eastern image on the West.

Language remains determinate of that which defines a human being, as Johann Herder postulated in his 1772 essay on the origin of language as he thought about the essential components of identity.[53] Language is especially determinate for what is or is not to be considered "literature," even literature understood in a multicultural manner. Certainly the claim of multicultural pluralism is that each language group could maintain its own linguistic traditions, and yet the reality (whether among the Yiddish-speaking Jews of North America or the French-speaking Huguenots of Prussia) is that multiculturalism is monolingualism. Heinz Schlaffer pointed to this in his attempt to define what is "German" in "German literature" when he noted, "German culture, which had appeared from a sacral language[,] was resacralized by Jews at the close of the nineteenth century."[54] Language became the true litmus test for "integration into German society in general." "By the early twentieth century," Schlaffer quite correctly opines, "if one does not understand the word 'German' to have a pure ethnic dimension, one can consider

the Jews and the more serious Germans" as claiming a complete identification with German culture because of their commitment to the written word
(138–40). This view becomes part of the mantra of exile Jewish writers between 1933 and 1945 in their claim that they were the "real German culture"
and thus preserved the German language from Nazi thugs.

In the most recent transformation of "Eastern" Jewish writers into
German writers, language remained central. Certainly for the survivor-author Jurek Becker, born a Polish speaker, it was the command of the language
that defined him as a "better German" than his classmates (and competi-
tors).[55] Today this question is worked out in the creations of Russian Jews
now writing in German. They are the German-language parallel to Gary
Shteyngart, the Russian Jew discussed earlier who turned his "American
Jewish" experience into his first novel, *The Russian Debutante's Handbook*
(2002). These Russian Jews, like the Polish-Jewish child survivor Jurek
Becker forty years before, are reinventing themselves in German and in
Germany. Like Becker they must find their way into a new language and
a new culture, one that many find inferior to Russian. The problem of language adaptation remains for the older generation of Russian-Jewish immigrants a major barrier to social and economic integration (as it is for most
of the other immigrant groups in Germany). It is of little wonder that the
Central Jewish Organization in Germany strongly suggested that "a good
knowledge of German" (not any stricter religious definition) be used as a
litmus test to limit further immigration of Jews after 2005 from the former
Soviet Union.[56] For the youngest writers, such as Lena Gorelik, "speaking
Russian" comes to be negatively coded by her German compatriots. It is
"speaking too loudly, speaking in a confused manner." That is, as she notes,
"simply speaking" (63). Language and audience are vital to these writers,
but they see themselves as the conduit for the Russian-Jewish experience for
their German-language readers.

Certainly the "hottest" of the "cool" multicultural Jewish writers to
come out of the newest Russian-Jewish Diaspora in the new Germany is
Wladimir Kaminer. Born in 1967 in Moscow, he was released from the
Soviet army in 1989. He arrived in the German Democratic Republic with
the first wave of young "Jews" invited by the dying GDR in 1990 when
there was a thought of some type of coming to terms with "world" Jewry
and Israel as allies in preserving the "transforming" socialist state. In an interview he noted, "I was young—twenty-two—so nobody was really calling

for me. I had friends there that I had met in Moscow. This was 1990; you didn't need a visa, not even a passport. All you needed was an invitation. And it was inexpensive."[57] By the end of the 1990s, he had become a cabaret and club performer (as a DJ spinning Russian club music, ska-punk) who brought his first volume, *Russendisko*, to the general public in 2000.[58] It was an immediate and huge success.

In *Russendisko*, the very notion of "being Jewish" as a unitary category is drawn into question. Kaminer accounts for the immigration of Jews—who are Russians, who claim to be Jews—to the GDR in 1990. These "Jews" were the ultimate multicultural conglomeration: "They could be Christians or Muslims or even atheists, blond, red-haired or black, with a retrousé nose or a hook nose. The only unifying factor was that their passports said they were Jewish. It was enough at the [refugee camp] at Marienfeld if one in the family was Jewish or a half or quarter Jew" (13). There was of course some attempt to provide a religious litmus test for these Jews, as we have seen. Here the ironic tone of the postmodern reflects a German sensibility about what it means to be Jewish. A rabbi asks a woman what Jews ate at Easter: She responded, "'Pickles and Easter cake.' 'Well,' she said, 'I know what you mean. We Jews eat Matzos.' Do you actually know what Matzos are, the Rabbi asked. 'But of course,' the woman answered gleefully, 'they are the cookies which are baked on an ancient receipt out of the blood of small children.' The Rabbi fainted dead away" (14). Are these Jews without knowledge of being Jewish or Jews who know well what is expected of them and ironically resist their transformation into members of a religion from members of an ethnicity? The Jews in the community take many of the new immigrants to heart but insist, for example, that uncircumcised males undergo the procedure in a gesture that redefines being Jewish in purely ritual terms (15). At least one does.

After this opening chapter, any confrontation with the question of a Jewish identity in Kaminer's first book vanishes. Kaminer seems to become a "Russian" similar to the hundreds of thousands of "late immigrants" (*Spätaussiedler*) from the former USSR and Central Europe who return to a virtual German "fatherland" from which their ancestors were seen to have emigrated in the seventeenth and eighteenth centuries. Indeed, after reunification both groups are treated identically as immigrants from the former USSR. Coming to Germany defines Kaminer as a Jew because of the German reader's expectation of what it means to fulfill a missing link in the multicultural world of Germany, a Germany in the 1990s "robbed" not so much of its Jews but of its connection with what is imagined to be authentic Jewry, the world of klezmer, the world of the East, the world of *Fiddler on the Roof*. That this Eastern world is totally Russified by the 1990s seems lost on the Germans, but not on Kaminer, who becomes a Jew only by becoming a German. The volume quickly becomes the tale of a young man adapting to a German multicultural ambiance in which he is part of the new German "multi-kulti" world as a Russian émigré.

Kaminer's own biography makes up the stuff of his literary work, and is therefore a window into the multiculturalism of the Berlin Republic, or at least into its fantasies. He thinks about the role of being a Jew only when he represents his life in the USSR. Anti-Semitism is not a feature of Germany but of the USSR. In *Militärmusik* (2001), being Jewish is seen as a potential disadvantage to party promotion (23).[59] Jewish actors and choreographers such as his employer Stein, who had worked at the Moscow Jewish Theater, had been persecuted as a dissident (40–41). Indeed, when Kaminer joins Stein in a dissident action—urinating on the stage at the Majakowski Theater—it is denounced officially as a "Zionist conspiracy" (49). Indeed many of the hoary, old anti-Semitic myths recycled. Thus Jewish scientists and engineers are accused of having poisoned Lake Baikal with a "Jewish cancer" that destroyed it (88).

Kaminer was, in his eyes, "never a real Russian, because the word 'Jew' stood in my passport, I was a member of the Komsomol, a bit of a hippy and a passive dissident" (54). As an outsider he moves elegantly to Germany, where all of that which excluded him makes it possible for him to function on a relatively high cultural level in Berlin society. Even in his next memoir, *Die Reise nach Trulala* (*The Trip to Trulala*; 2002), the entire residue of things Jewish vanishes from his forced memories of the USSR.[60] His German audience wants happy memories of the Russian past that are just primitive enough to warrant an exaltation of the Berlin present.

The anti-Semitism that defined "Jewishness" for Kaminer in the USSR seems to be missing in his 2001 account of the multicultural world of *Schönhauser Allee*, the working-class neighborhood where Kaminer lives.[61] In this volume, which focuses on his life in the Berlin Republic, all of the Jewish references vanish. Russians, Vietnamese, and Germans show up in various combinations and colors in the apartment blocks that make up this quarter of Berlin. It is true that he sees someone on the street who reminds him of Albert Einstein (51), but not even that moves him to think about himself or the fictive world he now creates as more than "multi-kulti," a world in which "Jewishness" is an invisible quality. Indeed, this may be one of the very few mentions of Einstein in a modern literary work that does not evoke his role as the Jewish genius. This is Kaminer's most successful creation of a utopian Berlin multicultural world in which all of the ethnicities and nationalities blur into a Russian-colored world. This is a hybridity in which the solvent is vodka. Kaminer finds it necessary to supply a bit of a philosophical afterword, noting that "group interests manifest themselves, human beings create various units, and exchange experiences with one another, attend yoga courses, and at some point can do virtually everything" (189). *Schönhauser Allee* comes to be the "real" setting, according to the author, of his new, safe, multicultural world. It is the place in which individual difference exists but is not pernicious.

In 2002, Kaminer collaborated with the photographer Helmut Höge on a volume entitled *Helden des Alltages: Ein lichtbildgestützter Vortrag über die seltsamen Sitten der Nachkriegzeit* (*Everyday Heroes: A Slide Lecture about the Unusual Habits of the Postwar Period*).[62] The photographs are of the most banal types: recording moments in the daily lives of "Germans," self-consciously presented without any aesthetic pretensions. The volume includes an essay by Kaminer entitled "People in a Park," which ruminates about the meaning of public art. The protagonist and his children pass a monument with an open book and two hands in the Arnimplatz. He and his children theorize about what this could be: a writer who always told the truth in his books and whose reward was to have his hands cut off, or merely a pair of gloves and a book left by a child on the way to kindergarten. His youngest has no theory but shakes the hand/glove each day as they pass.

Kaminer knows Germany now, and he understands that "this monument[,] as with all of the others in the capital city, actually has to do either with the reunification or the expulsion of the Jews [*Judenvertreibung*]" (27). Such public sculptures are often illegible to those who live in the area. Thus there are Holocaust monuments that seem to have no meaning: "The giant chair that lies tipped over in the Koppenplatz which should remind one of the expulsion of the Jews and which the artist has labeled 'the abandoned room'" (28). No Shoah, no murder of the Jews, only an expulsion: the very term is evocative but in no way condemnatory as are his memories of Soviet anti-Semitism. These public arenas, according to Kaminer, have lost any sense of the aesthetic message. The parks are full of drunks who appear in the morning and "form a living monument of the newest age." But this monument is no longer "German." "German" monuments are those understood now as reflecting the combination of the "expulsion of the Jews" (not their systematic murder) and the reunification.

This is because any new monument must reflect Kaminer's world of the new immigration. In one of the trees a glass has appeared, deposited carefully by one of the drinkers. Earlier the drunks simply mixed their beer and whiskey in their guts. "Through the merging of international customs the alcoholics have achieved a new quality of life, new perspectives are open to them. It even smells better" (29). Here the "Jewish" aspect of the world is subsumed in the rhetoric of Germany monuments to the past; the new immigrants (Russian Jews included) have added a new layer to the public experience and created their own monument. The "glass in the tree" is their monument to the cultural hybridity of the new multicultural world, which even smells better.

Kaminer's weakest book is, in light of his construction of a multicultural Germany, the most revealing. *Mein deutsches Dschungelbuch* (*My German Jungle Book*; 2003) is his account of a lecture tour throughout Germany.[63] Here he leaves the confines of his self-constructed *Schönhauser Allee* and enters into the small towns and byways of the Federal Republic. He is announced as "The Russian" or "The German Writer of Russian Descent" or "A Jewish Writer" (117). He answers, as he observes, to any and all of the three labels. In Fulda, he learns of the town myth that a Jew, driven from the town, was responsible for its bombing during the war because of his obsessive hatred of the town (127). The house seized from his family by the Nazis was hit six times! He finds older Germans suffering under the burden of the guilt that they believe that no one will allow them to avoid: "In spite of all this fact will always be my burden" (195). In Heidelberg, he hears a Russian band and their antiwar songs. His mind turns to his father, who had warned him that within every one there lies hidden a soldier. And then his thoughts turn to his half-brother in Israel under attack by the Scud missiles launched by Saddam Hussein (225). In Germany, unlike in the "multi-kulti" fantasy of Berlin, the past is present in ways that pierce the utopian notion of any hybrid or parallel multiculturalism. Kaminer claims that while his work seems autobiographical, "I wouldn't say my prose is autobiographical. It isn't about Wladimir Kaminer, it's about others. The narrator is transparent, a cipher. The reader doesn't learn any intimate details about the narrator's life; the focus is on the surrounding world, the past, the future, encounters. Dialogue is hugely important, because communication is."[64] The answer is that the "Jewishness" of Kaminer's self-representation in the Berlin Republic is on the very edges of how he needs to see and sell himself. It is part of the German past, and yet he is anxious not to exploit the German philo-Semitic desire to love all Jews, even the new immigrants if they are "Jewish" enough.

By 2004, Kaminer had become the "representative *Russian*" in Germany. His book *Ich mache mir Sorgen, Mama* (*I Am Concerned, Mama*; 2004) has only one reference to a Jew, and that is to the publisher of the daily Russian newspaper in Berlin.[65] When we enter into Kaminer's personal life, which also forms the center of this volume, his Jewish father, who had been unable to attain his own professional goals in the USSR because of his Jewish identity, has become a Russian pensioner in Berlin. All references to being Jewish are deleted from his family portrait. Most striking is the inclusion of an icon of the Virgin Mary on the "memory shelf" compiled by his wife. The question of a "hyphenated" identity remains, but it is now transmuted into that of the Russian in Berlin, much like Voltaire's or Samuel Johnson's exotic who comes to Europe amazed at the antics of its inhabitants. But these antics no longer contain any reference to anti-Semitic comments.

Kaminer arrives in the GDR as a young adult in 1990. His sense of autonomy is such that he believes that he can shape himself and shape the world he comes to inhabit. And in complex ways, given the remarkable success of his work, he is quite right. And yet the question of his "Jewish" perspective in the Federal Republic of Germany remains part of his public persona. For him, it is very different from Austria: "An awareness of what took place, and vigilance to ensure it never happens again—I mean, it took so little to unleash that madness—permits the Germans to consider the past with some remove, makes it possible to envision a future. It's totally different in Austria. I heard this joke about Austria recently. There's a documentary on television about concentration camps, and two old ladies on the bus are talking about it. 'What horror!' they're saying. 'You would never have something like this [on TV] under the Fuhrer.' There's absolutely no national remorse, no soul-searching at all."[66]

But it is very much in Austria that the other pole to this image of Jewish multiculturalism is to be found in the writing of Vladimir Vertlib.

He is labeled as the official multicultural Jewish writer in Austria. In awarding him the Anton Wildgans Prize for 2001, the president of the Austrian Industrial Organization, Peter Mitterbauer, noted that "Vladimir Vertlib is with his life story and his publications a personality that teaches us to transcend national and cultural boundaries [*mit seiner Lebensgeschichte und seinen Publikationen eine Persönlichkeit, die lehrt, staatliche und kulturelle Grenzen zu überwinden*]."[67] Vladimir Vertlib has picked up the gauntlet tossed by the survivor-author Edgar Hilsenrath as he chronicled his life as an émigré after his survival from the Nazi ghettos. Jewish writers from Jeremiah onward often frame their multicultural world in terms of perpetual exile. Vertlib, like Hilsenrath, chronicles his crossing of boundaries and oceans, always as an outsider who needs to belong and cannot seem to function even in selfconsciously multicultural worlds such as America.

Vertlib was born in 1966 in Leningrad, the son of a refusnik. The family moved in 1971 to Israel. After a very short and unsuccessful stay, they then moved to Vienna and then back again to Israel, to the United States, and then in 1981 to Austria. He has lived in Austria since 1981. In between were longer stages in Italy and the Netherlands waiting for visas. His first novel chronicles the waiting for deportation from the United States. *Abschiebung* (*Deportation*; 1995) is a first attempt to understand the "Jewishness" that drove the family into exile,[68] for his father was in no way a religious Jew; rather he found the pettiness of Soviet society so overwhelming that his solace in the world of the refusniks, the Jews who applied for permission to leave the Soviet Union, provided him with some sense of identity. This identity was certainly central to the childhood memories of the protagonist, who internalized the inherent difference of the Jews in the USSR: "She couldn't speak the phoneme 'R' in Russian. Many people claim that this is a typical Jewish feature of speech, and present this as one of the grounds for anti-Semitism" (26), unlike in Kaminer's or Shteyngart's world in which Jews are effortlessly integrated as Soviet citizens except for the machinations of the political system. Vertlib's Leningrad, however, places his father in a "third-class situation" when he seeks work. When he seeks work he is seen by the Russians as a Jew. They see "a typical Jewish face" (58). "Go to Palestine! What are you doing here, parasite. The Jews are our unhappiness! ... Hitler was right!" shouted the potential employer at him (59). The anti-Semitism that Vertlib mirrors is visceral and reflects a child's view of perpetual exclusion.

This initial attempt is magnified in his novel *Zwischenstation* (*Intermediate Station*; 1999), in which the entire range of the wandering is documented.[69] What is most striking is the account of how the protagonist becomes a writer. For Kaminer, this is an accidental incursion through popular culture. Here the protagonist finds a copy of Goethe's *The Sorrows of Young Werther* on the tram, and it becomes the (unread) key to his joining the world of the educated. His teacher assumes that anyone who has even heard of Goethe in her class is an intellectual, and if he is a Jew ... (159). At every station in this complex trip across Europe and America, the child protagonist serves as the translator and mediator for the adults. Whether in Holland or Italy, the worlds he inhabits are the multicultural world of the immigrant in conflict with the natives (often themselves immigrants.) The act of writing becomes a means of controlling and manipulating this world, and the tone is that of the ironic world of the Jewish multicultural.

Almost as an answer to the rootlessness of the perpetual émigré, Vertlib's next novel is a massive, historical memoir, *Das besondere Gedächtnis der Rosa Masur* (*The Special Memory of Rosa Masur*; 2001), which is framed as an autobiography written for a multicultural celebration of the 750th anniversary of the German city of Gigricht.[70] (The novel closes with an authorial claim that the historical facts presented are all correct.) There is a competition to have new immigrants present their life tales. It is complexly "multicultural," including a returned German Jew, an African asylum seeker, and the newly immigrated Russian Jew Rosa Masur, whose flights of autobiographical fancy provide the German reader with a sort of history of Eastern European Jewry from before World War I through the horrors of the Shoah to the present. It is full of the most outlandish tales coupled with true moments of pathos. What is "true" and what is "invented" are impossible to separate. Indeed, it mirrors the complex world of the Jews as represented in the novel (221), a world that consists of the telling of tales, to the discomfort of the young Israeli rabbi.

Indeed, the question is asked early on whether the Jews who are not inhabiting the camps set up for refugees from the GDR are "real" Jews. Her answer is simple: "I am no expert for Racial Science" (26). And indeed, in this search for the authentic "Jewish" within this cultural realm, we are confronted with variants on "Who or what is Jewish?" Thus the tale of one of Rosa's childhood playmates, who is convinced that she would only have success after the Soviet Revolution ("in the world where the bent noses rule"

[115]) as a Jew. She has lived this life even under the Nazis, and her son is convinced that she has invented the tale trying to claim a non-Jewish heritage; for, as he sees, the very shape of his nose proves the matter (116–17). But neither mother nor father are "Jewish" by any stretch of the imagination, even though they are treated and thus act as if they were.

It is this telling of stories that are attributed to the "Jews" (whoever they are) that is at the core of the novel. Rosa tells of her fanciful meeting with Stalin in order to get her son released from prison. Stalin praises the Jews for their linguistic ability (he is a world-renowned specialist for linguistics) and notes that this facility has allowed them to exist for two thousand years (385). The autobiography/fiction is completed, but the prize money is withdrawn by the city, pleading poverty. The novel closes as it opens with a search, now in the South of France, for the utopian space where all, especially Jews, can be at one with themselves.

Vladimir Vertlib's most recent novel, *Letzter Wunsch* (*Last Wishes*; 2003), is in a real sense the next stage to the émigré novel of multiculturalism.[71] Now the family of Gabriel Salzinger is established, at least marginally, again in the Jewish community in his fabled German city of Gigricht. When his father dies, the community suddenly discovers that his father's mother was not Jewish because she had undergone a "liberal" conversion to Judaism rather than an Orthodox one, and thus her son could not be buried in consecrated land. The burial, which had to take place within twenty-four hours according to Jewish ritual, is interrupted, and all are at a loss. The question of the authenticity of the Jewish experience in this world in which each culture must be authentic is here at the heart of this Jewish account of the new multiculturalism in Germany.

Even as a child in Germany, the protagonist was looked at with suspicion as not quite Jewish enough. He goes to the bathroom at his father's factory when a pedophile next to him looks down and says, "[Y]ou are not even a real Jew! ... Your Pipi is not mangled as it is usually with Jews" (227). After the case of his father's interrupted burial is made into a media event, he appears on television but as one who does not quite fit even in this multicultural area of the media: "Why do you have a foreign accent? You were born in Gigricht. Has that anything to do with Yiddish?" (312). His accent is Austrian, but it is heard as "Jewish." There is no resolution—the community will only offer to bury his father beyond the cemetery boundary.

He and a friend decide to resolve this once and for all by stealing the body and burying it at sea—where no one asks who is Jewish enough.

These novels are multicultural in a European sense, as "authors such as Vladimir Vertlib [with] their multicultural life stories open the domestic book world to the entirely new horizon of expectation, lift their perspective above our obsessive staring at their navel."[72] Jewish multiculturalism is thus the leaven in the European bread that transforms "mere" polylingualism into true multiculturalism. For Jews, there are the various multiculturalisms that they are forced to inhabit and that force them to reshape their sense of Jewish identity. Each does try to create a new multicultural world in his or her fictions, but they are all marred by the poisonous assumptions of the multicultural in worlds in which Jewish identity cannot be reduced to the categories of political correctness—no matter whose.

ELEVEN

POINTS OF CONFLICT
Cultural Values in "Green" and "Racial" Anti-Semitism

One of the "problems" of speaking about the parallels of Jewish and Muslim textual presentations in a multicultural world is the question of whether such parallels are poisoned by contemporary Muslim anti-Semitism or older Jewish attitudes toward Islam. Given the realities of contemporary politics, it is not always clesar how one should evaluate the patterns of opinion that may or may not turn out to be generalizations about one group or the other. For example, certainly there is no greater compliment that you can make to someone than to say that he or she is "intelligent." Within the history of anti-Semitism, however, this seemingly "philo-Semitic" compliment has regularly been used as a cudgel with which to attack Jews. The line between "anti-" and "philo-Semitic" attitudes toward the Jews is always blurred, but on the issue of Jewish superior intelligence, it is clearly missing. Being "smart" is seen as a problem for Jews. Recently there has been an increased interest in what has come to be called the "new" or "Green" (i.e., Islamic) anti-Semitism.[1] The argument has been made that in the beginning of this new century, we have entered into a "new" phase in the history of anti-Semitism.

There need to be basic guidelines for the comparative study of "old" and "new" forms of anti-Semitism that are sophisticated enough to provide the answer to whether these "new" forms are truly "new," just as the experiences of Muslims in the new multicultural world certainly are "new" but have strong analogies to the experiences of the Jews in the Enlightened world of the eighteenth century and thereafter. The question of radical breaks must be linked to the evident continuities in imagining the history of anti-Semitism. In his contribution to *A New Anti-Semitism? Debating Judeophobia in 21st Century Britain*, the noted historian of anti-Semitism Peter Pulzer observed, "When every civilian death is a war crime, that concept loses its significance. When every expulsion from a village is genocide, we no longer know how to recognize genocide. When Auschwitz is everywhere, it is nowhere."[2] Traditional models of anti-Semitism can be transmuted or given new functions. But in the new world, as in the old, it is also the case that not all criticism of individual Jewish (or Israeli) actions is anti-Semitic unless it assumes that these actions are the result of inherent qualities ascribed to the "Jews." That is, the questions of ruptures and/or continuities still rely on the generalizing function of anti-Semitic rhetoric to encompass all members of that constructed category, the "Jews." Is the "new" anti-Semitism truly "new," or is it the adaptation of older models and structures that stereotype (and thus create) the "Jew" for new or different purposes or audiences? Or does it continue to shape the nature of the "Jew" for other purposes than has been the case in the past? Or, indeed, does it merely have another functional adaptation and is it nothing more than the "old" anti-Semitism writ anew?

What I intend to do in this final chapter is to provide a litmus test for looking at the seemingly "philo-Semitic" continuities and discontinuities in anti-Semitism in their historical and cultural manifestations. If these guidelines are substantial enough, that should provide a subtle set of differences to measure the innovations and borrowings of the "new" forms of anti-Semitism. My case in point, given that much of the concern has been the appearance of a "Green" (Islamic) anti-Semitism of global proportions, will be a central text of the studies of the "new" anti-Semitism, a speech by the then Prime Minister of Malaysia Mahathir bin Mohamad in 2003.[3] An analysis of the specific cultural tradition of anti-Semitism embedded in this chapter will illustrate both the appropriation of "secular" models of anti-Semitism to support a model for the secularization of Islam as well as the discontinuity that such an appropriation signals. It will focus on a theme that seems to be one of philo-Semitism: the intellectual superiority of the Jews as a cohort.

To make this case, it is clear that anti-Semitism is a problem of the specific self-constituted groups that define themselves as "non-Jews." It is a problem for "Jews," however defined, but not a problem of "Jews."

This is not to say that individual Jews cannot be anti-Semitic—history and practice show that this type of identification with the aggressor is not only possible but also—as my book on *Jewish Self-Hatred* shows—frequent.[4] Anti-Semitism thus changes its shape, form, and thrust based on the needs of those self-defined "non-Jews" across history and cultures. The British Runnymede Commission on Anti-Semitism's report, issued in January 1994, claimed in its very first point, "Distinctions should be made between anti-Judaism, anti-Semitic racism and anti-Zionism."[5] This is true only if the function of these rhetorical positions is examined in their function for "non-Jewish" needs to define that group that they imagine constituting the "Jews." In truth, they are interchangeable based on the needs of the group.

Anti-Semitism is always present among the specific self-constituted groups that define themselves as "non-Jews." Such a construction increases in "times of crisis" for those specific self-constituted "non-Jews," whether or not such crises have anything to do with the "Jews" as imagined by the group. It is vital to understand that such reappearances in altered forms of anti-Semitic views and actions are not dependant on "Jewish" actions or the actions of a single Jew, but may use them in every and any way.

While it is true that anti-Semitism is a focused form of xenophobia, it has a quality and continuity that are historically determined to a much greater degree than in other forms of xenophobia. Again, it must be remembered that xenophobia is articulated in stereotypes of essential qualities ascribed to *all* members of an imagined group by another self-defined group. The group that is described may exist autonomously in the world, may be a composite, or may be completely invented. The qualities ascribed to this imagined construct may be negative (those "Jews" are arrogant, pushy, intrusive, and financially dishonest) or positive (those "Jews" are creative and intelligent). Thus, the question that will be addressed in this chapter—the appropriation of the thesis about the nature and form of Jewish intelligence by Islamic anti-Semitic discourse—answers the powerful question of whether so-called philo-Semitic images and discourses are not but the mirror image of anti-Semitic stereotypes. So-called positive images are as much qualities universally ascribed to a constituted group as are clearly negative images. They are just as laden with the desire to provide a form of control over the image of that construct category of the "Jews" as are negative images. In every case, it is a means of defining the group by creating the stereotype rather than referring to any quality of the myriad self-definitions of

Jews as they exist and existed in the world. We shall see how close positive ("Jews are smarter than we are") and negative ("Jews use their shrewdness to manipulate us") stereotypes truly are. What is striking about most positive stereotypes is that they often are seen to be learned when applied to the "Jews" as qualities desired in the group generating the stereotype: the Jews have done "X," which we too can do to have the qualities that we ascribed to them. But such attributes are always poisoned—the most positive quality if ascribed to the "Jews" comes to have pernicious undertones.

Anti-Semitism is focused by the self-definition of those groups of "non-Jews" who are forced to define themselves against the Jews as opposed to any other group. That is, the "Jews" that they create are essential to any inherent definition of the internal integrity of the groups that define them. Historically, anti-Semitism has arisen out of the splinter religious groups that defined themselves obsessively at their point of origin as *not Jewish*. This was inherent in their claims to a universal and exclusive religion as opposed to the narrowness and parochialism attributed to the "Jews." These groups develop into *Christianity* and *Islam*, and their definition of the "Jew" is a permanent part of the written record of the establishment of these religious groups in the Gospels and the Koran. These assumptions about difference become part of the habitus of secular Europe, which sees itself by the nineteenth century in conflict with religious self-definitions. These religions (and their secular forms) in constituting themselves are "different" from the "Jews" and are driven to claim the absolute essential need for universal conversion as opposed to Jewish religious exclusivity. This notion of universalism used a perverse model of Jewish diasporism in that it assumed the existence of a religious identity that had to exist globally but that was universally inclusive rather than selective. The absolute need for groups that are essentially identical to distinguish themselves from one another in the most absolute and inherent manner is what Sigmund Freud called the "narcissism of minor differences."

In the global, colonial, and postcolonial "West," anti-Semitism (and its manifestation as "anti-Judaism") took on secular form. As religious identity in Western Europe was secularized in the seventeenth and eighteenth centuries (but religious texts and practices were also maintained), the realm of "science" was used to provide a vocabulary through which to define the "Jew." Such views were not generally available in those cultures where this secularization does not take place. The rise of so-called scientific anti-Semitism came at a point where the culture of Western Europe was enmeshed in the warfare, to quote the nineteenth-century historian Andrew Dickson White, between theology and science—theology (not religion) seemed to have lost.[6] The reality was that the secularization of religious views of the "Jews" simply replaced one more compelling set of definitions (race) for older, seemingly less compelling definitions (religion). The sense of immutability and particularism inherent to one was simply and elegantly transformed into the other. In this transmutation, anti-Semitic rhetoric acquired a different vocabulary, a different emphasis, and often different cultural and political work. One of the forms that secular anti-Semitism took in the late nineteenth and early twentieth centuries, with the establishment of the modern national state in the age of secularized culture, was anti-Zionism—hardly an invention of contemporary "Green" anti-Semitism. Bernard Lewis has convincingly argued that Islamic leaders borrowed quite directly the "modern" (i.e., secular) form of anti-Semitism from their secular European counterparts.[7] With the globalization of anti-Semitism in both Western and Islamic cultural colonialism during the nineteenth and twentieth centuries, religious and secular models promiscuously borrowed from one another. And that seems still to be the case today.

My case in point is what has come to be a proof text of the "new" or "Green" (Islamic) anti-Semitism, the final, public speech by the then Prime Minister of Malaysia Mahathir bin Mohamad at the opening of the tenth session of the Islamic Summit Conference in Malaysia on 16 October 2003.[8] He argues that there is a sense of defeat in the Islamic world: "There is a feeling of hopelessness among the Muslim countries and their people. They feel that they can do nothing right. They believe that things can only get worse. The Muslims will forever be oppressed and dominated by the Europeans and the Jews. They will forever be poor, backward and weak. Some believe, as I have said, this is the Will of Allah, that the proper state of the Muslims is to be poor and oppressed in this world." The Jews are the wellspring for this domination and succeed precisely because they have harnessed modern (secular) science and technology. Muslims must not respond by violence: "Is there no other way than to ask our young people to blow themselves up and kill people and invite the massacre of more of our own people? It cannot be that there is no other way. 1.3 billion Muslims cannot be defeated by a few million Jews." By why are the Jews so powerful and so dangerous? How do they survive? "We are actually very strong. 1.3

billion people cannot be simply wiped out. The Europeans killed 6 million Jews out of 12 million. But today the Jews rule this world by proxy. They get others to fight and die for them." The "Jews" are "the enemy," because "we are up against a people who think." He credits and damns Jews with having "invented," among other things, human rights and democracy. "With these," he explained, "they have now gained control of the most powerful countries and they, this tiny community, have become a world power." Jews are "smart," but that is only a means to the ends of their control of the world. We Muslims, he states, must now become smart and must abandon the rigid interpretation of the Koran that rejected the scientific and technological tradition of early Islam. Become a player in the new world of knowledge, he states, and you too will be "smart" just as the Jews are. As Peter Lloyd, a commentator on the Australian Broadcasting Corporation, immediately noted about the speech, "Well, he went out with a bang.... He told the summit that Muslim people could only defeat Jews, the enemy of Islam, he called them, through the use of brains as well as brawn. And really it was a kind of a call to arms, a rallying speech to Muslims to exploit what he believes is the arrogance of the Jewish people, and to in some ways emulate their response to oppression over 2,000 years of pogroms by not hitting out but by thinking their way through and strategizing."[9] Intelligence and arrogance here are interchangeable, as indeed they are in the anti-Semitic rhetoric about "smart Jews."

The irony is that the search for the meaning of Jewish intelligence within the world of Islam that so captured this thinker seems to have deep roots in the modern era. In the 1830s, when the Jewish scholar Abraham Geiger asked what were the aspects of the nature of the Jews that seemed to him to fascinate Mohammed, he responded that

> Muhammad ... was no less afraid of [the Jews'] mental superiority and
> of appearing to them as ignorant; and so his first object must have been
> to conciliate them by an apparent yielding to their views. That the Jewish
> system of belief was even then a fully developed one, which penetrated
> the life of each member of the community, is proved both by its antiquity
> and by the fact that the Talmud had already been completed. Though
> the Jews of that region [the Arabian pennisula] were among the most
> ignorant, as is shown by the silence of the Talmud concerning them,
> and also by that which was borrowed from them and incorporated in

the Quran, yet very many traditions and pithy sayings survived in the mouth of the people, which doubtless gave to the Jews an appearance of intellectual superiority in those dark times and regions of ignorance and so gained for them honour in the sight of others. Thus it came about naturally that Muhammad wanted to learn their views and to include them in his community. It was not only the idea of swelling his society with these numbers of adherents that produced this wish in him, but also the way in which they defended their own cause and their mode of dealing with him. The fact that Muhammad very often came off second best in religious disputes is evident from several sayings, and particularly from the following very decided one: —"When thou seest those who busy themselves with cavilling at Our signs, depart from them until they busy themselves in some other subject; and if Satan cause thee to forget this precept, do not sit with the ungodly people after recollection." This remarkably strong statement, in which he makes God declare it to be a work of the devil to be present at controversies about the truth of his mission[,] shows how much Muhammad had to fear from argument. Intercourse with the Jews appeared to him to be dangerous for his Muslims also, and he warns them against too frequent communication or too close intimacy with the Jews. He naturally puts this forward on grounds, other than the right ones; but the real reason for the warning is obviously that Muhammad feared the power of the Jews to shake the faith of others in the religion revealed to him.[10]

For Geiger, who was quite aware of the charges made against Jews of his time as being only superficially clever, the projective identification with a Mohammed afraid of the ability of the Jews is telling. This view echoes Kant's argument in his early work on human anthropology that Jews and women have developed language as a weapon in light of their physical inability to confront their enemies. But for the Jewish scholar Geiger, Islam certainly stands in his mental world for Christianity, as Susannah Heschel has noted.[11] Christians are afraid of "smart Jews" because, as crypto-Jews themselves, they fear the point of their origin. Being too smart can have its downside, even within the construction of Islam.

Geiger's claim about the representation of the Jews in early Islam is, however, not without merit. His view is a restatement of an older view in the vocabulary of a secularizing Islam. When we turn to the textbooks of contemporary Egypt, very far away geographically and temporally from both Mohammed and Geiger, but also moored in the middle ground between modernity and Islam, we read of the necessity to "become acquainted with the Jews' character and the way they should be treated."[12] The Jews show "stubbornness, material greed, slander, hypocrisy, plotting against Islam and the Muslims" (64). This view is as old as the one expressed by the fourteenth-century historian Ibn Khaldun in his *Introduction to the Study of History*, in which he notes the "mendacity and deviousness" of the Jews (24).[13] This mendacity becomes the slyness of the Jews that underlies their ability through their "intelligence" to manipulate the modern world.

Indeed the very notion of the "smart Jew" is an invention or (perhaps better) a scientific refiguring of a means of speaking about the "essential" nature of the Jew. One of the most powerful theses that attempt to account for this within secular scientific anti-Semitism is the notion that the "dumb" Jews died off and only the "smart" ones survived. Indeed, being "smart" was the reason for their success. It was a weapon, as Immanuel Kant had already noted in the eighteenth century, that enabled them to combat their persecutors. By the nineteenth century, such superiority was given biological rationale. The view that Jewish superior intelligence has its roots in the persecution and winnowing of the Jews has a long and complex history in the English-speaking world. In the 1920s Ellsworth Huntington, a sociologist at Yale, argued that the rebellion against the Romans in the first century C.E. weeded out the violent and destructive Jews. What was left was Jewish superior intelligence but not necessarily a more moral people.[14] Huntington's views were expressly based on assumptions about a Jewish race understood in eugenic principles. Eugenics, that movement started by Charles Darwin's cousin Francis Galton, saw the potential for both positive and negative outcomes. Greater intelligence was generally seen by him as a positive outcome. This was certainly not the case for views of Jewish intelligence.

Francis Galton's central contentions about the diminished intelligence of Catholic Europe were based on the stupidity and crudity of Catholics as results of a failed eugenic project. The Anglican Galton replicated in this view the standard image of the Irish that haunted Victorian scientific racism of the time:

> The long period of the dark ages under which Europe has lain is due,
> I believe in a very considerable degree[,] to the celibacy enjoined by

religious orders on their votaries. Whenever a man or a woman was possessed of a gentle nature that fitted him or her to deeds of charity, to meditation, to literature or to art, the social condition of the time was such that they had no refuge elsewhere than in the bosom of the Church. But the Church chose to preach and exact celibacy.... She acted precisely as if she had aimed at selecting the rudest portion of the community to be, alone, the parents of future generations.[15]

This was an attack on the diminished intelligence of Catholic Europe before the Reformation—which again permitted the priests to marry. Such views were also to be read as critiques of the barbarism and vice of Catholic Europe—as seen through the eyes of the Reformation. This view is also re-read in Charles Darwin's comments on the decline of the Spanish Empire. He attributed this decline to the entry of "men of a gentle nature, those given to meditation or culture of mind," to "the bosom of a church which demanded celibacy." The "deteriorating influence on each successive generation" was "incalculable."[16] Like Galton, Darwin implies a positive and virtuous "Northern" as opposed to a degenerate "Southern" historical development. By the nineteenth century, this was displaced on the Irish-English dichotomy that haunted British politics and culture. In the contemporary discussions, it is not only the question of the decay of Catholic power (and the concomitant growth of Protestant or Northern European power) but also the development of Jewish superior intelligence as an answer to this "Catholic" degeneration.

In the Jewish eugenic rereadings of this argument during the period, the Jews come to hold the place of the figures of power, the "liberal" Protestants, in British, nineteenth-century science.[17] The Catholics remain as the exemplum of the mismanagement of their genetic "bank." Such a move is of course the traditional, post-Haskalah move of acculturated European Jews in England and in Germany. It is the powerful overidentification of Jewry and Judaism with Protestant identity. The confusion of these two models places the Jews in the position of the intellectual power of those who encourage their "best and their brightest" to reproduce. This is reflected in Galton's comment about the Jews in the 1890s who had left their appropriate places (such as Eastern Europe) and were now competing with the British throughout the globe for resources and the space to reproduce. The anxiety about genetic reproduction, the reproduction of the same, is linked to the anxiety about the reproduction of the Other and economic power.

While Jewish savants placed themselves in the privileged place of the Anglicans (and Protestants), non-Jewish scientists clearly saw the advantage of selection as a disadvantage when it came (solely) to the Jews. The Jew is certainly seen as "overintellectualized." And this "overintellectualization" is one of the sources of his pathological state. As the Heidelberg sociologist Alfred Weber noted at the turn of the twentieth century about the Jews, "The longer a people undergoes the process of civilization, the more in-tellectualized it is—to speak in a specifically biological manner: its genetic substance is implanted with intellectual gemmules, so that it is born with the tendency to place all of the aspects of its essence in the conscious which already reflects its personal fate."[18] Weber's understanding of the biological underpinning of Jewish intelligence links it to the process of moderniza-tion. Such a materialist reading of Jewish intelligence runs against the grain. Such views are absorbed into French cultural thought as well in the 1920s. Richard Griffiths argues that the myth about the superior intelligence of the Jews becomes part of the vocabulary of French social anti-Semitism by the 1920s and the publication of Jacques de Lacretelle's 1922 novel, *Silbermann*.[19] What is striking is that such attitudes seem not to conflict with a pro-Dreyfus (or liberal) position on the part of thinkers for whom the notion of an inherent Jewish difference would have been anathema if presented in social, rather than political, context. This seems to be the case in French letters well after the fall of the Vichy government.

If there is a "selection" (to use a word that by 1945 took on a very differ-ent cast) that determines the nature of the "Jews," no historical event would have had a greater impact than the Holocaust. After the Shoah, Cyril D. Darlington, professor of botany at Oxford and one of the last clear propo-nents of Galton's view of genius, argued for a historical selection of the Jews in Babylonian captivity—a division that separated the intelligent wheat (the leaders and priests) from the chaff. The genius of the Jews was isolated in exile, where it was forced to rely on itself and did not have to defend itself against the inroads of poorer genetic stock of those left behind.[20] Such views of the wheat and the chaff follow a rather primitive reading of Spencerian evolution through the means of historical selection. Indeed, here "clever-ness" as a means of survival comes to mark the quality of Jewish superior intelligence. But both views epitomize an understanding of the origins of

Jewish superior intelligence in the biological effects of the persecution of
the Jews—a view that is a clear holdover from mid-nineteenth-century
views. The question is whether such "genius" has any true value.

While intelligence testing came to be drawn more and more into question
during the American civil rights movement in the 1960s, the myth of Jewish
superior intelligence never faded away. The work of the intelligence testers,
however, gave way to a return to the older, Galtonian method, an innovation
of the presence of Jewish superior intelligence within the high culture, the
intellectual life of the day, for "genius" as measured in intelligence tests said
absolutely nothing about accomplishment. The model that had to be used
to establish the "Jews" as superior in American, post-Shoah culture was the
accomplishments of the Jews, for the abstract reduction to statistics did not
measure the positive or negative impact that "real" (named) Jews (whatever
their background or identity) had on high culture, and this impact came to
be understood as the bottom line for a "scientific" evaluation of the meaning
of Jewish superior intelligence. Only the examination of reference works,
of lists of "great men," could prove this impact. If the intelligence testers
through the 1940s reflected the sense of Jewish marginality, by the 1950s,
the sense of anxiety gives way to the use of the discussion of Jewish superior
intelligence as a means of establishment of the proof of Jewish rootedness in
American culture. The image of Jewish superior intelligence goes from being a sign of liminality to one of centrality. But it is poisoned with the con-
current notion that such intelligence is alien, coupled with a lack of culture
and the inherent ability to constructively use that intelligence.

It is a "scientific" formulation of the views that are espoused by individuals such as the Jewish mathematician Norbert Wiener and his friend
the Marxist mathematical geneticist J. B. S. Haldane and that the American
Jewish sociologist Lewis S. Feuer comes to call the "Wiener/Haldane" thesis.[21] According to Wiener, "The biological habits of the Christians tended to
breed out of the race whatever hereditary qualities make for learning whereas the biological habits of the Jew tended to breed these qualities in."[22] This
"thesis" has as its corollary that Christians could "breed in" these qualities again. Ernest van den Haag's 1969 conservative (and self-labeled non-
Jewish) reading of "Jewish intellectual superiority supported this view."[23]
The scientist van den Haag restated this view, suggesting that Jewish males
of higher intelligence were encouraged to reproduce, and, "literally for mil-
lennia, the brightest had the best chance to marry and produce children, and

their children had the best chance to survive infancy" (14). This argument goes one step further than the turn-of-the-twentieth-century Jewish sociologist Arthur Ruppin's view concerning the desire of rich Jewish men to have smart (but not necessarily rich) husbands for their daughters. This image of high-gain individuals reproducing and producing bright and healthy children is again a semblance of control. Infant morbidity and mortality may be factors of nutrition and/or exposure to contagious illness, but rarely or directly of the intelligence of the parents. As with the desire that the best and the brightest survived the concentration camps that haunts such work, van den Haag needs to ascribe Jewish survival to Jewish superior intelligence, for (as with other non-Jewish commentators) he must create a category that would be possible for any group to enter—a category of the transmission of acquired characteristics from and through judgments about good breeding. This occurs through the mechanism of selection, that is, the best and the brightest males are permitted to reproduce. Through them the heightened skills associated with intelligence are transmitted, and thus, in the next generation, only the smartest of the smart are permitted to reproduce, ad infinitum. Such views come to color the reading of Jewish superior intelligence even in the topic of Jewish humor. In at least one recent source, such jokes are read in light of the view of Jewish selection for intelligence.[24]

But there was another side to this coin. Van den Haag argued that Christians sacrificed their "good" genes by making their priests celibate; the Jews rewarded smart rabbis with the best wives and the most support for their families. Christian genes for intelligence were diminished, and genes for Jewish superior intelligence were reinforced. "The church offered the only career in which intellectual ability was rewarded, regardless of the origin of its bearer.... But the priesthood exacted a price: celibacy. Which meant that the most intelligent portion of the population did not have offspring; their genes were siphoned off, generation after generation, into the church, and not returned to the world's, or even the church's, genetic supply" (15). Is the reverse of Jewish superior intelligence Catholic inferior intelligence? It is an explanation for the history of anti-Semitism and the persecution of the Jews, for only stupid people, so such an argument could run, would do such things? But we can undo this now by allowing our ministers to marry. The sociologist Lewis Feuer noted a further error in this logic, pointing to a long history of anxiety about misalliances among Jewish families.[25] Few rich parents sought out poor scholars; they sought out equivalent marriages either with wealthy Jews or with the scions of established rabbinic families. The range of marriage structures among Jews in Europe was also altered by the Enlightenment and by the rise of the women's movement in Central Europe in the late nineteenth century. It is the reduction of all "Jewish" experience to a single model of genetic transmission that enabled van den Haag's argument to work.

Van den Haag's rationale concerning Jewish superior intelligence explained only those communities, such as the American Jewish community, that saw itself as "spared" the murderous assault of the Shoah. Only communities such as the American Jewish community, here read as the direct offspring of Eastern European Jewry, preserved the positive genetic result of such breeding for intelligence. Such a construction of the American Jewish experience and the uniformity of the American Jewish community provided a positive reading that was quite different from the alternative model, such as that represented in the fiction of Philip Roth during the 1970s. That model saw the survival of the Jews in the United States as accidental and, indeed, as the cause of a sense of guilt among American Jews. Survival, especially the survival of an intact Jewish community, is given a new meaning in theories of genetic selection. Survival comes to be read as the preservation of the genetic result of Eastern European Jewish breeding practices in the cultural, political, and intellectual achievements of American Jewry. The survival of American Jewry comes to be the acknowledgement that the traditions of Eastern European Jewry, as represented in the work of Mark Zborowski and Elizabeth Herzog, continue in spite of the Shoah.[26] It is not accidental that to make this argument of genetic selection, all of "modern" science, the science of race leading to the Shoah, is bracketed, and the new "scientists" return to a Galtonian model of selection.

In their *The Bell Curve* (1994), the late Jewish scholar Richard Herrnstein and his non-Jewish collaborator, Charles Murray, devote only one page to the highest group in terms of intelligence—"Ashkenazic Jews of European origins," who "test higher than any other ethnic group."[27] Based on this model that equates intelligence with virtue, we would come to expect that the higher the intelligence, the greater the protection against criminality and the greater the virtue of the group. According to Herrnstein and Murray, "Jews in America and Britain have an overall IQ mean somewhere between a half and a full standard deviation above the mean, with the source of the difference concentrated in the verbal component" (275). Such test scores, however, are not sufficient for them to establish the superior intelligence of the Jews; they also rely on "analyses of occupational and scientific attainment by Jews, which constantly show their disproportionate level of success, usually by orders of magnitude, in various inventories of scientific and artistic achievement." Jews are not only smart but also creative, and—following Max Weber's reading of American Protestant culture—this is a sign of their virtue, for worldly success is a sign of a virtuous life. They use two instruments to measure intelligence—(1) catalogues of accomplishments, and (2) multiple-choice testing—mirrors the history of the construction of the image of Jewish superior intelligence from the mid-nineteenth century to the present.[28] But it is equally important to understand that *the implication of such studies is the identification and quantifiability of virtue*, and that such rather crude types of analogies are just as likely to draw the virtue of the Jews into question as to posit them as the site of virtue. Such arguments are variants on the myths that attribute superior intelligence to the Jews as a cohort.

The van den Haag argument stresses that Jewish isolation and social pariahdom had a positive biological outcome—it enabled Jews to maintain their superior intelligence as they were not accountable to forms of social and cultural pressure that "deformed" the intelligence of the Christian cohort. The response of the non-Jewish academic answered by noting that one should not create a univocal category of "Christian" but accepting the category of "the Jew" as generated in the initial position. The third voice argues from the standpoint of not the beneficent value of isolation but rather the gradual elimination of differences, here not the racial or cultural difference of the Jew, but rather the difference of the new immigrant who is being acculturated into society and losing his or her edge of Jewish superior intelligence.

The structural relationship between the "Eastern European" model evolved by van den Haag, a model that is argued to have a much longer tradition, and the "American" model of the intellectual melting pot illustrates the tension seen within a group, university teachers, that sees itself as "intellectual." The first argument evokes a specter of Jewish superior intelligence that transcends the immigrant experience; the second, a desire to include oneself in a favorable gene pool to prove intellectual ability; and the third, a view that "after me, the deluge," that is, after the total integration of the Jews into the American body politic, Jewish superior intelligence will be eliminated. All of these views accept an idea of Jewish superior intelligence and relate to it as a given, staking their position as intellectuals around this "reality." These are all elaborations of the van den Haag–Galton thesis that see breeding as affecting "intelligence" over time.

Such a manipulation of the implications of Jewish superior intelligence can be seen in part in Kevin MacDonald's work, specifically his book *A People That Shall Dwell Alone: Judaism as a Group Evolutionary Strategy*.[29] MacDonald generally follows a "eugenic" argument, though he calls his own approach an "evolutionary" one (180). Here the implications of an "evolutionary psychological" model reveal the inherent biases in all narratives that wish to reconstruct the true "reason" why certain psychological traits exist. If they do not exist, of course, the narrative provides a reason why they must exist! The creation of such "family romances," to misuse Freud's phrase, is the reason that MacDonald was one of the expert witnesses called by David Irving in his unsuccessful prosecution of Deborah Lipstadt for slander. What he does argue in his trilogy—*A People That Shall Dwell Alone: Judaism as a Group Evolutionary Strategy* (Praeger, 1994); *Separation and Its Discontents: Toward an Evolutionary Theory of Anti-Semitism* (Praeger, 1998); and *The Culture of Critique: An Evolutionary Analysis of Jewish Involvement in Twentieth-Century Intellectual and Political Movements* (Praeger, 1998)—is that anti-Semitism can be understood as a natural by-product of a Darwinian strategy for Jewish survival. Like the parallel "Green" anti-Semitism of Mahathir bin Mohamad, he ascribed the invention of the modern world to the "Jews" as a sign of the corrosive effect of their peculiar intelligence, intelligence crafted as a weapon to use against the world in which they live. His publishers are less subtle and sell his book under the advertisement "Jewish Eugenics." Whatever the label, his work also relies on the model of eugenic selection with its roots in Galton's idea of "hereditary genius." He sees "Judaism" not merely as religious practice but also, in light of the nineteenth-century model of Moses as the first hygienist, as a "group strategy that is fairly (but not completely) closed to penetration from gentile gene pools" (ix). It is not completely clear that this was initially a conscious model. MacDonald places "biological drives" in the place of the Divinity in his model of how the history of the Jews developed. What was initially articulated within the laws of Judaism for biological reasons has now become an "unconscious" mode of selection made by the Jewish gene.

The Jews are, for MacDonald, the only group to "avoid the powerful tendencies toward cultural and genetic assimilation" (ix). Thus there seems to be a negative centrifugal force in the genetic pool driving closed, homogeneous groups into mixing and, giving the positive valence placed on "purity" in MacDonald's argument, into corruption. The Jews have maintained this biological separation through a "variety of cultural practices" such as "religious practices and beliefs, language and mannerisms, physical appearance, customs, occupations, and physically separated areas of residence which were administered by Jews according to Jewish civil and criminal law" (ix). This list of "cultural practices" is an odd one and needs further interpretation. That language and "mannerism" might well be understood as cultural one can accept; even the idea that there is a set of practices, such as infant male circumcision, that define the Jews who continue to practice them is probably true. But how "physical appearance" can be seen as a voluntary act, except in the question of costume, is puzzling. Do Jews culturally select their supposedly Jewish features? Is the Jewish nose elective? Indeed, MacDonald places a positive valence on the selection from within rather than measuring the selection from without. The idea of the ghetto, for example, seems to have arisen because of the desire to separate Jewish living spaces because Jews were becoming integrated into Venetian society, not because they were separate.

Among the various strategies that MacDonald sees as fostering this "group evolutionary strategy" is the tendency for Jews to favor their own kind through the use of charity (chapter 6) and in economic dealings (chapter 7). But at the very core of MacDonald's argument is the question of Jewish superior intelligence. He stresses the selection model—he sees selection as a result of catastrophes in which the survivors, such as those of the Babylonian captivity, formed a genetic elite—and he sees "the Talmudic academy … as an arena of natural selection for intelligence" (181). He also advocates a "gentile selection hypothesis" in which, because "of the hostile gentile environment, there were strong pressures that favored the resourceful, intelligent, and wealthy members of the Jewish community" (192). One need not repeat how bizarre such an argument is in American scholarship after the Shoah. It presumes an uninterrupted, historically pure practice of Jewish life that can be simply and directly traced back to the Biblical origins of the Jews. The historical discontinuities, especially the Shoah, are simply removed from consideration as part of a history of the Jews. This type of "evolutionary psychological" revisionism, which reinterprets the Shoah as the means to a reinforcement of Jewish separation, is odd. For MacDonald, "the Nazi holocaust" leads toward "a tendency to stress a unique Jewish identity, rather than to assimilate" (49). This instrumental use of the Shoah runs throughout this book. It shows a strange sense of "meaning" attributed to the extreme violence of the Shoah. It reads the "selection" that occurred as an act that furthers the quality of the Jewish genetic pool.

The manifestations of those features of the Jewish family that are seen as furthering Jewish superior intelligence are recorded in great detail. And his basis for this is the "virtually common knowledge" that Jewish parents are more supportive of the intellectual lives of their children (193). MacDonald, like the earlier post-Shoah investigators, relies on Zborowski and Herzog as the model for the ideal Jewish family with its emphasis on education and their seemingly visceral dismissal of the uneducated (185). Education is the sole goal—what is attributed to that educational process is only a positive experience. MacDonald thus again surveys the psychometric literature and tabulates, once again, the Nobel Prize winners. All of this Western Jewish experience grows out of the Eastern Jewish educational practices that abhorred secular learning and its methods. The ideal physical type of this intellectual child is "pale, emaciated, aflame with inner light" (207). This quote, taken from Zborowski and Herzog, points toward precisely the body type seen as destructive to Jewish superior intelligence by earlier generations of Jewish commentators. It is the point of jokes in the 1920s. Thus Werner Finck, one of the leading non-Jewish cabaret artists in Berlin during the 1920s, commented, when a heckler yelled "Jew Boy" at him, "You are mistaken, I only look that intelligent."[30] Or, to read this in the American context: Herbert Lindenberger, professor of comparative literature at Stanford University, writes about his uncle, a plastic surgeon, offering him a nose job in the 1950s. Uncle Fred states that his nephew's nose will be "bad for your career the way it is." Lindenberger replies that "in my particular field people usually took you for bright if they also took you for Jewish."[31] Such post-Enlightenment fantasies of the visible body of the Jew becoming invisible yet retaining its intellectual difference (itself an image of the traditional Jewish desire for learning) are extended in MacDonald's argument. Jewish superior intelligence does not stand alone for MacDonald. Jews also, according to MacDonald, have higher rates of certain mental illnesses, especially affective disorders (211). Mental illness and Jewish superior intelligence seem linked in the recent literature discussing the relationship between bipolar disorders and creativity. Here it is one further attribute of the Jewish gene pool.

It is evident that MacDonald recasts all of the hoary old myths about Jewish psychological difference and its presumed link to Jewish superior intelligence in contemporary psychobiological garb.[32] They become signs of Jewish virtue and the rationale for Jewish achievement, following the readings of the eugenists. But it is also an inherently American psychobiological approach to the question of Jewish superior intelligence, for all of the qualities read by MacDonald as signs of superiority in their historical context are qualities perceived as positive in American society. They are signs of success (and virtue) as well as of intelligence. And these qualities are repeatable, if only other groups will undertake the same pattern of selection as the Jews. Here the risk factors must also be taken into account, but the overall advantage of Jewish intelligence is so great as to compensate for other genetic anomalies.[33]

Thus different worlds breed different readings of the intelligence of the Jews. But in all cases this faulty intelligence, with its corrosive products such as human rights and social equality, undermines the dominant world in which the writer lives and which he wishes to improve. "Green" anti-Semitism of the Mahathir bin Mohamad mode, which wishes to both combat the "Jews" and improve the "Muslims," has evident parallels in the work of writers such as MacDonald. Mahathir bin Mohamad's image of the "Muslims" is as much of a construction in his argument as his image of the "Jews." He does not look at "successful" Muslims in the globalized Ummah, only at nation-states he sees as Islamic. Yet these arguments, which seem to pull both toward a scientific, secularizing notion of the "Jews," also reveal the oddly underlying arguments of a national religious conflict—between Catholics and Protestants—that has nothing explicit to do with the "Jews" yet is part of its initial formulation. Contemporary Islam, as Olivier Roy has noted, now tends to move in precisely the direction of such "modern" scientific or social arguments rather than the older, purely theological ones.[34] Here the rhetoric of Islam borrows from that of the older and newer anti-Semitism. So does anti-Semitism in the guise of philo-Semitism accomplish its political and social work.

NOTES

CHAPTER ONE

1. Rupert Jentzsch, "Das rituelle Schlachten von Haustieren in Deutschland ab 1933" (Ph. D. diss., Tierärztliches Hochschul, Hannover, 1998).
2. For deep background, see Jonathan M. Hess, *Germans, Jews, and the Claims of Modernity* (New Haven, Conn.: Yale University Press, 2002).
3. Elaine Sciolino, "Ban on Head Scarves Takes Effect in a United France," *New York Times*, 3 September 2004, A9.
4. "A Tragic Twist of the Scarf," *Economist*, 4 September 2004, 49.
5. Olivier Roy, *Globalised Islam: The Search for the New Ummah* (London: Hurst & Co., 2004), 24.
6. Tom Hundley, "'No Strikes, No Sit-ins' over France's Scarf Ban," *Chicago Tribune*, 8 September 2004, 6.
7. Here I reflect the debates about "secularization" that have dominated much of the past half-century from Carl Becker to Hannah Arendt to M. H. Abrams to Peter Berger to Hans Blumenberg's *The Legitimacy of the Modern Age* (trans. Robert M. Wallace [Cambridge, Mass.: MIT Press, 1983]) and beyond. Elizabeth Brient, "Hans Blumenberg and Hannah Arendt on the 'Unworldly Worldliness' of the Modern Age," *Journal of the History of Ideas* 61 (2000): 513–30.
8. Adam Sutcliffe, *Judaism and Enlightenment* (Cambridge: Cambridge University Press, 2003).
9. See Charles Taylor, "Models of Secularism," in *Secularism and Its Critics*, ed. Rajeev Bhargava (Delhi: Oxford University Press, 1998), 31–53; and Talal Asad, *Formations of the Secular: Christianity, Islam, Modernity* (Stanford, Calif.: Stanford University Press, 2003).
10. Richard W. Bulliet, *The Case for Islamo-Christian Civilization* (New York: Columbia University Press, 2004), 12.
11. Associated Press, "French Bishop Orders Recall of Anti-Semitic Bible," Thursday, 9 March 1995, AM cycle.
12. Susannah Heschel, *Abraham Geiger and the Jewish Jesus* (Chicago: University of Chicago Press, 1998).
13. Ignaz Goldziher, *Tagebuch*, ed. Alexander Scheiber (Leiden: Brill, 1978), 59.
14. Jonathan Sacks, *The Dignity of Difference: How to Avoid the Clash of Civilizations* (London: Continuum, 2002). See also Richard Harries, "[On] Jonathan Sacks, *The Dignity of Difference; How to Avoid the Clash of Civilisations* (2002)," *Scottish Journal of Theology* 57 (2004): 109–15.
15. David Biale, *Eros and the Jews* (Berkeley: University of California Press, 1997).
16. Y. Michal Bodemann and Gökce Yurdaku, "Diaspora lernen: Wie sich türkische Einwanderer an den Juden in Deutschland orientieren," *Süddeutsche Zeitung* (2 November 2005) and Y. Michal Bodemann and Gökce Yurdaku, "Geborgte Narrative: Wie sich türkische Einwanderer an den Juden in Deutschland orientieren," *Soziale Welt* 56 (2005): 11–33.

17. For an excellent case study of the adaptation of Judaism as religious practice in the American Diaspora, see Jenna Joselit, *The Wonders of America: Reinventing American Jewish Culture 1880–1950* (New York: Hill and Wang, 1994).

18. Alan Dundes, *The Blood Libel Legend* (Madison: University of Wisconsin Press, 1991).

19. Asad, *Formations of the Secular*, 180.

20. See Michael Mack, *German Idealism and the Jew* (Chicago: University of Chicago Press, 2003).

21. The complexity of this position is highlighted in the essays collected by Janet R. Jakobsen and Ann Pellegrini, eds., "World Secularisms at the Millennium," *Social Text* 18, no. 3 (2000). See specifically their introduction on 1–27.

22. See the essay by Ranu Samantrai, "Continuity or Rupture? An Argument for Secular Britain," *Social Text* 18, no. 3 (2000): 105–21.

23. Two polemical but informative books shape their argument about contemporary Islamic identity primarily around the rhetoric of the Israeli-Palestinian conflict rather than as part of the struggle about the modernization of Islam both within and beyond Europe: Jack Goody, *Islam in Europe* (London: Polity, 2004); and Gilles Kepel, *The War for Muslim Minds: Islam and the West*, trans. Pascale Ghazaleh (Cambridge, Mass.: Belknap Press of Harvard University Press, 2004). See also Ella Shohat, "Columbus, Palestine and Arab-Jews: Toward a Relational Approach to Community Identity," in *Cultural Readings of Imperialism: Edward Said and the Gravity of History*, ed. Keith Ansell-Pearson, Benita Parry, and Judith Squires (New York: St. Martin's, 1997), 88–105; and Asad, *Formations of the Secular*, 158–80.

24. Pierre Nora, ed., *Les France: Conflits et partages*, vol. 1 of *Les Lieux de mémoire* (Paris: Gallimard, 1993).

25. Zion Zohar, "Oriental Jewry Confronts Modernity: The Case of Rabbi Ovadiah Yosef," *Modern Judaism* 24 (2004): 120–49, here 132–33.

26. See Bassam Tibi, *Krieg der Zivilisationen* (Hamburg: Hoffmann & Campe, 1995). His work is available in English: Bassam Tibi, *The Challenge of Fundamentalism* (Berkeley: University of California Press, 2002); and Bassam Tibi, *Islam between Culture and Politics* (New York: Palgrave Macmillan, 2002).

27. Tariq Ramadan, *Western Muslims and the Future of Islam* (New York: Oxford University Press, 2003); and Feisal Abdul Rauf, *What's Right with Islam: A New Vision for Muslims and the West* (San Francisco: HarperSanFrancisco, 2004).

28. Samuel P. Huntington, "The Hispanic Challenge," *Foreign Policy* (March–April 2004): 1–16; this was later included in Samuel P. Huntington, *Who Are We: The Challenges to America's National Identity* (New York: Simon & Schuster, 2004).

29. Richard Rodriguez, *Brown: The Last Discovery of America* (New York: Penguin, 2003).

30. Gloria Anzaldúa, *Borderlands/La Frontera: The New Mestiza* (San Francisco: Spinsters/Aunt Lute, 1987), 79–81.

31. Christine Welsh, "Women in the Shadows: Reclaiming a Metis Heritage," *Descant* 24 (1993): 89–103.

32. Ruth Elizabeth Quiroa, "Literature as Mirror: Analyzing the Oral, Written, and Artistic Responses of Young Mexican-Origin Children to Mexican American–Themed Picture Storybooks" (Ph.D. diss., University of Illinois, Urbana, 2004).

33. Howard Adelman and John H. Simpson, eds., *Multiculturalism, Jews and Identities in Canada* (Jerusalem: Magnes Press, 1996).

34. Edward W. Said, *Culture and Imperialism* (New York: Alfred A. Knopf, 1993), 58.

35. Martin Bernal, *The Fabrication of Ancient Greece 1785–1985*, vol. 1 of *Black Athena: The Afroasiatic Roots of Classical Civilization* (New Brunswick, N.J.: Rutgers University Press, 1987). See David A. Hollinger, *Postethnic America: Beyond Multiculturalism* (New York: Basic Books, 1996), 126–27.

36. See for example the complexity outlined by Hana Wirth-Nesher, "Language as Homeland in Jewish-American Literature," in *Insider/Outsider: American Jews and Multiculturalism*, ed. David Biale, Michael Galchinsky, Susan Heschel (Berkeley: University of California Press, 1998), 212–30.

37. Asad, *Formations of the Secular*, 54.

38. Pierre Bourdieu and Loic Wacquant, "NewLiberalSpeak: Notes on the New Planetary Vulgate," trans. David Macey, March 2005, http://www.radicalphilosophy.com/print. asp?editorial_id=9956 (accessed 19 January 2006).

39. See Chicago Cultural Studies Group, "Critical Multiculturalism," reprinted in David Theo Goldberg, ed., *Multiculturalism: A Critical Reader* (Oxford: Blackwell, 1994), 107–40, here 135.

40. Irshad Manji, *The Trouble with Islam Today* (New York: St. Martin's Griffin, 2003), 199.

41. Paul Gilroy, *After Empire: Melancholia or Convivial Culture?* (London: Routtledge, 2004).

42. Norbert Elias, *The History of Manners*, vol. 1 of *The Civilizing Process*, trans. Edmund Jephcott (New York: Pantheon, 1978), 5.

43. Olivier Roy, *Globalised Islam*, 264–65.

44. See Philip Lewis, *Islamic Britain: Religion, Politics and Identity among British Muslims* (London: I. B. Tauris, 2002), for the background and history of this incident.

45. All quotes are in my translation and are taken from Zafer Senoçak, *Gefährliche Verwandtschaft* (Munich: Babel, 1998). On Senoçak, see Leslie A. Adelson, "Back to the Future: Turkish Remembrances of the GDR and Other Phantom Pasts," in *The Cultural After-Life of East Germany: New Transnational Perspectives*, ed. Leslie A. Adelson (Washington, D.C.: American Institute for Contemporary German Studies [AICGS], 2002), 93–109; Andreas Huyssen, "Diaspora and Nation: Migration into Other Pasts," *New German Critique* 88 (2003): 147–64; Katharina Gerstenberger, "Difficult Stories: Generation, Genealogy, Gender in Zafer Senoçak's *Gefährliche Verwandtschaft* and Monika Maron's *Pawels Briefe*," in *Recasting German Identity: Culture, Politics, and Literature in the Berlin Republic*, ed. Stuart Taberner and Frank Finlay (Woodbridge, UK: Camden House, 2002), 235–49; Sandra Hestermann, "The German-Turkish Diaspora and Multicultural German Identity: Hyphenated and Alternative Discourses of Identity in the Works of Zafer Senoçak and Feridun Zaimoglu," in *Diaspora and Multiculturalism: Common Traditions and New Developments*, ed. Monika Fludernik (Amsterdam: Rodopi, 2003), 235–49; Matthias Konzett, "Zafer Senoçak im Gesprach," *German Quarterly* 76 (2003): 131–39; Katharina Hall, "'Bekanntlich sind Dreiecksbeziehungen am kompliziertesten': Turkish, Jewish and German Identity in Zafer Senoçak's *Gefährliche Verwandtschaft*," *German Life and Letters* 56 (2003): 72–88; and Leslie A. Adelson, "The Turkish Turn in Contemporary German Literature and Memory Work," *Germanic Review* 77 (2002): 326–38.

46. Gershom Scholem, "Against the Myth of the German-Jewish Dialogue," in *On Jews and Judaism in Crisis*, ed. Werner J. Dannhauser (New York: Schocken, 1976), 61–64, here 61. See also Peter Schäfer and Gary Smith, eds., *Gershom Scholem. Zwischen den Disziplinen* (Frankfurt am Main: Suhrkamp, 1995).

47. Rudolf Virchow, "Gesamtbericht über die Farbe der Haut, der Haare und der Augen der Schulkinder in Deutschland," *Archiv für Anthropologie* 16 (1886): 275–475.

48. George L. Mosse, *Toward the Final Solution: A History of European Racism* (New York: Howard Fertig, 1975), 90–91.

CHAPTER TWO

1. John Efron, *Medicine and the German Jews: A History* (New Haven, Conn.: Yale University Press, 2001), 108–17.

2. Marianna Valverde, *Disease of the Will: Alcohol and the Dilemmas of Freedom* (Cambridge: Cambridge University Press, 1998); see specifically her chapter, "The Jews vs. The Irish," 115–19. This debate is presented in much greater detail by Charles R. Snyder, *Alcohol and the Jews: A Cultural Study of Drinking and Sobriety* (Carbondale: Southern Illinois University Press, 1978). See also Louis Lieberman, "Jewish Alcoholism and the Disease Concept," *Journal of Psychology and Judaism* 11 (1987): 165–80; K. C. M. Loewenthal, *Alcohol and Suicide Related Ideas and Behaviour among Jews and Protestants* (London: Economic and Social Research Council, 2002); and K. M. Loewenthal, M. Lee, A. K. Macleod, S. Cook, and V. Goldblatt, "Drowning Your Sorrows? Attitudes towards Alcohol in U.K. Jews and Protestants: A Thematic Analysis," *International Journal of Social Psychiatry* 49 (2003): 204–15.

3. Shoshana H. Shea, Tamara L. Wall, Lucinda G. Carr, and Ting-Kai Li, "ADH2 and Alcohol-Related Phenotypes in Ashkenazic Jewish American College Students," *Behavior Genetics* 10 (2001): 231–39.

4. D. A. Gilder, T. L. Wall, and C. L. Ehlers, "Psychiatric Diagnoses among Mission Indian Children with and without a Parental History of Alcohol Dependence," *Journal for the Study of Alcoholism* 63 (2002): 18–23.

5. "Researchers Find Gene Mutation That Protects against Addiction," *Pain & Central Nervous System Week*, 7 January 2002, 2.

6. J. H. Tucker, "To What Agent or Agents Are the Jews Indebted for Their Reported Exemption from Cholera," *Lancet* 64 (1854): 552.

7. Edward Greenhow, "Alleged Exemption of the Jews from Cholera," *Lancet* 65 (1865): 50; answered by J. H. Tucker, "Alleged Exemption of the Jews from Cholera," *Lancet* 65 (1865): 110.

8. "The Health of the Jews," *Lancet* 105 (1875): 484.

9. Thomas Lloyd, "Prompt Medical Attendance on the Poor: Plan amongst the Jews," *Lancet* 29 (1837): 456.

10. Kate M. Loewenthal, Andrew K. MacLeod, Susan Cook, Michelle Lee, and Vivienne Goldblatt, "Beliefs about Alcohol among UK Jews and Protestants: Do They Fit the Alcohol-Depression Hypothesis?" *Social Psychiatry and Psychiatric Epidemiology* 38 (2003): 122–27.

11. Shoshana Weiss, "Attitudes of Israeli Jewish and Arab High School Students toward Alcohol Control Measures," *Journal of Drug Education* 29 (1999): 41–52.

12. H. Bar, P. Eldar, and S. Weiss, "Alcohol Drinking Habits and Attitudes of the Adult Jewish Population in Israel 1987," *Journal of Drug Alcohol Dependency* 23 (1989): 237–45.

13. Rachel Lev-Wiesel, "The Right Stuff: Key Personality Characteristics That Indicate Success in Overcoming Addiction in Israel," in *Drug Problems: Cross-Cultural Policy and Program Development*, ed. Richard Isralowitz, Mohammed Afifi, and Richard Rawson (Westport, Conn.: Auburn House, 2002), 233–42.

14. Steven L. Berg, *Jewish Alcoholism and Drug Addiction: An Annotated Bibliography* (Westport, Conn.: Greenwood Press, 1993).

15. In general, see the more recent works by David Sorkin, *The Berlin Haskalah and German Religious Thought: Orphans of Knowledge* (London: Vallentine Mitchell, 2000); Michael A. Meyer, *Judaism within Modernity: Essays on Jewish History and Religion* (Detroit, Mich.: Wayne State University Press, 2001); Jonathan M. Hess, *Germans, Jews and the Claims of Modernity* (New Haven, Conn.: Yale University Press, 2002); Arno Herzig, *Judentum und Aufklärung: jüdisches Selbstverständnis in der bürgerlichen Öffentlichkeit* (Göttingen, Germany: Vandenhoeck & Ruprecht, 2002); and Jeremy Asher Dauber, *Antonio's Devils: Writers of the Jewish Enlightenment and the Birth of Modern Hebrew and Yiddish Literature*

(Stanford, Calif.: Stanford University Press, 2004). See also Steven M. Lowenstein, "The Pace of Modernization of German Jewry in the Nineteenth Century," *Leo Baeck Institute Yearbook* 21 (1976) 41-56; *The Mechanics of Change: Essays in the Social History of German Jewry* (Atlanta, Ga. : Scholars Press, 1992); *The Berlin Jewish Community, 1770-1830: Enlightenment, Family, and Crisis* (New York: Oxford University Press, 1994).

16. Norbert Elias, *The Civilizing Process*, trans. Edmund Jephcott, with some notes and revisions by the author (1939; rev. ed., Oxford: Basil Blackwell, 1982).

17. Jean Comaroff and John Comaroff, eds., *Modernity and Its Malcontents: Ritual and Power in Postcolonial Africa* (Chicago: University of Chicago Press, 1993), xv.

18. P. J. Bruns, "Vorschlag an die Juden, das Purimfest abzuschafen," *Berlinerische Monatschrift* (1790): 377–80. Paul Jakob Bruns was a polymath but was best known in his time as the author of *Neue systematische Erdbeschreibung von Africa* (Nuremberg, Germany: Schneider und Weigel, 1799) and *Beiträge zur kritischen Bearbeitung unbenutzter alter Handschriften und Urkunden*, 3 vols. (Brunswick, Germany: Reichard, 1802–1803). He also edited *Martin Luthers ungedruckte Predigten* (Helmstädt, Germany: Fleckeisen, 1796).

19. What Bruns does not do is to evoke the older image of the hanging of Haman as a parody of the Crucifixion. This image may well be part of the medieval rhetoric associated with the blood libel. See Cecil Roth, "The Feast of Purim and the Origins of the Blood Accusation," *Speculum* 4 (1933): 520–26; and Gerd Mentgen, "Über den Ursprung der Ritualmordfabel," *Aschkenas* 4 (1994): 405–16.

20. Johann Jakob Schudt, *Jüdische Merckwürdigkeiten* (Frankfurt am Main: n.p., 1714), vol. 2, sec. 6, ch. 35, 308–16.

21. Martin Luther, *Luther's Works: The Christian in Society IV*, vol. 47 of *Luther's Works* (Philadelphia: Fortress Press, 1971), 47:137–306, here 47:146.

22. Mikhail Bakhtin, *Problems of Dostoevsky's Poetics*, trans R. W. Rotsel, Theory & History of Literature (Minneapolis: University of Minnesota Press, 1984), 129–30.

23. [David Friedländer], "Freimüthige Gedanken eines Juden über den Vorschlag an die Juden, das Purimfest abzuschaffen," *Berlinische Monatschrift* (1790): 563–77. See Steven M. Lowenstein, *The Jewishness of David Friedländer and the Crisis of Berlin Jewry*, Braun Lectures in the History of the Jews in Prussia 3 (Ramat Gan, Israel: Bar-Ilan University Press, 1994).

24. Leopold Zunz, *Die Ritus des synagogalen Gottesdienstes, geschichtlich entwickelt*, 2 vols. (Berlin: J. Springer, 1855–1859), 2:69.

25. Bruns's rhetoric seems to have a history among "modern" theologians. See the Amsterdam theologian Philippe (Philipp) van (de) Limborch, *De veritate religionis Christianae, amica collatio cum erudito Judaeo* (Gouda: Apud Justum ab Hoeve, 1687), in his screed against all forms of Jewish ritual practice as defended by Uriel Acosta. It was in a missive to Limborch that John Locke formulated his famed "Letter on Toleration" (1685). This is his answer.

26. Adolf Freyherr Knigge, *Ueber den Umgang mit Menschen*, 3 vols., 3rd ed. (Frankfurt am Main: n.p., 1794); unless otherwise noted, the translations are from Baron Knigge, *Practical Philosophy of Social Life*, trans. P. Will, 2 vols. (London: T. Cadell, 1796).

27. Knigge, *Ueber den Umgang*, 3:115–20, here 3:117. See also Ruth Klüger, *Knigges Umgang mit Menschen* (Göttingen, Germany: Wallstein, 1996), 15–16.

28. See Nathan Rotenstreich, *The Recurring Pattern: Studies in Anti-Judaism in Modern Thought* (London: Weidenfeld & Nicolson, 1963), 23–47 on Kant.

29. Immanuel Kant, *Anthropologie in pragmatischer Hinsicht*, ed. Wilhelm Weischedel, in *Kant: Werke in Zehn Bände, Schriften zur Anthropologie, Geschichtsphilosophie, Politk und Pädagogik*, 2nd ed. (Darmstadt, Germany: Wissenschaftliche Buchgesellschaft, 1975), 10:399–690. All citations are to the pagination of the first edition ("A"), as noted in this edition; this is identical with all other Kant editions. Here, 10:A72–74. See E. M. Jellinek, "Immanuel Kant on

Drinking," *Quarterly Journal of Studies of Alcohol* 1 (1941): 777–80. This view that Jews drink less because of their visibility as Jews is argued in the mid-twentieth century by D. P. Glad, "Attitudes and Experiences of American-Jewish and American-Irish Male Youths as Related to Differences in Adult Rates of Inebriety," *Quarterly Journal of Studies of Alcohol* 8 (1947): 406–72.

30. Ibid., footnote to A131.

31. Hannah Arendt, *Lectures on Kant's Political Philosophy*, ed. Reinhold Beiner (Chicago: University of Chicago Press, 1982), 8.

32. Immanuel Kant, *Immanuel Kant's Menschenkunde: Nach handschriftlichen Vorlesungen: Nach handschriftlichten Vorlesungen*, ed. Friedrich Christian Starke (Leipzig, Germany: Die Expedition des europäischen Aufsehers, 1831), 299.

33. The idea that Jewish "sobriety" is a result of historical process has been put forth by Mark Keller, "The Great Jewish Drink Mystery," *British Journal of Addiction* 64 (1970): 287–96, who dates this to the reestablishment of the Second Temple. Keller assumes a uniformity of modern Jewish experience and of the image of this unitary stereotype of the Jew as sober. He does understand this as part of a process of social change and adaptation. See also L. D. Hankoff, "The Roots of Jewish Sobriety: Alcoholism in the First Century C.E.," *Koroth* 9 (1988) 62–72.

34. Andrew Barr, *Drink: A Social History of America* (New York: Carroll and Graf, 1999), 162.

35. James Samuelson, *A History of Drink: A Review, Social, Scientific, and Political* (London: Trübner & Co., 1878), 70–71.

36. Maurice Fishberg, *Health and Sanitation of the Immigrant Jewish Population of New York* (New York: Cowan, 1902), 16. See his summary statement: Maurice Fishberg, *The Jews: A Study of Race and Environment*, 2 vols. (New York: Harper, 1949).

37. Norman Kerr, *Inebriety: Its Etiology, Pathology, Treatment and Jurisprudence* (London: H. K. Lewis, 1889), 142, 145–46, here 146.

38. J. Snowman, "Jewish Eugenics," *Jewish Review* (1913): 159–74, here 166. See L. Chienisse, "Rassenpathologie und Alkoholismus bei den Juden," *Zeitschrift für die Demographie und Statistik der Juden* 6 (1910): 1–8, for French examples.

39. Fishberg, *Health and Sanitation*, 18.

40. Izak Goller, *A Purim-Night's Dream* (London: Ghetto Press, 1931), 21.

41. Robert Bales, "The 'Fixation Factor' in Alcohol Addiction: A Hypothesis Derived from a Comparative Study of Irish and Jewish Social Norms" (Ph.D. diss., Harvard University, 1944); and Robert Bales, "Cultural Differences in Rates of Alcoholism," *Quarterly Journal of Studies of Alcohol* 6 (1946): 480–99.

42. Maurice Samuel, *The World of Sholom Aleichem* (New York: Knopf, 1943), 131.

43. Jerome Rothenberg, "The Noble," from his *A Book of Writings* (New York: New Directions, 1974), 45. Part of the literary image of the Eastern Jew in (at least) Polish literature is his role as a tavern keeper, keeping the peasants drunk in order to exploit them. See Magdalena M. Opalski, *The Jewish Tavern-Keeper and His Tavern in Nineteenth Century Polish Literature* (Jerusalem: Zalman Shazar Center for Jewish History, 1986).

44. "Ansprache eines nüchteren Trunkenen in einer Versammlung trunkener Nüchterner, gehalten auf dem großen Marktplatz zwischen dem Rheine und der Oder am Purim 5617," *Jeschurun* 3 (1857): 377–82. See Robert Liberles, *Religious Conflict in Social Context: The Resurgence of Orthodox Judaism in Frankfurt am Main, 1838–1877* (Westport, Conn.: Greenwood Press, 1985).

45. "Die Bedeutung des Purimfestes," *Jeschurun* 20 (1887): 145–47. This is simply one of a number of such presentations. See "Zum Purimfeste," *Jeschurun* 19 (1886): 161–63; and the modern Hebrew poem by Elias Plessner, "Le-purim!" *Jeschurun* 20 (1887): 153.

46. Heinrich Graetz, "Der historische Hintergrund und die Abfassungszeit des Buches Esther und der Ursprung des Purim-Festes," *Monatsschrift für Geschichte und Wissenschaft des Judentums* 35 (1886): 425–42, 473–503, 521–42; and Moritz Steinschneider, "Purim und Parodie," *Monatsschrift für Geschichte und Wissenschaft des Judentums* 46 (1902): 275–80, 372–76, 473–78, 567–82; 47 (1903): 84–89, 169–80, 279–86, 360–70, 468–74; and 48 (1904): 242–47, 504–9. See also Max Steif, "Die Purimfeier in historischer Beleuchtung," *Ost und West* 5 (1905): 171–80; and the illustrations for "Purim-Maskenball bei den portugiesischen Juden in Holland im siebzehnten Jahrhundert," *Ost und West* 5 (1905): S171–72.

47. Kaufmann Kohler and Henry Malter, "Purim," *The Jewish Encyclopedia*, 12 vols. (New York: Funk and Wagnalls, 1901–1906), 7:274–79, here 7:277.

48. Jizchak Leib Perez, "Das ganze Jahr betrunken und am Purim nüchtern," trans. Alexander Eliasberg, *Neue jüdische Monatshefte* 1 (1917): 317–22.

49. *Die Welt* 4 (1900): 13.

50. Martin Buber, "Ein Purim-Prolog," *Die Welt* 5 (1901): 10–11.

51. See *Purim-Feier: Mittwoch, den 13. Weadar 5660 (14. März 1900) veranstaltet von den national-jüdischen Vereinen Berlins* (Berlin: n.p., 1900); Arthur Kahn, *Der Judentag* (Bonn: n.p., 1900); and Max I. Bodenheimer, *Der Zionismus in Deutschland und der Judentag* (Cologne: Verlag der Zionistischen Vereinigung für Deutschland, [1901]).

52. Max Jungmann, "Der deutsche Judentag," *Die Welt* 5 (1901): 10–11.

53. See Jack Zipes, ed. and trans., *The Operated Jew: Two Tales of Anti-Semitism* (New York: Routledge, 1991).

54. Hugo Hoppe, *Krankheiten und Sterblichkeit bei Juden und Nichtjuden mit besonderer Berücksichtigung der Alkoholfrage* (Berlin: S. Calvary, 1903), 42–43.

55. Moshe Werzberger, "Purim: Time for a Sober Look at Jews and Alcohol," http://www.orthodoxcaucus.org/projects/rove/werzberger.htm (accessed 19 January 2006).

CHAPTER THREE

1. David A. Hollinger, *Postethnic America: Beyond Multiculturalism* (New York: Basic Books, 1996), 92–93. This volume is part of an ongoing discussion about the nature of cultural and ethnic identity in America begun by Nathan Glazer and Daniel P. Moynihan, *Beyond the Melting Pot: The Negroes, Puerto Ricans, Jews, Italians, and Irish of New York City* (Cambridge, Mass.: MIT Press, 1963).

2. See my *Smart Jews: The Construction of the Idea of Jewish Superior Intelligence at the Other End of the Bell Curve*, the Inaugural Abraham Lincoln Lectures (Lincoln: University of Nebraska Press, 1996).

3. All quotations are from Georg Simmel, "The Stranger (1908) and The Web of Group Affiliations (1908)," reprinted in *Theories of Ethnicity: A Classical Reader*, ed. Werner Sollors (New York: New York University Press, 1996), 37–51. I am indebted to the work of my student Amos Morris-Reich, "The Beautiful Jew Is a Moneylender: Money and Individuality in Simmel's Rehabilitation of the 'Jew,'" *Theory, Culture & Society* 20 (2003): 127–42.

4. See the discussion of Simmel in Barbara Hahn, *The Jewess Pallas Athena: This Too a Theory of Modernity* (Princeton, N.J.: Princeton University Press, 2005), 81–86.

5. Andrew Cole, "What Hegel's Master/Slave Dialectic Really Means," *Journal of Medieval and Early Modern Studies* 34 (2004): 577–610.

6. Gabriel Josipovici, "Going and Resting," in *Jewish Identity*, ed. David Theo Goldberg and Michael Krausz (Philadelphia: Temple University Press, 1993), 309–21.

7. David Theo Goldberg, "Introduction: Multicultural Conditions," in his *Multiculturalism: A Critical Reader* (Oxford: Blackwell, 1994), 1–41, here 22.

8. Chandak Sengoopta, *Otto Weininger: Sex, Science, and Self in Imperial Vienna* (Chicago: University of Chicago Press, 2000); and David G. Stern and Béla Szabados, eds., *Wittgenstein Reads Weininger* (New York: Cambridge University Press, 2004).

9. Georg Simmel, "S. Lozinskij: Simmel's Briefe zur jüdischen Frage," in *Äesthetik und Soziologie um die Jahrhundertwende: Georg Simmel*, ed. Hannes Böhringer and Kalfride Gründer (Frankfurt am Main: Klostermann, 1976), 240–44, here 240. Cited by Amos Morris-Reich, "Three Paradigms of 'The Negative Jew': Identity from Simmel to Zizek," *Jewish Social Studies* 10 (2004): 179–214.

10. G. Wollstein, "Neue Kompromisse," *Der Jüdische Student* 15 (January 1917): 5.

11. Cited from Max Weber, "Ethnic Groups (1922)," in Sollors, *Theories of Ethnicity*, 56. See also Werner Sollors, ed., *The Invention of Ethnicity* (New York: Oxford University Press, 1988).

12. Reiner Grundmann and Nico Stehr, "Why Is Werner Sombart Not Part of the Core of Classical Sociology?" *Journal of Classical Sociology* 1 (2001): 257–87.

13. Jean Paul Sartre, *Anti-Semite and Jew: An Exploration of the Etiology of Hate*, intro. Michael Walzer (New York: Schocken, 1995). See Jonathan Judaken, "The Mirror Image and the Politics of Writing: Reflections on 'the Jew' in Sartre's Early Thought," *Historical Reflections/Réflexions Historiques* 25 (1999): 33–59; as well as S. Z. Charmé, "Authenticity, Multiculturalism and the Jewish Question," *Journal of the British Society for Phenomenology* 25 (1994): 183–88.

14. On Weber, I am indebted to David Nirenberg, "The Birth of the Pariah: Jews, Christian Dualism, and Social Science," *Social Research* 70 (2003): 201–36; Hans Liebeschutz, "Max Weber's Historical Interpretation of Judaism," *Year Book of the Leo Baeck Institute* 9 (1964): 41–68; and Hans Liebeschutz, *Das Judentum im deutschen Geschichtsbild von Hegel bis Max Weber* (Tübingen, Germany: Mohr, 1967); Arnaldo Momigliano, "A Note on Max Weber's Definition of Judaism as a Pariah Religion," *History and Theory* 19, no. 3 (1980): 313–18; and Eckart Otto, *Max Webers Studien des antiken Judentums: historische Grundlagen einer Theorie der Moderne* (Tübingen, Germany: Mohr, 2002). On the life of the concept, see Leon Botstein, "The Jew as Pariah: Hannah Arendt's Political Philosophy," *Dialectical Anthropology* 8 (1983): 47–73.

15. Max Weber, *Ancient Judaism*, trans. Hans H. Gerth and Don Martindale (New York: Free Press, 1967), 3.

16. Max Weber, *The Sociology of Religion*, trans. Ephraim Fischoff (Boston: Beacon Press, 1964), 108.

17. Ephraim Shmueli, "The 'Pariah-People' and Its 'Charismatic Leadership': A Revaluation of Weber's Ancient Judaism," *Proceedings of the American Academy of Jewish Research* 36 (1968): 167–247, here 170.

18. Max Weber, *The Protestant Ethic and the Spirit of Capitalism*, trans. Talcott Parsons (London: George Allen and Unwin, 1985), 165.

19. Joseph Deckert, *Jüdische Richter, Judeneid, Kol-nidre! Zeitgemäße Gedanken* (Vienna: Verlag der "Reichspost," 1898).

20. This report was submitted to Congress on 3 December 1910 and issued on 17 March 1911. A full text was published by Columbia University Press in 1912; see Franz Boas, *Changes in Bodily Form of Descendants of Immigrants* (New York: Columbia University Press, 1912). Boas summarized his findings (and chronicles the objections to this report) in Franz Boas, *Race, Language and Culture* (New York: Macmillan, 1940), 60–75. On Boas, see Leonard B. Glick, "Types Distinct from Our Own: Franz Boas on Jewish Identity and Assimilation," *American Anthropologist* 84 (1982): 545–65.

21. Werner Sombart, *The Jews and Modern Capitalism*, trans. M. Epstein (1911; reprint, Glencoe, Ill.: Free Press, 1951), 272.

22. *The Hirsch Chumash: The Five Books of the Torah*, trans. into German and commentary by Samson Raphael Hirsch, trans. into English by Daniel Haberman, ed. Elliott Bondi and David Bechhofer (Jerusalem: Feldheim Publishers, 2005): commentary to Genesis 9:7. See Mordechai Breuer, *Modernity within Tradition: The Social History of Orthodox Jewry in Imperial Germany*, trans. Elizabeth Petuchowski. (New York: Columbia University Press, 1992).

23. Moritz Goldstein, "Deutsch-jüdischer Parnass," *Der Kunstwart* 25 (1912): 281–94; and Moritz Goldstein, "German Jewry's Dilemma: The Story of a Provocative Essay," *Leo Baeck Institute Year Book* 2 (1957): 236–54. All references are quoted by Steven Aschheim, "1912: The Publication of Moritz Goldstein's 'The German-Jewish Parnassus' Sparks a Debate over Assimilation, German Culture, and the "Jewish Spirit,'" in *Yale Companion to Jewish Writing and Thought in Germany 1096–1996*, ed. Sander L. Gilman and Jack Zipes (New Haven, Conn.: Yale University Press, 1996), 299–305.

24. Franz Oppenheimer, "Stammesbewußtsein und Volksbewußtsein," *Jüdische Rundschau* 15 (25 February 1910): 278–81, here 280.

25. Hollinger, *Postethnic America*, 11.

26. Cited from Horace Kallen, "Democracy versus the Melting Pot: A Study of American Nationality (1915)," in Sollors, *Theories of Ethnicity*, 86. See also Erika Sunada, "Revisiting Horace M. Kallen's Cultural Pluralism: A Comparative Analysis," *Journal of American and Canadian Studies* 18 (2000): 51–76.

27. Eli Ben-Joseph, *Aesthetic Persuasion: Henry James, the Jews, and Race* (Lanham, Md.: University Press of America, 1996).

28. Randolph S. Bourne, "Trans-national America (1916)," in Sollors, *Theories of Ethnicity*, 103. See also Andrew Walzer, "The Cultural Criticism of Randolph Bourne: A Usable Past for Multicultural America?" *Canadian Review of American Studies/Revue Canadienne d'Etudes Américaines* 27 (1997): 1–22.

29. Anatole Leroy-Beaulieu, *Israel among the Nations: A Study of the Jews and Antisemitism*, trans. Frances Hellman (New York: G. P. Putnam's Sons, 1895), here 209.

30. Max Brod, *Franz Kafka: A Biography*, trans. G. Humphreys Roberts and Richard Winston (New York: Schocken, 1960), 128. See my *Franz Kafka* (London: Reaktion Press, 2005).

31. Kafka was not alone. See Laura Browder, "Self-made Jews: The Immigrants' Answer to Horatio Alger," in *Other Americans, Other Americas: The Politics and Poetics of Multiculturalism*, ed. Magdalena J. Zaborowska and Tim Caudery (Aarhus, Denmark: Aarhus University Press; 1998), 80–103.

32. Franz Kafka, *Amerika: The Man Who Disappeared*, trans. Michael Hofman (New York: New Directions, 1996), 3.

33. Ibid., 32.

34. Ibid., 89.

35. Ibid., 210.

36. Franz Kafka, *Letters to Milena*, trans. Philip Boehm (New York: Schocken, 1990), 136.

37. Richard Polenberg, *One Nation Divisible: Class, Race, and Ethnicity in the United States since 1938* (New York: Viking Press, 1980).

38. Everett V. Stonequist, *The Marginal Man: A Study in Personality and Culture Conflict* (New York: Charles Scribner's Sons, 1937), 76.

CHAPTER FOUR

1. See Ezra Mendelsohn, ed., *Modern Jews and Their Musical Agendas*, Studies in Contemporary Jewry 9 (Oxford: Oxford University Press, 1994).

2. In general, see the more recent works by David Sorkin, *The Berlin Haskalah and German Religious Thought: Orphans of Knowledge* (London: Vallentine Mitchell, 2000); Michael A. Meyer, *Judaism within Modernity: Essays on Jewish History and Religion* (Detroit, Mich.: Wayne State University Press, 2001); Jonathan M. Hess, *Germans, Jews and the Claims of Modernity* (New Haven, Conn.: Yale University Press, 2002); Arno Herzig, *Judentum und Aufklärung: jüdisches Selbstverständnis in der bürgerlichen Öffentlichkeit* (Göttingen, Germany: Vandenhoeck & Ruprecht, 2002); and Jeremy Asher Dauber, *Antonio's Devils: Writers of the Jewish Enlightenment and the Birth of Modern Hebrew and Yiddish Literature* (Stanford, Calif.: Stanford University Press, 2004).

3. Richard Wagner, "Judaism in Music," trans. William Ashton Ellis, in Richard Wagner, *Richard Wagner's Prose Works*, 7 vols. (London: Kegan Paul Trench Trubner, 1894), 3:79–100, here 3:88, 3:90. On the background and reception, see Jens Malte Fischer, *Richard Wagners "Das Judentum in der Musik": eine kritische Dokumentation als Beitrag zur Geschichte des Antisemitismus* (Frankfurt am Main: Insel, 2000).

4. Robert Knox, *The Races of Men: A Fragment* (London H. Renshaw, 1850), 131.

5. Again, it is interesting to note the attribution of a Jewish identity to a figure such as Rossini. Philip Gossett, the dean of Rossini scholars, wrote to me privately that "I cannot for the life of me imagine where Disraeli got that idea. It's a unicum [unique], to my knowledge. Indeed the frequently quoted remark of Rossini's about Meyerbeer, Halévy, and the Opéra was that Rossini had given up composing for that august institution until "the Jews finish with their Sabbath." That's more likely to be the way he thought about it! Rossini, by the way, DID have a world of respect for Meyerbeer and showed it in many different ways."

6. Benjamin Disraeli, *Coningsby, or the New Generation* (Harmondsworth, UK: Penguin, 1983), 271. See Daniel R. Schwarz, *Disraeli's Fiction* (London: Macmillan, 1979).

7. How different in the twentieth century in both high and popular culture. See David M. Schiller, *Bloch, Schoenberg, Bernstein: Assimilating Jewish Music* (Oxford: Oxford University Press, 2003); Andrea Most, *Making Americans: Jews and the Broadway Musical* (Cambridge, Mass.: Harvard University Press, 2004); and Jon Stratton, "Jews, Punk and the Holocaust: From the Velvet Underground to the Ramones—the Jewish-American Story," *Popular Music* 24 (2005): 79–105.

8. Quoted by Shirley Frank Levenson, "The Use of Music in *Daniel Deronda*," *Nineteenth-Century Fiction* 24 (1969): 317–34, here 318.

9. Ludwig Feuerbach, *The Essence of Christianity*, trans. Marian Evans [George Eliot] (London: John Chapman, 1854), 9.

10. Francis Galton, *Hereditary Genius: An Inquiry into Its Laws and Consequences* (London: Macmillan, 1869), 23 (on race), 4 (on Jews and Italians), 234 (on Heine). Galton's views were critiqued in his own days because of his inability to consider class as a factor. See Frank Challice Constable, *Poverty and Hereditary Genius: A Criticism of Mr. Francis Galton's Theory of Hereditary Genius* (London: A. C. Fifield, 1905). On the persistence of Galton's views, see Frederick Osborn, "Galton's 'Hereditary Genius,'" *Eugenics Review* 44 (1952–1953): 39–40. See also Ruth Leah Schwartz Cowan, "Sir Francis Galton and the Study of Heredity in the Nineteenth Century" (Ph.D. diss., Johns Hopkins University, 1969); Wolfgang Walter, *Der Geist der Eugenik: Francis Galtons Wissenschaftsreligion in Kultursoziologischer Perspektive* (Bielefeld: Universität Bielefeld, 1983); and Michael I. Kosacoff, "A Critical Examination of Some Assumptions of Psychometric Theory (Galton, Eugenics) (Ph.D. diss., New York University, 1986).

11. Joseph Jacobs, *The Jewish Race: A Study in National Character* (London: n.p., 1889), 13.

12. Joseph Jacobs, *Studies in Jewish Statistics: Social, Vital and Anthropometric* (London: D. Nutt, 1891), 45.

13. Sullivan's inclusion seems as odd as Rossini's, but the intent was to show the quality of "Jewish music," not to present any real lineage. See Sullivan's genealogy at "Are You Related to Sir Arthur Sullivan?" http://math.boisestate.edu/gas/other_sullivan/genealogy/sul_genealogy.html (accessed 19 January 2006).

14. Jacobs, *Studies in Jewish Statistics*, lix–lx.

15. Georg Simmel, "The Stranger," in *The Sociology of Georg Simmel*, ed. and trans. Kurt Wolff (New York: Free Press, 1950), 402–8, here 404.

16. Heinrich Berl, "Das Judentum in der abendländischen Musik," *Der Jude* 6 (1921): 495–505; Heinrich Berl, "Zum Problem einer jüdischen Musik," *Der Jude* 7 (1923): 309–20; and Heinrich Berl, *Das Judentum in Der Musik* (Stuttgart, Germany: Deutsche Verlags-Anstalt, 1926).

17. Max Brod, "Jüdische Volksmelodien," *Der Jude* 1 (1916): 344–45.

18. Kerry Murphy, "Race and Identity: Appraisals in France of Meyerbeer on His 1891 Centenary," *Nineteenth-Century Music Review* 1 (2004): 27–42.

19. Houston Stewart Chamberlain, *Die Grundlagen des Nuenzehnten Jahrhunderts* (Munich: F. Bruckmann, 1934), 1166–71.

20. Arno Nadel, "Jüdische Musik," *Der Jude* 7 (1923): 227–36.

21. Alfred Einstein, "Der Jude in der Musik," *Der Morgen* 2 (1927): 590–602.

22. Paul Nettl, *Alte jüdische Spielleute und Musiker* (Prague: J. Flesch, 1923).

23. Theodor Fritsch, *Fragen und Antworten über das Juden-Thema* (Leipzig, Germany: Verlag von Theodor Fritsch, 1892), 27.

24. Theodor Fritsch, *Statistik des Judenthums* (Leipzig, Germany: Verlag von Theodor Fritsch, 1892), 30.

25. Renee de Saussine, *Paganini* (New York: Hutchenson & Co., 1953), 113.

26. Best known is Arnold Zweig, *Bilanz der Deutschen Judenheit 1933: Ein Versuch* (Amsterdam: Querido Verlag, 1934); trans. in English as *Insulted and Exiled: The Truth about the German Jews* (London: John Miles, 1937).

27. Frederic Spotts, *Hitler and the Power of Aesthetics* (London: Hutchinson, 2002). In this regard, see the anti-Semitic compilation of "Jews in Music" in Theo Stengel and Herbert Gerigk, *Ausgemerzt! das Lexikon der Juden in der Musik und seine mörderischen Folgen* (Cologne: Dittrich, 1999).

28. Gdal Saleski, *Famous Musicians of a Wandering Race: Biographical Sketches of Outstanding Figures of Jewish Origin in the Musical World*, trans. Maurice M. Altermann and Celia Krieger (New York: Bloch Publishing Co., 1927), vii.

29. *Jews in Music*, Fireside Discussion Group 16 (Chicago: Anti-Defamation League of the B'nai Brith, [1936]), 3–4.

30. From JInfo.org, "Jewish Songwriters and Composers," http://wwwjinfo.org/Composers.html: "Amy Biancolli's biography *Fritz Kreisler: Love's Sorrow, Love's Joy* (Portland, Oregon: Amadeus Press, 1998) contains an extensive discussion of Kreisler's Jewish background, which he never acknowledged and which his wife adamantly denied (see Chapter 8: 'Kreisler the Catholic, Kreisler the Jew'). Biancolli cites a 1992 interview by David Sackson of Franz Rupp, Fritz Kreisler's piano accompanist in the 1930s. Rupp states that he once asked Kreisler's brother, the cellist Hugo Kreisler, about their Jewish background, to which Hugo responded simply, 'I'm a Jew, but my brother, I don't know.' According to Biancolli, Kreisler's father, Salomon Severin Kreisler (also called Samuel Severin Kreisler), a physician and amateur violinist from Krakow, was almost certainly Jewish. Fritz's mother, Anna, was a Roman Catholic and probably an 'Aryan.' According to Louis Lochner's 1950 biography *Fritz Kreisler* [New York: Rockliff, 1950], Kreisler was reared as a Roman Catholic. However, according to unpublished parts of the manuscript uncovered by Biancolli in the Library of Congress, he was baptized only at the age of twelve. The bottom line seems to be that

Kreisler was at least half-Jewish, and his reticence on the subject primarily an attempt to placate his highly anti-Semitic wife Harriet. ('Fritz hasn't a drop of Jewish blood in his veins!' she is said to have vehemently responded to an inquiry from Leopold Godowsky. Godowsky retorted: 'He must be very anemic.')"

31. Ritchie Robertson, ed., *The German-Jewish Dialogue: An Anthology of Literary Texts 1749–1993* (Oxford: Oxford University Press, 1999), 150.

32. All references are to Israel Zangwill, *Works*, 14 vols. (London: Globe, 1925), here 2:49–198. On Zangwill's politics, see David Vital, "Zangwill and Modern Jewish Nationalism," *Modern Judaism* 4 (1984): 243–53. On *The Melting Pot*, see Mark Slobin, "Some Intersections of Jews, Music, and Theater," in *From Hester Street to Hollywood: The Jewish-American Stage and Screen*, ed. Sarah Blacher Cohen (Bloomington: Indiana University Press, 1983), 29–43; David Biale, "The Melting Pot and Beyond: Jews and the Politics of American Identity," in *Insider/Outsider: American Jews and Multiculturalism*, ed. David Biale, Michael Galchinsky, and Susan Heschel (Berkeley: University of California Press, 1998), 17–33; and Edna Nahshon, "From the Ghetto to the Melting Pot: Israel Zangwill's Jewish Drama," *Jewish Quarterly* 46 (1999): 53–60.

33. See Heike Paul, "Multilingualism and Metaphors of Musicality: Israel Zangwill, Jeannette Lander, Ferdinand Kürnberger," in *German? American? Literature? New Directions in German-American Studies*, ed. Winfried Fluck and Werner Sollors (New York: Peter Lang, 2002), 359–82.

34. Joe Kraus, "How *The Melting Pot* Stirred America: The Reception of Zangwill's Play and Theater's Role in the American Assimilation Experience," *MELUS* 24 (1999): 3–19; and Guy Szuberla, "Zangwill's *The Melting Pot* Plays Chicago," *MELUS* 20 (1995): 20.

35. Yasmeen Abu-Laban and Victoria Lamont, "Crossing Borders: Interdisciplinarity, Immigration and the Melting Pot in the American Cultural Imaginary," *Canadian Review of American Studies* 27 (1997): 23–43.

36. Quoted by Andrew R. Heinze, *Jews and the American Soul: Human Nature in the Twentieth Century* (Princeton, N.J.: Princeton University Press, 2004), 27.

37. George Bernard Shaw, *The Perfect Wagnerite: A Commentary on the Ring of the Niblungs* (London: Grant Richards, 1898), 123.

38. B. L. Farjeon, *Aaron the Jew* (London: Hutchinson, 1895), 39. See Bryan Cheyette, "From Apology to Revolt: Benjamin Farjeon, Amy Levy, and the Post-Emancipation Anglo-Jewish Novel 1880–1900," *Jewish Historical Studies* 29 (1982–1986): 253–65.

39. George Bernard Shaw, *The Perfect Wagnerite: A Commentary on the Niblung's Ring* (London: Constable, 1906), Comments to Act I, scenes ii–iv.

40. H. G. Wells, cited in Michael Foot, *HG: The History of Mr. Wells* (New York: Counterpoint, 1995), 48.

41. Jacob Golomb, ed., *Nietzsche and Jewish Culture* (London: Routledge, 1997); and Werner Stegmaier and Daniel Krochmalnik, eds., *Jüdischer Nietzschianismus* (Berlin: de Gruyter, 1997). On the British context, see Dan Stone, *Breeding Superman: Nietzsche, Race and Eugenics in Edwardian and Interwar Britain* (Liverpool: Liverpool University Press, 2002).

42. On Zangwill's life, see Joseph H. Udelson, *Dreamer of the Ghetto: The Life and Works of Israel Zangwill* (Tuscaloosa: University of Alabama Press, 1990), esp. 190–98 and 289.

43. Israel Zangwill, "Letter," *Sentinel*, February 15, 1924.

44. "Afterword" to *The Melting Pot*, quoted by Udelson, *Dreamer of the Ghetto*, 198–99.

45. Israel Zangwill, "Singer vs. Schechter," *Jewish Chronicle*, October 26, 1900, 7.

46. Max Nordau, *Erinnerungen erzählt von ihm selbst und von der Gefährtin seines Lebens*, trans. S. O. Fangor (Leipzig, Germany: Renaissance Verlag, [1928]), 186.

47. Quoted in the translation from Joseph B. Maier, Judith Marcus, and Zoltán Tarr, eds., *German Jewry: Its History and Sociology: Selected Essays by Werner Cahnman* (New Brunswick, N.J.:

Transaction, 1989), 162–63. For the broader implications, see Jacques Le Rider, "La 'lutte des races' selon Ludwig Gumplowicz," *Lignes* 12 (1990): 220–16.

48. All references are to William Thackeray, *Vanity Fair* (1847; reprint, London: J. M. Dent, 1912).

49. Udelson, *Dreamer of the Ghetto*, 198.

50. Horace Kallen, "Democracy versus the Melting Pot: A Study of American Nationality (1915)," reprinted in *Theories of Ethnicity: A Classical Reader*, ed. Werner Sollors (New York: New York University Press, 1996), 67–92, here 92. Erika Sunada, "Revisiting Horace M. Kallen's Cultural Pluralism: A Comparative Analysis," *Journal of American and Canadian Studies* 18 (2000): 51–76.

51. David Schiff, *Gershwin: Rhapsody in Blue* (Cambridge: Cambridge University Press, 1997), 12.

52. Schiff, *Gershwin*, 12.

53. Gershom Scholem, "Against the Myth of the German-Jewish Dialogue," in *On Jews and Judaism in Crisis*, ed. Werner J. Dannhauser (New York: Schocken, 1976), 61–64, here 61. See also Peter Schäfer and Gary Smith, eds., *Gershom Scholem: Zwischen den Disziplinen* (Frankfurt am Main: Suhrkamp, 1995).

CHAPTER FIVE

1. See my "A View of Kafka's Treatment of Actuality in *Die Verwandlung*," *Germanic Notes* 2 (1971): 26–30.

2. Franz Kafka, *The Complete Stories*, ed. Nahum N. Glatzer (New York: Schocken, 1971), 89.

3. See John Hargraves, *Music in the Works of Broch, Mann, and Kafka* (Rochester, N.Y.: Camden House, 2001).

4. Helmut Kobligk, "'... ohne daß er etwas Böses getan hätte.' Zum Verständnis der Schuld in Kafkas Erzählungen 'Die Verwandlung' und 'Das Urteil,'" *Wirkendes Wort* 32 (1982): 391–404.

5. All references are to Anatole Leroy-Beaulieu, *Israel among the Nations: A Study of the Jews and Antisemitism*, trans. Frances Hellman (New York: G. P. Putnam's Sons, 1895), here 258. This was first published as Anatole Leroy-Beaulieu, that is, Henry Jean-Baptiste Anatole, *(Les) juifs et l'antisémitisme: Israél chez les nations* (Paris: Lévy, 1893). This went through at least seven printings in 1893 alone! Of his other works, see *La Révolution et le libéralisme; essais de critique et d'histoire* (Paris: Hachette, 1890); and his pamphlet *Les immigrants juifs et le judäisme aux États-Unis* (Paris: Librairie Nouvelle, 1905).

6. *Mischling* is a particularly offensive term from the pseudo-biological rhetoric of the late nineteenth century through the Nazi period. It evokes all of the questions of race, race-crossing, and racial purity that were inherent to the ideologies of the period. More recent multicultural readings of hybridity have attempted to recuperate this concept. I have chosen to keep the original German term, *Mischling*, rather than try to translate it either into contemporary English terminology or into the English scientific discourse of the fin de siècle. I have tried to show how this term comes to be incorporated within Kafka's world of images with all of its complicated negative associations.

7. Werner Sombart, *Die Zukunft der Juden* (Leipzig, Germany: Duncker & Humblot, 1912), 44.

8. W. W. Kopp, "Beobachtung an Halbjuden in Berliner Schulen," *Volk und Rasse* 10 (1935): 392.

9. Josefa Berens-Totenohl, *Der Femhof* (Jena, Germany: Eugen Diederichs, 1934), 29.

10. Max Warwar, "Der Flucht vor dem Typus," *Selbstwehr* 3 (April 30, 1909): 1–2.

11. On Kafka and the model of the "Orient," see the first-rate essay by Rolf J. Goebel, "Constructing Chinese History: Kafka's and Dittmar's Orientalist Discourse," *PMLA* 108 (1993): 59–71.

12. M. Lerche, "Beobachtung deutsch-jüdischer Rassenkreuzung an Berliner Schulen," *Die medizinische Welt* 1 (17 September 1927): 1222. In long letters to the editor, the Jewish sexologist Max Marcuse strongly dismissed the "anti-Jewish" presuppositions of Lerche's views, while at the same time Professor O. Reche of the University of Leipzig saw in her piece a positive contribution to racial science (*Die medizinische Welt* 1 [15 October 1927]: 1417–19). Lerche responded to Marcuse's call for a better science of race to approach the question of the *Mischling* with her own claim that her work was at best the tentative approach of a pedagogue. She also disavowed any "anti-Jewish bias" on the part of her study (*Die medizinische Welt* 1 [12 November 1927]: 1542).

13. Leroy-Beaulieu, *Israel among the Nations*, 261.

14. Ibid., 178.

15. Ibid., 194.

16. Ibid., 217–18.

17. Franz Kafka, *Letters to Friends, Family, and Editors*, ed. Max Brod, trans. Richard Winston and Clara Winston (New York: Schocken, 1977), 232.

18. Kafka, *Letters to Friends, Family, and Editors*, 232.

19. Ernst Lissauer, "Deutschtum und Judentum," *Kunstwart* 25 (1912): 6–12, here 8.

20. Franz Kafka, *The Diaries, 1914–1923*, ed. Max Brod, trans. Martin Greenberg and Hannah Arendt (New York: Schocken, 1949), 263.

21. Fritz Mauthner, *Erinnerungen. I. Prager Jugendjahre* (Munich: Georg Müller, 1918), 52–53.

22. Kafka, *Letters to Friends, Family, and Editors*, 286–89, here 289.

23. Franz Kafka, *Letters to Milena*, trans. Philip Boehm (New York: Schocken, 1990), 59.

24. Max Brod, *Franz Kafka: A Biography*, trans. G. Humphreys Roberts and Richard Winston (New York: Schocken, 1963), 74.

25. See Noëlie Vialles, *Animal to Edible*, trans. J. A. Underwood (Cambridge: Cambridge University Press, 1994); Meyer Kayserling, *Die rituale Schlachtfrage oder ist Schächten Thierquälerei?* (Aarau, Switzerland: n.p., 1867); Wilhelm Landsberg, *Das rituelle Schächten der Israeliten im Lichte der Wahrheit* (Kaiserlautern, Germany: E. Crusius, 1882); C. Bauwerker, *Das rituelle Schachten der Israeliten im Lichte der Wissenschaft* (Kaiserslautern, Germany: n.p., 1882); *Auszüge aus den Gutachten der hervorragendsten Physiologen und Veterinärärzte uber das "Schächten"* (Frankfurt am Main: Louis Golde, 1887); Komite zur Abwehr Antisemitischer Angriffe, ed., *Gutachten über das judisch-rituelle Schlachtverfahren ("Schächten")* (Berlin: E. Apolant, 1894); Friedrich Weichmann, *Das Schächten : (das rituelle Schlachten bei den Juden)* (Leipzig, Germany: I. C. Heinrichs, 1899); U. Liebling, "Das rituelle Fleischbeschau," *Österreiche Monatsschrift für Tierheilkunde* 12 (1900): 2241–50; Aaron Zebi Friedman, *Tub Taam, or a Vindication of the Jewish Mode of Slaughtering Animals for Food Called Shechitah* (New York: n.p., 1904); Hirsch Hildesheimer, *Das Schächten* (Berlin: n.p., 1905); Hirsch Hildesheimer, ed., *Neue Gutachten über das judische-rituelle Schlacht-verfahren (Schächten)* (Berlin: n.p., 1908); *Aus den Verhandlungen des Deutschen Reichstags über das Schachten: 18. Mai 1887, 25. April 1899 und 9. Mai 1899* (Berlin: n.p., 1909); Eduard Biberfeld, *Halsschnitt nicht Hirntertrümmerung* (Berlin: L. Lamm, 1911); Thomas Barlow Wood, *The Jewish Method of Slaughtering Animals for Food* (London: n.p., 1925); Board of Deputies of British Jews, *Opinions of Foreign Experts on the Jewish Method of Slaughtering Animals* (London: n.p., 1926); and Bela Galandauer, *Zur Physiologie des Schachtschnittes: ist das Schächten eine Tierquälerei?* (Berlin: Reichszentrale fur Schachtangelegenheiten, 1933). On slaughter and its ritual meaning, see Keith Thomas, *Man and the Natural World: Changing Attitudes in England, 1500–1800* (New York: Viking Penguin, 1984). This is still a topos for anti-Semitic writing; see Arnold Leese, *The Legalised Cruelty of Shechita: The Jewish Method of Cattle-Slaughter* (Reprinted: Hollywood, Calif.: Sons of Liberty, n.d.[1969], reprinted regularly through the 1980s).

26. Ferdinand Hueppe, *Handbuch der Hygiene* (Berlin: August Hirschwald, 1899), 275–77.

27. On the question of anti-Semitism and ritual slaughter, see Michael F. Metcalf, "Regulating Slaughter: Animal Protection and Antisemitism in Scandinavia, 1880–1941," *Patterns of Prejudice* 23 (1989): 32–48; Brian Klug, "Overkill: The Polemic against Ritual Slaughter," *Jewish Quarterly* 34 (1989): 38–42; Antony Kushner, "Stunning Intolerance: A Century of Opposition to Religious Slaughter," *The Jewish Quarterly* 36 (1989): 16–20; Brian Klug, "Ritual Murmur: The Undercurrent of Protest against Religious Slaughter of Animals in Britain in the 1980s," *Patterns of Prejudice* 23 (1989): 16–28; Temple Grandin, "Humanitarian Aspects of Shehitah in the United States," *Judaism* 39 (1990): 436–46; and Mordechai Breuer, *Modernity within Tradition: The Social History of Orthodox Jewry in Imperial Germany*, trans., Elizabeth Petuchowski (New York: Columbia University Press, 1992). On the general anxiety concerning health, blood, and slaughter, see Noëlie Vialles, *Le sang et la chair: Les abattoirs des pays de l'Adour* (Paris: Éditions de la Maison des sciences de l'homme, 1987).

28. Arthur Schopenhauer, *Parerga and Paralipomena*, ed. E. F. J. Payne (1851; reprint, Oxford: Oxford University Press, 2000), 2:375.

29. On anti-Semitism and *shehitah*, see Friedrich Külling, *Bei uns wie überall? Antisemitismus* (Zurich: Schweizer Israelitischer Gemeindebund, 1977), 249–385, from which these examples were taken.

30. On the general background of this question in England, see the debate outlined in Harriet Ritvo, *The Animal Estate: The English and Other Creatures in the Victorian Age* (Cambridge, Mass.: Harvard University Press, 1987). Two questions that are reflected in the anti-Semitic rhetoric against ritual slaughter and also turned into aspects of the debate about vivisection are the madness of the antivivisectionist and the notion of "sacrifice." See Craig Buettinger, "Antivivisection and the Charge of Zoophil-Psychosis in the Early Twentieth Century," *Historian* 55 (1993): 277–88; and Michael E. Lynch, "Sacrifice and the Transformation of the Animal Body into a Scientific Object: Laboratory Culture and Ritual Practice in the Neurosciences," *Social Studies of Science* 18 (1988): 265–89.

31. Cited by Ernst von Schwartz, *Das Betäubungslose Schächten der Israeliten* (Konstanz, Germany: Ackermann, 1905), 21.

32. See David Welch, *Propaganda and the German Cinema 1933–45* (Oxford: Clarendon, 1983); and Yizhak Ahren, Stig Hornshoj-Moller, and Christoph B. Melchers, *"Der ewige Jude"— wie Goebbels hetzte: Untersuchungen zum nationalsozialistischen Propagandafilm* (Aachen, Germany: Alano, 1990).

33. See Rupert Jentzsch, "Das rituelle Schlachten von Haustieren in Deutschland ab 1933" (Diss., Tierärztliches Hochschul, Hannover, 1998).

34. Talal Asad, *Formations of the Secular: Christianity, Islam, Modernity* (Stanford, Calif.: Stanford University Press, 2003), 156–57.

35. "A Kosher Knosh Explosion," *Guardian*, Saturday, 8 January 2005, 25.

36. See Leila Speisman, "Kosher and Healthy: Not Mutually Exclusive," *Canadian Jewish News* 10 February 2005, 7 and Shawna Wagman, "Funny, You Don't Look Kosher," *Canadian Business* 28 March 2005 / 10 April 2005, 87.

37. Olivier Roy, *Globalised Islam: The Search for the New Ummah* (London: Hurst & Co., 2004), 48 n. 39.

38. Roy, 272 n. 81.

39. "Farmers Urged to Go Halal," http://news.bbc.co.uk/1/hi/uk/2163101.stm (accessed 19 January 2006).

40. "Demand Grows for Halal Turkeys," http://news.bbc.co.uk/1/hi/uk/1724177.stm (accessed 19 January 2006).

41. Fareena Alam, "Are We Just What We Eat?" *(London) Guardian*, Sunday, 15 June 2003.

42. Craig S. Smith, "Poor and Muslim? Jewish? Soup Kitchen Is Not for You," *The New York Times* (28 February 2006):A4.

CHAPTER SIX

1. Richard Powers, *The Time of Our Singing* (New York: Picador, 2003), 15. Einstein is a leitmotif in the novel: see 8–9, 13, 40, 87–89, and, again on his violin playing, 522. The best study of the image of Einstein in literature remains Alan J. Friedman and Carol C. Donley, *Einstein as Myth and Muse* (Cambridge: Cambridge University Press, 1985).

2. Robyn Arianrhood, *Einstein's Heroes* (St. Lucia: University of Queensland Press, 2003), 148–49; and Joseph Eger, *Einstein's Violin: A Conductor's Notes on Music, Physics, and Social Change* (New York: Penguin/Tarcher, 2005).

3. Helen Dukas and Banesh Hoffmann, eds., *Albert Einstein: The Human Side: New Glimpses from His Archive* (Princeton, N.J.: Princeton University Press, 1979), 78.

4. I am clearly indebted to Richard Panek, *The Invisible Century: Einstein, Freud, and the Search for Hidden Universes* (New York: Viking, 2004); Fritz Stern, *Einstein's German World* (London: Allen Lane/Penguin Press, 2000); Max Jammer, *Einstein and Religion: Physics and Theology* (Princeton, N.J.: Princeton University Press, 1999); Michael R. Gilmore, "Einstein's God: Just What Did Einstein Believe about God?" *Skeptic: A Quarterly Publication of the Skeptics Society* 5 (1997): 62–64; Sachi Sri Kantha, "Scientific Productivity of Einstein, Freud and Landsteiner," *Medical Hypotheses* 46 (May 1996): 467–70; Kennee Switzer-Rakos, "Albert Einstein's Concept of the Jewish State," *Midstream* 31 (1985): 19–22; Regine Kather, "Die Wahrheit der Wissenschaft: 'Deutsche und Jüdische Physik,'" in *Bruch und Kontinuität: jüdisches Denken in der europäischen Geistesgeschichte*, ed. Eveline Goodman-Thau und Michael Daxner (Berlin: Akademie Verlag, 1995), 103–18; Uriel Tal, "Jewish and Universal Social Ethics in the Life and Thought of Albert Einstein," in *Albert Einstein: Historical and Cultural Perspectives, the Centennial Symposium in Jerusalem*, ed. Gerald Holton and Yehuda Elkana (Princeton, N.J.: Princeton University Press, 1982), 297–318; Peter Honigmann, "Albert Einsteins jüdische Haltung; gegen Assimilation—für Würde, Stolz und Wiedergeburt," *Tribüne* 98 (1986): 95–116; Felix Gilbert, "Einstein und das Europa seiner Zeit," *Historische Zeitschrift* 233 (1981): 1–33; Adolphe Nysenholc, "Judaïsme et science chez Einstein," *Connaissance d'Israël* 7–8 (1982): 5–17; Frederic Grunfeld, *Prophets without Honor: A Background to Freud, Kafka, Einstein and Their World* (New York: Holt, Rinehart & Winston, 1979); Yehuda Elkana and Adi Ophir, eds., *Einstein 1897–1979: Exhibition* (Jerusalem: Raphael Haim Hacohen, 1979); and Yosef Gotlieb, "Einstein the Zionist," *Midstream* 25 (1979): 43–48.

5. Dennis Overbye, *Einstein in Love: A Scientific Romance* (London: Bloomsbury, 2001), 6.

6. Albrecht Fölsing, *Albert Einstein: A Biography*, trans. Ewald Osers (New York: Viking, 1997), 26.

7. Ibid., 26.

8. Armin Hermann, *Einstein: Der Weltweise und sein Jahrhundert* (Munich: Piper, 1994), 158.

9. Ze'ev Rosenkranz, *Albert through the Looking Glass* (Jerusalem: Jewish National and University Library, 1998), 102.

10. Anton Reiser [Rudolf Kayser], *Albert Einstein: A Biographical Portrait* (New York: A. and C. Boni, 1930), 28.

11. Maja Winteler-Einstein, "Albert Einstein: A Biographical Sketch," in *The Collected Papers of Albert Einstein*, ed. J. Stachel (Princeton, N.J.: Princeton University Press, 1987), 1:xv–xxii.

12. Fölsing, *Albert Einstein*, 21.

13. Ibid., 41–42.

14. Alexander Moszkowski, *Einstein the Searcher: His Work Explained from Dialogues with Einstein* (London: Methuen, 1921), 221; first published in German in 1920 as *Einstein: Einblicke in seine Gedankenwelt, Gemeinverständliche Betrachtungen über die Relativitätstheorie und ein neues Weltsystem Entwickelt aus Gesprachen mit Einstein* (Berlin: Fontance, 1920).

15. Moszkowski, *Einstein the Searcher*, 222.
16. Albert Einstein, "Autobiographical Notes," in *Albert Einstein: Philosopher-Scientist*, ed. Paul Arthur Schlipp, Library of Living Philosophers (New York: Tudor Publishing, 1951), 3.
17. Lewis S. Feuer, *Einstein and the Generations of Science* (New Brunswick, N.J.: Transaction, 1982), xv.
18. Alice Calaprice, ed., *The Expanded Quotable Einstein* (Princeton, N.J.: Princeton University Press, 2000), 126. "I discovered for the first time [in 1914] that I was a Jew. I owed this discovery more to gentiles than Jews." Cited by Isaiah Berlin, "Einstein and Israel," *New York Review of Books*, 8 November 1979, 13–18, here 13.
19. Feuer, *Einstein and the Generations of Science*, xxvii.
20. Calaprice, *The Expanded Quotable Einstein*, 126.
21. Quoted by Gerald E. Tauber, "Einstein and Zionism," in *Einstein: A Centenary Volume*, ed. A. P. French (London: Heinemann, 1979), 199–207, here 199–200.
22. Sigmund Freud, *Standard Edition of the Complete Psychological Works of Sigmund Freud*, ed. and trans. J. Strachey, A. Freud, A. Strachey, and A. Tyson, 24 vols. (London: Hogarth, 1955–1974), 20:274. On Freud and Einstein, see Fölsing, *Albert Einstein*, 651.
23. Andrew R. Heinze, *Jews and the American Soul: Human Nature in the 20th Century* (Princeton, N.J.: Princeton University Press, 2004), 76.
24. Thorstein Veblen, "The Intellectual Pre-Eminence of Jews in Modern Europe," in his *Essays in Our Changing Order*, ed. Leon Ardzrooni (New York: Augustus M. Kelley, 1964), 219–31, here 219; first published in *Political Science Quarterly* (1919). That this essay is a projection of Veblen's sense of his own "Intellectual Pre-Eminence" was first discussed by Lewis Feuer, "Thorstein Veblen: The Metaphysics of the Interned Immigrant," *American Quarterly* 5 (1953): 99–112.
25. Charlie Chaplin, *My Autobiography* (London: Bodley Head, 1964), 146.
26. Steven Shapin, "The Philosopher and the Chicken: On the Dietetics of Disembodied Knowledge," in *Science Incarnate: Historical Embodiments of Natural Knowledge*, ed. Steven Shapin and Christopher Lawrence (Chicago: University of Chicago Press, 1998), 21–50.
27. *Jews in Music*, Fireside Discussion Group 16 (Chicago: Anti-Defamation League of the B'nai Brith, [1936]), 4.
28. Ritchie Robertson, ed., *The German-Jewish Dialogue: An Anthology of Literary Texts 1749–1993* (Oxford: Oxford University Press, 1999), 150.
29. Berlin, "Einstein and Israel," 13.
30. Fölsing, *Albert Einstein*, 54.
31. Overbye, *Einstein in Love*, 13.
32. Fölsing, *Albert Einstein*, 53.
33. Ibid., 53.
34. Overbye, *Einstein in Love*, 190.
35. Fölsing, *Albert Einstein*, 409.
36. Jamie Sayen, *Einstein in America: The Scientist's Conscience in the Age of Hitler and Hiroshima* (New York: Crown, 1985), 17.
37. Feuer, *Einstein and the Generations of Science*, xiv.
38. Regine Kather, "'Die Wissenschaft ist und bleibt international': das kosmopolitische Weltbild Albert Einsteins," *Menora* 6 (1995): 65–91.
39. Rabindranath Tagore, *The Religion of Man* (London: George, Allen & Unwin, 1931), app. 2, 222–25.
40. Friedrich Herneck, *Einstein Privat: Herta W. erinnert sich an die Jahre 1927 bis 1933* (Berlin: Der Morgen, 1978), 129.
41. Feuer, *Einstein and the Generations of Science*, xxvii.
42. Reproduced in William Cahn, *Einstein: A Pictorial Biography* (New York: Citadel, 1955), 62.

43. Dennis Brian, *Einstein: A Life* (New York: John Wiley, 1996), 193.

44. Fölsing, *Albert Einstein*, 547.

45. Peter A. Bucky with Allen G. Weakland, *The Private Albert Einstein* (Kansas City, Mo.: Andrews and McMeel, 1992), 85–87.

46. Albert Einstein, "Assimilation and Nationalism," in *About Zionism: Speeches and Letters*, ed. L. Simon (New York: Macmillan, 1931), cited in French, *Einstein*, 200.

47. Philip V. Bohlman, *"The Land Where Two Streams Flow": Music in the German-Jewish Community of Israel* (Urbana: University of Illinois Press, 1989).

48. William M. Kramer, "When Einstein Fiddled in Pasadena: A Nonscientific View of His California Years," *Western States Jewish History* 25 (1993): 99–140; and Abraham Hoffman, "Albert Einstein at Caltech, Pasadena, California 1930–1933," *Western States Jewish History* 36 (2003): 65–84.

49. Sayen, *Einstein in America*, 8.

50. Ibid., 14.

51. Brian, *Einstein*, 353.

52. Cited by Berlin, "Einstein and Israel," 14.

53. Cited in ibid., 14.

54. Ibid., 14.

55. *New York Times*, 11 May 1950, quoted in Calaprice, *The Expanded Quotable Einstein*, 141.

56. Arthur Hertzberg, ed., *The Zionist Idea* (New York: Atheneum, 1981), 255.

57. *Scotland on Sunday*, 13 February 1994.

58. Gershom Scholem, "Against the Myth of the German-Jewish Dialogue," in *On Jews and Judaism in Crisis*, ed. Werner J. Dannhauser (New York: Schocken, 1976), 61–64, here 61. See also Peter Schäfer and Gary Smith, eds., *Gershom Scholem: Zwischen den Disziplinen* (Frankfurt am Main: Suhrkamp, 1995).

CHAPTER SEVEN

1. All references are to the translation of N. O. Body, *My Life as a Woman*, ed. Hermann Simon, trans. Deborah Simon (Philadelphia: University of Pennsylvania Press, 2005). Simon's 1993 reprint presented the real identity of the anonymous author for the first time: *Aus eines Mannes Mädchenjahre* (Berlin: Hentrich, 1993). The original appeared in Berlin with Riecke in 1907. On Baer specifically, see David Brenner, "Re(-)dressing the 'German-Jewish': A Jewish Hermaphrodite in Wilhelmine Germany," in *Borders, Exiles, and Diasporas*, ed. Elazar Barkan and Marie-Denise Shelton (Stanford, Calif.: Stanford University Press, 1998), 32–45. On hermaphrodism in culture, see Stefan Hirschauer, *Die soziale Konstruktion der Transsexualität: über die Medizin und den Geschlechtswechsel* (Frankfurt am Main: Suhrkamp, 1993); Gesa Lindemann, *Das paradoxe Geschlecht: Transsexualität im Spannungsfeld von Körper, Leib und Gefühl* (Frankfurt am Main: Fischer Taschenbuch Verlag, 1993); Annette Runte, *Biographische Operationen: Diskurse der Transsexualität* (Munich: W. Fink, 1996); Jay Prosser, *Second Skins: The Body Narratives of Transsexuality* (New York: Columbia University Press, 1998); Kate More and Stephen Whittle, *Reclaiming Genders: Transsexual Grammars at the Fin de Siècle* (London: Cassell, 1999); and Jason Cromwell, *Transmen and FTMs: Identities, Bodies, Genders, and Sexualities* (Urbana: University of Illinois Press, 1999). Of extreme importance is the work of Alice Domurat Dreger: Alice Domurat Dreger, "Doubtful Sex: The Fate of the Hermaphrodite in Victorian Fiction," *Victorian Studies* 38 (1995): 335–70; idem, *Hermaphrodites and the Medical Invention of Sex* (Cambridge, Mass.: Harvard University Press, 1998); idem, "A History of Intersexuality: From the Age of Gonads to the Age of Consent," *Journal of Clinical Ethics* 9 (1998): 345–55; idem, ed., *Intersex in the Age of*

Ethics (Hagerstown, Md.: University Publishing Group, 1999); and idem, "Jarring Bodies: Thoughts on the Display of Unusual Anatomies," *Perspectives in Biology and Medicine* 43 (2000): 161–72.

2. Rainer Herrn, *Schnittmuster des Geschlechts – Transvestitismus und Transsexualität in der frühen Sexualwissenschaft* (Gießen: Psychosozial-Verlag, 2005).

3. Thus, the famed Philadelphia surgeon Samuel David Gross (1805–1884), the subject of Thomas Eakins's *The Gross Clinic*, undertook a castration and reconstruction in the 1850s. See S. D. Gross, "Case of Hermaphrodism, Involving the Operation of Castration and Illustrating a New Principle of Juridical Medicine," *American Journal of the Medical Sciences* NS 24 (1852): 386–90.

4. As early as his dissertation: see John Money, "Hermaphroditism. An Inquiry into the Nature of a Human Paradox" (Ph.D. diss., Harvard University, 1952).

5. Mireya Navarro, "When Gender Isn't a Given," *New York Times*, Sunday Style, 19 September 2004, 1, 6.

6. Milton Diamond and H. Keith Sigmundson, "Sex Reassignment at Birth: A Long Term Review and Clinical Implications," *Archives of Pediatric & Adolescent Medicine* 151 (1997): 298–304. A popular study is available by John Colapinto, *As Nature Made Him: The Boy Who Was Raised as a Girl* (New York: Perennial, 2002).

7. Hubert Kennedy, *Ulrichs: The Life and Works of Karl Heinrich Ulrichs* (Boston: Alyson, 1988).

8. Michel Foucault, ed., *Herculine Barbin: Being the Recently Discovered Memoirs of a Nineteenth-Century French Hermaphrodite*, trans. R. McDougall (New York: Pantheon, 1978).

9. See Klaus Müller, *Aber in meinem Herzen sprach eine Stimme so laut: Homosexuelle Autobiographien und medizinischen Pathographien im neunzehnten Jahrhundert* (Berlin: Rosa Winkel, 1991).

10. Havelock Ellis and J. A. Symonds, *Das konträre Geschlechtsgefühl* (Leipzig, Germany: G. Wigand, 1896).

11. Magnus Hirschfeld, *Berlins drittes Geschlecht* (Berlin: Hermann Seemann, [1905]).

12. Magnus Hirschfeld, "Drei Fälle von irrtümlicher Geschlechtsbestimmung, Medizinische Reform," *Wochenschrift für soziale Medizin, Hygiene und Medizinalstatistik* 15 (1906): 614.

13. Michel Foucault, *An Introduction*, vol. 1 of *The History of Sexuality*, trans. Robert Hurley (New York: Vintage, 1980), 43.

14. See Barbara Wedekind-Schwertner, "Daß ich eins und doppelt bin," in *Studien zur Idee der Androgynie unter besonderer Berücksichtigung Thomas Manns* (New York: Lang, 1984); and Andrea Raehs, *Zur Ikonographie des Hermaphroditen: Begriff und Problem von Hermaphroditismus und Androgynie in der Kunst*, European Dissertations (Europäische Hochschulschriften): Series (Reihe) XXVIII Art History (Kunstgeschichte), Bd. 113 (Frankfurt am Main: Peter Lang, 1990).

15. The best summary of his views are in his textbook: see Magnus Hirschfeld, *Sexualpathologie: Ein Lehrbuch für Ärzte und Studierende*, 3 vols. (Bonn: Marcus und Weber, 1917).

16. His work is very wide-ranging. See his early work (F. L. Neugebauer, *Zur Lehre von den angeborenen und erworbenen Verwachsungen und Verengerungen der Scheide: sowie des angeborenen Scheidenmangels mit Ausschluss der Doppelbildungen* [Berlin: A. Th. Engelhardt, 1895]) through to his classic essay: Franz von Neugebauer, "58 Beobachtungen von periodischen genitalen Blutungen mestruellen Anschein, pseudomenstruellen Blutungen, Menstruatio vicaia, Molimina menstrualia usw. bei Scheinzwitter," *Jahrbuch für sexuallen Zwischenstufen* 6 (1904): 277–326. His views are summarized in Franz Ludwig von Neugebauer, *Hermaphroditismus beim Menschen* (Leipzig, Germany: Werner Klinkhardt, 1908).

17. I cite from his English-language summary essay: Franz von Neugebauer, "Hermaphrodism in the Daily Practice of Medicine: Being Information upon Hermaphrodism Indispensable to the Practitioner," *British Gynaecological Journal* 19 (1903): 226–63.

18. Cesare Taruffi, *Hermaphrodismus und Zeugungsunfähigkeit: Eine systematische Darstellung des Missbildungen der menschlichen Geschlechtsorgane*, trans. R. Teuscher (Berlin: H. Barsdorf, 1903), 96–103.

19. Taruffi, *Hermaphrodismus und Zeugungsunfähigkeit*, 97.

20. Ferdinand-Valére Faneau de la Cour, *Du féminisme et de l'infantilisme chez les tuberculeux* (Paris: A. Parent, 1871).

21. Hermann Simon, "N. O. Body und kein Ende," in *Jüdische Welten: Juden in Deutschland vom 18. Jahrhundert bis in die Gegenwart*, ed. Marion Kaplan and Beate Meyer (Göttingen, Germany: Wallstein, 2005), 225–30.

22. See, for example, F. A. Forel, "Cas de menstruation chez un homme," *(Lausanne) Bulletin de la Societé médicale de la Suisse romande* (1869): 53–61; and W. D. Halliburton, "A Peculiar Case," *(St. Louis) Weekly Medical Review and Journal of Obstetrics* (1885): 392.

23. Paolo Albrecht, "Sulla Mestruazione ne maschio," *L'Anomalo* 2 (1880): 33.

24. Paul Näcke, "Kritisches zum Kapitel der normalen und pathologischen Sexualität," *Archiv für Psychiatrie und Nervenkrankheiten* 32 (1899): 356–86, here 364–65.

25. Wilhelm Fliess, *Die Beziehungen zwischen Nase und weiblichen Geschlechtsorganen, in ihrer biologischen Bedeutung dargestellt* (Leipzig: Deuticke, 1897) and his Zur Periodenlehre: Gesammelte Aufsätze (Jena: E. Diederichs, 1925). See also Sander L. Gilman, *The Case of Sigmund Freud: Medicine and Identity at the Fin de Siècle* (Baltimore: The Johns Hopkins University Press, 1993), 96-98.

26. Hirschfeld, *Sexualpathologie*, 2:1–92.

27. Thomas de Cantimpré, *Miraculorum et exemplorum memorabilium sui temporis libro duo* (Duaci [Douai, France]: Baltazris Belleri, 1605), 305–6.

28. Anatole Leroy-Beaulieu, *Israël chez les nations: les juifs et l'antisémitisme* (Paris: Calmann Lévy, 1893), 166–67.

29. Daniel Chwolson, *Die Blutanklage und sonstige mittelalterliche Beschuldigungen der Juden. Eine historische Untersuchung nach den Quellen* (Frankfurt am Main: J. Kauffmann, 1901), 7, 207–10.

30. Chrysostomus Dudulaelus, *Gründliche und Warhafftige Relation von einem Juden auss Jerusalem mit Nahmen Ahassverus* (n.p., 1602), Gathering: Diiir; reprinted as Chrysostomus Dudulaelus, *Evangelischer Bericht vom den Leben Jesu Christi …* (Stuttgart: J. Scheible, 1856), 126.

31. Theodor Fritsch, *Handbuch der Judenfrage* (Leipzig, Germany: Hammer, 1935), 409.

CHAPTER EIGHT

1. Roth and Kureishi, as they also are commentators on the contemporary scene, often have their literary works read as social science texts. See M. P. Kramer, "The Conversion of the Jews and Other Narratives of Self Definition: Notes towards the Writing of Jewish-American Literary History; or Adventures in Hebrew School," in *Ideology and Identity in Jewish American and Israeli Literature*, ed. Emily Budick (Albany: State University of New York Press, 2001): 177–96; and Philip Lewis, *Islamic Britain: Religion, Politics and Identity among British Muslims* (London: I. B. Tauris, 2002), 218.

2. See Andrew R. Heinze, *Adapting to Abundance: Jewish Immigrants, Mass Consumption, and the Search for American Identity* (New York: Columbia University Press, 1990).

3. Sylvia Huberman Scholnick, "Money versus Mitzvot: The Figure of the Businessman in Novels by American Jewish Writers," *Yiddish* 6 (1987): 48–55; and Nancy Von Rosk, "'Go, Make Yourself for a Person': Urbanity and the Construction of an American Identity in the Novels of Abraham Cahan and Anzia Yezierska," *Prospects* 26 (2001): 295–335.

4. Joel Rosenberg, "Rogin's Noise: The Alleged Historical Crimes of *The Jazz Singer*," *Prooftexts* 22 (2002): 221–39; Irv Saposnik, "Jolson, *the Jazz Singer* and the Jewish Mother: Or, How My Yiddishe Momme Became My Mammy," *Judaism* 43 (1994): 432–42; and Michael Alexander, "'Mammy, Don't You Know Me?' Al Jolson and the Jews," in his *Jazz Age Jews* (Princeton, N.J.: Princeton University Press, 2001), 131–79.

5. Chip Rhodes, "Ambivalence on the Left: Budd Schulberg's *What Makes Sammy Run?*" *Studies in American Fiction* 30 (2002): 65–83; R. J. Ellis, "'High Standards for White Conduct': Race, Racism and Class in *Dangling Man*," *Saul Bellow Journal* 16–17 (2000): 26–50; and Ravit Reichman, "The Medical Model and the Wartime Reading of *Dangling Man*: Or, What Can Joseph Recover?" *Saul Bellow Journal* 14 (1996): 28–42.

6. Oscar Handlin, *The Uprooted: The Epic Story of the Great Migrations That Made the American People* (Boston: Little, Brown, 1951), 6.

7. William Palmer, "David Riesman, Alexis de Tocqueville and History: A Look at *The Lonely Crowd* after Forty Years," *Colby Library Quarterly* 26 (1990): 19–27.

8. All references are to Philip Roth, *Goodbye, Columbus* (London: Penguin, 1986). See recently Roy Goldblatt, "As Plain as the Nose on Your Face: The Nose as the Organ of Othering," *Amerikastudien/American Studies* 48 (2003): 563–76; and Peter L. Rudnytsky, "Goodbye, Columbus: Roth's Portrait of the Narcissist as a Young Man," *Twentieth Century Literature: A Scholarly and Critical Journal* 51 (2005): 25–42.

9. William A. Francis, "Naming in Philip Roth's *Goodbye, Columbus*," *Literary Onomastics Studies* 15 (1988): 59–62.

10. Barbara Frey Waxman, "Jewish American Princesses, Their Mothers, and Feminist Psychology: A Rereading of Roth's 'Goodbye, Columbus,'" *Studies in American Jewish Literature* 7 (1988): 90–104.

11. Philip Roth, *American Pastoral* (Boston: Houghton Mifflin, 1997).

12. Alan W. France, "Reconsideration: Philip Roth's *Goodbye, Columbus* and the Limits of Commodity Culture," *MELUS* 15 (1988): 83–89.

13. Laurie Grobman, "African Americans in Roth's 'Goodbye Columbus,' Bellow's *Mr. Sammler's Planet* and Malamud's *The Natural*," *Studies in American Jewish Literature* 14 (1995): 80–89; and Barry Gross, "American Fiction, Jewish Writers, and Black Characters: The Return of 'The Human Negro' in Philip Roth," *MELUS* 11 (1984): 5–22.

14. Ted Hughes, "The God," from his *Birthday Letters* (London: Faber & Faber, 1998), 189.

15. On Roth's "Eli the Fanatic," see Hana Wirth-Nesher, "Resisting Allegory: Or, Reading 'Eli, the Fanatic' in Tel Aviv," *Prooftexts* 21 (2001): 103–12; Victoria Aarons, "Is It 'Good-for-the-Jews or No-Good-for-the-Jews'? Philip Roth's Registry of Jewish Consciousness," *Shofar* 19 (2000): 7–18; Martin Hellweg, "Philip Roth, 'Eli, the Fanatic' (1959)," in *Die amerikanische Short Story der Gegenwart: Interpretationen*, ed. Peter Freese (Berlin: Erich Schmidt, 1976), 215–25; Elliott M. Simon, "Philip Roth's 'Eli the Fanatic': The Color of Blackness," *Yiddish* 7 (1990): 39–48; and Sol Gittleman, "The Pecks of Woodenton, Long Island, Thirty Years Later: Another Look at 'Eli, the Fanatic,'" *Studies in American Jewish Literature* 8 (1989): 138–42.

16. Lazarus Bendavid, *Etwas zur Charackteristick der Juden*, ed. Michael Graetz and Dominique Bourel (1793; reprint, Jerusalem: Dinur Center, 1994).

17. All references are to Karl Emil Franzos, "Wunderkinder des Ghetto," in his *Aus der großen Ebene: Neue Kulturbilder aus Halb-Asien* (Stuttgart, Germany: Adolf Bonz, 1888), 23–60.

18. Joseph Skibell, *The English Disease* (Chapel Hill, N.C.: Algonquin Books of Chapel Hill, 2003). See also his *A Blessing on the Moon* (Chapel Hill, N.C.: Algonquin Books of Chapel Hill, 1997), which chronicled in a magical-realistic mode the afterlife of a Polish Jew murdered during the Shoah. Chaim Skibelski, according to the text an ancestor of the author, is killed along with the other Jewish citizens of a small Polish town and now wanders the

countryside, often accompanied by his rabbi, who has turned into a crow. This novel was also extremely well received; it won a number of awards and has been widely translated. Since it uses a conceit first employed to good ends by author Romain Gary in his novel *The Dance of Genghis Cohn* (*La Danse de Gengis Cohn*) (1967), one can see how much more subtle and critical Skibell's view (some forty years later) is in imagining this as a means of seeing the Shoah through contemporary eyes. Here, the Shoah becomes present in the contemporary world through the ghosts—real ghosts, not merely metaphors for memory. And Skibell is able to provide an alternative mode for understanding the Shoah. In *The English Disease*, he shows the pitfalls of a world captured by the need to overidentify with this world of the past to the detriment of the present.

19. All references are to Izak Goller, *The Five Books of Mr. Moses* (London: Methuen, 1929).

20. Goller is a great supporter of Zangwill. See his poetic eulogy of him reprinted in Izak Goller, *A Jew Speaks!* (Liverpool: T. Lynn, 1926), 69.

21. Bernard Reginster, "What Is a Free Spirit? Nietzsche on Fanaticism," *Archiv für Geschichte der Philosophie* 85 (2003): 51–85.

22. All quotations are from Hanif Kureishi, "My Son the Fanatic," from his *Love in a Blue Time* (London: Faber & Faber, 1997), 119–31. On Kureishi, see Stefano Manferlotti, *Dopo l'Impero: Romanzo ed etnia in Gran Bretagna* (Naples: Liguori, 1995); Ines Karin Böhner, *My Beautiful Laundrette und Sammy and Rosie Get Laid: Filmische Reflexion von Identitätsprozessen* (Frankfurt am Main: Peter Lang, 1996); Kenneth C. Kaleta, *Hanif Kureishi: Postcolonial Storyteller* (Austin: University of Texas Press, 1998); Ray Sangeeta, "The Nation in Performance: Bhabha, Mukherjee and Kureishi," in *Hybridity and Postcolonialism: Twentieth-Century Indian Literature*, ed. Monika Fludernik (Tübingen, Germany: Stauffenburg, 1998), 219–38; Anuradha Dingwaney Needham, *Using the Master's Tools: Resistance and the Literature of the African and South-Asian Diasporas* (New York: St. Martin's, 2000); Marina Kurten, "Negotiating Identities: Expressions of 'Culture' in British Migrant Literature," *Atlantic Literary Review* 3 (2002): 47–55; Chrissi Harris, "Insiders/Outsiders: Finding One's Self in the Cultural Borderlands," in *Literature and Ethnicity in the Cultural Borderlands*, ed. Jesus Benito and Anna Maria Manzanas (Amsterdam: Rodopi, 2002), 175–87; and Sukhdev Sandhu, "Pop Goes the Centre: Hanif Kureishi's London," in *Postcolonial Theory and Criticism*, ed. Laura Chrisman and Benita Parry (Cambridge: Brewer, 1999), 133–54.

23. All quotations are from Hanif Kureishi, *My Ear at His Heart: Reading My Father* (London: Faber & Faber, 2004).

24. John Clement Ball, "The Semi-Detached Metropolis: Hanif Kureishi's London," *ARIEL* 27 (1996): 7–27, here 9.

25. Cited by Lewis, *Islamic Britain*, 45.

26. S. Barton, *The Bengali Muslims of Bradford: Community Religions Project* (Leeds: University of Leeds, 1986), 177.

27. Olivier Roy, *Globalised Islam: The Search for the New Ummah* (London: Hurst & Co., 2004), 276.

28. Quoted by Lewis, *Islamic Britain*, 96.

29. Roy, *Globalised Islam*, 152.

30. Ibid., 219.

31. In 1997, Kureishi wrote a screenplay loosely based on his story. Directed by Udayan Prasad, *My Son the Fanatic* (1998) focuses on the world of Parvez played by Om Puri, who has made a career out of playing aging, confused Pakistani immigrants. In the film, his son, Farid (played Akbar Kurtha), is engaged to Madelaine Fingerhut, the "English" daughter of the local police chief. Parvez and his wife, Minoo (played by Gopai Desai), view this as a very good match as they are sure that their son would thus be accepted into English culture. The film

opens with Parvez's advocacy and Farid's rejection of hybridity as a model for multicultural-ism. The opening line has Farid ask, "Can you put keema with strawberries?" Farid breaks off the engagement, and in dismay Parvez confides in one of his regular fares, a prostitute named Bettina (Rachel Griffiths). It is only by degrees that Parvez realizes that his son has joined a fundamentalist Islamic sect. Farid invites an exploitative priest and his entourage to live in the family's house, and it is not long before the group has taken control of the house-hold, forcing Minoo to take refuge in the kitchen and swamping Parvez with debts. A visiting German businessman (Stellan Skarsgård) employs Parvez as a driver as well as procurer. His favorite partner, as it turns out, is Bettina. In the course of sharing confidences, Parvez and Bettina are surprised to find that they have enough in common to form the foundation for a relationship. Farid's sect has begun to drive the prostitutes, including Bettina, out of the neighborhood. Parvez is both agonized and relieved by the changes that are destroying his life. Unlike in the tale, he is wise enough to withdraw once he realizes that it is out of his con-trol. In order to capture the complexity of the interaction, Kureishi must add substantially to his account of the politics of conversion. No longer seen as a personal action, as in the story, in the film it now becomes a social moment impacted by an ironic image of a religious "cult." Kureishi's position is clearly critical (and "enlightened"). See Hanif Kureishi, *My Son the Fanatic* (London: Faber & Faber, 1997).

32. Roy, *Globalised Islam*, 144.
33. "Hidden Secrets," *Economist*, 22 September 2005, 101.

CHAPTER NINE

1. Barry Gross, "'Intellectual Overlordship': Blacks, Jews and Native Son," *Journal of Ethnic Studies* 5 (1977): 51–59; Evelyn M. Avery, "'Bittersweet Encounter': Blacks and Jews in the Fiction of Ethnic Women," in *The Ethnic American Woman: Problems, Protests, Lifestyle*, ed. Edith Blicksilver (Dubuque, Iowa: Kendall/Hunt, 1989), 420–25; Michael Galchinsky, "Glimpsing Golus in the Golden Land: Jews and Multiculturalism in America," *Judaism: A Quarterly Journal of Jewish Life and Thought* 43 (1994): 360–68; Emily Miller Budick, *Blacks and Jews in Literary Conversation* (Cambridge: Cambridge University Press, 1998); David Biale, Michael Galchinsky, and Susan Heschel, eds., *Insider/Outsider: American Jews and Multiculturalism* (Berkeley: University of California Press,1998); Milli Heyd, *Mutual Reflections: Jews and Blacks in American Art* (New Brunswick, N.J.: Rutgers University Press, 1999); Adam Zachary Newton, *Facing Black and Jew: Literature as Public Space in Twentieth-Century America* (Cambridge: Cambridge University Press, 1999); and Ethan Goffman, *Imagining Each Other: Blacks and Jews in Contemporary American Literature* (Albany: State University of New York Press, 2000).
2. David A. Hollinger, *Postethnic America: Beyond Multiculturalism* (New York: Basic Books, 1996), 25, 38.
3. Mark Slobin, *Fiddler on the Move: Exploring the Klezmer World* (New York: Oxford University Press, 2000)
4. Sander L. Gilman, *The Jew's Body* (New York: Routledge, 1991).
5. Audre Lorde, "The Master's Tools Will Never Dismantle the Master's House," in her *Sister Outsider* (Freedom, Calif.: Crossing Press, 1984), 110–13.
6. Peter Novick, *The Holocaust in American Life* (Boston: Houghton Mifflin, 1999).
7. All quotations are from Hanif Kureishi, "We're Not Jews," in his *Love in a Blue Time* (London: Faber and Faber, 1997), 41–51.
8. All quotations from the autobiography are from Hanif Kureishi, *My Ear at His Heart: Reading My Father* (London: Faber and Faber, 2004).

9. Paul Gilroy, *"There Ain't No Black in the Union Jack": The Cultural Politics of Race and Nation* (Chicago: University of Chicago Press, 1991).

10. Rita Felski, "Nothing to Declare: Identity, Shame, and the Lower Middle Class," *PMLA* 115 (2000): 33–45.

11. Gayatri Chakravorty Spivak, "The Burden of English," in *Orientalism and the Postcolonial Predicament: Perspectives on South Asia*, ed. Carol Breckenridge and Peter van der Veer (Philadelphia: University of Pennsylvania Press, 1993), 134–57.

12. Julian Barnes, *Metroland* (London: Cape, 1980), 32.

13. Y. Michal Bodemann, "Von Berlin nach Chicago und weiter. Georg Simmel und die Reise seines 'Fremden,'" *Berliner Journal für Soziologie* 8 (1998): 125–42.

14. Sarah Lyall, "Shadowy Party Heats Up British Racial Tensions," *New York Times*, Wednesday, 4 July 2001, A3. See also Susanne Schmid, "Exploring Multiculturalism: Bradford Jews and Bradford Pakistanis," *Journal for the Study of British Cultures* 4 (1997): 163–79.

15. All references are to Achmat Dangor, *Kafka's Curse: A Novella and Three Other Stories* (Cape Town: Kwela, 1997), 5–142. See also Loren Kruger, "Black Atlantics, White Indians, and Jews: Locations, Locutions, and Syncretic Identities in the Fiction of Achmat Dangor and Others," *South Atlantic Quarterly* 100, no. 1 (Winter 2001): 111–43.

16. "An Interview with Achmat Dangor," *Boldtype*, http://www.randomreference.com/bold-type/0399/dangor/interview.html (accessed 19 January 2006).

17. See Noel Ignatiev, *How the Irish Became White* (New York: Routledge, 1996); Karen Brodkin, *How Jews Became White Folks and What That Says about Race in America* (New Brunswick, N.J.: Rutgers University Press, 1998); Maurice Berger, *White Lies: Race and the Myths of Whiteness* (New York: Farrar, Straus & Giroux, 1999); Matthew Frye Jacobson, *Whiteness of a Different Color: European Immigrants and the Alchemy of Race* (Cambridge, Mass.: Harvard University Press, 1999); and Matthew Frye Jacobson and David Roediger, *Special Sorrows: The Diasporic Imagination of Irish, Polish, and Jewish Immigrants in the United States* (Berkeley: University of California Press, 2002).

18. Milton Shain, *The Roots of Antisemitism in South Africa* (Johannesburg: Witwatersrand University Press, 1994), 16; published in the series *Reconsiderations in Southern Africa History*, ed. Jeffrey Butler and Richard Elphick, and simultaneously published by the University of Virginia Press, 1994.

19. Ibid., 25.

20. Anatole Leroy-Beaulieu, *Israel among the Nations: A Study of the Jews and Antisemitism*, trans. Frances Hellman (New York: G. P. Putnam's Sons, 1895), 166–67.

21. D. Chwolson, *Die Blutanklage und sonstige mittelalterliche Beschuldigungen der Juden. Eine historische Untersuchung nach den Quellen* (Frankfurt am Main: Kauffmann, 1901), 7, 207–10.

22. Julius Preuss, "Die Beschneidung nach Bibel und Talmud," *Wiener klinische Rundschau* 11 (1897): 708–9; 724–27; J. Alkvist, "Geschichte der Circumcision," *Janus* 30 (1926): 86–104, 152–71; as well as Samuel Krauss, *Geschichte der jüdischen Ärzte vom frühsten Mittelalter bis zur Gleichberechtigung* (Vienna: A. S. Bettelheim-Stiftung, 1930), 157–58.

23. Sander L. Gilman, *Franz Kafka: The Jewish Patient* (New York: Routledge, 1995).

24. John Ezard, "Double First for Novel Newcomer Zadie Smith," *(London) Guardian*, 4 January 2001.

25. Zadie Smith, *White Teeth* (New York: Random House, 2000), here 271–72. On Smith, see Patricia Goldblatt, "School Is Still the Place: Stories of Immigration and Education," *MultiCultural Review* 13 (2004): 49–54; Dominic Head, "Zadie Smith's *White Teeth*: Multiculturalism for the Millennium," in *Contemporary British Fiction*, ed. Richard Lane, Rod Mengham, and Philip Tew (Cambridge: Polity, 2003), 106–19; Laura Moss, "The Politics of Everyday Hybridity: Zadie Smith's White Teeth," *Wasafiri* 39 (2003): 11–17; and

Kathleen O'Grady, "White Teeth: A Conversation with Author Zadie Smith," *Atlantis* 27 (2002): 105–11.

26. Zadie Smith, *The Autograph Man* (New York: Random House, 2002).

27. Salman Rushdie, *The Moor's Last Sigh* (New York: Knopf, 1995; London: Jonathan Cape, 1996). See Dohra Ahmad, "'This Fundo Stuff Is Really Something New': Fundamentalism and Hybridity in *The Moor's Last Sigh*," *Yale Journal of Criticism* 18 (2005): 1–20; Stephen Baker, "'You Must Remember This': Salman Rushdie's *The Moor's Last Sigh*," *Journal of Commonwealth Literature* 35 (2000): 43–54; Timothy Weiss, "At the End of East/West: Myth in Rushdie's *The Moor's Last Sigh*," *Jouvert* 4 (2000): 47; Liselotte Glage and Ruediger Kunor, eds., *The Decolonizing Pen: Cultural Diversity and the Transnational Imaginary in Rushdie's Fiction* (Trier, Germany: Wissenschaftlicher Verlag Trier, 2001); and Rachel Trousdale, "City of Mongrel Joy: Bombay and the Shiv Sena in *Midnight's Children* and *The Moor's Last Sigh*," *Journal of Commonwealth Literature* 39 (2004): 95–110. A "Jewish" take is Hillel Halkin, "Salman Rushdie Surrenders," *Commentary* 102, no. 1 (1996): 59.

28. Amitav Ghosh, *In an Antique Land: History in the Guise of a Traveler's Tale* (London: Granta Books, 1992; New Delhi: Ravi Dayal Publishers, 2000). All references are to the latter edition. See Anshuman A. Mondal, "Allegories of Identity: 'Postmodern' Anxiety and 'Post-Colonial' Ambivalence in Amitav Ghosh's *In an Antique Land* and *The Shadow Lines*," *Journal of Commonwealth Literature* 38 (2003): 19–36 and K. C. Beliappa, "Amitav Ghosh's *In an Antique Land*: An Excursion into Time Past and Time Present," in V. Kirpal, ed., *The Postmodern Indian Novel: Interrogating the 1980s and 1990s* (Bombay: Allied Publishers, 1996), 59–66.

29. Amitav Ghosh, "The Slave of Ms. H.6," *Subaltern Studies* 7 (1993), 159–220.

30. See Joshua Cohen, Matthew Howard, Martha C. Nussbaum, eds., *Is Multiculturalism Bad for Women?* (Princeton: Princeton University Press, 1999),

31. Vikram Seth, *Two Lives* (New York: HarperCollins, 2005).

32. Judie Newman, "Retrofitting the Raj: Ruth Prawer Jhabvala and the Uses and Abuses of the Past," in *British Women Writing Fiction*, ed. Abby H. P. Werlock (Tuscaloosa: University of Alabama Press, 2000), 70–89.

33. Somini Sengupta, "Storyteller in the Family," *The New York Times* 6 February 2006, B6.

34. Andrea Levy, *Small Island* (London: Review, 2004).

35. Monica Ali, *Brick Lane* (London: Black Swan, 2004).

36. Thomas Meinecke, *Hellblau* (Frankfurt am Main: Suhrkamp, 2001), 222–23. See also Sebastian Wogenstein, "Topographie des Dazwischen: Vladimir Vertlibs Das besondere Gedächtnis der Rosa Masur, Maxim Billers Esra und Thomas Meineckes Hellblau," *Gegenwartsliteratur* 3 (2004): 71–96.

37. Gish Jen, *Mona in the Promised Land: A Novel* (New York: Vintage, 1996). See Rachel C. Lee, *The Americas of Asian American Literature: Gendered Fictions of Nation and Transnation* (Princeton, N.J.: Princeton University Press, 1999).

38. Laura Accinelli, "Eye of the Beholder," *Los Angeles Times*, 23 January 1996, E1.

39. Chang-rae Lee, *Native Speaker* (New York: Riverhead, 1995).

40. Oscar Hijuelos, *A Simple Havana Melody (from When the World Was Good)* (New York: HarperCollins, 2002). See also Jose Miguel Oviedo, "Six Problems for Oscar Hijuelos: A Conversation with Jose Miguel Oviedo," *Latin American Literature and Arts* 63 (2001): 73–79; Amy Elias, "Oscar Hijuelos's *The Mambo Kings Play Songs of Love*, Ishmael Reed's *Mumbo Jumbo*, and Robert Coover's *The Public Burning*," *Critique: Studies in Contemporary Fiction* 41 (2000): 115–28; Alphy J. Plakkoottam, "Popular Fiction or Social Treatise? Oscar Hijuelos' *The Mambo Kings Play Songs of Love*," *Indian Journal of American Studies* 24 (1994): 48–52; Steven G. Kellman, "Oscar Hijuelos Plays Songs of Sisterly Love," *REDEN: Revista Espanola de Estudios Norteamericanos* 7 (1996): 35–41; Juan Bruce-Novoa, "Hijuelos'

Mambo Kings: Reading from Divergent Traditions," *Confluencia: Revista Hispanica de Cultura y Literatura* 10 (1995): 11–22; and Ilan Stavans, "Oscar Hijuelos, novelista," *Revista Iberoamericana* 57 (1991): 155–56.

CHAPTER TEN

1. Sander Gilman, "'We're Not Jews': Representing 'Jews' in Contemporary Multicultural Literature," *Modern Judaism* 23 (2003): 126–56.
2. Compare the various views of Claus Leggewie, *Multi Kulti* (Frankfurt am Main: Rotbuch Verlag, 1993); Werner Schiffauer, *Fremde in der Stadt* (Frankfurt am Main: Suhrkamp, 1997); and Sabine Kriechhammer-Yagmur, *Binationaler Alltag in Deutschland* (Berlin: Brandes & Apsel, 2001).
3. Theodor Adorno, *Minima Moralia: Reflections from Damaged Life* (London: New Left Books, 1951), 87.
4. Anita Desai, *Baumgartner's Bombay* (New York: A.A. Knopf, 1988), 20. See Pippa Brush, "German, Jew, Foreigner: The Immigrant Experience in Anita Desai's Baumgartner's Bombay," *Critical Survey* 8 (1996): 277-85. There is a substantial Anglo-Indian/Jewish literature of various inflections by women that wrestles with Desai's view beginning with one of the most interesting Indian-Jewish writers of the present day: Esther David, *By the Sabarmati* (New Delhi: Penguin Books, 1999); *The Walled City* (Madras: Manas, 1997); *The Book of Esther* (New Delhi; New York: Viking, 2002). Ruth Prawer Jhabvala's *Heat and Dust* (New York: Harper & Row, 1976), herself a Disapora German Jew, addresses the question of hybridity. The question of hybridity and location is raised by Marina Budhos, *House of Waiting* (New York: Global City Press, 1995) and her *The Professor of Light* (New York: G. P. Putnam's Sons, 1999), who writes about Diaspora Indians and Jews; Jael Silliman provides an autobiographical account of Jewish women in India in her *Jewish Portraits, Indian Frames: Women's Narratives from a Diaspora of Hope* (Hanover, N.H.: University Press of New England 2001; Calcutta: Seagull Books, 2001) and there is an extensive autobiography of Ruby Daniel with Barbara C. Johnson, *Ruby of Cochin, an Indian Jewish Woman Remembers* (Philadelphia: Jewish Publication Society, 1995). Non-Jewish novelists in India have also addressed the question of Jews as in Desai and Meera Mahadevan, *Shulamith* (New Delhi: Arnold-Heinemann Publishers [India], 1975).
5. Stuart Z. Charmé, "Varieties of Authenticity in Contemporary Jewish Identity," *Jewish Social Studies* 6 (2000): 133–55, here 133.
6. Michael P. Kramer, "Race, Literary History, and the 'Jewish Question,'" *Prooftexts* 21 (2001): 287–321, as well as the responses, 321–65; see also Hana Wirth-Nesher, ed., *What Is Jewish Literature?* (Philadelphia: Jewish Publication Society, 2002).
7. W. Lloyd Warner and Paul S. Lunt, "Ethnicity" (1942), cited in Werner Sollors, ed., *Theories of Ethnicity: A Classical Reader* (Washington Square, New York: New York University Press, 1996), 13.
8. Olivier Roy, *Globalised Islam: The Search for the New Ummah* (London: Hurst & Co., 2004), 124 n. 38.
9. Philippe Blasband, *Quand j'étais sumo* (Paris: Le Castor Astral, 2000), 97–110.
10. Philippe Blasband, *De cedres et de fumées* (Paris: Gallimard, 1990).
11. David Biale, "In Defense of Shaatnez: A Politics for Jews in a Multicultural America," in *Insider/Outsider: American Jews and Multiculturalism*, ed. David Biale, Michael Galchinsky, and Susannah Heschel (Berkeley: University of California Press, 1998), 123–34. See also Michael Galchinsky, "Glimpsing Golus in the Golden Land: Jews and Multiculturalism in America," *Judaism: A Quarterly Journal of Jewish Life and Thought* 43 (1994): 360–68.

12. Nadine Gordimer, "My Father Leaves Home," in her *Jump and Other Stories* (New York: Farrar, Straus & Giroux, 1991), 57–68, here 64.

13. Mark Kurlansky, "The Unclean," in his *The White Man in the Tree and Other Stories* (New York: Washington Square Books, 2000), 93–116.

14. Magdalena J. Zaborowska and Tim Caudery, eds., *Other Americans, Other Americas: The Politics and Poetics of Multiculturalism*, Publications of the English Department, University of Aarhus, vol. 28 (Aarhus, Denmark: Dolphin, 1998); and Andrew Furman, *Contemporary Jewish American Writers and the Multicultural Dilemma: The Return of the Exiled* (Syracuse, N.Y.: Syracuse University Press, 2001).

15. James Atlas, *Bellow: A Biography* (New York: Random House, 2000), 573–74.

16. A. B. Yehoshua, "*Mr Mani* and the Akedah," *Judaism* (Winter 2001): 61–65, here 64–65.

17. A. B. Yehoshua, *Mr. Mani*, trans. Hillel Halkin (San Diego, Calif.: Harcourt Brace & Co., 1992), 340. See most recently Adam Zachary Newton, "Not Quite Holocaust Fiction: A. B. Yehoshua's *Mr. Mani* and W. G. Sebald's *The Emigrants*," in *Teaching the Representation of the Holocaust*, ed. Marianne Hirsch and Irene Kacandes (New York: Modern Language Association of America, 2004), 422–30.

18. Elias Canetti, *The Voices of Marrakesch*, trans. J. A. Underwood (London: Marion Boyars, 1982), 40.

19. Nissim Ezekiel, "Background," from his *Collected Poems: 1952–1988* (Delhi: Oxford University Press 1989), 179. See John B. Beston, "An Interview with Nissim Ezekiel," *World Literature Written in English* 16 (1977): 87–94; Tabish Khair, "The Fissured Surface of Language in Indian English Poetry," *PN Review* 26 (2000): 7–9; Niranjan Mohanty, "Irony in the Poetry of Nissim Ezekiel," *World Literature Today* 69 (1995): 51–55; A. N. Dwivedi, "Modernity in Nissim Ezekiel's Poetry," *World Literature Today* 66 (1992): 432–34; and S. C. Narula, "Negative Affirmation in Nissim Ezekiel's Hymns and Psalms," *Ariel* 14 (1983): 57–71.

20. Ezekiel, "Wedding in Bombay," in Ezekiel, *Collected Poems*, 235.

21. Ezekiel, "Latter-Day Psalms," in ibid., 261.

22. Ezekiel, "How the English Lessons Ended," in ibid., 200–1.

23. Saul Bellow, *The Dean's December* (New York: Harper & Row, 1981); and Philip Roth, *The Prague Orgy* (London: Cape, 1985), also as the epilogue to *Zuckerman Bound* (New York: Farrar, Straus & Giroux, 1985), comprising *The Ghost Writer, Zuckerman Unbound, The Anatomy Lesson*, and "Epilogue" to *The Prague Orgy*. See also Sepp L. Tiefenthaler, "American-Jewish Fiction: The Germanic Reception," in *Handbook of American-Jewish Literature: An Analytical Guide to Topics, Themes, and Sources*, ed. Lewis Fried, Gene Brown, and Louis Harap (Westport, Conn.: Greenwood, 1988), 471–504; and Kristiaan Versluys, "Philip Roth: Prague Obsessions," in *Images of Central Europe in Travelogues and Fiction by North American Writers*, ed. Waldermar Zacharasiewicz (Tübingen, Germany: Stauffenburg, 1995), 313–19.

24. Lenka Reinerová, *Das Traumcafé einer Pragerin* (Berlin: Aufbau, 1996).

25. Benjamin Stein, *Das Alphabet des Juda Liva* (Zurich: Ammann, 1995). See Sander Gilman, "America and the Newest Jewish Writing in German," *German Quarterly* 73 (2000): 151–62.

26. Esther Dischereit, *als mir mein golem öffnete* (Passau, Germany: Karl Stutz, 1996). See also Todd Herzog, "Germans and Jews after the Fall of the Wall: The Promises and Problems of Hybridity," in *German Studies in the Post-Holocaust Age: The Politics of Memory, Identity, and Ethnicity*, ed. Adrian Del Caro and Janet Ward (Boulder: University Press of Colorado, 2000), 93–102; and Hartmut Steinecke, "Schreiben von der Shoah in der deutsch-jüdisch-en Literatur der 'zweiten Generation,'" *Zeitschrift für Deutsche Philologie* 123, supplement (2004): 246–59.

27. Michael Chabon, *The Amazing Adventures of Kavalier & Clay* (New York: Random House, 2000). See also Lee Behlman, "The Escapist: Fantasy, Folklore, and the Pleasures of the Comic Book in Recent Jewish American Holocaust Fiction," *Shofar: An Interdisciplinary Journal of Jewish Studies* 22 (2004): 56–71.

28. Sheli Teitelbaum, "Men in Tights," *Jerusalem Report*, 1 January 2001, 47.

29. Stuart Eskenazi, "Nextbook: Insights into the Jewish Soul through Literature," *Seattle Times*, Tuesday, 11 November 2003.

30. Chabon, *The Amazing Adventures of Kavalier & Clay*, 122.

31. Franz Kafka, *Amerika (the Man Who Disappeared)*, trans. Michael Hofman (New York: New Directions, 1996), 3.

32. Cynthia Ozick, *Bloodshed and Three Novellas* (New York: Knopf, 1976); and Cynthia Ozick, *The Puttermesser Papers* (New York: Knopf, 1997). See in this context Sarah Blacher Cohen, *Cynthia Ozick's Comic Art: From Levity to Liturgy* (Bloomington: Indiana University Press, 1994); as well as Sarah Blacher Cohen, "Cynthia Ozick and Her New Yiddish Golem," *Studies in American Jewish Literature* 6 (1987): 105–10.

33. Michael Chabon, *The Final Solution: A Story of Detection* (London: Fourth Estate, 2005); it first appeared in 2003 in the *Paris Review* in a shorter form.

34. Hana Wirth-Nesher, "Language as Homeland in Jewish-American Literature," in Biale, Galchinsky, and Heschel (1998), op. cit., 212–230.

35. David Baddiel, *The Secret Purposes* (London: Abacus, 2004), 363–404.

36. Paul Zakrzewski, ed., *Lost Tribe: Jewish Fiction from the Edge* (New York: Harper, 2003).

37. I quote from the translation by Catherine Tihanyi: Adam Biro, *Two Jews on a Train*, trans. Catherine Tihanyi (Chicago: University of Chicago Press, 2001), v.

38. Robert Birnbaum, "Interview: Jonathan Safran Foer," *IdentityTheory.com*, http://www.identitytheory.com/interviews/birnbaum108.html (accessed 19 January 2006).

39. Carol Eisenberg, "Young, Hip and 'Jewcy': A Generation Weaned on Irony and Multiculturalism Defines What It Means to Be ..." *Newsday*, 27 January 2004; and "Eminem Lyrics: 'White America,'" http://www.stlyrics.com/songs/e/eminem1371/whiteamerica64356.html (accessed 19 January 2006).

40. Eisenberg, "Young, Hip and 'Jewcy.'"

41. Dara Horn, *In the Image: A Novel* (New York: W. W. Norton, 2003).

42. Arthur Phillips, *Prague* (New York: Random House, 2002).

43. Gary Shteyngart, *The Russian Debutante's Handbook* (New York: Riverhead, 2002).

44. Daniel Zalewski, "From Russian with Tsoris," *New York Times Magazine*, 2 June 2002, 54–57.

45. Elena Lappin, *Foreign Brides* (London: Picador, 1999), 19–38. See also Susanne Schmid, "Exploring Multiculturalism: Bradford Jews and Bradford Pakistanis," *Journal for the Study of British Cultures* 4 (1997): 163–79.

46. See her defense of her brother in Elena Lappin, "Mein Bruder, der Biller," *Die Zeit*, Thursday, 10 October 2002.

47. Oliver Lubrich, "Zwischen den Sprachen—zwischen den Kulturen: Jüdische Einwanderer in Deutschland," in *Sprachraum ohne Grenzen: Spracherwerb in Europa*, ed. Claudia Hummel and Andreas Kruger, Ein Internationales Kolloquium, Berlin, 11–13 September 2001 (Berlin: Gesellschaft zur Forderung des internationalen Informationsaustausches, 2002), 57–69; Oliver Lubrich, "Are Russian Jews Post-colonial? Wladimir Kaminer and Identity Politics," *East European Jewish Affairs* 33 (2003): 35–53; and Tsypylma Darieva, *Russkij Berlin: Migranten und Medien in Berlin und London* (Munich: Lit, 2004). On the complexity of such constructions, see K. Postoutenko, "Imaginary Ethnicity: Jews and Russians in Russian Economical Mythology," *American Behavioral Scientist* 45 (2001): 282–95.

48. There are four "official religions," i.e., religions that are supported by a tax on their declared membership: "Roman" Catholicism, the Evangelical (Protestant) Church, Jehovah's Witnesses, and the state-acknowledged Jewish Community. "Islam," (however defined) the religion of the largest minority community, is not an "official" religion. See Jeffrey M. Peck, *Being Jewish in the New Germany* (New Brunswick, N.J.: Rutgers University Press, 2006).

49. The "official" Jewish community, recognized by the German government and supported by its supporters' taxes, early defined Jewish identity solely in terms of Orthodox religious practice.

50. "Integration jüdischer Kontingentflüchtlinge: Realität oder Utopie?" http://www.fh-potsdam.de/~Sozwes/werkstatt/adf/integration/integrationkontingent.html (accessed 19 January 2006).

51. Anna Sokhrina, *Shans na schast'e* (Saint Petersburg, Russia: Limbus Press, 1999), 123.

52. Lena Gorelik, *Meine weißen Nächte* (Munich: Schirmer Graf Verlag, 2004). On the fictionality of her text, see the interview with her in the *Münchener Merkur*, 7 November 2004: "I am not a hundred percent Anja, but I believe that each writer is—at least, if she writes in the first person—that one cannot avoid one's own experience. Certainly Anja is sometimes me, or I am sometimes Anja. Perhaps Anja is a bit more exaggerated, but sometimes is also understated."

53. *On the Origin of Language: Two essays. Jean-Jacques Rousseau Johann Gottfried Herder*, trans. John H. Moran and Alexander Gode (Chicago: University of Chicago Press, 1986), 87–166.

54. Heinz Schlaffer, *Die kurze Geschichte der deutschen Literatur* (Munich: Hanser, 2002).

55. See my *Jurek Becker: Die Biographie* (Berlin: Ullstein, 2002); as well as my *Jurek Becker • A Life in Five Worlds* (Chicago: University of Chicago Press, 2003), a version of the biography for the Anglophone world.

56. *Berlin Morgenpost*, 13 January 2005, 2.

57. Boris Fishman, "An Interview with Wladimir Kaminer," *Words without Borders*, http://www.wordswithoutborders.org/article.php?lab=Fishman (accessed 19 January 2006). All translations from the German are by the author.

58. Wladimir Kaminer, *Russendisko* (Munich: Manhattan, 2000). This is also available in an English translation as *Russian Disco*, trans. Michael Hulse (London: Ebury Press, 2002).

59. Wladimir Kaminer, *Militärmusik* (Munich: Manhattan, 2001).

60. Wladimir Kaminer, *Die Reise nach Trulala* (Munich: Manhattan, 2002).

61. Wladimir Kaminer, *Schönhauser Allee* (Munich: Manhattan, 2001).

62. Wladimir Kaminer and Helmut Höge, *Helden des Alltages: Ein lichtbildgestützter Vortrag über die seltsamen Sitten der Nachkriegzeit* (Munich: Manhattan, 2002).

63. Wladimir Kaminer, *Mein deutsches Dschungelbuch* (Munich: Manhattan, 2003).

64. Fishman, "An Interview with Wladimir Kaminer."

65. Wladimir Kaminer, *Ich mache mir Sorgen, Mama* (Munich: Manhattan, 2004).

66. Fishman, "An Interview with Wladimir Kaminer."

67. "Meldung: Anton Wildgans-Preis 2001 an Vladimir Vertlib," Buchkritik, http://www.buchkritik.at/meldung.asp?IDX=537 (accessed 19 January 2006).

68. Vladimir Vertlib, *Abschiebung* (Salzburg: Otto Müller, 1995). I am very grateful to Michael Bodemann, who suggested that I read these works by Vertlib. Vertlib has also looked at these questions from a social science point of view. See Vladimir Vertlib, *Osteuropäische Zuwanderung nach Österreich (1976–1991): unter besonderer Berücksichtigung der jüdischen Immigration aus der ehemaligen Sowjetunion; quantitative und qualitative Aspekte* (Vienna: Institut für Demographie, Österreichischen Akadamie der Wissenschaften, 1995); as well as his "Kosmopoliten, Zionisten, Landesverrater: Die ermordete jiddische Literatur der Sowjetunion," *Literatur-und-Kritik* 337–38 (1999): 62–70.

69. Vladimir Vertlib, *Zwischenstation* (Vienna: Deuticke, 1999). See also Sebastian Wogenstein, "Topographie des Dazwischen: Vladimir Vertlibs Das besondere Gedächtnis der Rosa Masur, Maxim Billers Esra und Thomas Meineckes Hellblau," *Gegenwartsliteratur* 3 (2004): 71–96.

70. Vladimir Vertlib, *Das besondere Gedächtnis der Rosa Masur* (Vienna: Deuticke, 2001).
71. Vladimir Vertlib, *Letzter Wunsch* (Vienna: Deuticke, 2003)
72. "Das besondere Gedächtnis der Rosa Masur: Roman von Vladimir Vertlib (2001, Deuticke)," http://www.lyrikwelt.de/rezensionen/rosamasur-r.htm (accessed 19 January 2006).

CHAPTER ELEVEN

1. See Phyllis Chesler, *The New Anti-Semitism: The Current Crisis and What We Must Do about It* (New York: Jossey-Bass, 2003); Gabriel Schoenfeld, *The Return of Anti-Semitism* (New York: Encounter, 2003); Abraham Foxman, *Never Again? The Threat of the New Anti-Semitism* (San Francisco: HarperSanFrancisco, 2003); and Alan Dershowitz, *The Case for Israel* (New York: John Wiley, 2003).
2. Paul Iganski and Barry Kosmin, eds., *A New Anti-Semitism? Debating Judeophobia in 21st Century Britain* (London: Profile Books 2003), 123.
3. All references are to the text as made available at http://www.oicsummit2003.org.my/speech_03.php on March 23, 2004.
4. Sander L. Gilman, *Jewish Self-hatred: Anti-Semitism and the Hidden Language of the Jews* (Baltimore: Johns Hopkins University Press, 1986).
5. Runnymede Commission on Anti-Semitism, *A Very Light Sleeper: The Persistence and Dangers of Anti-Semitism* (London: Runnymede Trust, 1994), 7.
6. Owen Chadwick, *The Secularization of the European Mind in the Nineteenth Century* (reprint, Cambridge: Cambridge University Press, 1990); and Andrew Dickson White, *A History of the Warfare of Science with Theology in Christendom* (New York: D. Appleton, 1898).
7. Bernard Lewis, *Semites and Anti-Semites: An Inquiry into Conflict and Prejudice* (New York: Norton, 1999), 117–39; and Jacob Lassner, "Abraham Geiger: A Nineteenth-Century Jewish Reformer on the Origins of Islam," in *The Jewish Discovery of Islam: Studies in Honor of Bernard Lewis*, ed. Martin Kraemer (Tel Aviv: Moshe Dayan Center for Middle Eastern and African Studies, 1999), 103–35.
8. This talk, more than any other recent text, has been a focus of the discussions of the "new" anti-Semitism. See Michael Kotzen, *The New Anti-Semitism: Sources, Symbols, and Significance* (Chicago: Jewish Federation, 2004), 1.
9. Broadcast on Thursday, 16 October 2003; see Peter Lloyd, reporter, "Dr Mahathir Calls for Muslim Unity," Australian Broadcasting Corporation, http://www.abc.net.au/pm/content/2003/s968775.htm (accessed 19 January 2006).
10. Abraham Geiger, *Judaism and Islam*, trans., F. M. Young (Madras: printed at M.D.C.S.P.C.K. Press, 1896), 6–7.
11. Susannah Heschel, *Abraham Geiger and the Jewish Jesus* (Chicago: University of Chicago Press, 1998).
12. Arnon Groiss, ed. and trans., *Jews, Christians, War and Peace in Egyptian School Textbooks* (New York: American Jewish Committee, 2004), 64.
13. Ibn Khaldun, *Introduction to the Study of History*, 3 vols., trans. Franz Rosenthal (New York: Pantheon, 1958), 3:305–6.
14. Ellsworth Huntington, *The Pulse of Progress* (New York: Scribner's, 1926), 176.
15. Francis Galton, *Hereditary Genius: An Inquiry into Its Laws and Consequences* (London: Macmillan, 1869), 357–58.
16. Charles Darwin, *The Descent of Man and Selection in Relation to Sex* (New York: H. M. Caldwell, 1874), 160. See Robert J. Richards, *Darwin and the Emergence of Evolutionary Theories of Mind and Behavior* (Chicago: University of Chicago Press, 1987).

17. On the question of Jewish eugenic thought, see John Efron, *Defenders of the Race: Jewish Doctors and Race Science in Fin-de Siècle Europe* (New Haven, Conn.: Yale University Press, 1994).

18. Arthur Landsberger, ed., *Judentaufe* (Munich: Georg Müller, 1912), 127. Compare the discussion of his brother's views concerning the nature of the Jew as pariah: Arnaldo Momigliano, "A Note on Max Weber's Definition of Judaism as a Pariah-Religion," *History and Theory* 19 (1980): 313–18; and Gary A. Abraham, *Max Weber and the Jewish Question: A Study of the Social Outlook of His Sociology* (Urbana: University of Illinois Press, 1992).

19. Richard Griffiths, "'The Clash of Races' and 'The Jewish Intelligence': A Specifically French Form of Social Anti-Semitism," *Patterns of Prejudice* 37 (2003): 51–63.

20. Cyril D. Darlington, *The Evolution of Man and Society* (New York: Simon & Schuster, 1969), 187–89.

21. Lewis S. Feuer, *Scientific Intellectual: The Psychological and Sociological Origins of Modern Science* (New York: Basic Books, 1963), 308; and more extensively in Lewis S. Feuer, "The Sociobiological Theory of Jewish Intellectual Achievement," in *Ethnicity, Identity, and History: Essays in Memory of Werner J. Cahnman*, ed. Joseph B. Maier and Chaim I. Waxman (New Brunswick, N.J.: Transaction, 1983), 93–125. Feuer rebuts this view in detail in his work, but assumes that such a thing as Jewish superior intelligence does evidence itself in the history of modern science, but for purely sociological reasons.

22. Norbert Wiener, *Ex-Prodigy: My Childhood and Youth* (New York: Simon & Schuster, 1953), 11. He is evoking a conversation with Haldane that echo the views of Haldane such as expressed in the Muirhead lectures given by him at Birmingham University in February and March 1937 and printed as J. B. S. Haldane, *Heredity and Politics* (London: Allen & Unwin, 1938), 162.

23. Ernest van den Haag, *The Jewish Mystique*, 2nd ed. (New York: Stein and Day, 1977), 13–25. This thesis has come to infiltrate even the joke books of the recent period; see Joseph Telushkin, *Jewish Humor: What the Best Jewish Jokes Say about the Jews* (New York: W. Morrow, 1992). Van den Haag identifies himself as not Jewish in the preface to this text.

24. Telushkin, *Jewish Humor*.

25. Feuer, "The Sociobiological Theory of Jewish Intellectual Achievement."

26. See their classic book *Life Is with People: The Jewish Little-Town of Eastern Europe* (New York: International Universities Press, 1952).

27. Richard J. Herrnstein and Charles Murray, *The Bell Curve: Intelligence and Class Structure in American Life* (New York: Free Press, 1994). The comments on Jewish superior intelligence are to be found on 275. On this comparison, see Seymour B. Sarason, "Jewishness, Blackishness, and the Nature-Nurture Controversy," *American Psychologist* 28 (1973): 962–71. Charles Murray continues this argument using the Galtonian tabulation method in his *Human Accomplishment: The Pursuit of Excellence in the Arts and Sciences, 800 B.C. to 1950* (New York: HarperCollins, 2003).

28. It also reflects the ambiguity of the image of the Jew in American history; see Louise Abbie Mayo, *The Ambivalent Image: Nineteenth-Century America's Perception of the Jew* (Cranbury, N.J.: Associated University Presses, 1988).

29. Kevin MacDonald, *A People That Shall Dwell Alone: Judaism as a Group Evolutionary Strategy*, Human Evolution, Behavior, and Intelligence series, ed. Seymour W. Itzkoff (Westport, Conn.: Praeger, 1994).

30. Hans Erman, *Berliner Geschichten, Geschichte Berlins: Historien, Episoden, Anekdoten* (Bad Herrenalb, Germany: Verlag für Internationalen Kulturaustausch, 1966), 444.

31. Herbert Lindenberger, "Between Texts: From Assimilationist Novel to Resistance Novel," *Jewish Social Studies 1* (1995): 48–68, here 51.

32. But MacDonald manipulates his sources rather shamelessly. Let me look at his appropriation of my work. He uses my work to argue for a Jewish linguistic separation, which was "an
important force for maintaining genetic and cultural separation" (89). Indeed, I argue quite
the opposite: that in the late medieval and early modern period, Jews had linguistically integrated themselves into the cultures of Western Europe and their separation was imposed on
them because of this integration. MacDonald argues that my discussion of hysteria and its
putative etiology in consanguineous marriages is proof that such marriages were common,
rather than the obvious fact, stressed by me, that "incest" was and is a culturally defined
category (107 n. 23). It is claimed that my work supports the idea that Jews were diagnosed
as having specific forms of mental illness and that this is an artifact of Jewish predisposition
to such illnesses rather than a label placed on the Jews and their mental states (211).

33. The fascination with this topic seems to have no end. See Jennifer Senior, "Are Jews Smarter?
What Genetic Science Tells Us," *New York Magazine*, 24 October 2005.

34. Olivier Roy, *Globalised Islam: The Search for the New Ummah* (London: Hurst & Co., 2004),
215.

INDEX

Aaron the Jew (Farjeon), 74
Abdul Rauf, Feisal, 11
Abie's Wild Irish Rose (Nichols), 82
About the Path Home: Verses of a Jew (Vom
        Heimweg: Verse eines Juden)
        (Zlocisti), 121
"Abrahamic" religions, 5–6
Abschiebung (Deportation) (Vertlib), 220
ADH2*2 allele, 24–25
ADH2*3 allele, 25
Adorno, Theodor, 180
Adversus Judaeos (Against the Jews) (John
        Chrysostom), 123
aesthetic surgery, 127–28, 170–71, 241
African Americans, 57, 62, 83, 145–46, 147,
        171
Afrocentric culture, 13
Against the Jews (Adversus Judaeos) (John
        Chrysostom), 123
Ahad Ha-am, xii, 108–9
Alam, Fareena, 97–98
Albert, Eugen d', 70
Albrecht, Paul, 122
alcohol: alcoholism seen as addiction,
        24–27; Eastern Jews' use of,
        34, 35–36, 37; Islam abjuring,
        43; Jews accused of indecorous
        consumption of, 27–28,
        41; Jews seen as immune to
        alcoholism, 23–28, 36, 41–42;
        in Kureishi's "My Son, the
        Fanatic," 139, 140, 141; Purim
        associated with, 7, 29, 30,
        32, 39–40, 42–43; in Roth's
        Goodbye, Columbus, 128–29
Alger, Horatio, 60, 61
Ali, Monica, 167–68
Aligarh University, 139
Alphabet of Juda Liva, The (Stein), 193–94

Altneuland (Herzl), 111
Amazing Adventures of Kavalier and Clay,
        The (Chabon), 196–200, 210
American Jews: cultural pluralism arising
        out of experience of, 45;
        as defined in terms of the
        Holocaust, 146; Eastern Jews
        driven to United States, 55;
        and Holocaust Museum,
        184, 203; in Jen's Mona in
        the Promised Land, 169–72;
        "Jewish" becoming religious
        label after Holocaust, 183; in
        Kafka's Amerika: The Man
        Who Disappeared, 60–62; in
        Lee's Native Speaker, 172–73;
        in New York City, 59, 197;
        Park's "marginal man" model
        of, 62–63; presence in American
        literature, 147–48, 186; and
        selection for Jewish intelligence,
        237, 238; in Shteyngart's The
        Russian Debutante's Handbook,
        205–8; as successful minority,
        125–26, 146, 147, 170, 176, 177;
        theories of difference of, 57–63;
        as "white" after the Holocaust,
        145, 152, 180
American Pastoral (Roth), 127–28
Amerika: The Man Who Disappeared
        (Kafka), 60–62, 85, 88, 197
Ancient Judaism (Weber), 52
animal rights, 96
anticruelty forces, 95
Anti-Defamation League of B'nai Brith, 72
anti-Judaism, 227, 228
Anti-Semite and Jew (Sartre), 52, 156
Anti-Semite's Catechism (Fritsch), 123

anti-Semitism, 225–42; as absolute evil
    after Holocaust, 151; as arising
    out of splinter religious groups,
    228; blood libel accusation,
    8, 123, 156, 215, 247n.19;
    as by-product of strategy
    for Jewish survival, 239–40;
    of Chamberlain, 70, 155;
    Dreyfus affair, 82, 89, 234; on
    the drunken Jew, 41; Einstein
    confronts, 102–3; German
    debate of 1880s about, 47;
    globalization of, 229; "Green"
    Islamic anti-Semitism, 225,
    226, 229–30, 239, 242; on
    Jewish assimilation, 88–89, 107;
    on Jewish mimicry, 69; among
    Jews, 227; philo-Semitism and,
    225, 226, 227, 242; pogroms,
    55, 74; ritual slaughter opposed
    by, 95; Simmel's "scientific"
    response to, 47; societies for
    combating, 71; in Soviet Union,
    216; of Wagner, 66–67, 82;
    Western European Jews fearing
    no changes would eliminate, 55;
    as xenophobia, 227; Zangwill on
    "East" as source of, 82
anti-Zionism, 227, 229
Anzaldúa, Gloria, 12
Apprenticeship of Duddy Kravitz, The
    (Richler), 207
Arendt, Hannah, 35
arranged marriages, 7, 169
Asad, Talal, 3, 8, 14, 96
Asch, Sholem, 182, 205
Asian-Americans: in Jen's Mona in the
    Promised Land, 169–72; in Lee's
    Native Speaker, 172–73
assimilation: of German Jews, 19, 47, 88–
    89; Hispanics not assimilating,
    11; Jews seen as resisting, 239–
    40; Lissauer on, 92; as litmus
    test of ethnicity, 183; of Turks
    in Germany, 21
Auer, Leopold, 72
Austria, 219–23

authenticity, 181, 193, 194, 213
Autograph Man, The (Smith), 162

Baal Shem Tov, 9
Bach, Johann Sebastian, 104, 106, 107, 109
"Bachelor Party" (Brownstein), 203
Baddiel, David, 202
Baer, Karl M.: as always male, 112, 113;
    ambiguous genitalia of, 112;
    autobiography of, 111; in B'nai
    Brith, 120; emigrates to Israel,
    124; as "French," 120; The
    International Trafficking in
    Girls, 115; masculinization of,
    119; and menstruation, 122,
    124; as N. O. Body, 111; raised
    as woman Martha Baer, 111,
    113; seen as feminized man,
    119; senses that he might be
    lesbian, 117; sex reassignment
    of, 111, 124
Bakhtin, Mikhail, 29–30
Bales, Robert, 37
Barbin, Herculine, 114–15
Barnes, Julian, 150–51
Baum, Oskar, 192
Bauman, Zygmunt, 51
Baumgartner's Bombay (Desai), 180–81
Becker, Jurek, 193, 194, 214
Beer, Michael, 53
Beethoven, Ludwig van, 104, 106
Bell Curve, The (Herrnstein and Murray),
    237–38
Bellow, Saul, 126, 147, 148, 186, 192
Bendavid, Lazarus, 131
Bender, Aimee, 203
Benedict, Julius, 68
Benny, Jack, 99
Bentham, Jeremy, 96
Bercovitch, Sacvan, 182
Berens-Totenohl, Josefa, 89
Bergman, Hugo, 105
Berl, Heinrich, 69–70
Berlin, Irving, 126
Berlin, Isaiah, 104, 108
Berlin's Third Sex (Hirschfeld), 115
Bernal, Martin, 13

Bernstein, Aaron, 101
besondere Gedächtnis der Rosa Masur, Das
  (*The Special Memory of Rosa
  Masur*) (Vertlib), 221–22
Besso, Michele, 104
Biale, David, 184
Bible for Christian Communities (*La Bible
  Latino-amércaine*) (Hurault), 4
Bildung. See high culture (*Bildung*)
bilingualism, 59
Biller, Maxim, 208
Biro, Adam, 203
Bismarck, Otto von, 79–80
Bizet, Georges, 69
Black, Stephen, 154
"Black Train" (Lappin), 208–10
Blasband, Philippe, 183–84, 186, 208
blood libel, 8, 123, 156, 215, 247n.19
B'nai Brith, 72, 120
Boas, Franz, 54–55, 250n.20
Bobrowski, Johannes, 193
Bodemann, Y. Michal, 6
Bonnivard, Odile, 98
Borrow, George, 53
Bourdieu, Pierre, 14–15
Bourne, Randolph S., 58, 59–60
Bradford Council of Mosques, 17
Breines, Paul, xiii
Breze, Lhaj Thami, 2
Brick Lane (Ali), 167–68
Bright Blue (Meinecke), 169
Brod, Max: and Einstein, 105; on Jewish
  music, 69; and Kafka, 60, 61,
  62, 86, 93; and Reinerová, 192
Browning, Robert, 74
Brownstein, Gabriel, 203
Bruns, Paul Jakob, 28–29, 30, 31, 247n.19
Buber, Martin, 14, 40–41, 69, 85, 88, 105,
  134–35
Budhos, Marina, 268n.4
Bulliet, Richard, 3–4
burial, 7, 27

Cahan, Abraham, 63, 125, 205
Canetti, Elias, 187–88
Cantipratanus, Thomas, 123
capitalism: Weber on Jews and, 54

Carey, Mariah, 169
carnival, 29–31
Castle, The (Kafka), 192
Catholics: Baer represents himself as, 121;
  Bible for Christian Communities,
  4; Einstein's exposure to, 101,
  102; and ethnicity, 182, 183;
  lack of decorum associated
  with, 30; priestly celibacy and
  intelligence, 232–33, 236
Central Jewish Organization (Germany),
  214
Chabon, Michael: *The Amazing Adventures
  of Kavalier and Clay*, 196–200,
  210; *The Final Solution*, 200;
  Mysteries of Pittsburgh, 196;
  Wonder Boys, 196
Chamberlain, Houston Stewart, 70, 155
Chaplin, Charlie, 103–4
"Charles Avison" (Browning), 74
Chekhov, Anton, 138
Chesnutt, Charles W., 57, 62
Chicago Cultural Studies Group, 15
"Child Prodigies in the Ghetto" (Franzos),
  132
cholera: Jews' reported exemption from, 26
"chosenness," 7
Christianity: defining itself as not Jewish,
  228, 231; and European
  constitution of 2005,
  4–5; European secularism
  as grounded in, xi, 3–4; in
  Ezekiel's work, 189; Judaism
  associated with Islam in,
  5–7; Luther, 30, 32. *See also*
  Catholics
Christie, Agatha, 116
Churchill, Winston, 149–50
Church of John F. Kennedy, The (Meinecke),
  168
Chwolson, Daniel, 123, 156
Çınar, Safter, 7
circumcision: as castration, 156; Christians
  see as meaningless ritual, 4; as
  damaging, 121–22; in Jewish
  separation, 240; as Mosaic, 31;
  as Muslim custom, 156; seen

as indecorous by host cultures, 7, 27
civil marriage, 6, 79
"clash of civilizations" thesis, ix, xiv
classical music, 65–84; performers versus composers, 68–71; in Zangwill's *The Melting Pot,* 73–84. *See also* violinists
clitoridectomy, 7, 164–65
Cochin Jews, 163
Cohen, Hermann (philosopher), 47
Cohen, Hermann (violinist), 69
Cohen and Son (play), 136
colonialism, 10, 149–50, 191
Comaroff, Jean and John, 28
comic books, 196, 198
commensality, 53
Commins, Dorothy, 108
compulsory baptism, 89
Congress for the Protection of Animals, 95
Congreve, William, 66
Coningsby (Disraeli), 67
conversion: Christianity and Islam's need for universal, 228; in Goller's *The Five Books of Mr. Moses,* 136; Kafka on, 85, 89, 92; in Levy's *Small Island,* 166; neofundamentalist Muslims on converting the West, 140–41; in Roth's "Eli the Fanatic," 134–35; seen as not changing innate nature of the Jew, 46; in Skibell's *The English Disease,* 135; Warwar on, 90
"Conversion of the Jews, The" (Roth), 142
cosmopolitanism: Bourne advocating, 58, 59; Jews as positive cosmopolitans, 188; Kureishi on Jewish, 150; Park on Jews as cosmopolites, 63; Senoçak and, 18, 21; in South African image of Jews, 157
Costa, Michael, 68–69
Costa-Lascoux, Jacqueline, 3
Crabb, David W., 25
creativity, 69–70, 91, 103
Crosland, Alan, 126

cross-dressing (transvestism), 116, 118
Cuban-Americans, 174–76
cultural diversity: Hirsch on, 56; Kallen on, 58; melting pot countered by, 13; as model of multiculturalism, 45
cultural nationalism, 108–9
cultural pluralism: as answer to melting pot, 82–83; arising from theories of Jewish cultural difference, 46; Bourne on, 60; conflict as well as harmony generated by, x–xi; in Germany, 212; Kallen on Jews as model for, 58–59; as model of the multicultural, xii–xiii, 45, 181; in Spiegelman's *Maus,* 184–85; writers countering claims of, 61
culture: "culture" versus "Culture," 16; multiculturalism taking as basis for identity, 13; popular, 12, 57, 126, 198. *See also* cultural diversity; cultural pluralism; high culture; multicultural, the

Dangerous Relations (*Gefährliche Verwandtschaft*) (Senoçak), 17–22, 171
Dangling Man (Bellow), 126
Dangor, Achmat, 152–57
Daniel, Ruby, 268n.4
Daniel Deronda (Eliot), 68
Darlington, Cyril D., 234
Darwin, Charles, 232, 233
David, Esther, 268n.4
Davids Geige (*David's Violin*) (Lateiner), 88
Day of Atonement (Raphaelson), 126
Dean's December, The (Bellow), 192
Death of a Salesman (Miller), 126
decorum: alcohol use leading to lack of, 27, 128; and genius as linked through Jewish experience, 103; Jews accused of lacking, 4, 27–28; Jews and culture of in Germany, 23–43; in Kafka's "The Metamorphosis," 87; Protestants on Catholic lack

of, 30; Purim seen as violating, 29–33; ritual slaughter seen as violating, 94, 96

Deportation (Abschiebung) (Vertlib), 220

Desai, Anita, 180–81, 268n.4

"Desire to Become an Indian" (Kafka), 85

Deux juifs dans un train: une autobiographie (Two Jews on a Train) (Biro), 203

Diaspora, modern. *See* modern Diaspora

Dickens, Charles, 60, 61, 82

difference: biological, 13, 45–46, 181; "bridging" by submerging, 6; conversation seen as answer to claims of, xi, xiv; as destructive as well as productive, xi; food as mark of, 98; Hirsch on, 38, 56; Jewish seen as divinely ordained, ix–x; Jewish seen as innate and immutable, 10, 46, 54–55, 59, 90, 122, 123, 146–47, 177; Jewish seen as physical, 146–47, 160, 174; Jewish sexual, 121–22; Jews as litmus test for importance of, ix, 45, 46, 55, 63–64, 147, 176; language as marker of, 150, 153; "narcissism of minor differences," 6, 11, 228; 9/11 and, ix; physical, 113–14, 146–47, 160, 174; Simmel's theory of the "stranger," 47–52; skin color as key to, 180; Sombart on Jewish, 54–55; Weber on Jewish, 52–54

Dischereit, Esther, 194–96

Disraeli, Benjamin, 67–68, 176, 252n.5

diversity, cultural. *See* cultural diversity

Dohm, Wilhelm von, 29, 31, 34

"Dreaming in Polish" (Bender), 203

Dreyfus affair, 82, 89, 234

drunkenness. *See* alcohol

"Drunk Every Day, Sober on Purim" (Peretz), 40

Dundes, Alan, 7–8

Dvorak, Antonin, 77

Eastern Europe: Holocaust tourism to, 201, 202; as Jewish space, 191–92; newest Jewish writing from, 210–23. *See also* Eastern Jews; Prague

Eastern Jews: in Dangor's "Kafka's Curse," 154, 157; driven to Western Europe and United states, 55, 151; educational practices of, 241; Einstein on anti-Semitism directed against, 102; Franzos's depiction of, 131–33; immigrants' moderate alcohol use, 37; Kafka as, 93; Kallen on New York, 59; lack of sobriety among, 34, 35–36; pogroms, 55, 74; in selection for Jewish intelligence, 237, 238; in Smith's *White Teeth,* 160; as tavern keepers, 248n.43; Yiddish, 73, 92, 93, 153, 154, 155. *See also* Russian Jews

East River (Asch), 205

Eckstein, Joseph, 169

education: Jewish emphasis on, 241

Efron, John, 24

Ehlers, Cindy L., 25

Ehrenfest, Paul, 105

Eichhorn, Johann Gottfried, 32

Einstein, Albert: on anti-Semitism, 102–3; and Belgian monarchs, 108; on cultural conventions in music, 105–6; as exemplary "smart" Jew, xiii; on Herzl, 104; on high culture as universal, 107–8; Jewish identity of, 101–3, 105, 108, 109; on Jewishness as indelible, 107; in Kaminer's *Schönhauser Allee,* 217; meets Kafka, 105; on Mozart, 101; musical benefits for Jewish causes, 106; on music and mathematics, 100; music lessons as a child, 100–101; playing skills erode, 106; in Prague, 105; religious education of, 101; as violinist, 98–109; violin used

as tool of seduction by, 104; on
    Zionism, 108
Einstein, Alfred, 70
Einstein, Mileva, 104
Eisenberg, Carol, 204
Elias, Norbert, 16, 28
Eliot, George, 68
"Eli the Fanatic" (Roth), 130–35, 137,
    142–43
Eliyahu of Vilnius (Vilna Gaon), 9
Ellis, Havelock, 115, 122
Elman, Mischa, 72, 106
Emerson, Ralph Waldo, 73
Emigrants, The (Sebald), 204
émigré novels, 205
Eminem, 203–4
English Disease, The (Skibell), 135
English language, 58, 61–62, 76, 150, 154,
    201
Enlightenment: Christianity associated
    with, 3–4; failure of, xii, 23,
    107; German Jews feeling
    indebted to, 19; Haskalah, 9, 66,
    139, 233; on Jewish institutional
    practices, 131; Jews and culture
    of decorum in Germany, 23–43;
    on ritual, 27–28; transformation
    required by, xiv
Escapist, The (comic book), 197, 199–200
Essence of Christianity (Feuerbach), 68
Esther, Book of, 32, 34
Eternal Jew, The (Hippler), 95
ethnicity: Jews seen as ethnic group,
    151, 182–83; Jews shift from
    religious to ethnic identity, 12,
    125–26; litmus tests of, 183;
    multiculturalism on religion
    as, 14; as subsuming other
    categories, 6, 182–83; Weber's
    definition of, 52. *See also* race
eugenics, 232, 233, 239
Europe: constitution of 2005, 4–5; Diaspora
    Judaism as model for Islam in
    multicultural, 1–22; "Jewish"
    becoming religious label
    after Holocaust, 183; radical
    secularization in Western, 6; as

site for New Hebraic Man to
    develop, 82. *See also* Eastern
    Europe; Enlightenment;
    France; Germany; Great Britain
*Everyday Heroes: A Slide Lecture about the
    Unusual Habits of the Postwar
    Period* (*Helden des Alltages*)
    (Kaminer and Höge), 217
Everything Is Illuminated (Foer), 200–202,
    203–4, 205, 210
evolutionary psychology, 239, 240
Ezekiel, Nissim, 188–91

Famous Musicians of a Wandering Race
    (Saleski), 71–72
fanatics: in Goller's *The Five Books of Mr.
    Moses,* 136; Hughes on, 130;
    in Kureishi's "My Son, the
    Fanatic," 137–43; Nietzsche
    on, 137; Orthodox Jews seen as,
    189; Roth's "Eli the Fanatic,"
    130–35
Fanta, Berta, 105
Farjeon, B. L., 74
Farrell, James, 182
fast food, 97
Faust (Gounod), 78
Felsenstein, Walter, 194
female circumcision, 7, 164–65
Femhof, Der (Berens-Totenohl), 89
feminization, 119–20
Feuer, Lewis S., 235, 236
Feuerbach, Ludwig, 68
Fichte, Johann Gottlieb, 9
Fiddler on the Roof (musical), 194, 205, 216
Fiedler, Leslie, 182, 183
Final Solution, The (Chabon), 200
Finck, Werner, 241
Fireside Discussion Group, 72, 104
Fishberg, Maurice, 36
Five Books of Mr. Moses, The (Goller), 136
Fliess, Wilhelm, 122–23
Florida Enchantment, A (Ganter and
    Redmond), 116
Foer, Jonathan Safran, 200–202, 203–4,
    205, 210

food: commensality, 53; in Ezekiel's work, 189; fast food, 97; halal meat, 1, 97–98; "identity" soup, 98; in Kafka's "The Metamorphosis," 94; kosher food, 1, 96–97, 185–86; as mark of difference, 98, 186; ritual slaughter, 1–2, 7, 8, 94–97

Forel, F. A., 122

Foucault, Michel, 114–15

Fowler, Robert, 95

France: Dreyfus affair, 82, 89, 234; "French" as racial category, 120; gay marriage debates in, 6; headscarves banned in public schools in, 1, 2–3, 9–10; "identity" soup in, 98; Lustiger, 183; Muslim versus Jewish population of, 10; Sikh turbans banned in public schools in, 2, 3; social anti-Semitism of, 234

Francophone multiculturalism, 203

Franzos, Karl Emil, 131–33

freedom of religion, 6

French Council of the Muslim Faith, 2

Freud, Sigmund, 6, 103, 122, 228

Friedländer, David, 31–34, 35, 39

Friedmann, Heinrich, 101

Friedrich, Walter, 106

Fritsch, Theodor, 70–71, 123

From Half-Asia (Franzos), 131, 132

Fugitive Pieces (Michaels), 209

Galton, Francis, 68, 232–33, 237, 239, 252n.10

Ganter, Archibald, 116

Gary, Romain, 264n.18

gay marriage, 6

Gefährliche Verwandtschaft (*Dangerous Relations*) (Senoçak), 17–22, 171

Geiger, Abraham, 5, 230–32

gender: culture seen as determining, 112–13

genetic illnesses, 169

genius, 68, 69, 70, 91, 103, 234–35, 239

German Democratic Republic (GDR), 193–94; in Becker's *Jacob the Liar,* 193–94; Kaminer comes to, 214–15, 219; Stein's *The Alphabet of Juda Liva* and, 193, 194

"German-Jewish Parnassus, The" (Goldstein), 56–57

German Jews: assimilation of, 19, 47, 88–89; fleeing Nazi Germany, 107; "German-Jewish symbiosis," 19, 51; German-language Jewish writers of Russian identity, 179–80; as marginal in German culture, 56–57; as Orientalists, 19; as pariah people for Weber, 52–54; seeing themselves as Germans, 18–21; as Simmel's "strangers," 47–52; sobriety of, 31–34; Sombart on immutability of, 54–55; success of, 176; in West Germany, 210–23

German language, 91, 93, 179–80, 213–14

Germany: Bismarck on German-Jewish crossbreeding, 79–80; Einstein encounters anti-Semitism in, 102–3; "French" as racial category in, 120; Jews and culture of decorum in, 23–43; Mölln murders, 6–7; multicultural literature in, 168–69; as "multi-kulti," 179, 211, 216, 217, 218; official religions in, 271n.48; rhetoric of victimization of Muslims in, 6–7; ritual slaughter opposed in, 2, 95, 96. *See also* German Democratic Republic (GDR); German Jews; Nazis; West Germany

Gershwin, George, 83

Ghosh, Amitav, 163–65

Gilroy, Paul, 16

Giscard d'Estaing, Valéry, 4–5

Glad, D. P., 248n.29

Gobineau, Joseph Arthur de, 120

Goethe, Johann Wolfgang von, 86, 221

Gold, Michael, 63, 185

Goldberg, Myla, 204
Goldstein, Moritz, 56–57
Goldziher, Ignaz, 5
Golem: in Chabon's *The Amazing
    Adventures of Kavalier and Clay*,
    196, 197–200; in Dischereit's
    *When My Golem Revealed
    Himself to Me*, 194–96; Judah
    Loew and creation of, 192,
    199; as link between past and
    present, 196
Golem (d'Albert), 70
Golem, Der (Meyrink), 194
Goller, Izak, 36–37, 136
Goncharov, Ivan, 207
Goodbye, Columbus (Roth), 126–27, 127–30,
    134, 142–43, 173
Gordimer, Nadine, 184–85
Gorelik, Lena, 212–13, 214, 271n.52
Gossett, Philip, 252n.5
Gounod, Charles, 78
Graetz, Heinrich, 40
graven images, 7, 53
Great Britain: in Ali's *Brick Lane*, 167–68;
    British Jews in highest reaches
    of class structure, 176; Disraeli,
    67–68, 176, 252n.5; in Goller's
    The Five Books of Mr. Moses,
    136; halal meat in, 97; Jewish
    immigrants after World War II,
    151; in Kureishi's "My Son, the
    Fanatic," 137–43; in Kureishi's
    "We're Not Jews," 148–51; in
    Levy's *Small Island*, 165–67;
    Muslim dress allowed in schools
    in, 10; Muslim population of,
    10; Race Relations Act of 1976,
    151; race riots of spring 2001,
    152; ritual slaughter opposed
    in, 95; Royal College of Music,
    68; Runnymede Commission on
    Anti-Semitism, 227; Sephardic
    Jews in, 8; in Smith's *The
    Autograph Man*, 162; in Smith's
    White Teeth, 158–62
"Green" anti-Semitism, 225, 226, 229–30,
    239, 242

Griffiths, Richard, 234
Grisi, Giulia, 67
Gross, Samuel David, 261n.3
Grüner, Ruben, 132
Gumplowicz, Ludwig, 79
"Gypsies," 53

Habermas, Jürgen, xi
halal meat, 1, 97–98
Haldane, J. B. S., 235, 273n.22
Halliburton, W. D., 122
Handlin, Oscar, 126
harmony: pluralism generating conflict as
    well as, x–xi
Harnack, Adolf, 49
Hartman, Geoffrey, 182, 183
Hasidim, 9
Haskalah (Jewish Enlightenment), 9, 66,
    139, 233
headscarves (*hijab*): banned in French
    public schools, 1, 2–3, 9–10;
    Jewish comparisons with, 7
Hebrew language, 212
Heeb (magazine), 204
Hegel, Georg Wilhelm Friedrich, 48, 58,
    177
Heifetz, Jascha, 72, 99
Heine, Heinrich, 63, 68, 91
Helden des Alltages (*Everyday Heroes*)
    (Kaminer and Höge), 217
Herder, Johann Gottfried, 50, 213
hermaphroditism, 111–24; Herculine
    Barbin, 114–15; fascination
    with, 113; feminization of the
    male as model, 119; and male
    menstruation, 122–24; as model
    for sexual difference, 115–16
Herrnstein, Richard, 237–38
Herzl, Theodor, 59, 73, 102, 104, 111, 122
Herzog, Elizabeth, 237, 241
Heschel, Susannah, 5, 231
high culture (*Bildung*): in Chabon's *The
    Amazing Adventures of Kavalier
    and Clay*, 198, 200; difference
    in development of, 31, 32;
    Hirsch as devotee of, 56; Jews
    in, xi, xiii, 13–14, 15, 19, 22,

46, 71; Jews transforming
themselves to experience, 66;
in Kafka's *Amerika: The Man
Who Disappeared,* 86; Muslims
engaged in, 17; self-control as
part of, 28; as universal, 107–8;
in Zangwill's *The Melting Pot,*
73–84. *See also* classical music
Hijuelos, Oscar, 174–76
Hilfsverein, 106
Hilsenrath, Edgar, 220
hip-hop, 204
Hippler, Fritz, 95
Hirsch, Samson Raphael, 38, 56
Hirschfeld, Magnus, 111–12, 114, 115, 116,
    119, 123
Hispanics, 11, 12
History of the Standard Oil Company
    (Tarbell), 61
Hitler, Adolf, 107
Hochhuth, Rolf, 80
Höge, Helmut, 217
Hollinger, David, 45, 145, 152
Holocaust (Shoah): American Jews as
    defined in terms of, 146, 176;
    American Jews as "white"
    after, 145, 152, 180; Bauman's
    dehistoricization of, 51; and
    British colonialism, 149–50;
    in Chabon's *The Amazing
    Adventures of Kavalier and
    Clay,* 199; in Chabon's *The
    Final Solution,* 200; in Foer's
    Everything Is Illuminated,
    201–2, 205; in Hijuelos's *A
    Simple Havana Melody (from
    When the World Was Good),*
    174, 175, 176; Holocaust envy,
    177; Holocaust tourism, 201,
    202, 203; Jewish-American
    writing focusing on, 147;
    "Jewish" becoming religious
    label after, 183; Jews as symbol
    of death and destruction after,
    177; Jews as ultimate victims
    due to, 158, 176; monuments to,
    217; in rhetoric of victimization

of Muslims, 6–7; seen as means
    of enforcing Jewish separation,
    240–41; as selecting for Jewish
    intelligence, 234, 237; as
    signaling inherent difference
    of Jews, 177; in Smith's *White
    Teeth,* 161–62; in Umanksy's
    "How to Make It to the
    Promised Land," 202–3
Holocaust Museum, 184, 203
Holyoake, George Jacob, xi
homosexuality: hermaphroditism as model
    for, 115–16; medical model of,
    114; physical difference lacking
    in, 113–14; "third sex" model
    of, 114, 115, 122
honor killings, 7
Hoppe, Hugo, 41–42
Horn, Dara, 204
"How to Make It to the Promised Land"
    (Umanksy), 202–3
Hueppe, Ferdinand, 94
Hughes, Ted, 130
Hugo, Victor, 113
Human Stain, The (Roth), 152, 157, 186
Humboldt, Wilhelm von, 29, 66
Hume, David, 33
humor: Jewish, 236, 273n.23
Hunchback of Notre Dame (Hugo), 113
Huntington, Ellsworth, 232
Huntington, Samuel P., ix, xiv, 11, 12
Hurault, Bernard, 4
Hurwitz, Adolf, 104
hybridity: American, 57; arising from
    theories of Jewish cultural
    difference, 46; atavism of,
    80; in Blasband's "A True
    Exile," 183–84; in Dangor's
    "Kafka's Curse," 157; in
    Eminem's "White America,"
    203–4; in Ghosh's *In an
    Antique Land,* 163–65; of
    Israeli society, 15–16; in Jen's
    Mona in the Promised Land,
    171–72; of the Jews, 187–88;
    Kafka rejects, 91–94; in Lee's
    Native Speaker, 173; in Levy's

Small Island, 165, 166; in Meinecke's work, 168, 169; in Mexico and Canada, 12–13; *Mischlinge*, 89, 91, 92, 255n.6; the multicultural as antithesis of, 13, 181; the multicultural associated with, 12–13, 45; in Rushdie's *The Moor's Last Sigh*, 162–63; in Senoçak's *Dangerous Relations*, 17–22; in Smith's *The Autograph Man*, 162; in Smith's *White Teeth*, 159–60; Thackeray on, 80; in Yehoshua's *Mr. Mani*, 186–87; in Zangwill's *The Melting Pot*, 77–78. *See also* hermaphroditism; intermarriage; melting pot

I am Concerned, Mama (*Ich mache mir Sorgen, Mama*) (Kaminer), 219
I and Thou (Buber), 134
Ibn Khaldun, 232
Ich mache mir Sorgen, Mama (*I am Concerned, Mama*) (Kaminer), 219
"identity" soup, 98
In an Antique Land (Ghosh), 163–65
intelligence: attributed to Jews, 154, 225, 226, 227–28, 230–45; genius, 68, 69, 70, 91, 103, 234–35, 239; "smart" Jews, xiii, 160, 194, 225, 230, 231, 232
intelligence (IQ) tests, 235, 237–38
intermarriage (mixed marriage): assimilation through, 21; Bismarck on, 79–80; Kallen on, 58; Weber on Jewish refusal of, 52, 53; Zangwill on, 78–79
Intermediate Station (*Zwischenstation*) (Vertlib), 221
International Trafficking in Girls, The (Baer), 115
In the Image (Horn), 204
Irving, David, 239
Islam: alcohol and drugs abjured by, 43; anti-Semitism in, 225, 226, 229–30, 239; becoming a heritage, 10–11; as center stage in post 9/11 world, ix; circumcision practiced by, 156; colonial experience of, 10; as considerable minority in Europe, 10; defining itself as not Jewish, 228; Diaspora Judaism as model for European Muslims, 1–22; in Ezekiel's work, 188–91; female circumcision in, 7, 164–65; in Ghosh's *In an Antique Land*, 163–65; Jews in Islamic world, 187–88; on Jews' superior intelligence, 230–32; Judaism associated with in Christianity, 5–7; in Kureishi's "My Son, the Fanatic," 137–43; in Kureishi's "We're Not Jews," 148–51; multiple national traditions of, 8; neofundamentalists, 16–17, 97, 140–41; as not ethnic marker, 151, 182–83; as not official religion in Germany, 271n.48; parallels with Jewish experience in Europe, 7–12; reduced to criterion of color, 137; re-Islamization, 142; rhetoric of victimization of Muslims, 6–7; in Rushdie's *The Moor's Last Sigh*, 162–63; Ummah, 3, 8, 17, 141, 143, 242; as "unassimilable" minority, 11–12
Israel: alcohol consumption in, 27; Israeli-Palestinian conflict, 10; Jews fleeing Germany to, 107; multiculturalism in, 183
Ives, Charles, 77

Jacobs, Joseph, 68–69
Jacob the Liar (*Jakob der Lügner*) (Becker), 193, 194
James, Henry, 59
jazz, 83, 126, 146
Jazz Singer, The (film), 126
Jen, Gish, 169–72

Jerusalem, 186–87
Jerusalem (Mendelssohn), 27
Jesenská, Milena, 62
Jewish Encyclopedia, The, 40
Jewish humor, 236, 273n.23
Jewish Self-Hatred (Gilman), 227
Jews: African Americans compared with, 57, 62, 145–46, 147; biological theories of difference of, 45–46; in classical music, 65–84; and constitution of multicultural ethic, 45–64; as cosmopolitan, 63, 150, 157, 188; defining Jewish literature, 179–91; difference seen as divinely ordained, ix–x; difference seen as innate and immutable, 10, 46, 54–55, 59, 90, 122, 123, 146–47, 177; difference seen as physical, 146–47, 160, 174; as economic man, xii, 49, 54, 60, 63, 125, 130; "foreignness" of, 18; genetic illnesses of, 169; Haskalah, 9, 66, 139, 233; as having no national homeland, 10; in high culture, xi, 13–14, 15, 19, 22, 46, 71; hybridity of, 187–88; immunity to alcoholism attributed to, 23–28, 36, 41–42; integration into Enlightenment Europe, 3–4; intelligence attributed to, 154, 225, 226, 227–28, 230–45; Islam associated with Judaism in Christianity, 5–7; in Islamic world, 187–88; "Jewish type," 90; as litmus test for importance of difference, ix, 45, 46, 55, 63–64, 147, 176; maintaining their religious identity, 11; as microcosm of the multicultural, 187–88; mimicry attributed to, 69, 160; as "modern" or "Western," 188; multiculturalism as seen from Jewish perspective, 179–223; multiple national traditions of, 8; in non-Jewish multicultural literature, 145–77; as now excluded from the multicultural, xiii, 180; as "Orientals," 90–91, 122; as overintellectualized, 234; parallels with Muslim experience in Europe, 7–12; as pariah people for Weber, 52–54, 59; particularism of, ix, 59–60, 228; performativity of Jewish identity, 184; as racial group, 151–52; redefined as a culture, 45–47; reform, 9, 29, 31; religion becoming a heritage, 10–11; religious definition of, 46; in secularized Judeo-Christian World, xi; seen as being beyond or without culture, xii; sexual difference attributed to, 121–22; shift from religious to ethnic identity, 12, 125–26, 151, 182–83; as Simmel's "strangers," 47–52; as small minority in Europe, 10; as "smart," xiii, 160, 194, 225, 230, 231, 232; stereotypes of, 32, 227–28; success of, 125–26, 176, 177, 185, 242; as symbol of death and destruction, 177; as ultimate victims, 158, 176; as "unassimilable" minority, 12, 158; as universal man, 188. *See also* anti-Semitism; Holocaust (Shoah); modern Diaspora; Orthodox Jews; Zionism
Jews and Medicine (Efron), 24
Jews and Modern Capitalism, The (Sombart), 54
Jews of Barnow, The (Franzos), 131
Jews without Money (Gold), 63, 185
Jhabvala, Ruth Prawer, 165, 268n.4
Joachim, Joseph, 69, 71
John Chrysostom, Saint, 123
"Josephine the Singer, or the Mouse Folk" (Kafka), 94
Josipovici, Gabriel, 51

Judah Loew, Maharal of Prague, 192, 199
"Judaism in Music" (Wagner), 66–67
Judeo-Christian tradition, xi, 5–6
Jungle, The (Sinclair), 60
Jungmann, Max, 41

Kafka, Franz, 85–98; *Amerika: The Man Who Disappeared*, 60–62, 85, 88, 197; authentically modern defined by, 14; on baptized Jews, 92; *The Castle*, 192; Chabon's *The Amazing Adventures of Kavalier and Clay* evoking, 197; "Desire to Become an Indian," 85; dreams of becoming a violinist, 87–88; as Eastern Jew, 93; Einstein meets, 105; hybridity rejected by, 91–94; "Josephine the Singer, or the Mouse Folk," 94; on the melting pot, xiii; "The Metamorphosis," 85, 86–87, 94, 111, 143, 198; as Prague Jew, 93, 206; "Report to an Academy," 85; Roth influenced by, 126; *Self-Defense* read by, 90; transformation as theme in writings of, 85–86; *The Trial*, 88; unmusicality of, 93–94; as vegetarian, 93, 94
"Kafka's Curse" (Dangor), 152–57
Kahler, Erich, 105
Kallen, Horace, 45, 58–59, 82–83, 181
Kaminer, Wladimir, 214–19; *Everyday Heroes: A Slide Lecture about the Unusual Habits of the Postwar Period*, 217; *I am Concerned, Mama*, 219; *Militärmusik*, 216; *My German Jungle Book*, 218–19; as representative Russian in Germany, 219; *Russendisko*, 215; *Schönhauser Allee*, 216–17; *The Trip to Trulala*, 216
Kandhalwi, Ihtesam al Hasan, 141
Kant, Immanuel, 34–35, 37, 41, 232
Kara, Yadé, 6
Kayser, Rudolf, 101

Keller, Mark, 248n.33
Kerr, Norman, 36
Kisch, Egon Erwin, 192
Kleiber, Erich, 107
klezmer, 83, 146, 179, 216
Knigge, Adolf, Freiherr von, 33–34, 36
Knox, Robert, 67
Kohn, Hans, 105
Kontingentflüchtlinge, 211
kosher food, 1, 96–97, 185–86
Kraft-Ebing, Richard, 114
Kramer, Michael P., 181–82, 183
Kreisler, Fritz, 72, 253n.30
Kulturbund, 109
Kureishi, Hanif: family history of, 137–38; "Love in a Blue Time," 151; *My Beautiful Laundrette*, 137; *My Ear at His Heart: Reading My Father*, 137; "My Son, the Fanatic," 137–43, 264n.31; Roth as influence on, 138; texts read as social science, 262n.1; "We're Not Jews," 148–51, 176, 184
Kurlansky, Mark, 185–86
Kurtz, Irma, 109

Lacretelle, Jacques de, 234
language: bilingualism, 59; English, 58, 61–62, 76, 150, 154, 201; German, 91, 93, 179–80, 213–14; Gumplowicz on, 79; in Jewish separation, 240, 274n.32; Jews learning that of nation where they dwelt, 35; Kafka as possessing no proper, 93; as marker of difference, 150, 153; as marker of ethnicity, 52, 183; minorities speaking different secular and religious, 7, 8–9; Russian-Jewish writers in Germany and, 213–14; Yiddish, 73, 92, 93, 153, 154, 155
Lappin, Elena, 208–10
Las Meninas (Velazquez), 113
Last Wishes (*Letzer Wunsch*) (Vertlib), 222–23

Lateiner, Joseph, 88
"Latter Day Psalms" (Ezekiel), 189–91
Lavater, Johann Caspar, 27
Lazarus, Emma, 205
Lee, Chang-rae, 172–73
Lee, Spike, 147
Leigh, Mike, 143
Le Pen, Jacques, 98
Lerche, M., 256n.12
Leroy-Beaulieu, Anatole, 60, 89, 91
Lessing, Gotthold Ephraim, 27, 53, 75
Letzer Wunsch (Last Wishes) (Vertlib),
        222–23
Levin's Mill (Levins Mühle) (Bobrowski),
        193
Levy, Amy, 74
Levy, Andrea, 165–67
Lewandowski, Alfred, 106
Lewandowski, Louis, 106
Lewis, Bernard, 229
Lewisohn, Ludwig, 63
Liebknecht, Karl, 95
Limborch, Philippe van, 247n.25
Lindenberger, Herbert, 241
Lipstadt, Deborah, 239
Lissauer, Ernst, 92
Locke, John, 29, 247n.25
Lombroso, Cesar, 91
Lonely Crowd, The (Riesman), 126
Lorde, Audre, 147
Lost Tribe (Zakrzewski), 202
"Love in a Blue Time" (Kureishi), 151
Lowenthal, Michael, 203
Lubavitcher movement, 135
Lunt, Paul, 182
Lustiger, Cardinal, 183
Luther, Martin, 30, 32

MacDonald, Kevin, 239–41, 274n.32
Mahathir bin Mohamad, 226, 229–30, 239,
        242
Mahler, Gustav, 69, 93, 135
Malamud, Bernard, 147
male menstruation, 122–24, 156
Man in the Brown Suit, The (Christie), 116
Manji, Irshad, 15–16
Marcuse, Max, 256n.12

"marginal man" model of Jews, 62–63
marriage: arranged, 7, 169; civil, 6, 79;
        gay, 6; secularization of, 6; in
        selection for Jewish intelligence,
        236–37. See also intermarriage
master-slave dialect, 48
Maus (Spiegelman), 184–85, 199
Mauthner, Fritz, 93
May, Karl, 61
Mecca-Cola, 141
medical multiculturalism, 26
Mein deutsches Dschungelbuch (My German
        Jungle Book) (Kaminer), 218–19
Meinecke, Thomas, 168–69
Melsa, Daniel, 81, 82
melting pot: "American symphony" as
        ultimate expression of, 83;
        cultural pluralism as answer
        to, 82–83; as the image of
        excision of national difference,
        73; Kallen on, 59, 82–83; as
        model of the multicultural, xiii;
        Riesman on, 126
Melting Pot, The (Zangwill), 73–84;
        economic success in, 125;
        Goller's The Five Books of Mr.
        Moses compared with, 136
Mendelssohn, Moses, 9, 27, 29, 35, 66
Mendelssohn-Bartholdy, Felix, 70, 107
Mendelssohn on the Roof (Weil), 192
Menem, Carlos, 183
menstruation, male, 122–24, 156
mental illness: Jewish superior intelligence
        and, 241–42
Menuhin, Yehudi, 72, 107
Merchant of Venice, The (Shakespeare),
        65–66
"Metamorphosis, The" (Kafka), 85, 86–87,
        94, 111, 143, 198
Métis, 12, 13
Metropolitan Documents series, 115
Meyerbeer, Giacomo, 53, 67
Meyrink, Gustav, 194
Michaels, Anne, 209
Militärmusik (Kaminer), 216
Miller, Arthur, 126
Miller, Henry, 205, 207

Mirvis, Tova, 203
Mischlinge, 89, 91, 92, 255n.6
Mitterbauer, Peter, 220
mixed marriage. *See* intermarriage (mixed marriage)
modern Diaspora: as exemplary case for multiculturalism, x; as model for Islam in multicultural Europe, 1–22; portable instruments of high culture as part of, 109. *See also* American Jews; Eastern Jews; German Jews
Mona in the Promised Land (Jen), 169–72
Money, John, 112–13
Montesquieu, Baron de, 33
Moor's Last Sigh, The (Rushdie), 162–63
Morini, Erika, 72
Moscheles, Ignaz, 70
Mosse, George, 21
Mozart, Wolfgang Amadeus, 101, 104, 109
Mr. Mani (Yehoshua), 186–87
muckrakers, 60, 61
multicultural, the: as American discourse of victimization, 15; as antithesis of hybridity, 13; continuities in debate over, xiii; cool multiculturalism, 204, 205, 208; on culture not race as basis of identity, 13; as destructive as well as productive, xi; Diaspora Judaism as model for Islam in multicultural Europe, 1–22; English as language of, 201; Francophone multiculturalism, 203; Hapsburg multiculturalism, 192; and "haves"/"have nots" contrast, 147; hip-hop multiculturalism, 204; hybridity as antithesis of, 13, 181; hybridity associated with, 12–13, 45; Jewish perspectives on, 179–223; Jews and constitution of ethic of, 45–64; Jews as microcosm of, 187–88; Jews as now excluded from, xiii, 180; Jews in contemporary

non-Jewish multicultural literature, 145–77; medical multiculturalism, 26; modern Diaspora as exemplary case for, x; 9/11 and, ix; performance not identity at core of new, 147; religion as ethnicity for, 14; spaces of, 191; transforming mere polylingualism into true multiculturalism, 223; twenty-first century skepticism about, 14–15; two models of, xii–xiii, 181; two primary ideas of, xi; variety of meanings of, 15; what groups count as, 146; as working best when focusing on economic limnality, 177, 184
Münsterberg, Hugo, 73
Murray, Charles, 237–38, 273n.27
music: jazz, 83, 126, 146; Kafka's unmusicality, 93–94; klezmer, 83, 146, 179, 216; and mathematics, 100; Weber on Jewish, 53. *See also* classical music
Musikvereine, 107
Muslim Degeneration and Its Only Remedy (Kandhalwi), 137
My Beautiful Laundrette (Kureishi), 137
My Ear at His Heart: Reading My Father (Kureishi), 137
My German Jungle Book (*Mein deutsches Dschungelbuch*) (Kaminer), 218–19
Mynona (Salomo Friedländer), 41
"My Son, the Fanatic" (Kureishi), 137–43, 264n.31
Mysteries of Pittsburgh (Chabon), 196

Näcke, Paul, 122
Nadel, Arno, 70
Nathan the Wise (Lessing), 27, 53, 75
nationalism, cultural, 108–9
Native Speaker (Lee), 172–73
Nazis: British colonialism compared with, 150; Einstein and, 107; in Hijuelos's *A Simple Havana*

Melody (from When the World Was Good), 175; Jewish musical performance restricted by, 109; on Jewish ritual slaughter, 95–96; Jews made visible by, 124. *See also* Holocaust (Shoah)
neofundamentalists, 16–17, 97, 140–41
neo-Orthodoxy, 55–56, 135
Nettl, Paul, 70
Neugebauer, Franz von, 116–18
New Arab poets, 14
"New Colossus, The" (Lazarus), 205
Newton, Isaac, 100, 104
New York City, 59, 197
Nichols, Anne, 82
Nietzsche, Friedrich, 76, 137
Nora, Pierre, 11
Nordau, Max, 78–79
Nose, The (Lappin), 208
nose jobs, 127, 128, 170–71, 241
Novick, Peter, 147
Nuriyev, Rudolf, 183

Oblomov (Goncharov), 207
On the Jews and Their Lies (Luther), 30
"Operated Goy, The" (Mynona), 41
"Operated Jew, The" (Panizza), 41
Oppenheimer, Franz, 57
"Ordinary Pain" (Lowenthal), 203
Orlando (Woolf), 116
Orthodox Jews: fanaticism of, 189; in Goller's *The Five Books of Mr. Moses*, 136; in Mirvis's "A Poland, a Lithuania, a Galicia," 203; neo-Orthodoxy, 55–56, 135; Purim and alcohol among, 42–43; in Skibell's *The English Disease*, 135
Ostwald, Hans, 115
Ozick, Cynthia, 182, 183, 198

Paganini, Niccolò, 71
Panizza, Oscar, 41
Pariah, The (Beer), 53
"pariah people" model for Jews, 52–54, 59
Park, Robert E., 62–63
particularism: Jewish, ix, 59–60, 228

Pasta, Giuditta, 67
Penslar, Derek, xii
People That Shall Dwell Alone, A: Judaism as a Group Evolutionary Strategy (MacDonald), 239
Peretz, Jizchak, 40
Petronius, 113
Philip, Arthur, 205
Philippson, Martin, 41
philo-Semitism, 225, 226, 227, 242
Philosophy of Money (Simmel), 49
pianists: Jews as, 104
Plath, Sylvia, 130
Plato, xi
pluralism, cultural. *See* cultural pluralism
pogroms, 55, 74
"Poland, A, a Lithuania, a Galicia" (Mirvis), 203
Polish Jews, 34, 35
political correctness, 186
popular culture, 12, 57, 126, 198
Powers, Richard, 99–100
Prague: in Chabon's *The Amazing Adventures of Kavalier and Clay*, 197, 198; hip Prague of 1990s, 192; as Jewish space, 191, 194; Kafka as Prague Jew, 93, 206; in Lappin's "Black Train," 208, 210; in Reinerová's work, 192–93; in Shteyngart's *The Russian Debutante's Handbook*, 206; in Stein's *The Alphabet of Juda Liva*, 193, 194, 196
Prague Orgy, The (Roth), 192
priestly celibacy, 232–33, 236
progress, xi, 35
Protestant Ethic and the Spirit of Capitalism (Weber), 54
Protocols of the Elders of Zion, 198
psychoanalysis, 93
Psychopathia Sexualis (Krafft-Ebing), 114
Pulzer, Peter, 226
Purim: Bruns on abandoning, 28–29, 30, 31; decorum seen as violated by, 29–33; drunkenness associated with, 7, 29, 30, 32, 39–40, 42–43; Friedländer's defense of,

31–34; as marking watershed in Jewish history, 40; as "not a holiday," 38; reconstitution of, 38–41; as secular holiday, 31; Zionist interpretation of, 40–41

"Purim Prologue, A" (Buber), 40–41

rabbis, 236, 237

Rabbit, Run (Updike), 129

race: contemporary medicine reintroducing, 26, 181; Jews seen as racial group in Britain, 151; in Meinecke's *Bright Blue*, 169; *Mischlinge*, 89, 91, 92, 255n.6; multiculturalism replacing with culture, 13; multicultural theory echoing discourse of, 180, 181; in scientific anti-Semitism, 229. *See also* ethnicity

Race Relations Act (1976), 151

Races of Men, The (Knox), 67

Ramadan, 7

Ramadan, Tariq, 11

Raphaelson, Samson, 125–26

Reche, O., 256n.12

Redmond, Fergus, 116

reform, 9, 29, 31

Reimer, David, 113

Reinerová, Lenka, 192–93

Reise nach Trulala, Die (*The Trip to Trulala*) (Kaminer), 216

relativity, theory of, 104

religion: becoming a heritage, 10–11; ethnicity as subsuming, 6, 182–83; as ethnicity for multiculturalism, 14; freedom of, 6; Judeo-Christian tradition, xi, 5–6; religious definition of Jews, 46; religious truth as not universal, x. *See also* Christianity; Islam; Jews; ritual; secularization

"Report to an Academy" (Kafka), 85

Reuben Sachs (Levy), 74

"Rhapsody in Blue" (Gershwin), 83

Richler, Mordecai, 207, 208

Riesman, David, 126

rights of women: Jews and Muslims seen as suppressing, 7

Rise of David Levinsky, The (Cahan), 63, 125

ritual: being Jewish through, 101; Enlightenment view of, 27–28; Hirsch on, 38; Judaism seen as religion of meaningless, 4; Muslim immigrants abandoning, 139–40; Nazi view of Jewish, 95–96; secular versus Mosaic, 31

ritual slaughter, 1–2, 7, 8, 94–97

Rodriguez, Richard, 12

Roosevelt, Theodore, 60, 73

Rosen, Max, 72

Roskies, David, ix

Rossini, Gioacchino, 67, 252n.5

Roth, Philip, 125–35; *American Pastoral*, 127–28; "The Conversion of the Jews," 142; "Eli the Fanatic," 130–35, 137, 142–43; *Goodbye, Columbus*, 126–27, 127–30, 134, 142–43, 173; *The Human Stain*, 152, 157, 186; and Jewish-American writing focusing on the Holocaust, 147; Kafka as influence on, 126; Kureishi influenced by, 138; *The Prague Orgy*, 192; on survival of American Jews, 237; texts read as social science, 262n.1

Rothenberg, Jerome, 37–38

Rothschild, Lord, 8

Roy, Olivier, 2, 16–17, 97, 183, 242

Royal College of Music, 68

Runnymede Commission on Anti-Semitism, 227

Ruppin, Arthur, 236

Rushdie, Salman, 17, 140, 162–63

Russendisko (Kaminer), 215

Russian Debutante's Handbook, The (Shteyngart), 205–8, 214

Russian Jews: in Germany, 210–23; in Shteyngart's *The Russian Debutante's Handbook*, 205–8

Sacks, Jonathan, ix–xi, xii, xiv, 6
Said, Edward, 13
Saleski, Gdal, 71–72
Samuels, Maurice, 37
Samuelson, James, 36
Sartre, Jean-Paul, 52, 156, 174
Satanic Verses (Rushdie), 17
Satyricon (Petronius), 113
Schechter, Salomon, 78
Schlaffer, Heinz, 213–14
Scholem, Gershom, 19–20, 83–84, 109
Schönberg, Arnold, 69
Schönhauser Allee (Kaminer), 216–17
Schopenhauer, Arthur, 95
Schudt, Johann Jakob, 29
Schulberg, Budd, 126
scientific anti-Semitism, 228–29, 232
Sebald, W. G., 204
Secret Purposes, The (Baddiel), 202
secularization: Christian basis of European,
    xi, 3–4; "Green" anti-Semitism
    and, 226; radical Western
    European, 6; and scientific anti-
    Semitism, 228–29
Seidel, Toscha, 72
selection: in accounting for Jewish
    intelligence, 233–42; eugenics,
    232, 233, 239
Self-Defense (Selbstwehr) (periodical), 90
Sengupta, Somini, 165
Senoçak, Zafer, 17–22, 171
Sephardic Jews, 8
Seth, Vikram, 165
Sex and Character (Weininger), 51
Shakespeare, William, 65–66
Shame of the Cities, The (Steffens), 61
Shammas, Anton, 182
Shapin, Steven, 104
Shaw, George Bernard, 74, 75–76
Shoah. *See* Holocaust (Shoah)
Sholem Aleichem, 194
Shteyngart, Gary, 204, 205–8, 214
Sikhs, 2, 3, 151
Silbermann (Lacretelle), 234
Silliman, Jael, 268n.4
Simmel, Georg: on networks of social
    affiliation, 48–49; Park on,

62–63; on sojourners, 161;
    theory of the "stranger," 47–52,
    103, 151, 168; on trade versus
    production, 49, 69; Weber and
    Sombart contrasted with, 54;
    Zionism rejected by, 51
Simon, Hermann, 120, 121
*Simple Havana Melody, A (from When the
    World Was Good)* (Hijuelos),
    174–76
Sinclair, Upton, 60
Skibell, Joseph, 135, 263n.18
slaughter, ritual, 1–2, 7, 8, 94–97
Small Island (Levy), 165–67
Smith, Zadie: *The Autograph Man*, 162;
    background of, 158; *White
    Teeth*, 158–62, 165, 167, 168
Sociology of Religion (Weber), 52–53
soft drinks, 141
Sokhrina, Anna, 211–12, 213
Solomon Gursky Was Here (Richler), 208
Sombart, Werner, 52, 54–55
Something on the Characteristics of the Jews
    (Bendavid), 131
South Africa: in Dangor's "Kafka's Curse,"
    152–57; Gordimer's models
    of Jewish identity in, 184–85;
    images of the Jew in, 153–54;
    Immigration Restriction Act of
    1902, 154–55
Soviet Jews. *See* Russian Jews
*Special Memory of Rosa Masur, The (Das
    besondere Gedächtnis der Rosa
    Masur)* (Vertlib), 221–22
Spiegelman, Art, 184–85, 199
Spielberg, Steven, 148
Statue of Liberty, 205
Steffens, Lincoln, 61
Stein, Benjamin, 193–94, 196
Steinschneider, Moritz, 40
Stonequist, Everett, 63
"stranger": Simmel's theory of the, 47–52,
    103, 151, 168
Sue, Eugène, 198
Sullivan, Arthur, 69, 253n.13
surgery, aesthetic, 127–28, 170–71, 241
Sutcliffe, Adam, 3

Switzerland, 1, 102
Symonds, John Addington, 115

Tagore, Rabindranath, 105–6
Talmudic training, 132, 240
Tarbell, Ida, 61
Taruffi, Cesare, 119
Taylor, Charles, 3
tea, 39
teshuvah, 134
Thackeray, William Makepeace, 80
"third sex" model, 114, 115, 122
Tibi, Bassam, 11
Time of Our Singing, The (Powers), 99–100
Tomboy (Meinecke), 168, 169
Torah im derekh eretz (Hirsch), 56
tourism: Holocaust, 201, 202, 203
Tower of Babel, x, xi
Transeau, Emma, 35–36
transformation: of Karl M. Baer, 111;
        in Chabon's *The Amazing
        Adventures of Kavalier and
        Clay*, 197, 198; classical
        music as site for Jewish, 66;
        and cultural collapse, 125; in
        Dangor's "Kafka's Curse,"
        152, 157; Dohm on Jewish,
        29; Jewish writers employing
        concept of, xiv; of Judaism in
        Western Diaspora, 9; in Kafka's
        "The Metamorphosis," 86–87,
        94; in Kafka's *The Trial*, 88; in
        Kafka's writings, 85–86; Knigge
        on Jewish, 33–34; in Kureishi's
        "My Son, the Fanatic," 139;
        as literary trope, 85; in Roth's
        work, 127, 129, 130, 131, 134,
        143; shift from religious to
        ethnic identity, 12, 125–26; in
        Skibell's *The English Disease*,
        135; Sombart on Jewish, 55. *See
        also* assimilation; conversion
transvestism (cross-dressing), 116, 118
Treitschke, Heinrich von, 47
Trial, The (Kafka), 88
Trip to Trulala, The (*Die Reise nach Trulala*)
        (Kaminer), 216

Tropic of Capricorn (Miller), 205
troubadours, 46
"True Exile, A" (Blasband), 183–84
Turkey, 5
Turko-German writing, 16
Two Jews on a Train (*Deux juifs dans un
        train: une autobiographie*) (Biro),
        203
Two Lives (Seth), 165
Two Thousand Years (Leigh), 143

Ukraine, 200–202
Ulrichs, Karl, 114, 115, 122
Umanksy, Ellen, 202–3
Ummah, 3, 8, 17, 141, 143, 242
"Unclean, The" (Kurlansky), 185–86
Ungar, Hermann, 192
Union of Islamic Organizations in France
        (UOIF), 2
United States: "American symphony,"
        83; multicultural literature in,
        169–76; as site for New Hebraic
        Man to develop, 82; as ultimate
        multicultural space, 199. *See
        also* American Jews
universalism, x, 228
Updike, John, 129
Uprooted, The (Handlin), 126
Up Stream (Lewisohn), 63

van den Haag, Ernest, 235–37, 238, 239,
        273n.23
Vanity Fair (Thackeray), 80
Veblen, Thorstein, 103
Velazquez, Diego, 113
Velvet Revolution, 192
Vera, or The Nihilists (Wilde), 75
Verband der Deutschen Juden, 41
Vertlib, Vladimir, 219–23; *Deportation*, 220;
        Intermediate Station, 221; *The
        Special Memory of Rosa Masur*,
        221–22
Vilna Gaon (Eliyahu of Vilnius), 9
violinists: Einstein as, 98–109; Jews as, 71,
        72, 100, 109; Kafka's hope of
        becoming, 87–88; in Kafka's
        "The Metamorphosis," 86–87;

Melsa, 81; in Zangwill's *The Melting Pot,* 73–84
Virchow, Rudolf, 21
Vom Heimweg: Verse eines Juden (About the Path Home: Verses of a Jew) (Zlocisti), 121

Wacquant, Loic, 14–15
Wagner, Richard: anti-Semitism of, 82; Einstein and, 104; Herzl listening to, 73, 104; "Judaism in Music," 66–67; Shaw on, 74, 75–76; in Zangwill's *The Melting Pot,* 74
Warner, W. Lloyd, 182
Warwar, Max, 90
Weber, Alfred, 234
Weber, Max, 52–54, 59, 238
Wegener, Paul, 194
Weil, Jiri, 192
Weininger, Otto, 51
Wells, H. G., 59, 76
Welsh, Christine, 12
"We're Not Jews" (Kureishi), 148–51, 176, 184
Werzberger, Moshe, 42–43
West Germany (Federal Republic of Germany): in Dischereit's *When My Golem Revealed Himself to Me,* 194–96; Russian Jewish immigrant writers in, 210–23; in Senoçak's *Dangerous Relations,* 17–22
What Makes Sammy Run (Schulberg), 126
When My Golem Revealed Himself to Me (Dischereit), 194–96
White, Andrew Dickson, 229
"White America" (Eminem), 203–4
Whiteman, Paul, 83
White Teeth (Smith), 158–62, 165, 167, 168
Wiener, Norbert, 235
Wilde, Oscar, 75
Wilhelm Meister novels (Goethe), 86
Winteler, Jost, 102
Winteler-Einstein, Maja, 101
Winternitz, Moritz, 105
Wissenschaft der Juden, 22

Wolff, Hermann, 70–71
Wollstein, G., 51
women: female circumcision, 7, 164–65; Jews and Muslims seen as suppressing rights of, 7
Wonder Boys (Chabon), 196
Wood (Meinecke), 168
Woolf, Virginia, 116
Wordsworth, William, 78
Wright, Richard, 147

xenophobia, 227

Yearbook of Sexual Intermediate Stages, 116
Yehoshua, A. B., 186–87
Yekl (Cahan), 205
Yellow Star, 124
Yiddish language, 73, 92, 93, 153, 154, 155
Yiddish theater, 61
Yom Kippur, 54, 126
Yosef, Ovadiah, 11
Yurdakul, Gökce, 6

Zakrzewski, Paul, 202
Zangwill, Israel: on intermarriage, 78–79; legacy of, 82; on Melsa, 81, 82; *The Melting Pot,* 73–84, 125, 136
Zborowski, Mark, 237, 241
Zimbalist, Efrem, 72
Zionism: anti-Zionism, 227, 229; Einstein on, 108; on German Jews as never truly Jewish, 51–52; Herzl, 59, 73, 102, 104, 111, 122; on Jewish culture in Germany, 57; and Jews as "Orientals," 122; and Nietzsche, 76; on Purim, 40–41; seen as enemy of the multicultural, 181; *Self-Defense,* 90; Simmel's rejection of, 51
Zlocisti, Theodor, 121
Zunz, Leopold, 33
Zweig, Stefan, 20–21
Zwischenstation (Intermediate Station) (Vertlib), 221